Oxford
Illustrated
Children's
Thesaurus

The perfect family thesaurus

OXFORD
UNIVERSITY PRESS

OXFORD
UNIVERSITY PRESS

Great Clarendon Street, Oxford OX2 6DP

Oxford University Press is a department of the University of Oxford.
It furthers the University's objective of excellence in research, scholarship,
and education by publishing worldwide in

Oxford   New York

Auckland   Cape Town   Dar es Salaam   Hong Kong   Karachi
Kuala Lumpur   Madrid   Melbourne   Mexico City   Nairobi
New Delhi   Shanghai   Taipei   Toronto

With offices in

Argentina   Austria   Brazil   Chile   Czech Republic   France   Greece
Guatemala   Hungary   Italy   Japan   Poland   Portugal   Singapore
South Korea   Switzerland   Thailand   Turkey   Ukraine   Vietnam

Oxford is a registered trade mark of Oxford University Press
in the UK and in certain other countries

© Oxford University Press 2010, 2018

Database right Oxford University Press (maker)

First published 2010
This edition 2018

British Library Cataloguing in Publication Data

Data available

ISBN: 978-0-19-276773-8

1 3 5 7 9 10 8 6 4 2

Printed in China

The Publishers would like to thank Shutterstock and
Wikipedia for permission to use their material. Every care has
been taken to trace copyright holders. However, if there have
been unintentional omissions or failure to trace copyright
holders, we apologise, and will, if informed, endeavour to
make corrections in any future edition.

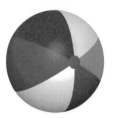

treasure chest

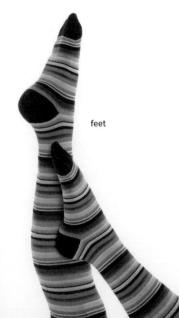

ball

feet

owl

scorpion

lion

How to use this thesaurus

This thesaurus will help you to find more interesting or more accurate words. Which words can you use besides 'fly' to describe how a bird moves? What do you call a line of mountains? Look up **bird** and **mountain** to find out. Imagine you are describing outer space. Look up **space** and **planet** for some ideas. There are also panels on overused words, word webs and writing tips to help you.

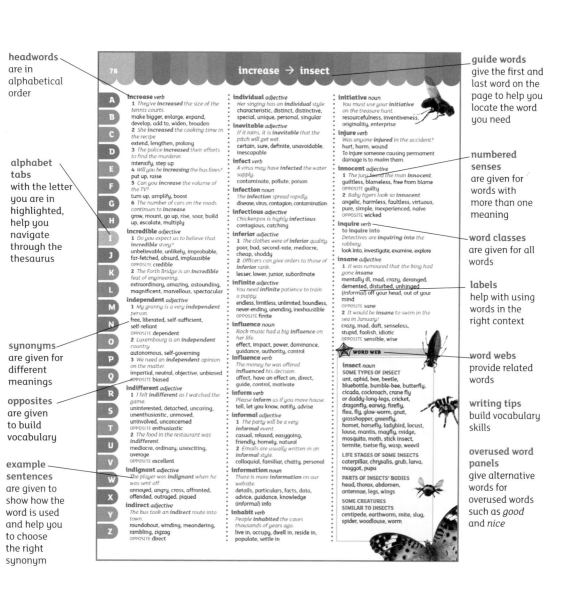

headwords are in alphabetical order

alphabet tabs with the letter you are in highlighted, help you navigate through the thesaurus

synonyms are given for different meanings

opposites are given to build vocabulary

example sentences are given to show how the word is used and help you to choose the right synonym

guide words give the first and last word on the page to help you locate the word you need

numbered senses are given for words with more than one meaning

word classes are given for all words

labels help with using words in the right context

word webs provide related words

writing tips build vocabulary skills

overused word panels give alternative words for overused words such as *good* and *nice*

---

78 increase → insect

increase verb
1 They've **increased** the size of the tennis courts.
make bigger, enlarge, expand, develop, add to, widen, broaden
2 She **increased** the cooking time in the recipe.
extend, lengthen, prolong
3 The police **increased** their efforts to find the murderer.
intensify, step up
4 Will you be **increasing** the bus fares?
put up, raise
5 Can you **increase** the volume of the TV?
turn up, amplify, boost
6 The number of cars on the roads continues to **increase**.
grow, mount, go up, rise, soar, build up, escalate, multiply

incredible adjective
1 Do you expect us to believe that **incredible** story?
unbelievable, unlikely, improbable, far-fetched, absurd, implausible
OPPOSITE credible
2 The Forth Bridge is an **incredible** feat of engineering.
extraordinary, amazing, astounding, magnificent, marvellous, spectacular

independent adjective
1 My granny is a very **independent** person.
free, liberated, self-sufficient, self-reliant
OPPOSITE dependent
2 Luxembourg is an **independent** country.
autonomous, self-governing
3 We need an **independent** opinion on the matter.
impartial, neutral, objective, unbiased
OPPOSITE biased

indifferent adjective
1 I felt **indifferent** as I watched the game.
uninterested, detached, uncaring, unenthusiastic, unmoved, uninvolved, unconcerned
OPPOSITE enthusiastic
2 The food in the restaurant was **indifferent**.
mediocre, ordinary, unexciting, average
OPPOSITE excellent

indignant adjective
The player was **indignant** when he was sent off.
annoyed, angry, cross, affronted, offended, outraged, piqued

indirect adjective
The bus took an **indirect** route into town.
roundabout, winding, meandering, rambling, zigzag
OPPOSITE direct

individual adjective
Her singing has an **individual** style.
characteristic, distinct, distinctive, special, unique, personal, singular

inevitable adjective
If it rains, it is **inevitable** that the pitch will get wet.
certain, sure, definite, unavoidable, inescapable

infect verb
A virus may have **infected** the water supply.
contaminate, pollute, poison

infection noun
The **infection** spread rapidly.
disease, virus, contagion, contamination

infectious adjective
Chickenpox is highly **infectious**.
contagious, catching

inferior adjective
1 The clothes were of **inferior** quality.
poor, bad, second-rate, mediocre, cheap, shoddy
2 Officers can give orders to those of **inferior** rank.
lesser, lower, junior, subordinate

infinite adjective
You need **infinite** patience to train a puppy.
endless, limitless, unlimited, boundless, never-ending, unending, inexhaustible
OPPOSITE finite

influence noun
Rock music had a big **influence** on her life.
effect, impact, power, dominance, guidance, authority, control

influence verb
The money he was offered **influenced** his decision.
affect, have an effect on, direct, guide, control, motivate

inform verb
Please **inform** us if you move house.
tell, let you know, notify, advise

informal adjective
1 The party will be a very **informal** event.
casual, relaxed, easygoing, friendly, homely, natural
2 Emails are usually written in an **informal** style.
colloquial, familiar, chatty, personal

information noun
There is more **information** on our website.
details, particulars, facts, data, advice, guidance, knowledge
(informal) info

inhabit verb
People **inhabited** the caves thousands of years ago.
live in, occupy, dwell in, reside in, populate, settle in

initiative noun
You must use your **initiative** on the treasure hunt.
resourcefulness, inventiveness, originality, enterprise

injure verb
Was anyone **injured** in the accident?
hurt, harm, wound
To injure someone causing permanent damage is to maim them.

innocent adjective
1 The jury found the man **innocent**.
guiltless, blameless, free from blame
OPPOSITE guilty
2 Baby tigers look so **innocent**.
angelic, harmless, faultless, virtuous, pure, simple, inexperienced, naïve
OPPOSITE wicked

inquire verb
to inquire into
Detectives are **inquiring** into the robbery.
look into, investigate, examine, explore

insane adjective
1 It was rumoured that the king had gone **insane**.
mentally ill, mad, crazy, deranged, demented, disturbed, unhinged
(informal) off your head, out of your mind
OPPOSITE sane
2 It would be **insane** to swim in the sea in January!
crazy, mad, daft, senseless, stupid, foolish, idiotic
OPPOSITE sensible, wise

WORD WEB

insect noun
SOME TYPES OF INSECT
ant, aphid, bee, beetle, bluebottle, bumble-bee, butterfly, cicada, cockroach, crane fly or daddy-long-legs, cricket, dragonfly, earwig, firefly, flea, fly, glow-worm, gnat, grasshopper, greenfly, hornet, horsefly, ladybird, locust, louse, mantis, mayfly, midge, mosquito, moth, stick insect, termite, tsetse fly, wasp, weevil

LIFE STAGES OF SOME INSECTS
caterpillar, chrysalis, grub, larva, maggot, pupa

PARTS OF INSECTS' BODIES
head, thorax, abdomen, antennae, legs, wings

SOME CREATURES SIMILAR TO INSECTS
centipede, earthworm, mite, slug, spider, woodlouse, worm

Have fun with these word activities

Use alliteration to describe these characters!

- pirate
- painter
- professor

You could use . . .
powerful, pleasant, peculiar, passionate, playful, pretty

Use alliteration to describe these characters!

- troll
- teddybear
- teacher

You could use . . .
terrible, terrific, ticklish, tedious, talkative

Use alliteration to describe these characters!

- farmer
- fairy
- firefighter

You could use . . .
friendly, famous, fantastic, fast, fashionable, fearless

Complete the similes.
The lion was as fierce as a ?

The elephant was as heavy as a ?

The custard was as lumpy as ?

The giraffe was as tall as a ?

The cabbage was as soggy as ?

Think of a word with the opposite meaning to the underlined words.
See how it changes the characters!

the <u>cheerful</u> clown

the <u>enormous</u> elephant

the <u>grumpy</u> giant

Find another word for 'say.'
'Walk the plank!'
? the princess.

'Help! Rescue me!'
? the pirate.

'Me too!'
? the parrot.

abandon *verb*
1 *The robbers **abandoned** the stolen car.*
leave, desert, forsake, leave behind, strand (*informal*) dump, ditch
2 *We **abandoned** our picnic because of the rain.*
cancel, give up, scrap, drop, abort, discard

ability *noun*
*Skin has a natural **ability** to heal itself.*
capability, competence, aptitude, talent, expertise, skill

able *adjective*
1 *Will you be **able** to come to my party?*
allowed, permitted, free, willing
OPPOSITE unable
2 *Penguins are very **able** swimmers.*
competent, capable, accomplished, expert, skilful, proficient, talented, gifted
OPPOSITE incompetent

abolish *verb*
*I wish someone would **abolish** homework!*
get rid of, do away with, put an end to, eliminate
OPPOSITE create

about *preposition*
*There are **about** two hundred children in the school.*
approximately, roughly, close to, around
to be about something
*The film is **about** a dog called Scruff.*
concern, deal with, involve

abrupt *adjective*
1 *The book came to a very **abrupt** end.*
sudden, hurried, hasty, quick, unexpected
OPPOSITE gradual
2 *The sales assistant had a very **abrupt** manner.*
blunt, curt, sharp, rude, gruff, impolite, tactless, unfriendly
OPPOSITE polite

absent *adjective*
*Why were you **absent** from school yesterday?*
away, missing
To be absent from school without a good reason is to **play truant**.
OPPOSITE present

absolute *adjective*
*The hypnotist asked for **absolute** silence.*
complete, total, utter, perfect

absolutely *adverb*
*This floor is **absolutely** filthy!*
completely, thoroughly, totally, utterly, wholly, entirely

abuse *verb*
1 *The rescued dog had been **abused** by its owners.*
mistreat, maltreat, hurt, injure, damage, harm, misuse
2 *The referee was **abused** by players from both teams.*
be rude to, insult, swear at (*informal*) call someone names

abuse *noun*
1 *They campaigned against the **abuse** of animals.*
mistreatment, misuse, damage, harm, injury
2 *A spectator yelled **abuse** at the referee.*
insults, name-calling, swear words

accelerate *verb*
*The bus **accelerated** when it reached the motorway.*
go faster, speed up, pick up speed
OPPOSITE slow down

accept *verb*
1 *I **accepted** the offer of a lift to the station.*
take, receive, welcome
OPPOSITE reject
2 *The club **accepted** my application for membership.*
approve, agree to, consent to
OPPOSITE reject
3 *Do you **accept** responsibility for the damage?*
admit, acknowledge, recognise, face up to
OPPOSITE deny
4 *They had to **accept** the umpire's decision.*
agree to, go along with, tolerate, put up with, resign yourself to

acceptable *adjective*
1 *Would a pound be **acceptable** as a tip?*
welcome, agreeable, appreciated, pleasant, pleasing, worthwhile
2 *She said my handwriting was not **acceptable**.*
satisfactory, adequate, appropriate, permissible, suitable, tolerable, passable
OPPOSITE unacceptable

accident *noun*
1 *There has been an **accident** at a fireworks display.*
misfortune, mishap, disaster, calamity, catastrophe

A person who is always having accidents is **accident-prone**.
2 *A motorway **accident** is causing traffic delays.*
collision, crash, smash
An accident involving a lot of vehicles is a **pile-up**.
A railway accident may involve a **derailment**.
3 *It was pure **accident** that led us to the secret passage.*
chance, luck, a fluke

accidental *adjective*
1 *The damage to the building was **accidental**.*
unintentional, unfortunate, unlucky
2 *The professor made an **accidental** discovery.*
unexpected, unforeseen, unplanned, fortunate, lucky, chance
OPPOSITE deliberate

account *noun*
1 *I wrote an **account** of our camping trip in my diary.*
report, record, description, history, narrative, story, chronicle, log (*informal*) write-up
2 *Money was of no **account** to him.*
importance, significance, consequence, interest, value

accurate *adjective*
1 *The detective took **accurate** measurements of the room.*
careful, correct, exact, meticulous, minute, precise
OPPOSITE inexact, rough
2 *Is this an **accurate** account of what happened?*
faithful, true, reliable, truthful, factual
OPPOSITE inaccurate, false

accuse *verb*
accuse of
*Miss Sharp **accused** her opponent **of** cheating.*
charge with, blame for, condemn for, denounce for
OPPOSITE defend

ache *noun*
*The **ache** in my tooth is getting worse.*
pain, soreness, throbbing, discomfort, pang, twinge

achieve *verb*
1 *He **achieved** his ambition to play rugby for Wales.*
accomplish, attain, succeed in, carry out, fulfil
2 *The singer **achieved** success with her first album.*
acquire, win, gain, earn, get, score

achievement *noun*
*To climb Mount Everest would be an **achievement**.*
accomplishment, attainment, success, feat, triumph

a
b
c
d
e
f
g
h
i
j
k
l
m
n
o
p
q
r
s
t
u
v
w
x
y
z

act *noun*
1 *Rescuing the boy from the river was a brave **act**.*
action, deed, feat, exploit, operation
2 *The best **act** at the circus involved three clowns.*
performance, sketch, item, turn

act *verb*
1 *We must **act** as soon as we hear the signal.*
do something, take action
2 *Give the medicine time to **act**.*
work, take effect, have an effect, function
3 *Stop **acting** like a baby!*
behave, carry on
4 *I **acted** the part of a pirate in the play.*
perform, play, portray, represent, appear as

action *noun*
1 *The driver's **action** prevented an accident.*
act, deed, effort, measure, feat
2 *The fruit ripens through the **action** of the sun.*
working, effect, mechanism
3 *The film was packed with **action**.*
drama, excitement, activity, liveliness, energy, vigour, vitality

active *adjective*
1 *Mr Aziz is very **active** for his age.*
energetic, lively, dynamic, vigorous, busy
2 *My uncle is an **active** member of the football club.*
enthusiastic, devoted, committed, dedicated, hard-working
OPPOSITE inactive

activity *noun*
1 *The town centre was full of **activity**.*
action, life, busyness, liveliness, excitement, movement, animation
2 *My mum's favourite **activity** is gardening.*
hobby, interest, pastime, pursuit, job, occupation, task

actual *adjective*
*Did you see the **actual** crime?*
real, true, genuine, authentic
OPPOSITE imaginary, supposed

actually *adverb*
*What did the teacher **actually** say to you?*
really, truly, definitely, certainly, genuinely, in fact

adapt *verb*
1 *I'll **adapt** the goggles so that they fit you.*
alter, change, modify, convert, reorganise, transform
2 *Our family **adapted** quickly to life in the country.*
become accustomed, adjust, acclimatise

add *verb*
*The poet **added** an extra line in the last verse.*
join on, attach, append, insert
to add to
*The herbs **add to** the flavour of the stew.*
improve, enhance, increase
to add up
1 *Can you **add up** these figures for me?*
count up, find the sum of, find the total of
(*informal*) tot up
2 (*informal*) *Her story just doesn't **add up**.*
be convincing, make sense

additional *adjective*
*There are **additional** toilets downstairs.*
extra, further, more, supplementary

adequate *adjective*
1 *A sandwich will be **adequate**, thank you.*
enough, sufficient, ample
2 *Your work is **adequate**, but I'm sure you can do better.*
satisfactory, acceptable, tolerable, competent, passable, respectable

adjust *verb*
1 *You need to **adjust** the TV picture.*
correct, modify, put right, improve, tune
2 *She **adjusted** the central heating thermostat.*
alter, change, set, vary, regulate

admire *verb*
1 *I **admire** her skill with words.*
think highly of, look up to, value, have a high opinion of, respect, applaud, approve of, esteem
OPPOSITE despise
2 *The travellers stopped to **admire** the view.*
enjoy, appreciate, be delighted by

admit *verb*
*Did he **admit** that he told a lie?*
acknowledge, agree, accept, confess, grant, own up
OPPOSITE deny

adopt *verb*
1 *Our school has **adopted** a healthy eating policy.*
take up, accept, choose, follow, embrace
2 *We have **adopted** a stray kitten.*
foster, take in

adore *verb*
1 *Rosie **adores** her big sister.*
love, worship, idolise, dote on
2 (*informal*) *I **adore** chocolate milk shakes!*
love, like, enjoy
OPPOSITE hate, detest

adult *adjective*
*An **adult** zebra can run at 80km an hour.*
grown-up, mature, full-size, fully grown
OPPOSITE young, immature

advance *verb*
1 *As the army **advanced**, the enemy fled.*
move forward, go forward, proceed, approach, come near, press on, progress, forge ahead, gain ground, make headway, make progress
OPPOSITE retreat
2 *Mobile phones have **advanced** in the last few years.*
develop, grow, improve, evolve, progress

advantage *noun*
*We had the **advantage** of the wind behind us.*
assistance, benefit, help, aid, asset
OPPOSITE disadvantage, drawback

adventure *noun*
1 *He told us about his latest **adventure**.*
enterprise, exploit, venture, escapade
2 *They travelled the world in search of **adventure**.*
excitement, danger, risk, thrills

advertise *verb*
*We made a poster to **advertise** the cake sale.*
publicise, promote, announce, make known (*informal*) plug

advice *noun*
*The website gives **advice** on building a bird table.*
guidance, help, directions, recommendations, suggestions, tips, pointers

advise *verb*
1 *What did the doctor **advise**?*
recommend, suggest, advocate, prescribe
2 *He **advised** me to rest.*
counsel, encourage, urge

affect *verb*
1 *Global warming will **affect** our climate.*
have an effect or impact on, influence, change, modify, alter
2 *The bad news **affected** us deeply.*
disturb, upset, concern, trouble, worry

afford *verb*
*I can't **afford** a new bike just now.*
have enough money for, pay for, manage, spare

afraid *adjective*
1 *We felt **afraid** as we approached the haunted house.*
frightened, scared, terrified, petrified, alarmed, fearful, anxious, apprehensive
OPPOSITE brave

2 *Don't be* **afraid** *to ask questions.*
hesitant, reluctant, shy

age noun
The book is set in the **age** *of the Vikings.*
period, time, era, epoch, days

aggressive adjective
Bats are not **aggressive** *creatures.*
hostile, violent, provocative, quarrelsome, bullying, warlike
OPPOSITE friendly

agile adjective
Mountain goats are extremely **agile**.
nimble, graceful, sure-footed, sprightly, acrobatic, supple, swift
OPPOSITE clumsy, stiff

agony noun
He screamed in **agony** *when he broke his leg.*
pain, suffering, torture, torment, anguish, distress

agree verb
1 *I'm glad that we* **agree**.
be united, think the same, concur
OPPOSITE disagree
2 *I* **agree** *that you are right.*
accept, acknowledge, admit, grant, allow
OPPOSITE disagree
3 *I* **agree** *to pay my share.*
consent, promise, be willing, undertake
OPPOSITE refuse

agreement noun
1 *There was* **agreement** *on the need for longer holidays.*
consensus, unanimity, unity, consent, harmony, sympathy, conformity
OPPOSITE disagreement
2 *The two sides signed an* **agreement**.
alliance, treaty
An agreement to end fighting is an **armistice** *or* **truce**.
A business agreement is a **bargain**, **contract** *or* **deal**.

aid noun
1 *We can climb out with the* **aid** *of this rope.*
help, support, assistance, backing, cooperation
2 *They agreed to send more* **aid** *to the poorer countries.*
donations, subsidies, contributions

aid verb
The local people **aided** *the police in their investigation.*
help, assist, support, back, collaborate with, cooperate with, contribute to, lend a hand to, further, promote, subsidise

aircraft noun

aeroplane

airship

helicopter

SOME TYPES OF AIRCRAFT
aeroplane, airliner, airship, biplane, bomber, fighter, glider, helicopter, hot-air balloon, jet, jumbo jet, seaplane

PARTS OF AIRCRAFT
cabin, cargo hold, cockpit, engine, fin, flap, flight deck, fuselage, joystick, passenger cabin, propeller, rotor, rudder, tail, tailplane, undercarriage, wing

PLACES WHERE AIRCRAFT TAKE OFF AND LAND
aerodrome, airfield, airport, airstrip, helipad, heliport, landing strip, runway

PEOPLE WHO FLY IN AIRCRAFT
pilot, aviator, balloonist, co-pilot, cabin crew, flight attendant, passengers

aim noun
What was the **aim** *of the experiment?*
ambition, desire, dream, goal, hope, intention, objective, purpose, target, wish

aim verb
1 *She* **aims** *to be a professional dancer.*
intend, mean, plan, propose, want, wish, seek
2 *He* **aimed** *his bow and arrow at the target.*
point, direct, take aim with, line up, level, train, focus

air noun
1 *We shouldn't pollute the* **air** *we breathe.*
atmosphere
2 *This room needs some* **air**.
fresh air, ventilation
3 *There was an* **air** *of mystery about the place.*
feeling, mood, look, appearance, sense

aircraft noun see panel above

alarm verb
The barking dog **alarmed** *the sheep.*
frighten, startle, scare, panic, agitate, distress, shock, surprise, upset, worry
OPPOSITE reassure

alarm noun
1 *Did you hear the* **alarm**?
signal, alert, warning, siren
2 *The sudden noise filled me with* **alarm**.
fright, fear, panic, anxiety, apprehension, distress, nervousness, terror, uneasiness

alien adjective
1 *The desert landscape looked* **alien** *to us.*
strange, foreign, unfamiliar, different, exotic
OPPOSITE familiar
2 *They saw the lights of an* **alien** *spaceship.*
extraterrestrial

alien noun
I wrote a story about **aliens** *from Mars.*
extraterrestrial, alien life-form, spaceman or spacewoman, starman or starwoman

AN ALIEN MIGHT BE
humanoid, insect-like, lizard-like, reptilian, intelligent, primitive, super-intelligent, telepathic

alien

BODY PARTS AN ALIEN MIGHT HAVE
antenna, blotches, scales, slime, sucker, tentacle, webbing

TRANSPORT AN ALIEN MIGHT USE
alien vessel, flying saucer, mothership, pod, spacecraft, spaceship, starship, time-machine, transporter beam

An alien might call someone from Earth an **Earthling**.

a b c d e f g h i j k l m n o p q r s t u v w x y z

alive *adjective*
Fortunately, my goldfish was still **alive**.
living, live, existing, in existence, surviving, breathing, flourishing
OPPOSITE dead

allow *verb*
1 They don't **allow** skateboards in the playground.
permit, let, authorise, approve of, agree to, consent to, give permission for, license, put up with, stand, support, tolerate
OPPOSITE forbid
2 Have you **allowed** enough time for the journey?
allocate, set aside, assign, grant, earmark

all right *adjective*
1 The survivors appeared to be **all right**.
well, unhurt, unharmed, uninjured, safe
2 The food in the hotel was **all right**.
satisfactory, acceptable, adequate, reasonable, passable
3 Is it **all right** to play music in here?
acceptable, permissable

almost *adverb*
1 I have **almost** finished the crossword.
nearly, practically, just about, virtually, all but, as good as, not quite
2 **Almost** a hundred people came to the concert.
about, approximately, around

alone *adjective, adverb*
1 Did you go to the party **alone**?
on your own, by yourself, unaccompanied
2 Zoe had no friends and felt very **alone**.
lonely, friendless, isolated, solitary, lonesome, desolate

also *adverb*
We need some bread, and **also** more butter.
in addition, besides, additionally, too, furthermore, moreover

alter *verb*
They have **altered** the route for the cycle race.
change, adjust, adapt, modify, transform, amend, make different, revise, vary

always *adverb*
1 The sea is **always** in motion.
constantly, continuously, endlessly, eternally, for ever, perpetually, unceasingly
2 This bus is **always** late.
consistently, continually, invariably, persistently, regularly, repeatedly

amaze *verb*
It **amazes** me to think that the Earth is billions of years old.
astonish, astound, startle, surprise, stun, shock, stagger, dumbfound
(*informal*) flabbergast

amazed *adjective*
I was **amazed** by the number of emails I received.
astonished, astounded, stunned, surprised, dumbfounded, speechless, staggered
(*informal*) flabbergasted

amazing *adjective*
The Northern Lights are an **amazing** sight.
astonishing, astounding, staggering, remarkable, surprising, extraordinary, incredible, breathtaking, phenomenal, sensational, stupendous, tremendous, wonderful, mind-boggling

ambition *noun*
1 She had great **ambition** when she was young.
drive, enthusiasm, enterprise, push, zeal
2 My **ambition** is to play tennis at Wimbledon.
goal, aim, intention, objective, target, desire, dream, wish, hope, aspiration

ambitious *adjective*
1 If you're **ambitious**, you will probably succeed.
enterprising, enthusiastic, committed, go-ahead, keen
OPPOSITE unambitious
2 I think your plan is too **ambitious**.
grand, big, large-scale

amount *noun*
1 I worked out the exact **amount** I'd need to buy the jacket..
sum, total, whole
2 There's a large **amount** of paper in the cupboard.
quantity, measure, supply, volume, mass, bulk

amuse *verb*
I think this joke will **amuse** you.
make you laugh, entertain, cheer up, divert
(*informal*) tickle

amusing *adjective*
I didn't find his jokes very **amusing**.
funny, witty, humorous, comic, comical, hilarious, diverting, entertaining
OPPOSITE unamusing, serious

ancient *adjective*
1 Does that **ancient** car still go?
old, old-fashioned, antiquated, out of date, obsolete
2 In **ancient** times, our ancestors were hunters.
early, primitive, prehistoric, remote, long past, olden
The times before written records were kept are **prehistoric** times.
The ancient Greeks and Romans lived in **classical** times.
OPPOSITE modern

anger *noun*
I was filled with **anger** when I read her letter.
rage, fury, indignation
(*old use*) wrath, ire
An outburst of anger is a **tantrum** or a **temper**.

anger *verb*
His cruelty towards his dog **angered** me.
enrage, infuriate, incense, madden, annoy, irritate, exasperate, antagonise, provoke
(*informal*) make your blood boil, make you see red
OPPOSITE pacify

angry *adjective*
Miss Potts turns purple when she gets **angry**.
cross, furious, enraged, infuriated, irate, livid, annoyed, incensed, exasperated, fuming, indignant, raging, seething
(*informal*) mad
To become angry is to **lose your temper**.
OPPOSITE calm

animal *noun*
see panel opposite

announce *verb*
1 The head **announced** that sports day was cancelled.
declare, state, proclaim, report
2 The DJ **announced** the next record.
present, introduce, lead into

announcement *noun*
1 The head reads the **announcements** in assembly.
notice
2 The prime minister issued an **announcement**.
statement, declaration, proclamation, pronouncement
3 I heard the **announcement** on TV.
report, bulletin, news flash

annoy *verb*
1 I was **annoyed** that I missed the bus.
irritate, bother, displease, exasperate, anger, upset, vex, trouble, worry
OPPOSITE please
2 Please don't **annoy** me while I'm working.
pester, bother, harass, badger, nag, plague, trouble, try (*informal*) bug

🕸 **WORD WEB**

animal *noun*
*Wild **animals** roam freely in the safari park.*
creature, beast, brute
A word for wild animals in general is **wildlife**.
A scientific word for animals is **fauna**.

VARIOUS KINDS OF ANIMAL
amphibian, arachnid, bird, fish, insect, invertebrate, mammal, marsupial, mollusc, reptile, rodent, vertebrate

An animal that eats meat is a **carnivore**.
An animal that eats plants is a **herbivore**.
An animal that eats many things is an **omnivore**.
Animals that sleep most of the winter are **hibernating animals**.
Animals that are active at night are **nocturnal animals**.

SOME ANIMALS THAT LIVE ON LAND
aardvark, antelope, ape, armadillo, baboon, badger, bat, bear, beaver, bison, buffalo, camel, cheetah, chimpanzee, chinchilla, chipmunk, deer, dormouse, elephant, elk, fox, gazelle, gibbon, giraffe, gnu, gorilla, grizzly bear, hare, hedgehog, hippopotamus, hyena, jackal, jaguar, kangaroo, koala, lemming, lemur, leopard, lion, llama, lynx, mongoose, monkey, moose, mouse, ocelot, opossum, orang-utan, otter, panda, panther, platypus, polar bear, porcupine, rabbit, rat, reindeer, rhinoceros, skunk, squirrel, stoat, tapir, tiger, vole, wallaby, weasel, wildebeest, wolf, wolverine, wombat, yak, zebra

SOME ANIMALS THAT LIVE IN THE SEA
dolphin, porpoise, seal, sea lion, walrus, whale

SOME EXTINCT ANIMALS
dinosaur, dodo, quagga

gorilla

PARTS OF AN ANIMAL'S BODY
antler, claw, fang, foreleg, hind leg, hoof, horn, jaws, mane, muzzle, paw, snout, tail, trotter, tusk, whisker, fur, coat, fleece, hide, pelt

MALE AND FEMALE ANIMALS
A male elephant or whale is a **bull** and a female is a **cow**.
A male fox is a **dog** and a female is a **vixen**.
A male goat is a **billy goat** and a female is a **nanny goat**.
A male hare or rabbit is a **buck** and a female is a **doe**.
A male horse is a **stallion** and a female is a **mare**.
A female lion is a **lioness**.
A female pig is a **sow**.
A male sheep is a **ram** and a female is a **ewe**.
A female tiger is a **tigress**.
A male wolf is a **dog** and a female is a **bitch**.

✏ **WRITING TIPS**

You can use these words to describe an **animal**.
TO DESCRIBE *HOW AN ANIMAL MOVES*
bound, creep, crouch, dart, gallop, gambol, leap, lumber, nuzzle, pad, paw, pounce, roam, scuttle, skip, slink, slither, spring, stamp, stampede, trot, waddle *The jaguar **padded** along silently.*
TO DESCRIBE *AN ANIMAL'S BODY*
agile, nimble, sinewy, wiry; lumbering, majestic, mighty, muscular, powerful *The cheetah stretched its long, **sinewy** body.*
TO DESCRIBE *AN ANIMAL'S SKIN OR COAT*
coarse, fluffy, furry, glistening, glossy, hairy, leathery, matted, prickly, scaly, shaggy, shiny, silky, sleek, slimy, slippery, smooth, spiky, thick, thorny, tough, wiry, woolly; mottled, piebald, spotted, striped *The otters' coats were **smooth** and **silky**.*

YOUNG ANIMALS
A young beaver is a **kit**.
A young fox or lion is a **cub**.
A young goat is a **kid**.
A young hare is a **leveret**.
A young horse is a **foal**, **colt** (male) or **filly** (female).
A young pig is a **piglet**.
A young otter or seal is a **pup**.
A young sheep is a **lamb**.

HOMES OF WILD ANIMALS
den, lair
A badger lives in a **sett**.
A beaver or otter lives in a **lodge**.
A fox lives in an **earth**.
A rabbit lives in a **burrow** or **warren**.
A squirrel lives in a **drey**.

SOUNDS MADE BY ANIMALS
bark, bay, bellow, buzz, gnash, growl, grunt, hiss, howl, jabber, purr, roar, snap, snarl, snort, snuffle, squeak, trumpet, whimper, whine, yap, yelp, yowl

A sheep **bleats**.
A donkey **brays**.
A frog **croaks**.
Cattle **low** or **moo**.
A cat **mews** or **miaows**.
A horse **neighs** or **whinnies**.

lemur

giraffe

zebra

skunk

lion

tortoise

annoying adjective
*My brother has a lot of **annoying** habits.*
irritating, exasperating, maddening, provoking, tiresome, trying, vexing, troublesome

answer noun
1 *Did you get an **answer** to your letter?*
reply, response, acknowledgement, reaction
A quick or angry answer is a **retort**.
2 *The **answers** to the quiz are on the next page.*
solution, explanation

answer verb
1 *You haven't **answered** my question.*
give an answer to, reply to, respond to, react to, acknowledge
2 *'I'm quite well,' I **answered**.*
reply, respond, return
To answer quickly or angrily is to **retort**.

anxious adjective
1 *Are you **anxious** about your exams?*
nervous, worried, apprehensive, concerned, uneasy, fearful, edgy, fraught, tense, troubled, (informal) uptight, jittery
OPPOSITE calm
2 *I'm **anxious** to do my best.*
eager, keen, impatient, enthusiastic, willing

apologise verb
*The ogre **apologised** for being rude.*
make an apology, say sorry, express regret, repent, be penitent

apparent adjective
*There was no **apparent** reason for the crash.*
obvious, evident, clear, noticeable, detectable, perceptible, recognisable, conspicuous, visible
OPPOSITE concealed

appeal verb
to appeal for
*The prisoners **appealed for** our help.*
request, beg for, plead for, cry out for, entreat, ask earnestly for, pray for
to appeal to
*That kind of music doesn't **appeal** to me.*
attract, interest, fascinate, tempt

appear verb
1 *Snowdrops **appear** in the spring.*
come out, emerge, become visible, come into view, develop, occur, show, crop up, spring up, surface
2 *Our visitors didn't **appear** until midnight.*
arrive, come, turn up
(informal) show up

3 *It **appears** that the baby is asleep.*
seem, look
4 *I once **appeared** in a musical.*
act, perform, take part, feature

appearance noun
1 *They were startled by the **appearance** of the ghost.*
approach, arrival, entrance, entry
2 *Mr Hogweed had a grim **appearance**.*
air, aspect, bearing, look

appetite noun
1 *When I was ill, I completely lost my **appetite**.*
hunger
2 *Explorers have a great **appetite** for adventure.*
desire, eagerness, enthusiasm, passion, keenness, wish, urge, taste, thirst, longing, yearning, craving, lust, zest

apply verb
1 *The nurse told me to **apply** the ointment generously.*
administer, put on, lay on, spread
2 *My brother has **applied** for a new job.*
make an application for, ask for, request
3 *The rules **apply** to all our members.*
be relevant, relate, refer
4 *The vet **applied** all her skill to save the animal's life.*
use, employ, exercise, utilise

appreciate verb
1 *He **appreciates** good music.*
enjoy, like, love
2 *I **appreciate** her good qualities.*
admire, respect, regard highly, approve of, value, esteem
OPPOSITE despise
3 *I **appreciate** that you can't afford much.*
realise, recognise, understand, comprehend, know, see
4 *Dad hopes that the value of our house will **appreciate**.*
grow, increase, go up, mount, rise

approach verb
1 *The lioness **approached** her prey.*
draw near to, move towards, come near to, advance on
2 *I **approached** the head to ask if we could have a party.*
speak to, contact, go to
3 *The volunteers **approached** their work cheerfully.*
begin, undertake, embark on, set about

approach noun
1 *We could hear the **approach** of heavy footsteps.*
arrival, advance, coming

2 *Dad made an **approach** to the bank manager for a loan.*
application, appeal, proposal
3 *I like her positive **approach**.*
attitude, manner, style, way
4 *The easiest **approach** to the castle is from the west.*
access, entry, entrance, way in

appropriate adjective
*It's not **appropriate** to wear jeans to a wedding.*
suitable, proper, fitting, apt, right, tactful, tasteful, well-judged
OPPOSITE inappropriate

approval noun
1 *We cheered to show our **approval**.*
appreciation, admiration, praise, high regard, acclaim, respect, support
OPPOSITE disapproval
2 *The head gave her **approval** to our plan.*
agreement, consent, authorisation, assent, go-ahead, permission, support, blessing
OPPOSITE refusal

approve verb
*The head **approved** my request for a day off school.*
agree to, consent to, authorise, allow, accept, pass, permit, support, back
OPPOSITE refuse

approximate adjective
*What is the **approximate** length of the journey?*
estimated, rough, nexact, near
OPPOSITE exact

approximately adverb
*The film will finish at **approximately** five o'clock.*
roughly, about, around, round about, close to, nearly, more or less

area noun
1 *From the plane we saw a big **area** of desert.*
expanse, stretch, tract
A small area is a **patch**.
An area of water or ice is a **sheet**.
2 *I live in an urban **area**.*
district, locality, neighbourhood, region, zone, vicinity

argue verb
1 *You two are always **arguing** over something.*
quarrel, disagree, differ, fall out, fight, have an argument, squabble, wrangle, bicker
OPPOSITE agree
2 *We **argued** over the price of the cloth.*
bargain, haggle
3 *He **argued** that it was my turn to walk the dog.*
claim, assert, try to prove, maintain, reason, suggest

A B C D E F G H I J K L M N O P Q R S T U V W X Y Z

argument noun
1 *They was an **argument** over who should pay for the meal.*
disagreement, quarrel, dispute, row, clash, controversy, debate, difference, fight, squabble, altercation
2 *Did you follow the **argument** of the book?*
line of reasoning, theme, outline, gist

WORD WEB

armour noun
PARTS OF A MEDIEVAL KNIGHT'S ARMOUR
breastplate, cuirass (breast and back plate), gauntlet, greave (shin guard), habergeon (sleeveless coat), helmet, visor

Armour made of linked rings is **chain mail**.
An outfit of armour is a **suit of armour**.

arrange verb
1 *The books are **arranged** in alphabetical order.*
sort, order, put in order, group, organise, categorise, classify, collate, display, sort out, set out, lay out, line up
2 *Do you need any help **arranging** the party?*
plan, organise, prepare, set up, see to

arrangement noun
1 *They have improved the **arrangement** of the garden.*
layout, organisation, design, planning
2 *Did you change the **arrangement** of my books?*
order, grouping, display, distribution, spacing
3 *We have an **arrangement** to use the swimming pool.*
agreement, deal, bargain, contract, scheme

arrive verb
*When is the train due to **arrive**?*
appear, come, turn up, show up, get in
*When a plane arrives it **lands** or **touches down**.*
to arrive at
*We **arrived at** the castle before midnight.*
get to, reach

arrogant adjective
*His **arrogant** manner annoys me.*
boastful, conceited, proud, haughty, self-important, bumptious, pompous, snobbish, superior, vain
(*informal*) cocky, snooty, stuck-up
OPPOSITE modest

art noun see panel below

article noun
1 *Have you any **articles** for the jumble sale?*
item, object, thing
2 *Did you read my **article** in the magazine?*
essay, report, piece of writing

artificial adjective
1 *Organic gardeners don't use **artificial** fertilisers.*
man-made, synthetic, unnatural, manufactured
OPPOSITE natural
2 *She had an **artificial** flower in her buttonhole.*
fake, false, imitation, unreal, bogus, counterfeit
OPPOSITE genuine, real

ashamed adjective
*He was **ashamed** because of what he had done.*
sorry, remorseful, repentant, embarrassed, shamefaced, abashed, mortified, apologetic, penitent
(*informal*) red-faced
OPPOSITE unashamed, unrepentant

ask verb
1 *I **asked** them to be careful with the parcel.*
beg, entreat, appeal to, implore, plead with
2 *'Are you ready?' I **asked**.*
demand, enquire, inquire, query, question
3 *I'm going to **ask** you to my party.*
invite
(*formal*) request the pleasure of your company

asleep adjective
*I didn't hear the phone because I was **asleep**.*
sleeping, dozing, having a nap, napping
(*formal*) slumbering
*A patient asleep for an operation is **anaesthetized** or **under sedation**.*

WORD WEB

art noun and **artist** noun
SOME ARTISTS AND CRAFTSPEOPLE
animator, blacksmith, carpenter, cartoonist, designer, draughtsman, draughtswoman, embroiderer, engraver, goldsmith, graphic designer, illustrator, knitter, mason, painter, photographer, potter, printer, quilter, sculptor, silversmith, weaver

SOME ARTS AND CRAFTS
animation, basketry, batik, beadwork, carpentry, carving, collage, crochet, cross-stitch, decoupage, drawing, embroidery, enamelling, engraving, etching, graphics, illustration, jewellery, knitting, metalwork, modelling, mosaics, needlework, origami, painting, patchwork, photography, pottery, printing, quilting, screen printing, sculpture, sewing, sketching, spinning, stained glass, stamping, stencilling, tapestry, weaving, woodwork

artistic adjective
*Mum's flower arrangements are very **artistic**.*
creative, imaginative, aesthetic, attractive, beautiful, tasteful
OPPOSITE ugly

potter

photographer

a b c d e f g h i j k l m n o p q r s t u v w x y z

An animal asleep for the winter is **hibernating**.
OPPOSITE awake
to fall asleep We waited until the giant **fell asleep**.
drop off, doze, nod off
To fall asleep quickly is **to go out like a light**.

assemble verb
1 A crowd **assembled** to watch the rescue.
gather, come together, converge, accumulate, crowd together, flock together, meet, convene
OPPOSITE disperse
2 We **assembled** our luggage at the front door.
collect, gather, bring together, pile up, put together
3 The general **assembled** his troops.
round up, rally, muster

assembly noun
There was a large **assembly** of people in the market square.
gathering, meeting, crowd, throng
An assembly for worship is a **service**.
A large assembly to show support for something, often out of doors, is a **rally**.
An assembly to discuss political matters is a **council** or **parliament**.
An assembly to discuss and learn about a particular topic is a **conference** or **congress**.

assistance noun
1 Do you need **assistance** with your luggage?
help, aid, support, encouragement
2 We bought new sports equipment with the **assistance** of a local firm.
backing, collaboration, cooperation, sponsorship, subsidy, support

assistant noun
The magician was training a new **assistant**.
helper, partner, colleague, associate, supporter

assorted adjective
I bought a bag of sweets with **assorted** flavours.
various, different, mixed, diverse, miscellaneous, several

assortment noun
There was an **assortment** of sandwiches to choose from.
variety, mixture, selection, array, choice, collection, diversity

assume verb
1 I **assume** you'd like some chocolate.
suppose, presume, imagine, believe, guess, expect, gather, suspect, think
2 The bandit **assumed** a disguise.
put on, adopt, dress up in, wear

assure verb
I **assure** you that I will take care of your dog.
promise, give your word to

astonish verb
It **astonished** us to learn that the house was haunted.
amaze, astound, surprise, stagger, shock, dumbfound, leave speechless, startle, stun, take aback, take by surprise
(informal) flabbergast, take your breath away

astonishing adjective
The volcano was an **astonishing** sight.
amazing, astounding, staggering, remarkable, surprising, extraordinary, incredible, breathtaking, phenomenal, sensational, stupendous, tremendous, wonderful

athletic adjective
You need to be **athletic** to run in a marathon.
fit, active, energetic, strong, muscular, powerful, robust, sturdy, vigorous, well-built
(informal) sporty
OPPOSITE feeble, puny

WORD WEB

astronaut noun
The **astronauts** climbed aboard the space shuttle.
spaceman or spacewoman

THINGS AN ASTRONAUT MIGHT USE OR WEAR
spacesuit, jet pack, oxygen tank, gloves, helmet, moonboots or spaceboots, visor

PLACES AN ASTRONAUT MIGHT VISIT
alien planet, moonbase, spacelab, space shuttle, space station, starbase

atrocious adjective
Everyone was shocked by the **atrocious** crime.
wicked, terrible, dreadful, abominable, brutal, savage, barbaric, bloodthirsty, callous, cruel, diabolical, evil, fiendish, horrifying, merciless, outrageous, sadistic, terrible, vicious, villainous

attach verb
Attach this label to the parcel.
fasten, fix, join, tie, bind, secure, connect, link, couple, stick, affix, add, append
OPPOSITE detach

attack noun
1 The pirates' **attack** took us by surprise.
assault, strike, charge, rush, raid, ambush, invasion, onslaught
An attack with big guns or bombs is a **blitz** or **bombardment**.
An attack by planes is an **air raid**.

satellite

2 *The newspaper published an* **attack** *on his character.*
criticism, outburst, abuse, tirade
3 *I had a sneezing* **attack** *in assembly.*
bout, fit, spasm
(*informal*) turn

attack verb
1 *The travellers were* **attacked** *by highwaymen.*
assault, beat up, mug, set on, assail
To attack someone else's territory is to **invade** or **raid** it.
To attack someone from a hidden place is to **ambush** them.
To attack the enemy with bombs or heavy guns is to **bombard** them.
To attack by rushing at the enemy is to **charge**.
To attack a place suddenly is to **storm** it.
If an animal attacks you, it might **savage** you.
2 *He* **attacked** *her reputation.*
abuse, criticise, denounce
OPPOSITE defend

attempt verb
They will **attempt** *to reconstruct a Viking ship.*
try, endeavour, strive, seek, aim, make an effort

attend verb
Are you going to **attend** *the end-of-term concert?*
go to, appear at, be present at
to attend to
1 *Please* **attend** *carefully* **to** *my instructions.*
listen to, pay attention to, follow carefully, heed, mark, mind, note, notice, observe, think about
2 *Who will* **attend to** *the washing up?*
deal with, see to
3 *The nurses* **attended to** *the wounded.*
take care of, care for, look after, help, mind, tend

attitude noun
I'm trying to take a more positive **attitude** *to life.*
outlook, approach, behaviour, stance, frame of mind, disposition, view, position, manner, mood

attract verb
1 *Do you think our exhibition will* **attract** *people?*
interest, appeal to, fascinate, tempt, entice
2 *Baby animals* **attract** *big crowds at the zoo.*
draw, pull in

attractive adjective
1 *Miranda was a very* **attractive** *young woman.*
beautiful, pretty, good-looking, handsome, gorgeous, glamorous, striking, fetching, charming, lovely, delightful, pleasing, fascinating, captivating, enchanting
OPPOSITE unattractive, repulsive
2 *There are some* **attractive** *bargains in the sale.*
appealing, agreeable, interesting, desirable, tempting, irresistible

authority noun
1 *I have the head's* **authority** *to go home early.*
permission, consent, approval
2 *The king had the* **authority** *to execute the prisoners.*
power, right, influence
3 *My uncle is an* **authority** *on steam trains.*
expert, specialist

automatic adjective
1 *We took our car through the* **automatic** *car wash.*
automated, mechanical, programmed, computerised
2 *My sneezing was an* **automatic** *response to the pepper.*
instinctive, involuntary, impulsive, spontaneous, reflex, natural, unconscious, unthinking

available adjective
1 *There are no more seats* **available**.
obtainable, free
2 *Is there a phone* **available** *in the library?*
accessible, ready, usable, at hand, handy, within reach, convenient

average adjective
It was an **average** *kind of day at school.*
everyday, ordinary, normal, typical, usual, regular, commonplace, familiar
OPPOSITE unusual, extraordinary

avoid verb
1 *The driver tried hard to* **avoid** *the collision.*
get out of the way of, avert, dodge, keep clear of, steer clear of, fend off, shun
2 *The outlaws* **avoided** *capture for months.*
elude, evade, run away from, escape from
3 *How did you manage to* **avoid** *the washing up?*
get out of, shirk

awake adjective
Hester lay **awake** *all night worrying.*
wide awake, restless, sleepless, conscious, astir

Not being able to sleep is to be suffering from **insomnia**.
OPPOSITE asleep

award noun
Kirsty got a national **award** *for gymnastics.*
prize, trophy, medal

aware adjective
aware of
The spy was **aware of** *the dangers of the mission.*
acquainted with, conscious of, familiar with, informed about
OPPOSITE ignorant of

awful adjective
1 *The weather was* **awful** *last weekend.*
bad, dreadful, terrible, appalling, dire, abysmal
(*informal*) rubbish, lousy
2 *The teacher complained about our* **awful** *behaviour.*
disgraceful, shameful, disobedient, naughty
3 *Cinderella's stepmother was an* **awful** *woman.*
unpleasant, disagreeable, nasty, horrid, detestable, unkind, unfriendly
4 *The country was shocked by the* **awful** *crime.*
horrifying, shocking, atrocious, abominable, outrageous
5 *I feel* **awful** *about forgetting your birthday.*
sorry, ashamed, embarrassed, guilty, remorseful

awkward adjective
1 *The parcel was an* **awkward** *shape.*
bulky, inconvenient, unmanageable, unwieldy
OPPOSITE convenient
2 *The giant was very* **awkward** *with his knife and fork.*
clumsy, unskilful, bungling
OPPOSITE skilful
3 *We found ourselves in a very* **awkward** *situation.*
difficult, troublesome, trying, perplexing, tough
OPPOSITE straightforward, easy
4 *Are you trying to be* **awkward**?
obstinate, stubborn, uncooperative, unhelpful, exasperating
OPPOSITE cooperative
5 *I felt* **awkward** *as I didn't know anyone at the party.*
embarrassed, uncomfortable, uneasy, out of place, at ease
OPPOSITE comfortable, at ease

a b c d e f g h i j k l m n o p q r s t u v w x y z

Bb

baby noun
infant, child
A baby who has just been born is a **newborn**.
A baby just learning to walk is a **toddler**.
The time when someone is a baby is their **babyhood**.

babyish adjective
My brother thinks that dolls are babyish.
childish, immature, infantile
OPPOSITE grown-up, mature

back noun
We always sit at the back of the bus.
end, rear, tail end
OPPOSITE front

back adjective
The back door of the cabin was locked.
end, rear, tail
The back legs of an animal are its **hind** legs.
OPPOSITE front

back verb
1 *A big lorry was backing into our driveway.*
go backwards, reverse
2 *I'm backing the blue team to win the race.*
bet on, put money on
3 *The council is backing the plan to build a skate park.*
support, sponsor, endorse

background noun
1 *I drew a mermaid with the sea in the background.*
OPPOSITE foreground
2 *The first chapter deals with the background to the war.*
circumstances of, history of, lead-up to
3 *My mother's family has a Swedish background.*
tradition, upbringing, ancestry

OVERUSED WORDS

bad adjective
Try to vary the words you use for **bad**. Here are some other words you could use.

FOR A *BAD PERSON*
wicked, evil, cruel, malevolent, malicious, vicious, villainous, mean, nasty, beastly, monstrous, corrupt, deplorable, detestable, immoral, infamous, shameful, sinful *Gobo was a detestable king who was loathed by his subjects.*
A bad person is a **scoundrel**, **rogue** or **rascal**.
A bad character in a story or film is a **villain** or (*informal*) **baddy**.
OPPOSITE good, virtuous
FOR A *BAD ACCIDENT* OR *BAD ILLNESS*
serious, severe, grave, distressing, acute *Ingrid has a severe case of chickenpox.*
OPPOSITE minor
FOR *BAD BEHAVIOUR*
naughty, mischievous, disobedient, disgraceful, wrong *That mischievous kitten drank my milk!*
OPPOSITE exemplary, angelic
FOR A *BAD EXPERIENCE* OR *BAD NEWS*
unpleasant, unwelcome, disagreeable, horrible, awful, terrible, dreadful, horrific, appalling, shocking, hideous, disastrous, ghastly, frightful, abominable, diabolical
The letter contained disagreeable news.
Another word for a bad experience is an **ordeal**.
OPPOSITE good, excellent
FOR A *BAD HABIT* OR SOMETHING THAT IS *BAD FOR YOU*
harmful, damaging, dangerous, undesirable, detrimental, injurious
Fizzy drinks can be harmful to your teeth.
FOR *BAD WEATHER*
harsh, hostile, unfavourable, adverse, miserable
(*informal*) lousy *Penguins face hostile weather in the Antarctic.*
OPPOSITE fine, favourable
FOR FOOD THAT HAS *GONE BAD*
mouldy, rotten, off, decayed, sour, spoiled, rancid *The strawberries have started to go mouldy.*
OPPOSITE fresh
TO *FEEL BAD* ABOUT SOMETHING
guilty, ashamed, sorry, remorseful, repentant *Scrooge feels repentant by the end of the story.*
OPPOSITE unashamed, unrepentant

---

bad adjective
This has been a bad week for all of us.
awful, horrible, terrible
OPPOSITE good, fine, excellent

bad-tempered adjective
Trolls are always bad-tempered before breakfast.
cross, grumpy, irritable, moody, quarrelsome, fractious, ill-tempered, short-tempered, cantankerous, crotchety, snappy, testy, sullen
OPPOSITE good-tempered, cheerful

bag noun
I put my wet clothes in a plastic bag.
sack, carrier, holdall, satchel, handbag, shoulder bag
A bag you carry on your back is a **backpack** or **rucksack**.

ball noun
Wind the string into a ball.
sphere, globe, orb
A small ball of something is a **pellet** or **globule**.

ban verb
Skateboards are banned from the playground.
forbid, prohibit, bar, exclude, outlaw
OPPOSITE allow, permit

band noun
1 *The king was surrounded by a band of courtiers.*
company, group, gang, party, troop, crew
2 *I play piano in the junior jazz band.*
group, ensemble, orchestra
3 *The team captain wears a red arm band.*
strip, stripe, ring, line, belt, hoop

bang noun
1 *There was a loud bang as the balloon burst.*
blast, boom, crash, thud, thump, pop, explosion, report
2 *He got a bang on the head from the low ceiling.*
bump, blow, hit, knock, thump, punch, smack, whack, clout
(*informal*) wallop

bang *verb*
*Miss Crabbit **banged** her fist on the desk and scowled.*
hit, thump, strike, bash, slam, wham

banish *verb*
*The king's brother was **banished** forever.*
exile, expel, deport, send away, eject

bank *noun*
1 *The temple was built on the **banks** of the River Nile.*
edge, side, shore, margin, brink
2 *We rolled our Easter eggs down a grassy **bank**.*
slope, mound, ridge, embankment

banquet *noun*
*There was a **banquet** on the queen's birthday.*
dinner, feast

bar *noun*
1 *Did you eat the whole **bar** of chocolate?*
block, slab, chunk, wedge
A bar of gold or silver is an **ingot**.
A bar of soap is a **cake**.
2 *The window had iron **bars** across it.*
rod, pole, rail, stake, beam, girder

bar *verb*
1 *Two athletes were **barred** from competing in the race.*
ban, prohibit, exclude, keep out
2 *A fallen tree **barred** our way.*
block, hinder, impede, obstruct, stop, check

bare *adjective*
1 *I put suncream on my **bare** arms and legs.*
naked, nude, exposed, uncovered, unclothed, undressed
2 *The wolf had a **bare** patch on its back.*
bald, hairless
3 *We slept outside on the **bare** mountain.*
barren, bleak, treeless
4 *Inside, the dungeon was cold and **bare**.*
empty, unfurnished, vacant
5 *There wasn't a **bare** patch of wall left.*
blank, plain, clear, empty
6 *There is only room to pack the **bare** essentials.*
basic, minimum

barely *adverb*
*We **barely** had time to get dressed.*
hardly, scarcely, only just

bargain *noun*
1 *We made a **bargain** with the captain to take us ashore.*
deal, agreement, promise, pact

2 *That camera you bought was a **bargain**.*
good buy, special offer
(*informal*) snip, steal

bargain *verb*
*He refused to **bargain** with the pirates for his life.*
argue, do a deal, haggle, negotiate

bark *verb*
*The guard dog began to **bark** fiercely.*
woof, yap, yelp, growl

barrel *noun*
*The smugglers carried **barrels** of gunpowder.*
cask, drum, tub, keg, butt

barrier *noun*
1 *Spectators were asked to stay behind the **barrier**.*
wall, fence, railing, barricade
A barrier across a road is a **roadblock**.
2 *His shyness was a **barrier** to making friends.*
obstacle, hurdle, drawback, handicap, hindrance, stumbling block

base *noun*
1 *The footprints stop at the **base** of the pyramid.*
bottom, foot
2 *The dolls' house comes with a wooden **base**.*
foundation, support
A base under a statue is a **pedestal** or **plinth**.
3 *The mountaineers returned to their **base**.*
headquarters, camp, depot

basic *adjective*
1 *These are the **basic** moves in ice-skating.*
main, chief, principal, key, central, essential, fundamental, crucial
2 *My knowledge of French is very **basic**.*
elementary, simple
OPPOSITE advanced

bathe *verb*
1 *It was too cold to **bathe** in the sea.*
swim, go swimming, splash about, take a dip
To walk about in shallow water is to **paddle**.
To walk through deep water is to **wade**.
2 *The nurse gently **bathed** the wound.*
clean, cleanse, wash, rinse

battle *noun*
*The **battle** between our countries raged for many years.*
fight, clash, conflict, action, engagement, hostilities, struggle

beach *noun*
*We found these shells on the **beach**.*
sands, seashore, seaside, shore

beam *noun*
1 *Wooden **beams** ran across the ceiling.*
bar, timber, joist, plank, post, rafter, boom, spar, strut, support
2 *A **beam** of sunlight entered the cave.*
ray, shaft, stream, gleam
A strong narrow beam of light used in various devices is a **laser**.

bear *verb*
1 *The rope won't **bear** my weight.*
carry, support, hold, take
2 *The messenger **bore** a letter from the king.*
bring, carry, convey, transport, take, transfer
3 *The gravestone **bears** an old inscription.*
display, show, have
4 *The stench in the cave was too much to **bear**.*
put up with, cope with, stand, suffer, tolerate, endure, abide
5 *The lioness has **borne** three cubs.*
give birth to

beast *noun*
*In the darkness, they heard a wild **beast** howl.*
animal, creature
You might call a large or frightening beast a **brute** or **monster**.

beat *verb*
1 *It's cruel to **beat** an animal with a stick.*
hit, strike, thrash, batter, whip, lash, flog
(*informal*) whack, wallop
2 *I **beat** my brother at chess for the first time.*
defeat, conquer, vanquish, win against, get the better of, overcome, overwhelm, rout, thrash, trounce
(*informal*) hammer
3 ***Beat** the eggs, milk and sugar together.*
whisk, whip, blend, mix, stir
4 *Can you feel your heart **beating**?*
pound, thump, palpitate
to beat someone up
*The bully threatened to **beat** me **up**.*
assault, attack

a
b
c
d
e
f
g
h
i
j
k
l
m
n
o
p
q
r
s
t
u
v
w
x
y
z

beat noun
1 Can you feel the **beat** of your heart?
pulse, throb
2 Reggae music has a strong **beat**.
rhythm, accent, stress

beautiful adjective
1 The fairy queen looked **beautiful** by moonlight.
attractive, good-looking, pretty, gorgeous, glamorous, radiant, elegant, enchanting, dazzling, stunning, magnificent, resplendent
A man who is pleasing to look at is **good-looking** or **handsome**.
OPPOSITE ugly, unattractive
2 It was a **beautiful** day for a bicycle trip.
fine, excellent, glorious, marvellous, sunny, superb, splendid, wonderful
OPPOSITE dull, gloomy, drab
3 The Northern Lights are a **beautiful** sight.
glorious, magnificent, picturesque, scenic, spectacular, splendid
4 The nightingale has a **beautiful** song.
harmonious, mellifluous, melodious, sweet-sounding
OPPOSITE grating

beckon verb
The guard was **beckoning** me to approach.
signal, gesture, motion, gesticulate

become verb
1 I soon **became** frustrated with the video game.
begin to be, turn, get
2 Eventually, the tadpoles will **become** frogs.
grow into, change into, develop into, turn into
3 That style of hat **becomes** you.
look good on, suit, flatter

bed noun
1 The children slept on hard, wooden **beds**.
bunk, mattress
A bed for a baby is a **cot**, **cradle** or **crib**.
Two single beds one above the other are **bunk beds**.
A bed on a ship or train is a **berth**.
A bed made of net or cloth hung up above the ground is a **hammock**.
2 We planted daffodils in the flower **beds**.
plot, patch, border
3 These creatures feed on the **bed** of the ocean.
bottom, floor
OPPOSITE surface

beg verb
He **begged** me not to let go of the rope.
ask, plead with, entreat, implore, beseech

begin verb
1 The hunters **began** their search at dawn.
start, commence, embark on, set about
OPPOSITE end, finish, conclude
2 When did the trouble **begin**?
start, commence, arise, emerge, appear, originate, spring up
OPPOSITE end, stop, cease

beginning noun
The house was built at the **beginning** of last century.
start, opening, commencement, introduction, establishment, foundation, initiation, launch, dawn
The beginning of the day is **dawn** or **daybreak**.
The beginning of a journey is the **starting point**.
The beginning of a stream or river is the **origin** or **source**.
A piece of writing at the beginning of a book is an **introduction**, **preface** or **prologue**.
A piece of music at the beginning of a musical or opera is a **prelude** or **overture**.
OPPOSITE end, conclusion

behave verb
Our neighbour is **behaving** very strangely.
act, react, perform
to behave yourself
We promised to **behave ourselves** in the car.
be good, be on your best behaviour

behaviour noun
I give my puppy treats for good **behaviour**.
actions, conduct, manners, attitude

belief noun
1 She was a woman of strong religious **beliefs**.
faith, principle, creed, doctrine
2 It is my **belief** that he stole the money.
opinion, view, conviction, feeling, notion, theory

believable adjective
None of the characters in the book are **believable**.
credible, plausible
OPPOSITE unbelievable, implausible

believe verb
1 I don't **believe** anything he says.
accept, have faith in, rely on, trust
OPPOSITE disbelieve, doubt
2 I **believe** they used to live in Canada.
assume, feel, know, presume, reckon, suppose, think

belong verb
1 This ring **belonged** to my grandmother.
be owned by

2 Do you **belong** to the sports club?
be a member of, be connected with

belongings plural noun
Don't leave any **belongings** on the bus.
possessions, property, goods, things

bend verb
This drinking straw **bends** in the middle.
curve, turn, twist, curl, coil, loop, arch, warp, wind
A word for things which bend easily is **flexible** or (informal) **bendy**.
OPPOSITE straighten
to bend down
I **bent down** to tie my shoelaces.
stoop, bow, crouch, duck, kneel

bend noun
Watch out for the sharp **bend** in the road.
curve, turn, angle, corner, twist, zigzag

bend

bent adjective
1 After the crash, the car was a mass of **bent** metal.
curved, twisted, coiled, looped, buckled, crooked, arched, folded, warped
(informal) wonky
2 The witch had a **bent** back and walked with a stick.
crooked, hunched, curved, arched, bowed

best adjective
1 She is our **best** goalkeeper.
top, leading, finest, foremost, supreme, star, outstanding, unequalled, unrivalled
OPPOSITE worst
2 We did what we thought was **best**.
most suitable, most appropriate

betray verb
1 He **betrayed** us by telling the enemy our plan.
be disloyal to, be a traitor to, cheat, conspire against, double-cross
Someone who betrays you is a **traitor**.
To betray your country is to commit **treason**.
2 The look in her eyes **betrayed** her true feelings.
reveal, show, indicate, disclose, divulge, expose, tell

better adjective

1 *Which of these songs do you think is **better**?*
superior, finer, preferable
2 *I had a cold, but I'm **better** now.*
recovered, cured, healed, improved, well

beware verb

***Beware!** There are thieves about.*
be careful! watch out! look out! take care! be on your guard!
beware of
***Beware of** the bull.*
watch out for, avoid, mind, heed, keep clear of

biased adjective

*A referee should not make a **biased** decision.*
prejudiced, partial, one-sided, partisan, unfair
OPPOSITE impartial

big adjective

*The giant owned three pairs of **big** boots.*
large, huge, great, massive, enormous, gigantic, colossal, mammoth
(*informal*) whopping, ginormous, humungous
OPPOSITE small, little, tiny

! OVERUSED WORDS

Try to vary the words you use for **big**. Here are some other words you could use.

FOR A *BIG PERSON* OR *BIG CREATURE*
burly, giant, hefty, hulking, mighty, monstrous, towering *The **mighty** robot clanked as it moved.*
FOR A *BIG OBJECT*
bulky, heavy, hefty, weighty *What could be inside that **bulky** envelope?*
FOR A *BIG ROOM* OR *BIG BOX*
roomy, sizeable, spacious *Inside, the spaceship was surprisingly **roomy**.*
OPPOSITE cramped
FOR A *BIG DISTANCE*
immense, infinite, vast *A **vast** stretch of ocean lay before them.*
FOR A *BIG AMOUNT* OR *BIG HELPING*
ample, considerable, substantial *We each got an **ample** helping of porridge.*
OPPOSITE meagre, paltry
FOR A *BIG DECISION* OR *BIG MOMENT*
grave, important, serious, significant *Yesterday was the most **significant** day in my short life.*
OPPOSITE unimportant, minor

🕸 WORD WEB

bird noun
A female bird is a **hen**.
A male bird is a **cock**.
A young bird is a **chick**, **fledgling** or **nestling**.
A family of chicks is a **brood**.
A group of birds is a **colony** or **flock**.
A group of flying birds is a **flight** or **skein**.
A person who studies birds is an **ornithologist**.

SOME COMMON BRITISH BIRDS
blackbird, blue tit, bullfinch, bunting, chaffinch, crow, cuckoo, dove, greenfinch, jackdaw, jay, linnet, magpie, martin, nightingale, pigeon, raven, robin, rook, skylark, sparrow, starling, swallow, swift, thrush, tit, wagtail, waxwing, woodpecker, wren, yellowhammer

BIRDS OF PREY
buzzard, eagle, falcon, hawk, kestrel, kite, merlin, osprey, owl, sparrowhawk, vulture

FARM AND GAME BIRDS
chicken, duck, goose, grouse, partridge, pheasant, quail, turkey

Birds kept by farmers are called **poultry**.

SEA AND WATER BIRDS
albatross, auk, bittern, coot, cormorant, crane, curlew, duck, gannet, goose, guillemot, gull, heron, kingfisher, kittiwake, lapwing, mallard, moorhen, oystercatcher, peewit, pelican, penguin, puffin, seagull, snipe, stork, swan, teal

BIRDS FROM OTHER COUNTRIES
bird of paradise, budgerigar, canary, cockatoo, flamingo, humming bird, ibis, kookaburra, lovebirds, macaw, mynah bird, parakeet, parrot, toucan

flamingo

eagle

BIRDS WHICH CANNOT FLY
emu, kiwi, ostrich, peacock, penguin

PARTS OF A BIRD'S BODY
beak, bill, claw, talon, breast, crown, throat, crest, feather, down, plumage, plume, wing

SOME TYPES OF BIRD HOME
nest, nesting box, aviary, coop, roost

SOUNDS MADE BY BIRDS
cackle, caw, cheep, chirp, chirrup, cluck, coo, crow, gabble, honk, peep, pipe, quack, screech, squawk, trill, tweet, twitter, warble
A turkey **gobbles**.
An owl **hoots**.

SPECIAL NAMES
A female peacock is a **peahen**.
A young duck is a **duckling**.
A young goose is a **gosling**.
A young swan is a **cygnet**.
An eagle's nest is an **eyrie**.
A place where rooks nest is a **rookery**.

✏ WRITING TIPS

You can use these words to describe a **bird**.
1 TO DESCRIBE *HOW A BIRD MOVES*
circle, dart, flit, flutter, fly, glide, hop, hover, peck, perch, preen, skim, soar, swoop, waddle, wheel
*A pair of swallows **flitted** among the rooftops.*

2 TO DESCRIBE *A BIRD'S FEATHERS*
bedraggled, downy, drab, fluffy, gleaming, iridescent, ruffled, smooth, speckled *The peacock displayed its **iridescent** tail.*

lovebirds

owl

ostrich

a b d e f g h i j k l m n o p q r s t u v w x y z

A
B
C
D
E
F
G
H
I
J
K
L
M
N
O
P
Q
R
S
T
U
V
W
X
Y
Z

bit noun
1 *Mum divided the cake into eight **bits**.*
piece, portion, part, section, segment, share, slice
2 *These jeans are a **bit** long for me.*
a little, slightly, rather, fairly, somewhat, quite

bite verb
1 *I **bit** a chunk out of my apple.*
munch, nibble, chew, crunch, gnaw, (informal) chomp
2 *Take care. These animals can **bite**.*
nip, pinch, pierce, wound
When an animal tries to bite you it **snaps** at you.
When an insect bites you it **stings** you.
A fierce animal **mauls** or **savages** its prey.

bitter adjective
1 *The medicine had a **bitter** taste.*
sour, sharp, acid, acrid, tart
OPPOSITE sweet
2 *His brother was still **bitter** about the quarrel.*
resentful, embittered, disgruntled, aggrieved
OPPOSITE contented
3 *The wind blowing in from the sea was **bitter**.*
biting, cold, freezing, icy, piercing, raw, wintry, (informal) perishing
OPPOSITE mild

black adjective, noun
*The pony had a shiny **black** coat.*
coal-black, jet-black, pitch-black, ebony, raven
You can also describe a black night as **pitch-dark**.
Someone in a bad mood is said to look **as black as thunder**.
Common similes are **as black as coal** and **as black as night**.

blame verb
*Don't **blame** me if you miss the bus.*
accuse, criticise, condemn, reproach, scold

blank adjective
1 *There are no **blank** pages left in my jotter.*
empty, bare, clean, plain, unmarked, unused
2 *The old woman gave us a **blank** look.*
expressionless, faceless, vacant

blaze noun
*Firefighters fought the **blaze** for hours.*
fire, flames, inferno

blaze verb
*Within a few minutes the campfire was **blazing**.*
burn brightly, flare up

bleak adjective
1 *The countryside was **bleak** and barren.*
bare, barren, desolate, empty, exposed, stark

2 *The future looks **bleak** for the club.*
gloomy, hopeless, depressing, dismal, grim, miserable
OPPOSITE promising

blend verb
1 ***Blend** the flour with a tablespoon of water.*
beat together, mix, stir together, whip, whisk
2 *The paint colours **blend** well with each other.*
go together, match, fit, harmonise
OPPOSITE clash

blind adjective
*Polar bear cubs are born **blind**.*
sightless, unsighted, unseeing
A common simile is **as blind as a bat**.
OPPOSITE sighted, seeing
blind to
*The captain was **blind to** his own faults.*
ignorant of, unaware of, oblivious to
OPPOSITE aware of

bliss noun
*Having a whole day off school was sheer **bliss**.*
joy, delight, pleasure, happiness, heaven, ecstasy
OPPOSITE misery

blob noun
*The alien left **blobs** of green slime on the carpet.*
drop, lump, spot, dollop, daub, globule

block noun
1 *A **block** of ice fell from the glacier.*
chunk, hunk, lump, piece
2 *There must be a **block** in the drainpipe.*
blockage, jam, obstacle, obstruction
block verb
1 *A tall hedge **blocked** our view of the house.*
obstruct, hamper, hinder, interfere with
2 *A mass of leaves had **blocked** the drain.*
clog, choke, jam, plug, stop up, congest (informal) bung up

bloodthirsty adjective
*The **bloodthirsty** pirates rattled their swords.*
brutal, cruel, barbaric, murderous, inhuman, pitiless, ruthless, savage, vicious

bloom noun
*The pear tree was covered in white **blooms**.*
flower, blossom, bud
bloom verb
*The daffodils **bloomed** early this year.*
blossom, flower, open
OPPOSITE fade

blot noun
*The old map was covered with ink **blots**.*
spot, blotch, mark, blob, splodge, smudge, smear, stain
blot verb
to blot something out
*The new tower block **blots out** the view.*
conceal, hide, mask, obliterate, obscure

blow noun
1 *He was knocked out by a **blow** on the head.*
knock, bang, bash, hit, punch, clout, slap, smack, swipe, thump (informal) wallop, whack
2 *Losing the hockey match was a terrible **blow**.*
shock, upset, setback, disappointment, catastrophe, misfortune, disaster, calamity
blow verb
*The wind was **blowing** from the east.*
blast, gust, puff, fan
To make a shrill sound by blowing is to **whistle**.

blunder noun
*Forgetting her birthday was a terrible **blunder**.*
mistake, error, fault, slip, slip-up, gaffe
(informal) howler

blunt adjective
1 *This pencil is **blunt**.*
dull, worn, unsharpened
OPPOSITE sharp, pointed
2 *Her reply to my question was very **blunt**.*
abrupt, frank, direct, outspoken, plain, tactless
OPPOSITE tactful

blurred adjective
*The background of the photograph is all **blurred**.*
indistinct, vague, blurry, fuzzy, hazy, out of focus
OPPOSITE clear, distinct

blush verb
*The actor **blushed** with embarrassment.*
flush, go red, colour

boast verb
*The knight was always **boasting** about his fencing skills.*
brag, show off, crow, gloat, swagger
(informal) blow your own trumpet

boastful adjective
*Giants are **boastful** creatures and brag about everything.*
arrogant, big-headed, conceited, vain, bumptious
(informal) cocky, swanky
OPPOSITE modest, humble

WORD WEB

boat *noun*
*Several fishing **boats** were moored in the harbour.*
ship, craft, vessel

SOME TYPES OF BOAT OR SHIP
barge, canoe, catamaran, cruise liner, dhow, dinghy, dugout, ferry, freighter, gondola, hovercraft, hydrofoil, junk, launch, lifeboat, motor boat, oil tanker, paper boat, punt, raft, rowing boat, schooner, skiff, speedboat, steamship, tanker, trawler, tug, yacht

MILITARY BOATS OR SHIPS
aircraft carrier, battleship, destroyer, frigate, gunboat, minesweeper, submarine, warship

SOME BOATS USED IN THE PAST
brigantine, clipper, coracle, cutter, galleon, galley, man-of-war, paddle steamer, schooner, trireme, windjammer

kayak

The left side of a boat is called **port**.
The right side of a boat is called **starboard**.
A shed where boats are stored is a **boathouse**.

canoe

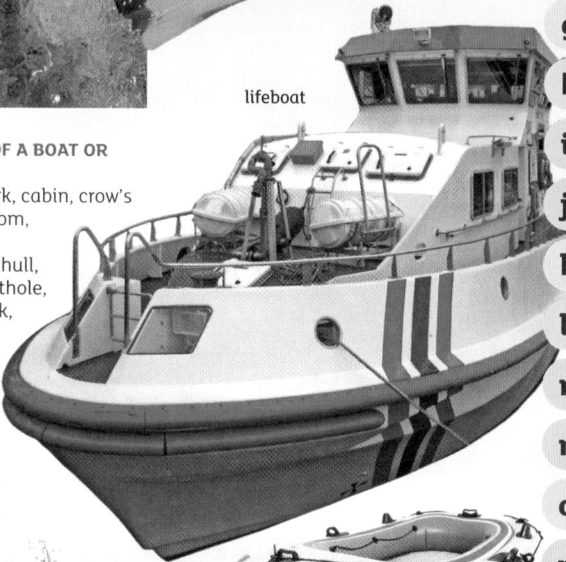

lifeboat

WORDS FOR PARTS OF A BOAT OR SHIP
boom, bridge, bulwark, cabin, crow's nest, deck, engine room, fo'c'sle or forecastle, funnel, galley, helm, hull, keel, mast, poop, porthole, propeller, quarterdeck, rigging, rudder, sail, tiller

SPECIAL NAMES
The front part of a boat is the **bow** or **prow**.
The back part of a boat is the **stern**.

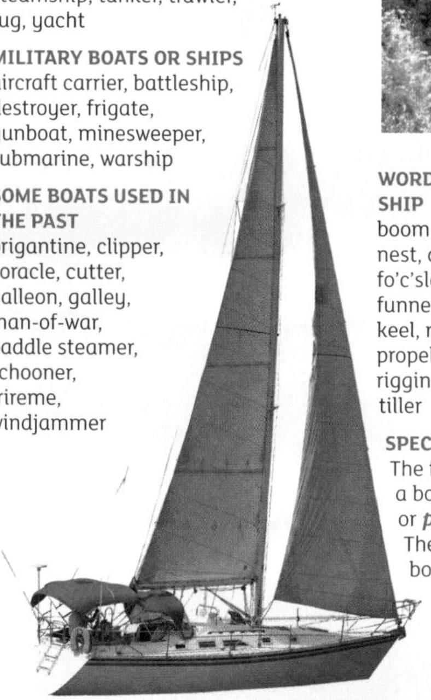

yacht

cruise liner

dinghy

a
b
c
d
e
f
g
h
i
j
k
l
m
n
o
p
q
r
s
t
u
v
w
x
y
z

A
B
C
D
E
F
G
H
I
J
K
L
M
N
O
P
Q
R
S
T
U
V
W
X
Y
Z

🕷 WORD WEB

body noun
The study of the human body
is **anatomy**.
The main part of your body except
your head, arms, and legs is your
trunk or **torso**.
The shape of your body is your
build, **figure** or **physique**.
A person's dead body is a **corpse**.
The dead body of an animal is a
carcass.

**OUTER PARTS OF THE HUMAN
BODY**
abdomen, ankle, arm, armpit,
breast, buttocks, calf, cheek, chest,
chin, ear, elbow, eye, finger, foot,
forehead, genitals, groin, hand,
head, heel, hip, instep, jaw, knee,
kneecap, knuckle, leg, lip, mouth,
navel, neck, nipple, nose, pores,
shin, shoulder, skin, stomach,
temple, thigh, throat, waist, wrist

**INNER PARTS OF THE HUMAN
BODY**
arteries, bladder, bowels, brain,
eardrum, glands, gullet, gums,
guts, heart, intestines, kidneys,
larynx, liver, lung, muscles, nerves,
ovaries, pancreas, prostate,
sinews, stomach, tendons, tongue,
tonsil, tooth, uterus, veins,
windpipe, womb

bog noun
We felt our boots sinking into the **bog**.
swamp, quagmire, quicksand, fen

boisterous adjective
Baby dragons can be loud and
boisterous.
lively, noisy, rowdy, unruly,
wild, disorderly
OPPOSITE restrained, calm

bold adjective
1 It was a **bold** move to attack
the fortress.
brave, courageous, daring,
adventurous, audacious, confident,
enterprising, fearless, heroic, valiant,
intrepid, plucky
OPPOSITE cowardly
2 The poster uses large letters in
bold colours.
striking, strong, bright, loud,
showy, conspicuous, eye-catching,
noticeable, prominent
OPPOSITE inconspicuous, subtle

bolt verb
1 Did you remember to **bolt** the door?
fasten, latch, lock, secure, bar
2 The horses **bolted** when they
heard the thunder.
dash away, dart, flee, sprint, run
away, rush off

3 Don't **bolt** your food.
gobble, gulp, guzzle, wolf down

book verb
1 Have you **booked** a seat on the
train?
order, reserve
2 I've **booked** the disco for the party.
arrange, engage, organise

border noun
1 The town is on the **border** between
France and Germany.
boundary, frontier
2 I drew a thin line around the
border of the picture.
edge, margin, perimeter
A decorative border round the top of
a wall is a **frieze**.
A border round the bottom of
a skirt is a **hem**.
A decorative border on fabric is
a **frill**, **fringe** or **trimming**.

boring adjective
The film was so **boring** I fell asleep.
dull, dreary, tedious, tiresome,
unexciting, uninteresting, dry,
monotonous, uninspiring, insipid,
unimaginative, uneventful, humdrum
OPPOSITE interesting, exciting

bossy adjective
Stop being so **bossy** towards your
sister.
domineering, bullying, dictatorial,
officious, tyrannical
An informal name for a bossy person
is **bossy boots**.

bother verb
1 Would it **bother** you if I played
some music?
disturb, trouble, upset, annoy,
irritate, pester, worry, vex, exasperate
(informal) bug, hassle
2 Don't **bother** to phone tonight.
make an effort, take trouble, concern
yourself, care, mind

bother noun
It's such a **bother** to remember
the password.
nuisance, annoyance, irritation,
inconvenience, pest, trouble,
difficulty, problem
(informal) hassle

bottom noun
1 We camped at the **bottom** of
the mountain.
foot, base
OPPOSITE top, peak
2 The wreck sank to the **bottom**
of the sea.
bed, floor
OPPOSITE surface
3 A wasp stung me on the **bottom**.
backside, behind, buttocks, rear,
rump, seat
(informal) bum

bottom adjective
I got the **bottom** mark in the test.
least, lowest
OPPOSITE top

bounce verb
The ball **bounced** twice before it
reached the net.
rebound, ricochet, spring, leap

bound verb
The puppies **bounded** across the lawn.
leap, bounce, jump, spring, skip,
gambol, caper, frisk

box noun
case, chest, crate, carton, packet
A small box for jewellery or treasure
is a **casket**.
A large box for luggage is a **trunk**.

boy noun
lad, youngster, youth
(informal) kid

brain noun
You'll need to use your **brain** to solve
this riddle.
intelligence, intellect, mind, reason,
sense, wit

branch noun
1 A robin perched on a **branch** of
the tree.
bough, limb
2 I've joined the local **branch** of the
Kennel Club.
section, division, department, wing

branch verb
Follow the track until it **branches**
into two.
divide, fork

brand noun
Which **brand** of ice cream do you
like?
make, kind, sort, type, variety, label
The sign of a particular brand of
goods is a **trademark**.

brave adjective
It was **brave** of you to save the cat
from drowning.
courageous, heroic, valiant, fearless,
daring, gallant, intrepid, plucky
A common simile is **as brave
as a lion**.
OPPOSITE cowardly

bravery noun
The police dog was awarded a medal
for **bravery**.
courage, heroism, valour,
fearlessness, daring, nerve, gallantry,
grit, pluck
(informal) guts, bottle
OPPOSITE cowardice

break noun
1 Can you see any **breaks** in the
chain?
breach, crack, hole, gap, opening,
split, rift, puncture, rupture, fracture,
fissure

2 *Let's take a **break** for coffee.*
interval, pause, rest, lull,
time-out
(*informal*) breather

break verb
1 *The vase fell off the shelf and
broke.*
smash, shatter, fracture, chip, crack,
split, snap, splinter
(*informal*) bust
2 *The burglar was arrested for
breaking the law.*
disobey, disregard, violate, flout
3 *In her last race, she **broke** the
world record.*
beat, better, exceed, surpass, outdo

breathe verb
To breathe in is to **inhale**.
To breathe out is to **exhale**.
To breathe heavily when you have
been running is to **pant** or **puff**.
The formal word for breathing is
respiration.

breed verb
1 *Salmon swim upstream to **breed**
every year.*
reproduce, have young, multiply,
procreate, spawn
2 *Bad hygiene **breeds** disease.*
cause, produce, generate, encourage,
promote, cultivate, induce

breed noun
*What **breed** of dog is that?*
kind, sort, type, variety
The evidence of how a dog has been
bred is its **pedigree**.

breezy adjective
*This morning the weather was bright
and **breezy**.*
windy, blowy, blustery, gusty, fresh,
draughty

bridge noun
A bridge you can walk over is a
footbridge.
A bridge to carry water is an
aqueduct.
A long bridge carrying a road or
railway is a **viaduct**.

brief adjective
1 *We paid a **brief** visit to our cousins
on the way home.*
short, quick, hasty, fleeting,
temporary
2 *Give me a **brief** account of what
happened.*
short, concise, abbreviated,
condensed, compact, succinct

bright adjective
1 *We saw the **bright** lights of the
town in the distance.*
shining, brilliant, blazing, dazzling,
glaring, gleaming
OPPOSITE dull, dim, weak

2 *Bright colours will make the
poster stand out.*
strong, intense, vivid
Colours that shine in the dark are
luminous colours.
OPPOSITE dull, faded, muted
3 *Her teachers thought she was very
bright.*
clever, intelligent, gifted, sharp,
quick-witted
(*informal*) brainy
A common simile is **as bright as a
button**.
OPPOSITE stupid, dull-witted
4 *Miranda gave me a **bright** smile.*
cheerful, happy, lively, merry, jolly,
radiant
OPPOSITE sad, gloomy
5 *The day was cold, but **bright**.*
sunny, fine, fair, clear, cloudless
OPPOSITE dull, cloudy, overcast

brilliant adjective
1 *The fireworks gave off a **brilliant**
light.*
bright, blazing, dazzling, glaring,
gleaming, glittering, glorious,
shining, splendid, vivid
OPPOSITE dim, dull
2 *Brunel was a **brilliant** engineer.*
clever, exceptional, outstanding,
gifted, talented
OPPOSITE incompetent, talentless
3 (*informal*) *I saw a **brilliant** film
last week.*
excellent, marvellous, outstanding,
wonderful, superb
(*informal*) fantastic, fabulous

bring verb
1 *Can you **bring** the shopping in
from the car?*
carry, fetch, deliver, bear, transport
2 *You can **bring** a friend to the
party.*
invite, conduct, escort, guide, lead
3 *The war has **brought** great sorrow
to our people.*
cause, produce, lead to, result in,
generate
to bring something about
*The new coach **brought about** some
changes.*
cause, effect, create, introduce, be
responsible for
to bring someone up
*In the story, Tarzan is **brought up**
by apes.*
rear, raise, care for, foster, look after,
nurture, educate, train
to bring something up
*I wish you hadn't **brought up** the
subject of money.*
mention, talk about, raise, broach

brisk adjective
1 *Mr Hastie went for a **brisk** walk
every evening.*
lively, fast-paced, energetic, bracing,

invigorating, vigorous, refreshing
OPPOSITE slow, leisurely
2 *The flower shop does a **brisk** trade
around Easter.*
busy, lively, bustling, hectic
OPPOSITE quiet, slack, slow

broad adjective
1 *The streets in the city were **broad**
and straight.*
wide, open, large, roomy, spacious,
vast, extensive
OPPOSITE narrow
2 *Just give me a **broad** outline
of what happened.*
general, rough, vague, loose,
indefinite, imprecise
OPPOSITE specific, detailed

broken adjective
1 *Don't use that computer—it's
broken.*
faulty, defective, damaged, out of
order
OPPOSITE working
2 *After losing all his money, Forbes
was a **broken** man.*
crushed, defeated, beaten, spiritless

brush verb
1 *Jill spent ages **brushing** her
hair for the party.*
groom, comb, tidy
2 *A bird **brushed** against my cheek
as it flew past.*
touch, contact, rub, scrape

brutal adjective
*The bandits launched a **brutal**
attack.*
savage, vicious, cruel, barbaric,
bloodthirsty, callous, ferocious,
inhuman, merciless, pitiless, ruthless,
sadistic
OPPOSITE gentle, humane

bubble verb
*A green liquid **bubbled** in the witch's
cauldron.*
boil, seethe, gurgle, froth, foam

bubbly adjective
1 *Bubbly drinks get up my nose.*
fizzy, sparkling, effervescent
2 *Sophie has a bright and **bubbly**
personality.*
cheerful, lively, vivacious, spirited,
animated

buckle noun
*The pirate wore a belt with a large
silver **buckle**.*
clasp, fastener, fastening, clip, catch
buckle verb
1 *Please **buckle** your seat belts.*
fasten, secure, clasp, clip, do up,
hook up
2 *The bridge **buckled** when the giant
stepped on to it.*
bend, warp, twist, crumple, cave in,
collapse

a
b
c
d
e
f
g
h
i
j
k
l
m
n
o
p
q
r
s
t
u
v
w
x
y
z

A
B
C
D
E
F
G
H
I
J
K
L
M
N
O
P
Q
R
S
T
U
V
W
X
Y
Z

budge *verb*
The window was stuck and wouldn't ***budge***.
give way, move, shift, stir

bug *noun*
1 *Birds help to control* ***bugs*** *in the garden.*
insect, pest
2 *(informal) I can't get rid of this stomach* ***bug***.
infection, virus, germ, disease, illness
3 *There are a few* ***bugs*** *in the computer program.*
fault, error, defect, flaw
(*informal*) gremlin

build *verb*
Dad is going to ***build*** *a shed in the garden.*
construct, erect, put together, put up, set up, assemble
to build up
1 *I'm* ***building up*** *a collection of vinyl records.*
accumulate, assemble, collect, put together
2 *We felt the tension* ***building up*** *in the crowd.*
increase, intensify, rise, grow, mount up, escalate

WORD WEB

building *noun*
The new ***building*** *will have seven storeys.*
construction, structure, dwelling
A person who designs buildings is an ***architect***.

lighthouse

BUILDINGS WHERE PEOPLE LIVE
apartment, barracks, bungalow, castle, cottage, farmhouse, flat, fort, fortress, house, mansion, palace, skyscraper, tenement, terrace, tower, villa

BUILDINGS WHERE PEOPLE WORK
factory, garage, lighthouse, mill, shop, store, warehouse

BUILDINGS WHERE PEOPLE WORSHIP
abbey, cathedral, chapel, church, monastery, mosque, pagoda, shrine, synagogue, temple

OTHER TYPES OF BUILDING
cabin, cafe, cinema, college, gallery, hotel, inn, library, museum, observatory, police station, post office, power station, prison, pub or public house, restaurant, school, shed, theatre

build *noun*
Charlotte was a girl of slender ***build***.
body, form, frame, figure, physique

bulge *noun*
There was a large ***bulge*** *in the robber's sack.*
bump, hump, lump, swelling, protuberance

bulge *verb*
The creature had eyes which ***bulged*** *out of its head.*
stick out, swell, puff out, protrude

bulky *adjective*
The parcel is too ***bulky*** *to go through the letterbox.*
big, large, hefty, substantial, sizeable, cumbersome, unwieldy
OPPOSITE small, compact

bully *verb*
Some of the children were afraid of being ***bullied***.
persecute, torment, intimidate, terrorise, push around

bump *verb*
1 *The baby* ***bumped*** *his head on the table.*
hit, strike, knock, bang

PARTS YOU MIGHT FIND INSIDE A BUILDING
balcony, basement, cellar, conservatory, corridor, courtyard, crypt, dungeon, foyer, gallery, lobby, porch, quadrangle, room, staircase, veranda

PARTS YOU MIGHT FIND OUTSIDE A BUILDING
arch, balustrade, bay window, bow window, buttress, chimney, colonnade, column, dome, dormer window, drainpipe, eaves, foundations, gable, gutter, masonry, parapet, pediment, pillar, pipes, roof, tower, turret, vault, wall, window, windowsill

CASTLES AND FORTIFIED BUILDINGS
château, citadel, fort, fortress, motte and bailey, palace, stronghold, tower

PARTS OF A CASTLE
bailey, barbican, battlement, buttress, courtyard, donjon, drawbridge, dungeon, gate, gateway, keep, magazine, moat, motte, parapet, portcullis, postern, rampart, tower, turret, wall, watchtower

2 *My bicycle* ***bumped*** *up and down over the cobbles.*
bounce, shake, jerk, jolt
to bump into
1 *The taxi* ***bumped into*** *the car in front of it.*
collide with, bang into, run into, crash into
2 *I* ***bumped into*** *one of my friends in the bookshop.*
meet, come across, run into

bump *noun*
1 *We felt a* ***bump*** *as the plane landed.*
thud, thump, bang, blow, knock
2 *How did you get that* ***bump*** *on your head?*
lump, swelling, bulge

bumpy *adjective*
1 *The car jolted up and down on the* ***bumpy*** *road.*
rough, uneven, irregular, lumpy
OPPOSITE smooth, even
2 *We had a* ***bumpy*** *ride in a jeep over muddy tracks.*
bouncy, jerky, jolting, lurching, choppy

bunch *noun*
1 *The jailer jangled a* ***bunch*** *of keys.*
bundle, cluster, collection, set
2 *She picked a* ***bunch*** *of flowers.*
bouquet, posy, spray
3 *(informal) They're a friendly* ***bunch*** *of people.*
group,
set,
circle,
band,
gang,
crowd

bundle *noun*
I found a ***bundle*** *of old newspapers.*
bunch, batch, pile, stack, collection, pack, bale

burn *verb*
1 *We could see the campfire* ***burning*** *in the distance.*
be alight, be on fire, blaze, flame, flare, flicker
To burn without flames is to ***glow*** or ***smoulder***.
2 *The captain ordered them to* ***burn*** *the enemy ship.*
set fire to, incinerate, reduce to ashes
To start something burning is to ***ignite***, ***kindle*** or ***light*** it.
To burn something slightly is to ***char***, ***scorch*** or ***singe*** it.
To hurt someone with boiling liquid or steam is to ***scald*** them.
To burn a dead body is to ***cremate*** it.

skyscraper

To burn a mark on an animal is to **brand** it.

burst verb
The balloon **burst** when my brother sat on it.
puncture, rupture, break, give way, split, tear

bury verb
1 The document was **buried** under a pile of old letters.
cover, conceal, hide, secrete
2 They say the old witch was **buried** in that graveyard.
inter, entomb

bushy adjective
The troll had **bushy** green eyebrows.
hairy, thick, dense, shaggy, bristly

business noun
1 My uncle runs a restaurant **business**.
company, firm, organisation
2 The new bookshop does a lot of **business**.
trade, trading, buying and selling, commerce
3 What sort of **business** do you want to go into?
work, job, career, employment, industry, occupation, profession, trade
4 He left early to attend to some urgent **business**.
matter, issue, affair, problem, point, concern, question

bustle verb
Miss Flyte **bustled** about the kitchen making tea.
rush, dash, hurry, scurry, scuttle, fuss

busy adjective
1 Mum is **busy** making my birthday cake just now.
occupied, engaged, employed, working, slaving away, beavering away
(informal) hard at it, up to your eyes
A common simile is as busy as a bee.
OPPOSITE idle
2 Christmas is a very **busy** time for shops.
active, hectic, frantic, lively
OPPOSITE quiet, restful
3 Is the town always this **busy** on Saturdays?
crowded, bustling, hectic, lively, teeming
OPPOSITE quiet, peaceful

buy verb
I'm saving up to **buy** a skateboard.
get, pay for, purchase, acquire
OPPOSITE sell

C c

cabin noun
The outlaws hid in a **cabin** in the woods.
hut, shack, shed, lodge, chalet, shelter

cafe noun
We had lunch in a **cafe** overlooking the river.
cafeteria, coffee shop, tearoom, snack bar, buffet, canteen, bistro, brasserie

cage noun
A large cage or enclosure for birds is an **aviary**.
A cage or enclosure for poultry is a **coop**.
A cage or enclosure for animals is a **pen**.
A cage or box for a pet rabbit is a **hutch**.

calculate verb
I **calculated** that it would take an hour to walk home.
work out, compute, figure out, reckon, add up, count, total
To calculate something roughly is to **estimate**.

call noun
1 We heard a **call** for help from inside the cave.
cry, exclamation, scream, shout, yell
2 Grandad made an unexpected **call**.
visit, stop, stay
3 There's not much **call** for suncream in winter.
demand, need

call verb
1 'Stop that racket!' **called** the janitor.
cry out, exclaim, shout, yell
2 It was too late at night to **call** my friends.
phone, ring, telephone
3 The headteacher **called** me to her office.
summon, invite, send for, order
4 The doctor **called** to see if I was feeling better.
visit, pay a visit, drop in, drop by
5 They **called** the baby Jessica.
name, baptise, christen, dub
6 What is your new book going to be **called**?
name, title, entitle

calm adjective
1 The weather was too **calm** to fly our kites.
still, quiet, peaceful, tranquil, serene, windless
OPPOSITE stormy, windy

2 The sea was **calm**, and we had a pleasant voyage.
smooth, still, flat, motionless, tranquil
OPPOSITE rough, choppy
3 I tried to stay **calm** before my judo exam.
cool, level-headed, patient, relaxed, sedate, unemotional, unexcitable, untroubled
OPPOSITE anxious, nervous

cancel verb
We had to **cancel** the race because of the weather.
abandon, call off, scrap, drop
(informal) scrub, ditch, axe
To cancel something after it has already begun is to **abort** it.
To put something off until later is to **postpone** it.
To cancel items on a list is to **cross out**, **delete** or **erase** them.

capture verb
1 The bank robbers were **captured** by police this morning.
catch, arrest, apprehend, seize, take prisoner
(informal) nab, nick
2 The castle has never been **captured** by enemy forces.
occupy, seize, take, take over, win

care noun
1 The old wizard's face was full of **care**.
worry, anxiety, trouble, concern, burden, responsibility, sorrow, stress
2 I took great **care** with my handwriting.
attention, concentration, thought, thoroughness, meticulousness
OPPOSITE carelessness
3 Jake left his pet hamster in my **care**.
charge, keeping, protection, safe keeping, supervision
to take care
Please **take care** crossing the road.
be careful, be on your guard, look out, watch out
to take care of someone or something
My granny **takes care of** me after school.
care for, look after, mind, watch over, attend to, tend

care verb
Do you **care** which team wins the World Cup?
mind, bother, worry, be interested, be troubled, be bothered, be worried
to care for someone or something
1 The veterinary hospital **cares for** sick animals.
take care of, look after, attend to, tend, nurse
2 I don't really **care for** broccoli.
like, be fond of, be keen on, love

a
b
c
d
e
f
g
h
i
j
k
l
m
n
o
p
q
r
s
t
u
v
w
x
y
z

career noun
*Max had a successful **career** as a racing driver.*
job, occupation, profession, trade, business, employment, calling

careful adjective
1 *You must be more **careful** with your spelling.*
accurate, conscientious, thorough, thoughtful, meticulous, painstaking, precise
OPPOSITE careless, inaccurate
2 *Dad kept a **careful** watch on the bonfire.*
attentive, cautious, watchful, alert, wary, vigilant
OPPOSITE careless, inattentive
to be careful
*Please **be careful** with those scissors.*
take care, be on your guard, look out, watch out

careless adjective
1 *This is a very **careless** piece of work.*
messy, untidy, thoughtless, inaccurate, slapdash, shoddy, scrappy, sloppy, slovenly
OPPOSITE careful, accurate
2 *I was **careless** and cut my finger.*
inattentive, thoughtless, absent-minded, heedless, irresponsible, negligent, reckless
OPPOSITE careful, attentive

carnival noun
*The whole village comes out for the annual **carnival**.*
fair, festival, fête, gala, parade, procession, show, celebration, pageant

carry verb
1 *I helped Mum to **carry** the shopping to the car.*
take, transfer, lift, fetch, bring, lug
2 *Aircraft **carry** passengers and goods.*
transport, convey
3 *The rear axle **carries** the greatest weight.*
bear, support, hold up
to carry on
*We **carried on** in spite of the rain.*
continue, go on, persevere, persist, keep on, remain, stay, survive
to carry something out
*The soldiers **carried out** the captain's orders.*
perform, do, execute, accomplish, achieve, complete, finish

carve verb
1 *The statue was **carved** out of stone.*
sculpt, chisel, hew
2 *Mum **carved** the chicken for Sunday dinner.*
cut, slice

case noun
1 *I loaded my **case** into the boot of the car.*
suitcase, trunk
*A number of suitcases that you take on holiday is your **baggage** or **luggage**.*
2 *What's in those **cases** in the attic?*
box, chest, crate, carton, casket
3 *This has been a clear **case** of mistaken identity.*
instance, occurrence, example, illustration
4 *It was one of Sherlock Holmes's most famous **cases**.*
inquiry, investigation
5 *She presented a good **case** for abolishing hunting.*
argument, line of reasoning

casual adjective
1 *It was just a **casual** remark, so don't take it too seriously.*
accidental, chance, unexpected, unintentional, unplanned
OPPOSITE deliberate
2 *The restaurant had a **casual** atmosphere.*
easy-going, informal, relaxed
OPPOSITE formal
3 *The teacher complained about our **casual** attitude.*
apathetic, careless, slack, unenthusiastic
OPPOSITE enthusiastic

catastrophe noun
*The drought is a **catastrophe** for the farmers.*
disaster, calamity, misfortune, mishap, tragedy

catch verb
1 *My friends yelled at me to **catch** the ball.*
clutch, grab, grasp, grip, hang on to, hold, seize, snatch, take
2 *One of the anglers **caught** a fish.*
hook, net, trap
3 *The police hoped to **catch** the thief red-handed.*
arrest, capture, corner
(informal) nab
4 *I hope you don't **catch** my cold.*
become infected by, contract, get
(informal) go down with
5 *You must hurry if you want to **catch** the bus.*
be in time for, get on

catch noun
1 *The angler got a large **catch** of salmon.*
haul
2 *The car is so cheap that there must be a **catch**.*
problem, obstacle, snag, difficulty, disadvantage, drawback, trap, trick

3 *All the windows are fitted with safety **catches**.*
fastening, latch, lock, bolt, hook

cause noun
1 *What was the **cause** of the trouble?*
origin, source, start
*You can also talk about the **reasons** for the trouble.*
2 *You've got no **cause** to complain.*
grounds, basis, motive
3 *The sponsored walk is for a good **cause**.*
purpose, object

cause verb
*A single spark from the fire could **cause** an explosion.*
bring about, create, generate, lead to, give rise to, result in, provoke, arouse

caution noun
1 *We decided to proceed with **caution**.*
care, attention, watchfulness, wariness, vigilance
2 *The traffic warden let him off with a **caution**.*
warning, reprimand, telling-off
(informal) ticking-off

cautious adjective
*My grandad is a **cautious** driver.*
careful, attentive, watchful, wary, vigilant, hesitant
OPPOSITE reckless

cease verb
*The fighting **ceased** at midnight.*
come to an end, end, finish, stop, halt
OPPOSITE begin

celebrate verb
1 *Let's **celebrate**!*
enjoy yourself, have a good time, be happy, rejoice
2 *What shall we do to **celebrate** Granny's birthday?*
commemorate, observe, keep

celebration noun
*We had a big **celebration** for my cousin's wedding.*
festivity, party, feast, festival, banquet, jamboree

celebrity noun
*The awards were handed out by a TV **celebrity**.*
famous person, personality, public figure, VIP, star, idol

cemetery noun
*A famous author is buried in the local **cemetery**.*
graveyard, burial ground, churchyard
*A place where dead people are cremated is a **crematorium**.*

central adjective
1 *We are now in the **central** part of the building.*
middle, core, inner, interior
OPPOSITE outer

2 *Who are the **central** characters in the story?*
chief, crucial, essential, fundamental, important, main, major, principal, vital
OPPOSITE unimportant

centre noun
*The library is in the **centre** of the town. The burial chamber is in the **centre** of the pyramid.*
middle, heart, core, inside, interior
The centre of a planet or a piece of fruit is the **core**.
The centre of an atom or a living cell is the **nucleus**.
The centre of a wheel is the **hub**.
The point at the centre of a see-saw is the **pivot**.
The edible part in the centre of a nut is the **kernel**.
OPPOSITE edge, outside, surface

ceremony noun
1 *We watched the **ceremony** of the opening of parliament.*
rite, ritual, formalities
A ceremony where someone is given a prize is a **presentation**.
A ceremony where someone is given a special honour is an **investiture**.
A ceremony to celebrate something new is an **inauguration** or **opening**.
A ceremony where someone becomes a member of a society is an **initiation**.
A ceremony to make a church or other building sacred is a **dedication**.
A ceremony to remember a dead person or a past event is a **commemoration**.
A ceremony held in a church is a **service**.
2 *They had a quiet wedding without a lot of **ceremony**.*
formality, pomp, pageantry, spectacle

certain adjective
1 *My mum was **certain** she would win the cookery competition.*
confident, convinced, positive, sure, determined
OPPOSITE uncertain
2 *We have **certain** proof that the painting is a forgery.*
definite, clear, convincing, absolute, unquestionable, reliable, trustworthy, undeniable, infallible, genuine, valid
OPPOSITE unreliable
3 *The damaged plane faced **certain** disaster.*
inevitable, unavoidable
OPPOSITE possible
4 *Her new book is **certain** to be a bestseller.*
bound, sure

chain noun
1 *The anchor was attached to a **chain**.*
One ring in a chain is a **link**.
A chain used to link railway wagons together is a **coupling**.

2 *The police formed a **chain** to keep the crowd back.*
line, row, cordon
3 *Holmes described the **chain** of events that led to the murder.*
series, sequence, succession, string

champion noun
1 *She is the current world **champion** at ice skating.*
title-holder, prizewinner, victor, winner, conqueror
2 *Martin Luther King was a **champion** of civil rights.*
supporter, advocate, defender, upholder, patron, backer

championship noun
*Fifteen schools took part in the karate **championship**.*
competition, contest, tournament

chance noun
1 *They say there's a **chance** of rain later.*
possibility, likelihood, probability, prospect, danger, risk
2 *I haven't had a **chance** to reply yet.*
opportunity, time, occasion
3 *The director took a **chance** in hiring an unknown actor.*
gamble, risk
by chance
*I found the house quite **by chance**.*
by accident, accidentally, by coincidence
An unfortunate chance is **bad luck** or a **misfortune**.
A fortunate chance is **good luck** or a **fluke**.

change verb
1 *They've **changed** the programme for the concert.*
alter, modify, rearrange, reorganise, adjust, adapt, vary
2 *The town has **changed** a lot since Victorian times.*
alter, become different, develop, grow, move on
3 *Can I **change** these jeans for a bigger size, please?*
exchange, replace, switch, substitute
(informal) swap
to change into
*Tadpoles **change into** frogs.*
become, turn into, be transformed into

change noun
*There has been a slight **change** of plan.*
alteration, modification, variation, difference, break
A change to something worse is a **deterioration**.
A change to something better is an **improvement** or a **reform**.
A very big change is a **revolution** or **transformation** or **U-turn**.
A change in which one person or thing is replaced by another is a **substitution**.

chaos noun
*After the earthquake, the city was in **chaos**.*
confusion, disorder, mayhem, uproar, tumult, pandemonium, anarchy, bedlam, muddle, shambles
OPPOSITE order

chaotic adjective
*Alice finds that life in Wonderland is **chaotic**.*
confused, disorderly, disorganised, muddled, topsy-turvy, untidy, unruly, riotous
OPPOSITE orderly, organised

chapter noun
*I read a **chapter** of my book last night.*
part, section, division
One section of a play is an **act** or **scene**.
One part of a serial is an **episode** or **instalment**.

character noun
1 *Her **character** is quite different from her sister's.*
personality, temperament, nature, disposition, make-up, manner
2 *Our neighbour is a well-known **character** in our street.*
figure, personality, individual, person
3 *Which **character** would you like to play in Peter Pan?*
part, role

charge noun
1 *The admission **charge** is five euros.*
price, rate
The charge made for a ride on public transport is the **fare**.
The charge made to post a letter or parcel is the **postage**.
A charge made to join a club is a **fee** or **subscription**.
A charge made for certain things by the government is a **duty** or a **tax**.
A charge made to use a private road, bridge or tunnel is a **toll**.
2 *The robbers face several criminal **charges**.*
accusation, allegation
3 *Many soldiers were killed in the **charge**.*
assault, attack, onslaught, raid
4 *My best friend left her hamster in my **charge**.*
care, keeping, protection, custody, trust
to be in charge of something
*An experienced sailor was **in charge of** the crew.*
manage, lead, command, direct, supervise, run

charge verb
1 *The library **charges** ten pence for a photocopy.*
ask for, make you pay
2 *A man has been **charged** with attempted robbery.*
accuse (of)

a b c d e f g h i j k l m n o p q r s t u v w x y z

3 *The cavalry charged the enemy line.*
attack, assault, storm, rush

charm verb
Winnie the Pooh has charmed readers all over the world.
bewitch, captivate, delight, enchant, entrance, fascinate, please

charming adjective
We drove through some charming scenery.
delightful, attractive, pleasant, pleasing, likeable, appealing

chart noun
1 *The explorer stopped to consult his chart.*
map
2 *This chart shows the average rainfall for each month.*
diagram, graph, table

chase verb
The wolves chased a deer through the forest.
pursue, run after, follow, track, trail, hunt

chatty adjective
Frank is usually shy, but today he's quite chatty.
talkative, communicative
OPPOSITE silent

cheap adjective
1 *We got a cheap flight to London.*
inexpensive, affordable, bargain, cut-price, discount, reasonable
2 *These tyres are made from cheap rubber.*
inferior, shoddy, second-rate, worthless, trashy
(*informal*) tacky, tatty
OPPOSITE superior, good-quality

cheat verb
1 *She was cheated into buying a fake diamond ring.*
deceive, trick, swindle, double-cross, hoax
(*informal*) con, diddle, fleece, fool, rip off
2 *Anyone who cheats in the quiz will be disqualified.*
copy, crib

cheat noun
Don't trust him—he's a cheat.
cheater, deceiver, swindler, fraud, impostor, hoaxer

check verb
1 *Have you checked your work carefully?*
examine, inspect, look over, scrutinise
2 *The heavy snow checked their progress towards the Pole.*
hamper, hinder, block, obstruct, delay, hold back, slow, slow down, halt, stop

check noun
I need to run some checks on your computer.
test, examination, inspection, check-up

cheeky adjective
Don't be so cheeky!
disrespectful, facetious, flippant, impertinent, impolite, impudent, insolent, insulting, irreverent, mocking, rude, saucy, shameless
OPPOSITE respectful

cheer verb
1 *We cheered when our team scored a goal.*
clap, applaud, shout, yell
OPPOSITE jeer
2 *The good news cheered us.*
comfort, console, gladden, delight, please, encourage, uplift
OPPOSITE sadden

cheerful adjective
The sun was shining, and we set out in a cheerful mood.
happy, good-humoured, light-hearted, merry, jolly, joyful, joyous, glad, pleased, optimistic, lively, elated, animated, bright, buoyant, jovial, gleeful, chirpy
OPPOSITE sad

chest noun
I found some old books in a chest in the attic.
box, crate, case, trunk

chew verb
Are you still chewing that toffee?
eat, gnaw, munch

chief noun
The pirates chose Redbeard as their chief.
leader, ruler, head, commander, captain, chieftain, master, governor, president, principal
(*informal*) boss

chief adjective
1 *The chief ingredients in a trifle are jelly, custard and cream.*
main, central, key, principal, crucial, basic, essential, important, vital, major, primary, foremost, fundamental, indispensable, necessary, significant, predominant, prominent
OPPOSITE unimportant, minor, trivial
2 *Albert was Queen Victoria's chief advisor.*
head, senior

child noun
1 *The book festival is aimed especially at children.*
boy or girl, infant, juvenile, youngster, youth, lad or lass
(*informal*) kid, tot, nipper
2 *How many children do you have?*
son or daughter, descendant, offspring

A child who expects to inherit a title or fortune from parents is an **heir** or **heiress**.
A child whose parents are dead is an **orphan**.
A child looked after by a guardian is a **ward**.

childish adjective
It's childish to make rude noises.
babyish, immature, juvenile, infantile
OPPOSITE mature

chilly adjective
1 *It's a chilly evening, so wrap up well.*
cold, cool, frosty, icy, crisp, fresh, raw, wintry
(*informal*) nippy
OPPOSITE warm
2 *The librarian gave me a very chilly look.*
unfriendly, hostile, unwelcoming, unsympathetic
OPPOSITE friendly

chip noun
1 *There were chips of broken glass on the pavement.*
bit, piece, fragment, scrap, sliver, splinter, flake, shaving
2 *This mug's got a chip in it.*
crack, nick, notch, flaw

chip verb
I chipped a cup while I was washing up.
crack, nick, notch, damage

choice noun
1 *My bike had a flat tyre, so I had no choice but to walk.*
alternative, option
2 *She wouldn't be my choice as team captain.*
preference, selection, pick, vote
3 *The greengrocer has a good choice of vegetables.*
range, selection, assortment, array, mixture, variety, diversity

choke verb
1 *This tie is so tight it's choking me.*
strangle, suffocate, stifle, throttle
2 *Thick fumes made the firefighters choke.*
cough, gasp

choose verb
1 *We had a show of hands to choose a winner.*
select, appoint, elect, vote for
2 *I chose the blue shoes to go with my dress.*
decide on, select, pick out, opt for, plump for, settle on, single out
3 *Lola chose to stay at home.*
decide, make a decision, determine, prefer, resolve

chop verb
1 *Chop the celery into large chunks.*
cut, split

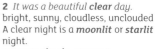

2 *They **chopped** down the undergrowth to make a path.*
hack, slash
To chop down a tree is to **fell** it.
To chop off an arm or leg is to **amputate** it.
To chop a branch off a tree is to **lop** it.
To chop food into small pieces is to **dice** or **mince** it.

chunk noun
*I bit a **chunk** out of my apple.*
piece, portion, lump, block, hunk, slab, wedge

circle noun
1 *We arranged the chairs in a **circle**.*
ring, round, hoop, loop, band
A flat, solid circle is a **disc**.
A three-dimensional round shape is a **sphere**.
An egg shape is an **oval** or **ellipse**.
The distance round a circle is the **circumference**.
The distance across a circle is the **diameter**.
The distance from the centre to the circumference is the **radius**.
A circular movement is a **revolution** or **rotation**.
A circular trip round the world is a **circumnavigation**.
A circular trip of a satellite round a planet is an **orbit**.
2 *She has a wide **circle** of friends.*
group, set, crowd

city noun
The chief city of a country or region is the **metropolis**.
An area of houses outside the central part of a city is the **suburbs**.
A word meaning 'to do with a town or city' is **urban**.
A word meaning 'to do with a city and its suburbs' is **metropolitan**.

claim verb
1 *You can **claim** your prize for the raffle here.*
ask for, request, collect, demand, insist on
2 *The professor **claims** to be an expert on dinosaurs.*
declare, assert, allege, maintain, argue, insist

clap verb
1 *The audience **clapped** loudly at the end of the concert.*
applaud, cheer
2 *Suddenly, a hand **clapped** me on the shoulder.*
slap, hit, pat, smack

class noun
1 *There are 26 children in our **class**.*
form, set, stream
The other pupils in your class are your **classmates**.

2 *There are many different **classes** of plants.*
category, group, classification, division, set, sort, type, kind, species
3 *The ancient Romans divided people into social **classes**.*
level, rank, status

clean adjective
1 *Can you bring me a **clean** cup, please?*
spotless, washed, scrubbed, swept, tidy, immaculate, hygienic, sanitary
An informal word meaning 'very clean' is **squeaky-clean**.
A common simile is **as clean as a whistle**.
OPPOSITE dirty
2 *I began my diary on a **clean** piece of paper.*
blank, unused, unmarked, empty, bare, fresh, new
OPPOSITE used
3 *This plaster will keep the wound **clean**.*
sterile, sterilised, uninfected
4 *You can get **clean** water from this tap.*
pure, clear, fresh, unpolluted, uncontaminated
5 *The referee said he wanted a **clean** fight.*
fair, honest, honourable, sporting, sportsmanlike
OPPOSITE dishonourable

clean verb
1 *We **cleaned** the house from top to bottom. I tried to **clean** the mud off my boots.*
wash, wipe, mop, scour, scrub, polish, dust, sweep, vacuum, rinse, wring out, hose down, sponge, shampoo, swill
To clean clothes is to **launder** them.
OPPOSITE dirty, mess up
2 *The nurse **cleaned** the wound with an antiseptic wipe.*
cleanse, bathe, disinfect, sanitise, sterilise
OPPOSITE infect, contaminate

clear adjective
1 *We saw fish swimming in the **clear** pool.*
clean, pure, colourless, transparent
A common simile is **as clear as crystal**.
A simile which means the opposite is **as clear as mud**.
OPPOSITE opaque

2 *It was a beautiful **clear** day.*
bright, sunny, cloudless, unclouded
A clear night is a **moonlit** or **starlit** night.
OPPOSITE cloudy, overcast
3 *The instructions on the map were quite **clear**.*
plain, understandable, intelligible, lucid, unambiguous
OPPOSITE ambiguous, confusing
4 *The actor spoke his words with a **clear** voice.*
distinct, audible
A common simile is **as clear as a bell**.
OPPOSITE muffled
5 *The signature is not **clear**.*
legible, recognisable, visible
OPPOSITE illegible
6 *My camera takes nice **clear** pictures.*
sharp, well defined, focused
OPPOSITE unfocused
7 *Is your conscience is **clear**?*
innocent, untroubled, blameless
OPPOSITE guilty
8 *There's a **clear** difference between a male blackbird and a female.*
obvious, definite, noticeable, conspicuous, perceptible, pronounced
OPPOSITE imperceptible
9 *They made sure the road was **clear** for the ambulance.*
open, empty, free, passable, uncrowded, unobstructed
OPPOSITE congested

clear verb
1 *I **cleared** the weeds from the flower bed.*
get rid of, remove, eliminate, strip
2 *The plumber **cleared** the blocked drain.*
unblock, unclog, clean out, open up
To clear a channel is to **dredge** it.
3 *I **cleared** the misty windows.*
clean, wipe, polish
4 *If the fire alarm goes, **clear** the building.*
empty, evacuate
5 *The fog **cleared** slowly.*
disappear, vanish, disperse, evaporate, melt away
6 *The forecast said that the weather will **clear**.*
become clear, brighten, fair up
7 *He was **cleared** of all the charges against him.*
acquit, free, release
8 *The runners **cleared** the first hurdle.*
go over, get over, jump over, pass over, vault
  to clear up
  *Please **clear up** this mess before you go.*
  clean up, tidy up, put right, put straight

a
b
c
d
e
f
g
h
i
j
k
l
m
n
o
p
q
r
s
t
u
v
w
x
y
z

climb

clever adjective

1 *Dr Hafiz is very clever and can read hieroglyphics.*
intelligent, bright, gifted, able, knowledgeable
(*informal*) brainy, smart
OPPOSITE unintelligent
An informal name for a clever person is a **brainbox**.
An uncomplimentary synonym is **clever clogs** or **smartypants**.
2 *The elves were very clever with their fingers.*
accomplished, capable, gifted, skilful, talented
If you are clever at a lot of things, you are **versatile**.
OPPOSITE unskilful
3 *They are clever enough to get away with it.*
quick, sharp, shrewd, smart
Uncomplimentary synonyms are **artful**, **crafty**, **cunning**, **wily**.
OPPOSITE stupid

climax noun

The climax of the film is a stunning car chase.
high point, highlight, peak, crisis
OPPOSITE anticlimax

climb verb

1 *It took us several hours to climb the mountain.*
ascend, clamber up, go up, scale
2 *The plane climbed into the clouds.*
lift off, soar, take off
3 *The road climbs steeply up to the castle.*
rise, slope
to climb down
3 *It's harder to climb down rock than to get up it.*
descend, get down from
We all told him he was wrong, so he had to climb down.
admit defeat, give in, surrender

cling verb

to cling to someone or **something**
1 *The baby koala clung to its mother.*
clasp, grasp, clutch, embrace, hug

2 *Ivy clings to the wall.*
adhere to, fasten on to, stick to

clip verb

1 *The sheets of paper were clipped together.*
pin, staple
2 *Dad clipped the hedges in the back garden.*
cut, trim
To cut unwanted twigs off a tree or bush is to **prune** it.

close adjective

1 *Our house is close to the shops.*
near, nearby, not far
To be actually by the side of something is to be **adjacent**.
OPPOSITE far, distant
2 *Anisha and I are close friends.*
intimate, dear, devoted, fond, affectionate
3 *The police made a close examination of the stolen car.*
careful, detailed, painstaking, minute, thorough
OPPOSITE casual

4 *It was an exciting race because it was so close.*
equal, even, level, well-matched
5 *Open the window—it's very close in here.*
humid, muggy, stuffy, clammy, airless, stifling, suffocating
OPPOSITE airy

close verb

1 *Don't forget to close the lid.*
shut, fasten, seal, secure
2 *The road has been closed to traffic for the parade.*
barricade, block, obstruct, stop up
3 *The band closed the concert with my favourite song.*
finish, end, complete, conclude, stop, terminate
(*informal*) wind up

clothes noun see panel above

cloudy adjective

1 *The day was cold and cloudy.*
dull, overcast, grey, dark, dismal, gloomy, sunless
OPPOSITE cloudless

🕸 WORD WEB

clothes *plural noun*
What clothes are you taking on holiday?
clothing, garments, outfits, dress, attire, garb, finery
(*informal*) gear, togs, get-up
A set of clothes to wear is a **costume**, **outfit** or **suit**.
An official set of clothes worn for school or work is a **uniform**.

SOME ITEMS OF CLOTHING
blouse, caftan, camisole, chador or chuddar, dhoti, dress, dungarees, frock, gown, jeans, jersey, jodhpurs, jumper, kilt, kimono, leggings, miniskirt, pinafore, polo shirt, pullover, robe, sari, sarong, shirt, shorts, skirt, slacks, smock, suit, sweater, sweatshirt, trousers, trunks, T-shirt, tunic, waistcoat

OUTER CLOTHES
anorak, apron, blazer, cagoule, cape, cardigan, cloak, coat, dressing gown, duffel coat, fleece, gilet, hoodie, greatcoat, jacket, mackintosh, oilskins, overalls, overcoat, parka, poncho, raincoat, shawl, stole, tracksuit, windcheater

UNDERWEAR
boxer shorts, bra, briefs, crop top, drawers, knickers, pants, petticoat, slip, socks, stockings, tights, underpants, vest

CLOTHES FOR SLEEPING IN
nightdress or (*informal*) nightie, pyjamas

CLOTHES WORN IN THE PAST
corset, doublet, frock coat, gauntlet, ruff, toga

ACCESSORIES WORN WITH CLOTHES
belt, braces, cravat, earmuffs, glove, sash, scarf, shawl, tie

PARTS OF A GARMENT
bodice, button, buttonhole, collar, cuff, hem, lapel, pocket, seam, sleeve, waistband, zip

THINGS USED TO DECORATE CLOTHES
beads, frills, fringes, lace, ruffles, sequins, tassels

SOME KINDS OF HAT
balaclava, baseball cap, bearskin, beret, boater, bonnet, bowler, cap, deerstalker, fez, helmet, mitre, mortarboard, panama hat, skull cap, sombrero, sou'wester, stetson, sun-hat, tam-o'-shanter, top hat, trilby, turban

✏ WRITING TIPS

You can use these words to describe **clothes**:
baggy, casual, chic, dowdy, drab, fashionable, fine, flashy, flattering, frilly, frumpy, glamorous, ill-fitting, loose, luxurious, old-fashioned, ornate, ragged, roomy, shabby, skimpy, smart, sporty, stylish, tattered or in tatters, threadbare, tight-fitting, trendy, worn

2 *We couldn't see any fish in the* **cloudy** *water.*
muddy, murky, hazy, milky
OPPOSITE clear, transparent

club *noun*
1 *The warrior brandished a wooden* **club.**
stick, baton, truncheon
2 *Would you like to join our book* **club?**
group, society, association, organisation, circle, union

clue *noun*
1 *I don't know the answer. Can you give me a* **clue?**
hint, suggestion, indication, pointer, tip, idea
2 *'This footprint is an important* **clue,'** *said the detective.*
piece of evidence, lead

clumsy *adjective*
The **clumsy** *gnome was always breaking things.*
careless, awkward, ungainly, inept
An informal name for a clumsy person is **butterfingers.**
OPPOSITE graceful

clutter *noun*
Clear up all this **clutter.**
mess, muddle, junk, litter, rubbish, odds and ends

coach *verb*
He was **coached** *by a former champion.*
train, teach, instruct

coarse *adjective*
1 *The blanket was made of* **coarse** *woollen material.*
rough, harsh, scratchy, bristly, hairy
OPPOSITE soft
2 *We were shocked by their* **coarse** *table manners.*
rude, offensive, impolite, improper, indecent, crude, vulgar
OPPOSITE polite, refined

coat *noun*
1 *The detective was wearing a thick winter* **coat.**
see **clothes** panel opposite
2 *The fox had a reddish brown* **coat.**
hide, pelt, skin, fur, hair
A sheep's coat is a **fleece.**
3 *The front door needs a* **coat** *of paint.*
layer, coating, covering

coat *verb*
We ate marshmallows **coated** *with chocolate.*
cover, spread, smear, glaze

coax *verb*
Sam **coaxed** *the hamster back into its cage.*
persuade, tempt, entice

coil *noun*
The snake twisted itself into a **coil.**
spiral, twist, curl, twirl, screw, corkscrew, whirl, whorl, roll, scroll A coil of wool or thread is a **skein.**

coil *verb*
The snake **coiled** *itself round a branch.*
curl, loop, roll, spiral, turn, twist, twirl, wind, writhe

cold *adjective*
1 *Wrap up warm in this* **cold** *weather.*
freezing, chilly, frosty, icy, raw, arctic, bitter, cool, crisp, snowy, wintry, (*informal*) perishing
A common simile is **as cold as ice.**
OPPOSITE hot, warm
2 *I tried to shelter from the* **cold** *wind.*
biting, bitter, keen, penetrating, piercing
3 *I was* **cold** *in spite of my woolly hat.*
freezing, frozen, chilly, chilled, shivering, shivery
To be so cold that you become ill is to suffer from **hypothermia.**
OPPOSITE hot, warm
4 *The cyclops gave us a* **cold** *stare from his one eye.*
unfriendly, unkind, unfeeling, distant, cool, heartless, indifferent, reserved, stony, uncaring, unemotional, unsympathetic
OPPOSITE warm, friendly

collapse *verb*
1 *Many buildings* **collapsed** *in the earthquake.*
fall down, fall in, cave in, give way, crumple, buckle, disintegrate, tumble down
2 *Some of the runners* **collapsed** *in the heat.*
faint, pass out, fall over, keel over

collect *verb*
1 *Squirrels* **collect** *nuts for the winter.*
gather, accumulate, hoard, heap, pile up, store up, stockpile, amass
2 *A crowd* **collected** *to watch the fire.*
assemble, gather, come together, converge
OPPOSITE scatter, disperse
3 *We* **collected** *a large sum for charity.*
raise, take in
4 *She* **collected** *the car from the garage.*
fetch, get, obtain, bring
OPPOSITE drop off, hand in

collection *noun*
Would you like to see my fossil **collection?**
assortment, set, accumulation, array, hoard, pile
A collection of books is a **library.**
A collection of poems or short stories is an **anthology.**

collide *verb*
to collide with *The runaway trolley* **collided with** *a wall.*
bump into, crash into, run into, smash into, hit, strike

collision *noun*
The **collision** *dented the front wheel of my bike.*
bump, crash, smash, knock, accident
A collision involving a lot of vehicles is a **pile-up.**

colossal *adjective*
A **colossal** *statue towered above us.*
huge, enormous, gigantic, immense, massive, giant, mammoth, monumental, towering, vast
OPPOSITE small, tiny

✎ WRITING TIPS

colour *noun*
You can use these words to describe a **colour.**

TO DESCRIBE *A PALE COLOUR*
delicate, faded, light, muted, neutral, pastel, washed-out

TO DESCRIBE *A STRONG COLOUR*
bright, fluorescent, garish, loud, neon, vibrant, zingy

---

colourful *adjective*
1 *The rose garden is* **colourful** *in the summer.*
multicoloured, showy, vibrant, bright, brilliant, gaudy
OPPOSITE colourless
2 *The book gives a* **colourful** *account of life on an island.*
exciting, interesting, lively, vivid, striking, rich, picturesque
OPPOSITE dull

column *noun*
1 *The roof of the temple was supported by stone* **columns.**
pillar, post, support, shaft
2 *A* **column** *of soldiers wound its way across the desert.*
line, file, procession, row, string
3 *I sometimes read the sports* **column** *in the newspaper.*
article, piece, report, feature

combine *verb*
1 *We* **combined** *our pocket money to buy a kite.*
put together, add together, join, merge, unite, amalgamate
OPPOSITE divide
2 **Combine** *the mixture with water to make a paste.*
mix, stir together, blend, mingle, bind
OPPOSITE separate

a b c d e f g h i j k l m n o p q r s t u v w x y z

come verb
1 We expect our guests to **come** in the afternoon.
arrive, appear, visit
OPPOSITE go
2 When you hear a cuckoo, you know that summer is **coming**.
advance, draw near
to come about
Can you tell me how the accident **came about**?
happen, occur, take place, result
to come across
I **came across** an old friend of mine.
find, discover, chance upon, meet, bump into
to come to
1 Tell me when you **come to** the last chapter.
reach, get to, arrive at
2 What did the repair bill **come to**?
add up to, amount to, total

comfort noun
1 My teddy bear was a **comfort** to me when I was ill.
reassurance, consolation, encouragement, support, relief
2 If I had a million pounds, I could live in **comfort**.
ease, luxury, contentment, well-being, prosperity, luxury, affluence

comfort verb
The coach tried to **comfort** the team after they lost.
cheer up, console, reassure, encourage, hearten, sympathise with, soothe

comfortable adjective
1 The bed was so **comfortable** that Goldilocks fell fast asleep.
cosy, snug, relaxing, easy, soft, warm, roomy, padded, plush
(informal) comfy
OPPOSITE uncomfortable
2 We'll need **comfortable** clothes for travelling.
casual, informal, loose-fitting
3 Our cat leads a **comfortable** life.
contented, happy, pleasant, agreeable, well-off, prosperous, luxurious, affluent

command noun
1 The general gave the **command** to attack.
order, instruction, commandment, edict
2 Captain Nemo has **command** of the whole crew.
charge, control, authority (over), power (over), management, supervision
3 My sister has a good **command** of Spanish.
knowledge, mastery, grasp, understanding, ability (in), skill (in)

command verb
1 The officer **commanded** his troops to fire.
order, instruct, direct, tell, bid
2 The captain **commands** the ship.
control, direct, be in charge of, govern, head, lead, manage, administer, supervise

comment noun
He made some nasty **comments** about his boss.
remark, statement, observation, opinion, mention, reference
A hostile comment is a **criticism**.

commit verb
The thieves were planning to **commit** another robbery.
carry out, do, perform, execute

common adjective
1 Colds are a **common** complaint in winter.
commonplace, everyday, frequent, normal, ordinary, familiar, well known, widespread
OPPOSITE rare
2 'Good morning' is a **common** way to greet people.
typical, usual, regular, routine, standard, customary, conventional, habitual, traditional
OPPOSITE uncommon
3 My friends and I have a **common** interest in music.
shared, mutual, joint

commotion noun
Football supporters were causing a **commotion** outside.
disturbance, row, fuss, trouble, disorder, unrest, agitation, turmoil, uproar, racket, rumpus, upheaval, riot, fracas, furore, hullabaloo, brouhaha, pandemonium, bedlam

communicate verb
1 Steve **communicated** his boredom with a yawn.
express, make known, indicate, convey, disclose, announce, pass on, proclaim, publish, report
2 Nowadays, we **communicate** by email.
contact each other, correspond, be in touch

company noun
1 My cousin works for a computer **company**.
business, firm, corporation, organisation, establishment
2 Shrek shunned the **company** of other ogres.
fellowship, companionship, friendship, society

compare verb
Can you **compare** these sets of figures?
contrast, juxtapose, relate, set side by side

to compare with
This copy can't **compare with** the original painting.
compete with, rival, emulate, equal, match

compete verb
Five schools will be **competing** in the hockey tournament.
participate, perform, take part, enter
to compete against
We are **competing against** a strong team this week.
oppose, play against, contend with

competent adjective
You have to be a **competent** swimmer to join the club.
able, capable, skilful, skilled, accomplished, proficient, experienced, expert, qualified, trained
OPPOSITE incompetent

competitor noun
The **competitors** lined up for the start of the race.
contestant, contender, challenger, participant, opponent, rival
People who take part in an exam are **candidates** or **entrants**.

complain verb
Miss Grouch spent most of her life **complaining**.
moan, protest, grumble, grouse, gripe, whinge, make a fuss
to complain about
I wrote a letter **complaining about** the noise.
protest about, object to, criticise, find fault with
OPPOSITE praise

complaint noun
1 They received hundreds of **complaints** about the film.
criticism, objection, protest, moan, grumble
2 You have a nasty stomach **complaint**.
disease, illness, ailment, sickness, infection
(informal) upset

complete adjective
1 Your training as a witch is not yet **complete**.
completed, ended, finished, accomplished, concluded
OPPOSITE unfinished
2 Have you got a **complete** set of cards?
whole, entire, full, intact
OPPOSITE incomplete
3 My birthday party was a **complete** disaster.
total, utter, sheer, absolute, thorough, downright, perfect, pure

A B C D E F G H I J K L M N O P Q R S T U V W X Y Z

complete verb
*We have **completed** all the tasks on the sheet.*
finish, end, conclude, carry out, perform

complex adjective
*Defusing a bomb is a **complex** task.*
complicated, difficult, elaborate, detailed, intricate, involved
(*informal*) fiddly
OPPOSITE simple

complicated adjective
*The plot of the film is very **complicated**.*
complex, intricate, involved, difficult, elaborate, convoluted
OPPOSITE simple, straightforward

compliments plural noun
*It was nice to get **compliments** about my cooking.*
praise, appreciation, approval, congratulations, tribute
Compliments which you don't deserve are **flattery**.
OPPOSITE insults

compose verb
*Beethoven **composed** nine symphonies.*
create, devise, produce, make up, think up, write
to be composed of
*This quilt is **composed of** pieces of patchwork.*
be made of, consist of, comprise

compulsory adjective
*The wearing of seat belts is **compulsory**.*
required, obligatory, necessary
OPPOSITE optional

conceal verb
1 *The dog tried to **conceal** its bone.*
hide, cover up, bury
2 *We tried to **conceal** our hiding place.*
disguise, mask, screen, camouflage, make invisible
3 *Don't **conceal** the truth.*
keep quiet about, keep secret, hush up, suppress

conceited adjective
*He was so **conceited** when he won first prize!*
boastful, arrogant, proud, vain, self-satisfied
(*informal*) big-headed, cocky
OPPOSITE modest

concentrate verb
*I had to **concentrate** to hear what she was saying.*
be attentive, think hard, focus

concern verb
1 *This conversation doesn't **concern** you.*
affect, involve, be important to, matter to, be relevant to, relate to

2 *It **concerns** me that we are destroying the rain forests.*
bother, distress, trouble, upset, worry

concern noun
1 *My private life is no **concern** of theirs.*
affair, business
2 *Global warming is a great **concern** to us all.*
worry, anxiety, fear
3 *She's the head of a business **concern**.*
company, firm, enterprise, establishment

concerned adjective
1 *After waiting an hour, Julia began to feel **concerned**.*
worried, bothered, troubled, anxious, upset, distressed
2 *We're writing a letter to all those **concerned**.*
involved, connected, related, affected

conclusion noun
1 *The **conclusion** of the film was a bit puzzling.*
close, end, finale, finish, completion, culmination
2 *'What is your **conclusion**, Inspector?'*
decision, judgement, opinion, verdict, deduction

condemn verb
1 *The manager **condemned** the behaviour of the players.*
criticise, disapprove of, denounce, deplore, reproach
OPPOSITE praise
2 *The judge **condemned** the men to death.*
sentence
OPPOSITE acquit

condition noun
1 *Is your bike in good **condition**?*
state, order, repair
2 *A dog needs exercise to stay in good **condition**.*
fitness, health, shape
3 *It's a **condition** of membership that you pay a subscription.*
requirement, obligation, term

confess verb
*The goblin **confessed** that he had stolen the gold.*
admit, own up to, acknowledge, reveal

confidence noun
1 *We can face the future with **confidence**.*
hope, optimism, faith
OPPOSITE doubt
2 *I wish I had her **confidence**.*
self-confidence, assurance, boldness, conviction

confident adjective
1 *I am **confident** that we will win.*
certain, sure, positive, optimistic
OPPOSITE doubtful
2 *She is a **confident** sort of person.*
self-confident, assertive, bold, fearless, unafraid

confirm verb
1 *The strange events **confirmed** his belief in ghosts.*
prove, justify, support, back up, reinforce
OPPOSITE disprove
2 *I phoned to **confirm** my appointment at the dentist.*
verify, make official
OPPOSITE cancel

confront verb
*I decided to **confront** her and demand an apology.*
challenge, stand up to, face up to
OPPOSITE avoid

confuse verb
1 *I was **confused** by the directions on the map.*
puzzle, bewilder, mystify, baffle, perplex
2 *You must be **confusing** me with someone else.*
mix up, muddle

confusion noun
1 *There was great **confusion** when the lights went out.*
chaos, commotion, fuss, uproar, turmoil, pandemonium, bedlam, hullabaloo
2 *There was a look of **confusion** on her face.*
bewilderment, puzzlement, perplexity

congratulate verb
*We **congratulated** the winners.*
praise, applaud, compliment
OPPOSITE criticise

connect verb
1 *What's the best way to **connect** these wires?*
join, attach, fasten, link, couple, fix together, tie together
OPPOSITE separate
2 *The fingerprints **connected** him with the crime.*
make a connection between, associate, relate

connection noun
*There is a close **connection** between our two families.*
association, relationship, link

conquer verb
1 *Extra troops were sent to **conquer** the enemy forces.*
beat, defeat, overcome, vanquish, get the better of, overwhelm, crush, rout
2 *Gaul was **conquered** by Caesar.*
seize, capture, take, win, occupy, possess

a
b
c
d
e
f
g
h
i
j
k
l
m
n
o
p
q
r
s
t
u
v
w
x
y
z

conscientious *adjective*
Elves are very conscientious workers.
hard working, careful, dependable, reliable, responsible, dutiful, meticulous, painstaking, thorough
OPPOSITE careless

conscious *adjective*
1 *The patient was conscious throughout the operation.*
awake, alert, aware
OPPOSITE unconscious
2 *She made a conscious effort to improve her work.*
deliberate, intentional, planned
OPPOSITE accidental

consequence *noun*
1 *He drank the potion without thinking of the consequences.*
effect, result, outcome, sequel, upshot
2 *The loss of a few pence is of no consequence.*
importance, significance

consider *verb*
1 *The detective considered the problem carefully.*
think about, examine, contemplate, ponder on, reflect on, study, weigh up, meditate about
2 *I consider this to be my best work.*
believe, judge, reckon

considerate *adjective*
It was considerate of you to lend me your umbrella.
kind, kind-hearted, helpful, obliging, sympathetic, thoughtful, unselfish, caring, charitable, neighbourly
OPPOSITE selfish

consist *verb*
to consist of
1 *The planet consists largely of craters.*
be made of, be composed of, comprise, contain, include, incorporate
2 *His job consists mostly of answering the phone.*
involve

consistent *adjective*
1 *These plants need to be kept at a consistent temperature.*
steady, constant, regular, stable, unchanging
2 *Fortunately, our goalkeeper is a consistent player.*
predictable, dependable, reliable

console *verb*
He did his best to console me when my dog died.
comfort, soothe, sympathise with, support

conspicuous *adjective*
1 *The clock tower is a conspicuous landmark.*
prominent, notable, obvious, eye-catching, unmistakable, visible
2 *I had made some conspicuous mistakes.*
clear, noticeable, obvious, evident, glaring

constant *adjective*
1 *There is a constant noise of traffic on the motorway.*
continual, continuous, never-ending, non-stop, ceaseless, incessant, interminable, endless, everlasting, permanent, perpetual, unending, persistent, relentless
OPPOSITE changeable
2 *My dog has been my constant friend for many years.*
faithful, loyal, dependable, reliable, firm, true, trustworthy, devoted
OPPOSITE unreliable

construct *verb*
We constructed a tree house in the back garden.
build, erect, assemble, make, put together, put up, set up
OPPOSITE demolish

consult *verb*
1 *You should consult the dentist about your sore tooth.*
ask, get advice from, speak to
2 *If you don't know how to spell a word, consult your dictionary.*
refer to

contact *verb*
I'll contact you when I have some news.
call, call on, get in touch with, notify communicate with, speak to, talk to, correspond with, phone, ring, write to

contain *verb*
1 *This box contains odds and ends.*
hold
2 *A dictionary contains words and definitions.*
include, incorporate, comprise, consist of

contemplate *verb*
1 *The princess contemplated herself in the mirror.*
look at, view, observe, survey, watch, stare at, gaze at
2 *The robbers contemplated what to do next.*
think about, consider, ponder, study, reflect on, weigh up, meditate about

contempt *noun*
The knight stared at his enemy with a look of contempt.
hatred, scorn, loathing, disgust, dislike, distaste
OPPOSITE admiration

contented *adjective*
After her meal, the cat looked very contented.
happy, pleased, content, satisfied, fulfilled, serene, peaceful, relaxed, comfortable, tranquil, untroubled
OPPOSITE discontented

contest *noun*
The tennis final was an exciting contest.
competition, challenge, fight, bout, encounter, struggle, game, match, tournament

contestant *noun*
There are twenty contestants in the spelling competition.
competitor, participant, player, contender

continual *adjective*
I get sick of their continual arguing.
constant, persistent, perpetual, repeated, frequent, recurrent, eternal, unending
OPPOSITE occasional

continue *verb*
1 *We continued our search until it got dark.*
keep up, prolong, sustain, persevere with, pursue
(*informal*) stick at
2 *This rain can't continue for long.*
carry on, last, persist, endure, keep on, go on, linger
3 *We'll continue our meeting after lunch.*
resume, proceed with, pick up

continuous *adjective*
We had continuous rain all through our holiday.
never-ending, non-stop, ceaseless, everlasting, incessant, unbroken, unceasing, uninterrupted
An illness which continues for a long time is a *chronic* illness.
OPPOSITE intermittent

contract *noun*
The actress has signed a contract for a new film.
agreement, deal, undertaking
A contract between two countries is an *alliance* or *treaty*.
A contract to end a dispute about money is a *settlement*.

contract *verb*
1 *Metal contracts when it gets colder.*
reduce, lessen, shrink, tighten
OPPOSITE expand
2 *The crew contracted a mysterious illness.*
catch, develop, get

contrast verb
1 *We were asked to* **contrast** *two of our favourite poems.*
compare, juxtapose, distinguish between
2 *Her handwriting* **contrasts** *with mine.*
clash, differ (from)

contrast noun
There is a sharp **contrast** *between the two paintings.*
difference, distinction, opposition
OPPOSITE similarity

contribute verb
Will you **contribute** *something to our charity collection?*
donate, give, provide
(*informal*) chip in
to contribute to
The sunny weather **contributed to** *our enjoyment.*
add to, help, aid, encourage, enhance

control noun
The captain had complete **control** *over the crew.*
authority, power, command, government, management, direction, leadership, guidance

control verb
1 *The government* **controls** *the country's affairs.*
be in control of, be in charge of, manage, run, command, direct, lead, guide, govern, administer, regulate, rule, superintend, supervise
2 *Can't you* **control** *that dog?*
manage, handle, restrain
3 *They built a dam to* **control** *the floods.*
check, curb, hold back, contain

convenient adjective
1 *Is there a* **convenient** *place to put my umbrella?*
suitable, appropriate, available, nearby, accessible
OPPOSITE inconvenient
2 *Mum has a* **convenient** *tool for opening jars.*
handy, helpful, useful, labour-saving, neat

conventional adjective
The **conventional** *way to greet someone is to shake hands.*
customary, traditional, usual, accepted, common, normal, ordinary, everyday, routine, standard, regular, habitual
OPPOSITE unconventional

conversation noun
An informal conversation is a **chat** *or* **gossip**.
A more formal conversation is a **discussion**.
A very formal conversation is a **conference**.
Conversation in a play or novel is **dialogue**.

WORD WEB

cook verb
To cook food for guests or customers is to **cater** for them.
Cooking as a business is **catering**.
The art or skill of cooking is **cookery**.

SOME WAYS TO COOK FOOD
bake, barbecue, boil, braise, brew, broil, casserole, deep-fry, fry, grill, poach, roast, sauté, simmer, steam, stew, toast

OTHER WAYS TO PREPARE FOOD
baste, blend, chop, dice, grate, grind, infuse, knead, liquidise, marinade, mince, mix, peel, purée, sieve, sift, stir, whisk

SOME ITEMS THAT ARE USED FOR COOKING
baking tin or tray, barbecue, blender, bowl, carving knife, casserole, cauldron, chopping board, colander, cooker, dish, food processor, frying pan, grill, ladle, liquidiser, microwave, mincer, oven, pan, pot, rolling pin, saucepan, skewer, spatula, spit, strainer, toaster, whisk, wok, wooden spoon

blender

---

convert verb
1 *We have* **converted** *our attic into a games room.*
change, adapt, alter, transform
2 *I never used to like football, but my cousin* **converted** *me.*
change someone's mind, persuade, convince, win over

convince verb
The prisoner **convinced** *them that he was innocent.*
persuade, assure, satisfy, make believe, win round

convincing adjective
I tried to think of a **convincing** *excuse.*
persuasive, believable, credible, plausible

cook verb see panel above

cool adjective
1 *The weather is* **cool** *for the time of year.*
chilly, coldish
OPPOSITE hot, warm
2 *Would you like a* **cool** *glass of lemonade?*
chilled, iced, refreshing
OPPOSITE hot
3 *Clifford remained* **cool** *when everyone else panicked.*
calm, level-headed, relaxed, unexcitable, unflustered
(*informal*) laid-back
A common simile is **as cool as a cucumber**.
OPPOSITE frantic
4 (*informal*) *Those trainers are really* **cool**!
chic, fashionable, smart
(*informal*) trendy

cooperate verb
to cooperate with
The scouts **cooperated with** *each other to build a fire.*
work with or together with, collaborate with, aid, assist, support

cope verb
Shall I help you, or can you **cope** *on your own?*
manage, carry on, get by, make do, survive
to cope with
I can't **cope with** *all this homework!*
deal with, handle, manage, get through

copy noun
That isn't the original painting—it's a **copy**.
replica, reproduction, duplicate, imitation, likeness
A copy made to deceive someone is a **fake** or a **forgery**.
A living organism which is identical to another is a **clone**.

copy verb
1 *I* **copied** *the poem into my notepad.*
duplicate, reproduce, write out
To copy something in order to deceive is to **fake** or **forge** it.
2 *My parrot can* **copy** *my voice.*
imitate, impersonate, mimic

core noun
It is very hot at the earth's **core**.
centre, inside, middle, heart, nucleus

core

corner noun
1 *I'll meet you at the **corner** of the road.*
turn, turning, junction, crossroads, intersection
The place where two lines meet is an **angle**.
2 *I sat in a quiet **corner** and read her letter.*
alcove, recess, nook

correct adjective
1 *Your answers are all **correct**.*
right, accurate, exact, faultless
2 *I hope he has given us **correct** information.*
true, genuine, authentic, precise, reliable, factual
3 *What is the **correct** way to address this letter?*
proper, acceptable, regular, appropriate, suitable
OPPOSITE wrong

correct verb
1 *I have to **correct** my spelling mistakes.*
alter, put right, make better, improve
2 *Miss Nicol spent the day **correcting** exam papers.*
mark

correspond verb
to correspond with
1 *Her version of the story doesn't **correspond with** mine.*
agree with, match, be similar to, be consistent with, tally with
2 *Carol **corresponds with** a friend in Paris.*
write to, communicate with, send letters to

corrupt adjective
***Corrupt** officials had accepted millions of pounds in bribes.*
dishonest, criminal, untrustworthy
(*informal*) bent, crooked
OPPOSITE honest

cost noun
*The bill shows the total **cost**.*
price, charge, amount, payment, fee, figure, expense, expenditure, tariff
The cost of travelling on public transport is the **fare**.

costume noun
*The Irish dancers were wearing national **costumes**.*
outfit, dress, clothing, suit, attire, garment, garb
(*informal*) get-up
A costume you dress up in for a party is **fancy dress**.
A set of clothes worn by soldiers or members of an organisation is a **uniform**.

cosy adjective
*It's good to feel **cosy** in bed when it's cold outside.*
comfortable, snug, soft, warm, secure
OPPOSITE uncomfortable

count verb
1 *I'm **counting** the days until my birthday.*
add up, calculate, compute, estimate, reckon, figure out, work out, total
2 *It's playing well that **counts**, not winning.*
be important, be significant, matter
to count on
*You can **count on** me to support you.*
depend on, rely on, trust, bank on

country noun
1 *England and Wales are separate **countries**.*
nation, state, land, territory
A country ruled by a king or queen is a **kingdom**, **monarchy** or **realm**.
A country governed by leaders elected by the people is a **democracy**.
A democratic country with a President is a **republic**.
2 *We went for a picnic in the **country**.*
countryside, landscape, outdoors, scenery
A word meaning 'to do with the country' is **rural** and its opposite is **urban**.
OPPOSITE town, city

courage noun
*The rescue dogs showed great **courage**.*
bravery, boldness, daring, fearlessness, nerve, pluck, valour, heroism, grit
(*informal*) guts
OPPOSITE cowardice

course noun
1 *The hot-air balloon was drifting off its **course**.*
direction, path, route, way, progress, passage
2 *The war changed the **course** of history.*
development, progression, sequence, succession

cover verb
1 *A coat of paint will **cover** the graffiti.*
conceal, disguise, hide, obscure, mask, blot out
2 *She **covered** her face with her hands.*
shield, screen, protect, shade, veil
3 *An encyclopedia **covers** many subjects.*
deal with, include, contain, incorporate

cover noun
1 *The **cover** of the book was torn.*
wrapper
A cover for a letter is an **envelope**.
A cover for a book is a **jacket**.
A cover to keep papers in is a **file** or **folder**.
2 *On the bare hillside, there was no **cover** from the storm.*
shelter, protection, defence, shield, refuge, sanctuary

covering noun
*There was a light **covering** of snow on the hills.*
coating, coat, layer, blanket, carpet, film, sheet, skin, veil

cowardly adjective
*It was **cowardly** to run away.*
timid, faint-hearted, spineless, gutless
(*informal*) yellow, chicken
OPPOSITE brave

cower verb
*A frightened creature was **cowering** in the corner.*
cringe, shrink, crouch, flinch, quail

crack noun
1 *There's a **crack** in this cup.*
break, chip, fracture, flaw, chink, split
2 *The outlaw hid in a **crack** between two rocks.*
gap, opening, crevice, rift, cranny
3 *The detective heard the **crack** of a pistol shot.*
bang, fire, explosion, snap, pop
4 *She gave the robber a **crack** on the head.*
blow, bang, knock, smack, whack
5 *I had a **crack** at writing a poem.*
try, attempt, shot, go

crack verb
*A brick fell down and **cracked** the pavement.*
break, fracture, chip, split, shatter, splinter

craft noun
1 *I'd like to learn the **craft** of weaving.*
art, skill, technique, expertise, handicraft
2 *All sorts of craft were in the harbour.*
boats, ships, vessels

crafty adjective
*The evil sorceress had a **crafty** plan.*
cunning, clever, shrewd, scheming, sneaky, sly, tricky, wily, artful

cram verb
1 *We can't **cram** any more people in—the car is full.*
pack, squeeze, crush, force, jam, compress
2 *My sister is **cramming** for her maths exam.*
revise, study
(*informal*) swot

cramped *adjective*
The seating on the train was a bit cramped.
confined, narrow, restricted, tight, uncomfortable, crowded
(*informal*) poky
OPPOSITE roomy

crash *noun*
1 *I heard a loud crash from the kitchen.*
bang, smash
2 *We saw a nasty crash on the motorway.*
accident, collision, smash, bump
A crash involving a lot of vehicles is a *pile-up*.
A train crash may involve a *derailment*.

crash *verb*
The car crashed into a lamp post.
bump, smash, collide, knock

crawl *verb*
I saw a caterpillar crawling along a leaf.
creep, edge, inch, slither, clamber

crawl

craze *noun*
This game is the latest craze in the playground.
fad, trend, vogue, fashion, enthusiasm, obsession, passion

crazy *adjective*
1 *The dog went crazy when it was stung by a wasp.*
mad, insane, frenzied, hysterical, frantic, berserk, delirious, wild
(*informal*) loopy, nuts
2 *It was a crazy idea to try to build a space rocket!*
absurd, ridiculous, ludicrous, daft, idiotic, senseless, silly, stupid, foolhardy, preposterous
(*informal*) bonkers, barmy, wacky
OPPOSITE sensible

create *verb*
1 *The cats were creating a racket outside.*
make, cause, produce
2 *We have created a website for our chess club.*
set up, start up, bring about, bring into existence, originate
You *write* a poem or story.
You *compose* music.
You *draw* or *paint* a picture.
You *carve* a statue.
You *invent* or *think up* a new idea.
You *design* a new product.
You *devise* a plan.
You *found* a new club or organisation.
You *manufacture* goods.

You *generate* electricity.
You *build* or *construct* a model or a building.

creative *adjective*
My aunt is a very creative person.
artistic, imaginative, inventive, original, inspired
OPPOSITE unimaginative

creator *noun*
Walt Disney was the creator of Mickey Mouse.
inventor, maker, originator, producer, deviser
The creator of a design is an *architect* or *designer*.
The creator of goods for sale is a *manufacturer*.

creature *noun*
A wild-looking creature emerged from the swamp.
animal, beast, being

creep *verb*
1 *I watched the lizard creep back into its hiding place.*
crawl, edge, inch, slither, wriggle
2 *I crept out of bed without waking the others.*
move quietly, sneak, tiptoe, slip, slink, steal

creepy *adjective*
There were creepy noises coming from the cellar.
scary, frightening, eerie, ghostly, weird, sinister, uncanny, unearthly
(*informal*) spooky

crisis *noun*
The election result caused a crisis in the country.
emergency, problem, difficulty, predicament

crisp *adjective*
1 *Fry the bacon until it's crisp.*
crispy, crunchy, brittle
OPPOSITE soft, soggy, limp
2 *It was a crisp winter morning.*
cold, fresh, frosty

critical *adjective*
1 *Some people made critical comments about my hairstyle.*
negative, disapproving, derogatory, uncomplimentary, unfavourable
OPPOSITE complimentary
2 *This match is critical for our team's chances of success.*
crucial, important, vital, serious, decisive
OPPOSITE unimportant

criticise *verb*
She criticised us for being so careless.
blame, condemn, disapprove of, find fault with, reprimand, reproach, scold, berate
OPPOSITE praise

crooked *adjective*
1 *The wizard bent his wand into a crooked shape.*
bent, twisted, warped, knarled
OPPOSITE straight
2 (*informal*) *The crooked salesman was selling fake diamonds.*
criminal, dishonest, corrupt, illegal, unlawful
(*informal*) bent
OPPOSITE honest

cross *verb*
1 *There is a bus stop where the two roads cross.*
criss-cross, intersect
2 *You can cross the river at the footbridge.*
go across, pass over, traverse, ford, span

cross *adjective*
My mum will be cross if we're late.
angry, annoyed, upset, vexed, bad-tempered, ill-tempered, irritable, grumpy, testy, irate
OPPOSITE pleased

crouch *verb*
The outlaws crouched silently in the bushes.
squat, kneel, stoop, bend, duck, bob down, hunch, huddle

crowd *noun*
1 *A crowd of people waited outside the theatre.*
gathering, group, assembly, bunch, cluster, throng, mob, multitude, crush, horde, swarm
2 *There was a huge crowd for the tennis final.*
audience, spectators, gate, attendance

crowd *verb*
1 *People crowded on the pavement to watch the parade.*
gather, collect, assemble, congregate, mass, flock, muster
2 *Hundreds of people crowded into the hall.*
push, pile, squeeze, pack, cram, crush, jam, bundle, herd

crowd

crowded *adjective*
The shops are always crowded at Christmas time.
full, packed, teeming, swarming, overflowing, jammed, congested
OPPOSITE empty

a b c d e f g h i j k l m n o p q r s t u v w x y z

crude adjective
1 *The refinery processes **crude** oil.*
raw, natural, unprocessed, unrefined
OPPOSITE refined
2 *We made a **crude** shelter out of twigs.*
rough, clumsy, makeshift, primitive
OPPOSITE skilful
3 *The teacher told them to stop using **crude** language.*
rude, obscene, coarse, dirty, foul, impolite, indecent, vulgar
OPPOSITE polite

cruel adjective
*I think hunting is a **cruel** way to kill animals.*
brutal, savage, vicious, fierce, barbaric, bloodthirsty, barbarous, heartless, ruthless, merciless, inhuman, sadistic, uncivilised, beastly
OPPOSITE kind, humane, gentle

crumb noun
*We put out some **crumbs** of bread for the birds.*
bit, fragment, scrap, morsel

crumble verb
1 *The walls of the castle were beginning to **crumble**.*
disintegrate, break up, collapse, fall apart, decay, decompose
2 *The farmer **crumbled** some bread into his soup.*
crush, grind, pound, pulverise

crunch verb
1 *The dog was **crunching** on a bone.*
chew, munch, chomp, grind
2 *I heard heavy footsteps **crunching** up the path.*
crush, grind, pound, smash

crush verb
1 *He **crushed** his anorak into his schoolbag.*
squash, squeeze, mangle, pound, press, bruise, crunch, scrunch
To crush something into a soft mess is to **mash** or **pulp** it.
To crush something into a powder is to **grind** or **pulverise** it.
To crush something out of shape is to **crumple** or **smash** it.
2 *Our soldiers **crushed** the attacking army.*
defeat, conquer, vanquish, overcome, overwhelm, quash, trounce, rout

crush noun
*There was a **crush** of people at the front gates.*
crowd, press, mob, throng, jam, congestion

cry verb
1 *Someone was **crying** for help from the burning house.*
call, shout, yell, exclaim, roar, bawl, bellow, scream, screech, shriek

2 *The baby started to **cry** when she dropped her toy.*
sob, weep, bawl, blubber, wail, shed tears, snivel
When someone starts to cry, their eyes **well up with tears**.

cry noun
*The wounded man let out a **cry** of pain.*
call, shout, yell, roar, howl, exclamation, bellow, scream, screech, shriek, yelp

cuddle verb
*My baby brother **cuddles** a teddy bear in bed.*
hug, hold closely, clasp, embrace, caress, nestle against, snuggle against

cunning adjective
*The pirates had a **cunning** plan to seize the ship.*
clever, crafty, devious, wily, ingenious, shrewd, artful, scheming, sly, tricky

cup noun
A tall cup with straight sides is a **mug**.
A tall cup without a handle is a **beaker** or **tumbler**.
A decorative drinking cup is a **goblet**.

cure verb
1 *These pills will **cure** your headache.*
ease, heal, help, improve, make better, relieve
OPPOSITE aggravate
2 *No one can **cure** the problem with my computer.*
correct, mend, sort, repair, fix, put an end to, put right

cure noun
*I wish they could find a **cure** for colds.*
remedy, treatment, antidote, medicine, therapy

curious adjective
1 *We are all very **curious** about the secret chamber.*
inquisitive, inquiring, interested (in), intrigued, agog
An uncomplimentary word is **nosy**.
OPPOSITE uninterested, indifferent
2 *What is that **curious** smell?*
odd, strange, peculiar, abnormal, queer, unusual, extraordinary, funny, mysterious, puzzling, weird

curl verb
1 *The snake **curled** itself around a branch.*
wind, twist, loop, coil, wrap, curve, turn, twine
2 *Steam **curled** upwards from the cauldron.*
coil, spiral, twirl, swirl, furl, snake, writhe, ripple

curl noun
*The girl's hair was a mass of golden **curls**.*
wave, ringlet, coil, loop, twist, roll, scroll, spiral

curly adjective
*My new doll has **curly** black hair.*
curled, curling, wavy, frizzy, crinkly, ringletted
OPPOSITE straight

current noun
*The wooden raft drifted along with the **current**.*
flow, tide, stream
A current of air is a **draught**.

current adjective
1 *The shop sells all the **current** teenage fashions.*
modern, contemporary, present-day, up to date, topical, prevailing, prevalent
OPPOSITE past, old-fashioned
2 *Have you got a **current** passport?*
valid, usable, up to date
OPPOSITE out of date
3 *Who is the **current** prime minister?*
present, existing
OPPOSITE past, former

curse noun
1 *Long ago, a wizard put a **curse** on the family.*
jinx, hex
2 *When the gardener hit his finger, he let out a **curse**.*
swear word, oath

curve noun
*Try to draw a straight line without any **curves**.*
bend, curl, loop, turn, twist, arch, arc, bow, bulge, wave
A curve in the shape of a new moon is a **crescent**.
A curve on a road surface is a **camber**.

curve verb
*The road ahead **curves** round to the right.*
bend, wind, turn, twist, curl, loop, swerve, veer, snake, meander

curved adjective
*The wall was painted with a series of **curved** lines.*
curving, curvy, curled, looped, coiled, rounded, bulging, bent, arched, bowed, twisted, crooked, spiral, winding, meandering, serpentine, snaking, undulating
A surface which is curved like the inside of a circle is **concave**.
A surface which is curved like the outside of a circle is **convex**.

custom noun
1 *It's our **custom** to give presents at Christmas.*
tradition, practice, habit, convention, fashion, routine, way

2 *The shop is having a sale to attract more **custom**.*
customers, buyers, trade, business

cut *verb*
1 *The woodcutter **cut** the tree trunk to make logs.*
chop, slit, split, chip, notch, axe, hack, hew, cleave
To cut off a limb is to **amputate** or **sever** it.
To cut down a tree is to **fell** it.
To cut branches off a tree is to **lop** them.
To cut twigs off a growing plant is to **prune** it.
To cut something up to examine it is to **dissect** it.
To cut stone to make a statue is to **carve** it.
To cut an inscription in stone is to **engrave** it.
2 *The cook **cut** the apples into small pieces.*
chop, slice, dice, grate, mince, shred
3 *I'm going to get my hair **cut** in the holidays.*
trim, clip, crop, snip, shave
To cut wool off a sheep is to **shear** it.
To cut grass is to **mow** it.
To cut corn is to **harvest** or **reap** it.
4 *Josh **cut** his foot on a sharp stone.*
gash, slash, nick, stab, pierce, wound
5 *This letter is too long—I'll need to **cut** it.*
shorten, condense, edit
6 *The shop has **cut** its prices by 10%.*
lower, reduce, decrease
If you cut something by half, you **halve** it.

cut *noun*
*I got a nasty **cut** when I was slicing bread.*
gash, wound, injury, nick, slash, scratch, slit, snip

damage *verb*
*Many books were **damaged** in the fire.*
harm, spoil, mar, break, impair, weaken, disfigure, deface, mutilate, scar
To damage something beyond repair is to **destroy**, **ruin** or **wreck** it.
To damage something deliberately is to **sabotage** or **vandalise** it.

damp *adjective*
1 *Don't wear those clothes if they are **damp**.*
moist, soggy, clammy, dank

WORD WEB

dance *noun*
SOME KINDS OF DANCE OR DANCING
ballet, ballroom dancing, barn dance, belly dancing, bolero, break-dancing, cancan, disco, flamenco, folk dance, Highland dancing, hornpipe, jazz dance, jig, jive dancing, limbo dancing, line-dancing, mazurka, morris dance, quadrille, reel, rumba, samba, Scottish country dancing, square dance, step dancing, street dance, tap dancing, tarantella

A person who writes the steps for a dance is a **choreographer**.

SOME BALLROOM DANCES
foxtrot, minuet, polka, quickstep, tango, waltz

GATHERINGS WHERE PEOPLE DANCE
ball, ceilidh, disco

breakdancing

ballet

flamenco

ballroom dancing

---

2 *I don't like this **damp** weather.*
drizzly, foggy, misty, rainy, wet
Weather which is both damp and warm is **humid** or **muggy** weather.
OPPOSITE dry

dance *verb*
*I could have **danced** for joy.*
caper, cavort, frisk, frolic, gambol, hop about, jig about, jump about, leap, prance, skip, whirl

danger *noun*
1 *Who knows what **dangers** lie ahead?*
peril, jeopardy, trouble, crisis, hazard, menace, pitfall, threat, trap
OPPOSITE safety
2 *The forecast says there's a **danger** of frost.*
chance, possibility, risk

dangerous *adjective*
1 *We were in a **dangerous** situation.*
hazardous, perilous, risky, precarious, treacherous, unsafe, alarming, menacing
(*informal*) hairy
2 *The police arrested him for **dangerous** driving.*
careless, reckless
3 *A **dangerous** criminal had escaped from prison.*
violent, desperate, ruthless, treacherous
4 *It's wicked to empty **dangerous** chemicals into the river.*
harmful, poisonous, deadly, toxic
OPPOSITE harmless, safe

---

dangle *verb*
*There was a bunch of keys **dangling** from the chain.*
hang, swing, sway, droop, wave about, flap, trail

dare *verb*
1 *I wouldn't **dare** to make a parachute jump.*
have the courage, take the risk
2 *They **dared** me to climb the tree.*
challenge, defy

daring *adjective*
*It was a very **daring** plan.*
bold, brave, adventurous, courageous, fearless, intrepid, plucky, valiant
A daring person is a **daredevil**.
OPPOSITE timid

dark *adjective*
1 *It was a very **dark** night.*
black, dim, murky, shadowy, gloomy, dingy
OPPOSITE bright
2 *She wore a **dark** green coat.*
OPPOSITE pale, light

dash *verb*
1 *We **dashed** home because it was raining.*
hurry, run, rush, race, hasten, sprint, speed, tear, zoom
2 *She **dashed** her cup against the wall.*
throw, hurl, knock, smash

a b c d e f g h i j k l m n o p q r s t u v w x y z

data *plural noun*
I entered all the data into the computer.
information, details, facts
Data can be in the form of *figures*, *numbers* or *statistics*.

dawn *noun*
1 *I was woken at dawn by the birds singing outside.*
daybreak, sunrise, first light
OPPOSITE dusk, sunset
2 *It was the dawn of the modern age.*
beginning, start, birth, origin

day *noun*
1 *Badgers sleep during the day.*
daytime
OPPOSITE night
2 *Things were different in my grandfather's day.*
age, time, era, epoch, period

dazed *adjective*
He had a dazed expression on his face.
confused, bewildered, muddled, perplexed

dazzle *verb*
1 *My eyes were dazzled by the bright lights.*
daze, blind
2 *The acrobats dazzled the audience with their skill.*
amaze, astonish, impress, fascinate, awe

dead *adjective*
1 *A dead fish floated by the side of the river.*
deceased, lifeless
Instead of 'the king who has just died', you can say 'the *late* king'.
A dead body is a *carcass* or *corpse*.
A common simile is *as dead as a doornail*.
OPPOSITE alive
2 *This battery is dead.*
flat, not working, worn out
3 *The town centre is dead at this time of night.*
dull, boring, uninteresting, slow
OPPOSITE lively

deadly *adjective*
The witch gave her a deadly dose of poison.
lethal, fatal, harmful, dangerous, destructive
OPPOSITE harmless

deafening *adjective*
We complained about the deafening noise.
loud, blaring, booming, thunderous, penetrating

deal *verb*
1 *Who is going to deal the cards?*
give out, distribute, share out
2 *My uncle used to deal in second-hand cars.*
do business, trade
to deal with something
1 *I can deal with this problem.*
cope with, sort out, attend to, see to, handle, manage, control, grapple with, look after, solve
2 *The book deals with the history of Rome.*
be concerned with, cover, explain about

deal *noun*
She made a deal with the garage for her new car.
arrangement, agreement, contract, bargain

dear *adjective*
1 *She is a very dear friend.*
close, loved, valued, beloved
OPPOSITE distant
2 *I didn't buy the watch because it was too dear.*
expensive, costly
(*informal*) pricey
OPPOSITE cheap

debate *noun*
We had a debate about animal rights.
discussion, argument, dispute
Something which people argue about a lot is a *controversy*.

debate *verb*
1 *We debated whether it is right to kill animals for food.*
discuss, argue
2 *I debated what to do next.*
consider, ponder, deliberate, weigh up, reflect on

decay *verb*
Dead leaves fall to the ground and decay.
decompose, rot, disintegrate, break down

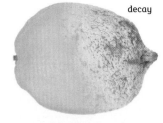

decay

deceitful *adjective*
Don't trust him—he's a deceitful person.
dishonest, underhand, insincere, duplicitous, false, cheating, hypocritical, lying, treacherous, two-faced, sneaky
OPPOSITE honest

deceive *verb*
The spy had been deceiving them for years.
fool, trick, delude, dupe, hoodwink, cheat, double-cross, mislead, swindle, take in
(*informal*) con, diddle

decent *adjective*
1 *Do the decent thing and own up.*
honest, honourable
2 *My friend's jokes were not decent.*
polite, proper, respectable, fitting, acceptable, appropriate, suitable
OPPOSITE indecent
3 *I haven't had a decent meal for ages!*
satisfactory, agreeable, good, nice
OPPOSITE bad

decide *verb*
1 *We decided to finish our work instead of going out to play.*
choose, make a decision, make up your mind, opt, elect, resolve
2 *The referee decided that the player was offside.*
conclude, judge, rule
3 *The last lap decided the result of the race.*
determine, settle

decision *noun*
1 *Can you tell me what your decision is?*
choice, preference
2 *The judge announced his decision.*
conclusion, judgement, verdict, findings

decisive *adjective*
1 *A decisive piece of evidence proved that he was innocent.*
crucial, convincing, definite
OPPOSITE uncertain
2 *A referee needs to be decisive.*
firm, forceful, strong-minded, resolute, quick-thinking
OPPOSITE hesitant

declare *verb*
He declared that he was innocent.
announce, state, assert, make known, pronounce, proclaim, swear

decline *verb*
1 *Our enthusiasm declined as the day went on.*
become less, decrease, diminish, lessen, weaken, dwindle, flag, wane, tail off
OPPOSITE increase
2 *Why did you decline my invitation to lunch?*
refuse, reject, turn down
OPPOSITE accept

decorate *verb*
1 *We decorated the Christmas tree with tinsel.*
ornament, adorn, beautify, prettify, deck, festoon

To decorate a dish of food is to **garnish** it.
To decorate clothes with lace or ribbon is to **trim** them.
2 *Dad is going to **decorate** my bedroom next weekend.*
paint, paper or wallpaper
(*informal*) do up, make over
3 *The firefighters were **decorated** for their bravery.*
award or give a medal to, honour, reward

decrease *verb*
1 *We **decreased** speed.*
reduce, cut, lower, slacken
2 *Our enthusiasm **decreased** as the day went on.*
become less, decline, decrease, diminish, lessen, weaken, dwindle, flag, wane, tail off, shrink, subside
OPPOSITE increase

dedicate *verb*
*He **dedicates** himself entirely to his art.*
commit, devote

deed *noun*
*They thanked the rescue team for their heroic **deed**.*
act, action, feat, exploit, effort, achievement

deep *adjective*
1 *The pond is quite **deep** in the middle.*
OPPOSITE shallow
2 *The letter expressed his **deep** regret.*
intense, earnest, genuine, sincere
OPPOSITE insincere
3 *Veronica fell into a **deep** sleep.*
heavy, sound
OPPOSITE light
4 *The actor spoke in a **deep** and sombre voice.*
low, bass
OPPOSITE high

defeat *verb*
*The Greeks attacked and **defeated** the Trojans.*
beat, conquer, vanquish, triumph over, win a victory over, overcome, overpower, crush, rout, trounce
To defeat someone in chess is to **checkmate** them.
To be defeated is to **lose**.

defeat *noun*
*The team suffered a humiliating **defeat**.*
failure, humiliation, rout, trouncing
OPPOSITE victory

defect *noun*
*Cars are tested for **defects** before they leave the factory.*
fault, flaw, imperfection, shortcoming, failure, weakness
A defect in a computer program is a **bug**.

defence *noun*
1 *What was the accused woman's **defence**?*
justification, excuse, explanation, argument, case
2 *The castle was built as a **defence** against enemy attack.*
protection, guard, safeguard, fortification, barricade, shield

defend *verb*
1 *They tried to **defend** themselves against the enemy.*
protect, guard, keep safe
OPPOSITE attack
2 *He gave a speech **defending** his actions.*
justify, support, stand up for, make a case for
OPPOSITE accuse

defiant *adjective*
*The prisoner cursed with a **defiant** look in his eye.*
rebellious, insolent, aggressive, challenging, disobedient, obstinate, quarrelsome, uncooperative, stubborn, mutinous
OPPOSITE submissive, compliant

definite *adjective*
1 *Is it **definite** that we're going to move?*
certain, sure, fixed, settled, decided
2 *The doctor saw **definite** signs of improvement.*
clear, distinct, noticeable, obvious, marked, positive, pronounced, unmistakable
OPPOSITE indefinite

definitely *adverb*
*I'll **definitely** phone you tomorrow.*
certainly, for certain, positively, surely, unquestionably, without doubt, without fail
OPPOSITE perhaps

defy *verb*
1 *The rebel army decided to **defy** the king.*
disobey, refuse to obey, resist, stand up to, confront
OPPOSITE obey
2 *I **defy** you to come up with a better idea.*
challenge, dare
3 *The jammed door **defied** our efforts to open it.*
resist, withstand, defeat, frustrate, beat

delay *verb*
1 *Don't let me **delay** you.*
detain, hold up, keep waiting, make late, hinder, slow down
2 *They **delayed** the race because of bad weather.*
postpone, put off, defer
3 *You'll miss the bus if you **delay**.*
hesitate, linger, pause, wait, dawdle, loiter

(*informal*) hang about or around, drag your feet

delay *noun*
*There has been a **delay** with the building work.*
hold-up, wait, pause

deliberate *adjective*
1 *That remark was a **deliberate** insult.*
intentional, planned, calculated, conscious, premeditated
OPPOSITE accidental, unintentional
2 *He walked with **deliberate** steps across the room.*
careful, steady, cautious, slow, unhurried
OPPOSITE hasty, careless

deliberately *adverb*
*Did you say that **deliberately** to hurt my feelings?*
on purpose, intentionally
OPPOSITE accidentally, unintentionally

delicate *adjective*
1 *The blouse has **delicate** embroidery on the cuffs.*
dainty, exquisite, intricate, neat
2 *Take care not to damage the **delicate** material.*
fragile, fine, flimsy, thin
3 ***Delicate** plants should be protected from frost.*
sensitive, tender
OPPOSITE tough, hardy
4 *The child was born with a **delicate** constitution.*
frail, weak, feeble, sickly, unhealthy
OPPOSITE strong
5 *The pianist's fingers had a **delicate** touch.*
gentle, light, soft

delicious *adjective*
*The food at the banquet was **delicious**.*
tasty, appetising, mouth-watering, delectable
(*informal*) scrumptious, yummy
OPPOSITE horrible, disgusting

delight *noun*
*Imagine my **delight** when I saw my friend again!*
happiness, joy, pleasure, enjoyment, bliss, ecstasy

delight *verb*
*The puppet show **delighted** the children.*
please, charm, entertain, amuse, divert, enchant, entrance, fascinate, thrill
OPPOSITE dismay

delighted *adjective*
*The **delighted** crowd cheered the winners.*
pleased, happy, joyful, thrilled, ecstatic, elated, exultant

a b c d e f g h i j k l m n o p q r s t u v w x y z

deliver verb
1 *Does anyone **deliver** mail to the island?*
convey, bring, hand over, distribute, present, supply, take round
2 *The head **delivered** a lecture on good behaviour.*
give, make, read out

demand verb
1 *I **demanded** a refund for my train fare.*
insist on, claim, call for, require, want
2 *'What do you want?' **demanded** a voice inside.*
ask, enquire, inquire

demand noun
1 *The king refused the **demands** of his people.*
request, claim, requirement
2 *There is not much **demand** for ice lollies in winter.*
need, call

demolish verb
*They **demolished** a building to make way for the road.*
destroy, flatten, knock down, level, pull down, tear down, bulldoze
OPPOSITE build, construct

demonstrate verb
1 *The teacher **demonstrated** how warm air rises.*
show, exhibit, illustrate
2 *Animal rights campaigners were **demonstrating** in the street.*
protest, march, parade

demonstration noun
1 *I watched a **demonstration** of the new computer game.*
show, display, presentation
2 *Everyone joined the **demonstration** against world poverty.*
protest, rally, march, parade
(*informal*) demo

den noun
*We built a **den** in the garden.*
hideout, shelter, hiding place, secret place
*The den of a wild animal is its **lair**.*

dense adjective
1 *The accident happened in **dense** fog.*
thick, heavy
2 *A **dense** crowd waited in the square.*
compact, packed, solid
3 *I'm being rather **dense** today!*
stupid, slow

dent noun
*There was a large **dent** in the car door.*
indentation, depression, hollow, dip, dimple

deny verb
1 *The boy **denied** that he had stolen the money.*
reject, dispute, disagree with, contradict, dismiss, oppose
OPPOSITE admit, accept
2 *Her parents **deny** her nothing.*
refuse, deprive of, withhold
OPPOSITE give

depart verb
1 *What time is the train due to **depart**?*
leave, set off, get going, set out, start, begin a journey
OPPOSITE arrive, get in
2 *It looks as if the robbers **departed** in a hurry.*
leave, exit, go away, retreat, withdraw, make off
(*informal*) clear off, scram, scarper
OPPOSITE arrive

depend verb
to depend on someone
*I **depend on** you to help me.*
rely on, count on, bank on, trust
to depend on something
*My success will **depend on** good luck.*
be decided by, rest on, hinge on

dependable adjective
*Are these friends of yours **dependable**?*
reliable, trustworthy, loyal, faithful, trusty, honest, sound, steady
OPPOSITE unreliable

depressed adjective
*After his friends left, he began to feel **depressed**.*
disheartened, dejected, discouraged, downcast, downhearted, unhappy, sad, low, gloomy, glum, melancholy, miserable, despondent, desolate, in despair
(*informal*) down
OPPOSITE cheerful

derelict adjective
*They plan to pull down those **derelict** buildings.*
dilapidated, crumbling, decrepit, neglected, deserted, abandoned, ruined

descend verb
1 *After admiring the view, we began to **descend** the mountain.*
climb down, come down, go down, move down
*To descend through the air is to **drop** or **fall**.*
*To descend through water is to **sink**.*
2 *The road **descends** gradually into the valley.*
drop, fall, slope, dip, incline
OPPOSITE ascend
to be descended from someone
*She's **descended from** a French family.*
come from, originate from

describe verb
1 *An eyewitness **described** how the accident happened.*
report, tell about, depict, explain, outline
2 *Friends **described** him as a quiet, shy man.*
portray, characterise, represent, present

description noun
1 *I wrote a **description** of our day at the seaside.*
report, account, story
2 *Write a **description** of your favourite character in the play.*
portrait, representation, sketch

descriptive adjective
*The author writes in a very **descriptive** style.*
expressive, colourful, detailed, graphic, vivid

desert verb
*He **deserted** his friends when they needed him most.*
abandon, leave, forsake, betray
(*informal*) walk out on
*To desert someone in a place they can't get away from is to **maroon** or **strand** them.*

deserted adjective
*By midnight, the streets of the town were **deserted**.*
empty, unoccupied, uninhabited, vacant
OPPOSITE crowded

deserve verb
*You **deserve** a break after all your hard work.*
be worthy of, be entitled to, have earned, merit, warrant

design noun
1 *This is the winning **design** for the new art gallery.*
plan, drawing, outline, blueprint, sketch
*A first example of something, used as a model for making others, is a **prototype**.*
2 *Do you like the **design** of this wallpaper?*
style, pattern, arrangement, composition

design verb
*She **designs** all her own clothes.*
create, develop, invent, devise, conceive, think up

desire verb
*The magic mirror will show you what you most **desire**.*
wish for, long for, want, crave, fancy, hanker after, yearn for, pine for, set your heart on, have a yen for

desire noun
My greatest **desire** is to swim with dolphins.
wish, want, longing, ambition, urge, craving, fancy, hankering, yearning
A desire for food is **appetite** or **hunger**.
A desire for drink is **thirst**.
Excessive desire for money or other things is **greed**.

desolate adjective
1 Jamie felt **desolate** when his goldfish died.
depressed, dejected, miserable, sad, melancholy, hopeless, wretched, forlorn
OPPOSITE cheerful
2 No one wants to live in that **desolate** place.
bleak, depressing, dreary, gloomy, dismal, cheerless, inhospitable, deserted, uninhabited, abandoned, godforsaken
OPPOSITE pleasant

despair noun
The defeated knight was overcome by **despair**.
depression, desperation, gloom, hopelessness, misery, anguish, dejection, melancholy, pessimism, wretchedness
OPPOSITE hope

desperate adjective
1 The shipwrecked crew were in a **desperate** situation.
difficult, critical, grave, serious, severe, drastic, dire, urgent, extreme
2 The hills were home to a band of **desperate** outlaws.
dangerous, violent, reckless

despise verb
I **despise** people who cheat at cards.
hate, loathe, feel contempt for, deride, have a low opinion of, look down on, scorn, sneer at
OPPOSITE admire

destiny noun
Destiny brought us together
fate, fortune

destroy verb
1 An avalanche **destroyed** the village.
demolish, devastate, crush, flatten, knock down, level, pull down, shatter, smash, sweep away
2 He tried to **destroy** the good work we had done.
ruin, wreck, sabotage, undo

destruction noun
1 The hurricane caused **destruction** all along the coast.
devastation, damage, demolition, ruin, wrecking
OPPOSITE creation

2 Global warming may cause the **destruction** of many animal species.
elimination, annihilation, obliteration, extermination, extinction
OPPOSITE conservation

detach verb
The camera lens can be **detached** for cleaning.
remove, separate, disconnect, take off, release, undo, unfasten, part
To detach a caravan from a vehicle is to **unhitch** it.
To detach railway wagons from a locomotive is to **uncouple** them.
To detach something by cutting it off is to **sever** it.
OPPOSITE attach

detail noun
Her account of what happened was accurate in every **detail**.
fact, feature, particular, aspect, item, point, respect

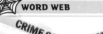 **WORD WEB**

detective noun
Detective Dewar solved the case of the stolen tiara.
investigator, sleuth
(informal) private eye

THINGS A DETECTIVE MIGHT LOOK FOR
clues, evidence, eyewitness, fingerprints, footprints, murder weapon, tracks; criminal, crook, culprit, felon, suspect

THINGS A DETECTIVE MIGHT DO
analyse, comb (an area), deduce, deduct, detect, dig up, ferret out, follow a hunch, follow a lead or a tip-off, interrogate or question (a witness), investigate, pursue, shadow, solve (a case), stake out (a hiding place), tail or track down (a suspect)

An informal name for a story in which a detective solves a crime is a **whodunnit**.

deteriorate verb
1 The queen's health had begun to **deteriorate**.
worsen, decline, degenerate, get worse, go downhill
2 The walls will **deteriorate** if we don't maintain them.
decay, disintegrate, crumble
OPPOSITE improve

determination noun
Marathon runners show great **determination**.
resolve, commitment, will-power, courage, dedication, drive, grit, perseverance, persistence, spirit
(informal) guts

determined adjective
1 Boudicca must have been a **determined** woman.
resolute, decisive, strong-minded, assertive, persistent, tough, firm
OPPOSITE weak-minded
2 I'm **determined** to finish the race.
committed, resolved

detest verb
I **detest** the smell of boiled cabbage.
dislike, hate, loathe
Informal expressions are **can't bear** and **can't stand**.
OPPOSITE love

develop verb
1 The zoo is **developing** its education programme.
expand, extend, enlarge, build up, diversify
2 Her piano playing has **developed** this year.
improve, progress, evolve, advance, get better
3 The plants will **develop** quickly in the spring.
grow, flourish
4 How did he **develop** that posh accent?
get, acquire, pick up, cultivate

device noun
The TV comes with a remote control **device**.
tool, implement, instrument, appliance, apparatus, gadget, contraption
(informal) gizmo

devious adjective
1 The mad professor had a **devious** plan to take over the world.
cunning, deceitful, dishonest, furtive, scheming, sly, sneaky, treacherous, wily
2 Because of the roadworks, we took a **devious** route home.
indirect, roundabout, winding, meandering
OPPOSITE direct

a b c d e f g h i j k l m n o p q r s t u v w x y z

A B C D E F G H I J K L M N O P Q R S T U

devoted adjective
*She's a **devoted** supporter of our team.*
loyal, faithful, dedicated, enthusiastic, committed
OPPOSITE apathetic

devour verb
*He **devoured** a whole plateful of sandwiches.*
eat, consume, guzzle, gobble up, gulp down, swallow
(*informal*) scoff, wolf down

diagram noun
*We drew a **diagram** of the life cycle of a frog.*
chart, plan, sketch, outline

diary noun
*I write all about my birthday party in my **diary**.*
journal, daily record
A diary describing a voyage or mission is a **log** or **logbook**.
A diary in which you insert pictures and souvenirs is a **scrapbook**.
A diary published on a website is a **blog**.

die verb
1 *My sister's hamster **died** last week.*
expire, pass away, perish
(*informal*) snuff it, kick the bucket, croak
To die of hunger is to **starve**.
2 *The flowers will **die** if they don't have water.*
wither, wilt, droop, fade
to die out
*When did the dinosaurs **die out**?*
become extinct, cease to exist, come to an end, disappear, vanish

differ verb
*The two men **differed** in their beliefs.*
disagree, conflict, argue, clash, contradict each other, oppose each other, quarrel
OPPOSITE agree
to differ from
*My style of painting **differs from** hers.*
be different from, contrast with

difference noun
1 *Can you see any **difference** between these two colours?*
contrast, distinction
OPPOSITE similarity
2 *This money will make a **difference** to their lives.*
change, alteration, modification, variation

different adjective
1 *We have **different** views about global warming.*
differing, contradictory, opposite, clashing, conflicting
2 *It's important that the teams wear **different** colours.*
contrasting, dissimilar, distinguishable
3 *The packet contains sweets of **different** flavours.*
various, assorted, mixed, several, diverse, numerous, miscellaneous
4 *Let's go somewhere **different** on holiday this year.*
new, original, fresh
5 *Everyone's handwriting is **different**.*
distinct, distinctive, individual, special, unique

difficult adjective
1 *This crossword is really **difficult**. We were faced with a **difficult** problem.*
hard, complicated, complex, involved, intricate, baffling, perplexing, puzzling
(*informal*) tricky, thorny, knotty
OPPOSITE simple
2 *It is a **difficult** climb to the top of the hill.*
challenging, arduous, demanding, taxing, exhausting, formidable, gruelling, laborious, strenuous, tough
OPPOSITE easy
3 *Mum says I was a **difficult** child when I was little.*
troublesome, awkward, trying, tiresome, annoying, disruptive, obstinate, stubborn, uncooperative, unhelpful
OPPOSITE cooperative

difficulty noun
1 *The explorers were used to facing **difficulty**.*
trouble, adversity, challenges, hardship
2 *There are some **difficulties** with your application.*
problem, complication, hitch, obstacle, snag

dig verb
1 *We spent the afternoon **digging** the garden.*
cultivate, fork over, turn over
2 *Rabbits **dig** holes in the ground.*
burrow, excavate, tunnel, gouge out, hollow out, scoop out
3 *Did you **dig** me in the back?*
poke, prod, jab

dignified adjective
*Lady Snodgrass was a very **dignified** old lady.*
refined, stately, distinguished, noble, sedate, solemn, proper, grave, grand, august
OPPOSITE undignified

dim adjective
1 *I could see the **dim** outline of a figure in the mist.*
indistinct, faint, blurred, fuzzy, hazy, shadowy, vague
OPPOSITE clear
2 *The light in the cave was rather **dim**.*
dark, dull, dingy, murky, gloomy
OPPOSITE bright

din noun
*I can't hear you because of that awful **din**!*
noise, racket, row, clatter, hullabaloo

dingy adjective
*How can we brighten up this **dingy** room?*
dull, drab, dreary, dowdy, colourless, dismal, gloomy, murky
OPPOSITE bright

🕸 WORD WEB

dinosaur noun
SOME TYPES OF DINOSAUR
apatosaurus, archaeopteryx, brachiosaurus, diplodocus, gallimimus, iguanodon, megalosaurus, pterodactylus, stegosaurus, triceratops, tyrannosaurus rex, velociraptor

BODY PARTS WHICH A DINOSAUR MAY HAVE
dorsal plates, bony frill, fleshy fin, horn, wings, crest

A person who studies dinosaurs and other fossils is a **palaeontologist**.

dip *verb*
I dipped my hand in the water.
immerse, lower, plunge, submerge, dunk

dip *noun*
1 *There was a dip in the road ahead.*
hollow, hole, depression, slope
2 *It was so hot we decided to have a dip in the sea.*
swim, bathe

direct *adjective*
1 *It would be quicker to take the direct route.*
straight, shortest
OPPOSITE indirect
2 *Please give me a direct answer.*
straightforward, frank, honest, sincere, blunt, plain, outspoken, candid, unambiguous
OPPOSITE evasive

direct *verb*
1 *Can you direct me to the station?*
guide, point, show the way, give directions to
2 *A new manager has been apppointed to direct the company.*
manage, run, be in charge of, control, administer, superintend, supervise, take charge of
To direct an orchestra is to **conduct** it.
3 *The conductor directed us to begin playing.*
instruct, command, order, tell

dirt *noun*
1 *The floor was covered in dirt.*
filth, grime, mess, muck, mud, dust
2 *Chickens scratched about in the dirt.*
earth, soil, clay, loam, mud

dirty *adjective*
1 *Those dirty clothes need to be washed.*
unclean, filthy, grimy, grubby, soiled, stained, messy, mucky, muddy, sooty, foul
(*informal*) manky, grotty
OPPOSITE clean
2 *We refused to drink the dirty water.*
impure, polluted, murky, cloudy
OPPOSITE pure
3 *The other team used dirty tactics.*
unfair, dishonest, illegal, mean, unsporting
OPPOSITE honest
4 *The comedian used a lot of dirty words.*
rude,

offensive, coarse, crude, improper, indecent, obscene
OPPOSITE decent

disadvantage *noun*
It's a disadvantage to be small if you play basketball.
drawback, handicap, hindrance, inconvenience, downside, snag

disagree *verb*
My sister and I often disagree about music.
argue, differ, clash, quarrel, squabble, bicker, fall out
OPPOSITE agree
to disagree with
He disagrees with everything I say.
argue with, contradict, oppose, object to

disagreement *noun*
We had a disagreement over who should pay for the meal.
argument, dispute, difference of opinion, quarrel, row, clash, squabble, conflict
OPPOSITE agreement

disappear *verb*
1 *The markings will disappear as the chicks grow older.*
become invisible, vanish, fade, clear, disperse, dissolve
2 *The thief disappeared around the corner.*
run away, escape, flee, go away, withdraw
OPPOSITE appear

disappoint *verb*
She didn't want to disappoint her fans by cancelling the show.
let down, fail, dissatisfy, displease, upset
OPPOSITE please, satisfy

disappointed *adjective*
I'm disappointed that you can't come to my party.
saddened, unhappy, upset, let down, unsatisfied, displeased
OPPOSITE pleased, satisfied

disapprove *verb*
to disapprove of
My aunt disapproves of watching television.
object to, take exception to, dislike, deplore, condemn, criticise, denounce, frown on
(*informal*) take a dim view of
OPPOSITE approve of

discipline *noun*
Discipline is important in the army.
order, control

discourage *verb*
1 *Don't let her criticism discourage you.*
demoralise, depress
(*informal*) put you off

2 *The burglar alarm will discourage thieves.*
deter, dissuade, prevent, restrain, stop, hinder

discover *verb*
I discovered some old toys in the attic.
find, come across, spot, stumble across, uncover
To discover something that has been buried is to **unearth** it.
To discover something that has been under water is to **dredge it up**.
To discover something you have been pursuing is to **track it down**.
OPPOSITE hide

discovery *noun*
Scientists have made an exciting new discovery.
find, breakthrough

discrimination *noun*
1 *She shows discrimination in her choice of music.*
good taste, good judgement
2 *The school has a policy against racial discrimination.*
prejudice, bias, intolerance, unfairness
Discrimination against people because of their sex is **sexism**.
Discrimination against people because of their race is **racism**.

discuss *verb*
I discussed the idea with my parents.
talk about, confer about, debate

a
b
c
d
e
f
g
h
i
s
u
v
w
x
y
z

discussion noun
We had a lively **discussion** about pocket money.
conversation, argument, exchange of views
A formal discussion is a **conference** or **debate**.

disease noun
He suffers from a serious **disease**.
illness, ailment, sickness, complaint, affliction
(informal) bug

disgrace noun
1 He never got over the **disgrace** of being caught cheating.
humiliation, shame, embarrassment, dishonour
2 The way he treats it is a **disgrace**!
outrage, scandal

disgraceful adjective
We were shocked by her **disgraceful** behaviour.
shameful, shocking, appalling, outrageous, scandalous
OPPOSITE honourable

disguise verb
I tried to **disguise** my feelings.
conceal, hide, cover up, camouflage, mask
to disguise yourself as
The spy **disguised himself as** a hotel porter.
dress up as, pretend to be

disguise noun
I didn't recognise him in that **disguise**.
costume, camouflage, make-up, mask

disgust noun
The sight of the carcass filled me with **disgust**.
repulsion, repugnance, distaste, dislike, horror, loathing, detestation
OPPOSITE liking

disgust verb
The smell of rotten eggs **disgusts** me.
repel, revolt, sicken, appal, offend, distress, shock, horrify
(informal) put you off, turn your stomach
OPPOSITE please

disgusting adjective
The brew in the cauldron looked **disgusting**.
repulsive, revolting, horrible, sickening, loathsome, nasty, repellent, repugnant, offensive, appalling, nauseating
(informal) yucky, icky, gross
OPPOSITE delightful, pleasing

dishonest adjective
1 They were taken in by a **dishonest** salesman.
deceitful, cheating, corrupt, disreputable, untrustworthy, immoral, lying, swindling, thieving
(informal) bent, crooked, dodgy, shady

2 The author makes some **dishonest** claims.
false, misleading, untruthful, fraudulent, devious

dishonesty noun
The MP was accused of **dishonesty**.
deceit, cheating, corruption, insincerity, lying, deviousness
(informal) crookedness
OPPOSITE honesty

disintegrate verb
The cloth is so old that it's starting to **disintegrate**.
break up, fall apart, break into pieces, crumble, decay, decompose

dislike noun
His colleagues regarded him with intense **dislike**.
hatred, loathing, detestation, disapproval, disgust, revulsion
OPPOSITE liking

dislike verb
I **dislike** people who hunt wild animals.
hate, loathe, detest, disapprove of
OPPOSITE like

disloyal adjective
The rebels were accused of being **disloyal** to the king.
unfaithful, treacherous, faithless, false, unreliable, untrustworthy
OPPOSITE loyal

dismal adjective
1 How can we brighten up this **dismal** room?
dull, drab, dreary, dingy, colourless, cheerless, gloomy, murky
OPPOSITE bright, cheerful
2 (informal) It was a **dismal** performance by the home team.
dreadful, awful, terrible, feeble, useless, hopeless
(informal) pathetic
OPPOSITE bright, cheerful

dismay noun
We listened with **dismay** to the bad news.
distress, alarm, shock, concern, anxiety, gloom

dismiss verb
1 The teacher **dismissed** the class.
send away, discharge, free, let go, release
2 The firm **dismissed** ten workers.
sack, give the sack, give notice to, make redundant
(informal) fire
3 The weather was so bad that we **dismissed** the idea of having a picnic.
discard, drop, reject

disobedient adjective
She said she had never known such a **disobedient** child.
naughty, badly behaved, undisciplined, uncontrollable, unmanageable, unruly, ungovernable, troublesome, defiant, disruptive, mutinous, rebellious, contrary
OPPOSITE obedient

disobey verb
1 You will be penalised if you **disobey** the rules.
break, ignore, disregard, defy, violate
2 Soldiers are trained never to **disobey**.
be disobedient, rebel, revolt, mutiny
OPPOSITE obey

display verb
We planned the best way to **display** our work.
demonstrate, exhibit, present, put on show, set out, show, show off
To display something boastfully is to **flaunt** it.

display noun
We set out a **display** of our art work.
exhibition, show, presentation, demonstration

disrespectful adjective
She was very **disrespectful** towards her parents.
rude, bad-mannered, insulting, impolite, insolent, cheeky
OPPOSITE respectful

disrupt verb
Bad weather has **disrupted** the tennis tournament.
interrupt, upset, interfere with, throw into confusion or disorder

dissatisfied adjective
I was **dissatisfied** with my piano playing.
displeased, disappointed, discontented, frustrated, annoyed
OPPOSITE satisfied

distance noun
What is the **distance** from Earth to the Sun?
measurement, space, extent, reach, mileage
The distance across something is the **breadth** or **width**.
The distance along something is the **length**.
The distance between two points is a **gap** or **interval**.

distant adjective
1 I'd love to travel to **distant** countries.
faraway, remote, out-of-the-way, inaccessible, exotic
OPPOSITE close

2 *His **distant** manner puts me off.*
unfriendly, unapproachable, formal, reserved, withdrawn, cool, haughty, aloof
OPPOSITE friendly

distinct *adjective*
1 *There is a **distinct** improvement in your handwriting.*
definite, evident, noticeable, obvious, perceptible
OPPOSITE imperceptible
2 *It was a small photo, but the details were quite **distinct**.*
clear, distinguishable, plain, recognisable, sharp, unmistakable, visible, well defined
OPPOSITE indistinct
3 *Organise your essay into **distinct** sections.*
individual, separate

distinguish *verb*
1 *It was impossible to **distinguish** one twin from the other.*
tell apart, pick out, discriminate, differentiate, make a distinction, decide
2 *In the dark we couldn't **distinguish** who was walking past.*
identify, tell, make out, determine, perceive, recognise, single out

distress *verb*
*We could see that the bad news **distressed** her.*
upset, disturb, trouble, worry, alarm, dismay, torment
OPPOSITE comfort

distribute *verb*
1 *The coach **distributed** water to the players at half-time.*
give out, hand round, circulate, dispense, issue, share out, take round (*informal*) dish out, doll out
2 ***Distribute** the seeds evenly.*
scatter, spread, disperse

distrust *verb*
*I **distrusted** the professor from the moment I met him.*
doubt, mistrust, question, suspect, be suspicious or wary of, be sceptical about, feel uncertain or uneasy or unsure about
OPPOSITE trust

disturb *verb*
1 *Don't **disturb** the baby when she's asleep.*
bother, interrupt, annoy, pester
2 *They were **disturbed** by the bad news.*
distress, trouble, upset, worry, alarm, frighten
3 *Please don't **disturb** the papers on my desk.*
muddle, mix up, move around, mess about with

ditch *noun*
*We dug a **ditch** to drain away the water.*
trench, channel, drain, gully

dive *verb*
1 *The mermaid **dived** into the water.*
plunge, jump, leap
A dive in which you land flat on your front is a **bellyflop**.
2 *The eagle **dived** towards its prey.*
pounce, swoop

dive

divide *verb*
1 *We **divided** the class into two groups.*
separate, split, break up, move apart, part
OPPOSITE combine
2 *I **divided** the cake between my friends.*
distribute, share out, give out, allot, deal out, dispense
3 *Which way do we go? The path **divides** here.*
branch, fork
OPPOSITE converge

dizzy *adjective*
*Going on a roundabout makes me feel **dizzy**.*
dazed, giddy, faint, reeling, unsteady

do *verb*
1 *My friend always knows what to **do** in a crisis.*
act, behave, conduct yourself
2 *The vet has a lot of work to **do** this morning.*
attend to, cope with, deal with, handle, look after, perform, undertake
3 *It took me half an hour to **do** the washing-up.*
accomplish, achieve, carry out, complete, execute, finish
4 *I need to **do** all of these sums.*
answer, puzzle out, solve, work out
5 *Staring at the sun can **do** damage to your eyes.*
bring about, cause, produce, result in
6 *If you don't have lemonade, water will **do**.*
be acceptable, be enough, be satisfactory, be sufficient, serve

dock *noun*
*A boat was waiting for us at the end of the **dock**.*
harbour, quay, jetty, wharf, landing stage, dockyard, pier, port, marina

dodge *verb*
*I just managed to **dodge** the snowball.*
avoid, evade, side-step

dominate *verb*
*The visiting team **dominated** the game.*
control, direct, monopolise, govern, take control of, take over

donation *noun*
*The museum relies on **donations** from the public.*
contribution, gift, offering

done *adjective*
1 *All my thank you letters are **done**.*
finished, complete, over
2 *The cake will be brown on top when it's **done**.*
cooked, ready

doomed *adjective*
*The expedition was **doomed** from the start.*
ill-fated, condemned, fated, cursed, jinxed, damned

door *noun*
A door in a floor or ceiling is a **hatch** or **trapdoor**.
The plank or stone underneath a door is the **threshold**.
The beam or stone above a door is the **lintel**.
The device on which most doors swing is the **hinge**.

dot *noun*
*She was furious when she saw **dots** of paint on the carpet.*
spot, speck, fleck, point, mark
The dot you always put at the end of a sentence is a **full stop**.
on the dot
(*informal*) *We left the house at nine o'clock **on the dot**.*
exactly, precisely

double *adjective*
*You enter the room through a **double** set of doors.*
dual, twofold, paired, twin, matching, duplicate

double *noun*
*She's so like you—she's almost your **double**.*
twin
(*informal*) lookalike, spitting image, dead ringer
A living organism created as an exact copy of another living organism is a **clone**.

doubt *noun*
1 *Have you any **doubt** about his honesty?*
distrust, suspicion, mistrust, hesitation, reservation, scepticism
OPPOSITE confidence

a b c d e f g h i j k l m n o p q r s t u v w x y z

2 *There is no **doubt** that you will pass your exam.*
question, uncertainty, ambiguity, confusion
OPPOSITE certainty

doubt *verb*
*There is no reason to **doubt** her story.*
distrust, feel uncertain or uneasy or unsure about, question, mistrust, suspect, be sceptical about, be suspicious or wary of
OPPOSITE trust

doubtful *adjective*
*He looked **doubtful**, but agreed to let us go.*
unsure, uncertain, unconvinced, hesitant, distrustful, sceptical, suspicious
OPPOSITE certain

doze *verb*
*Dad often **dozes** in the evening.*
rest, sleep, nod off
(*informal*) drop off

drab *adjective*
*That dress is too **drab** to wear to the party.*
dull, dingy, dreary, cheerless, colourless, dismal, gloomy, grey
OPPOSITE bright, cheerful

draft *noun*
*I jotted down a **draft** of my story.*
outline, plan, sketch, rough version

draft *verb*
*I began to **draft** my story.*
outline, plan, prepare, sketch, work out

drag *verb*
*The tractor **dragged** the car out of the ditch.*

pull, tow, tug, draw, haul, lug
OPPOSITE push

drain *verb*
1 *If they **drain** the marsh, lots of waterbirds will die.*
dry out, remove water from
2 *She **drained** the oil from the engine.*
draw off, empty
3 *The water slowly **drained** away.*
trickle, ooze, seep
4 *The tough climb **drained** my energy.*
use up, consume, exhaust

drastic *adjective*
*After being without food for three days, the explorers needed to take **drastic** action.*
desperate, extreme, radical, harsh, severe
OPPOSITE moderate

draw *verb*
1 *I **drew** some pictures of the flowers in our garden.*
sketch, trace, doodle
2 *I'm not very good at **drawing** faces.*
depict, portray, represent
3 *The horse was **drawing** a cart.*
pull, tow, drag, haul, tug, lug

4 *We expect tomorrow's match to **draw** a big crowd.*
attract, bring in, pull in
5 *The two teams **drew** 1–1.*
finish equal, tie
to draw near
*As the spaceship **drew near**, I began to get nervous.*
approach, advance, come near

drawback *noun*
*It's a **drawback** to be small if you play basketball.*
disadvantage, difficulty, handicap, obstacle, inconvenience, hindrance, downside, snag

dread *noun*
*Our teacher has a **dread** of spiders.*
fear, horror, terror, phobia (about), anxiety (about)

dreadful *adjective*
1 *There has been a **dreadful** accident at sea.*
horrible, terrible, appalling, horrendous, distressing, shocking, upsetting, tragic, grim
2 *The weather at the weekend was **dreadful**.*
bad, awful, terrible, abysmal, abominable, dire, foul, nasty
OPPOSITE good, pleasant

dream *noun*
*A bad dream is a **nightmare**.*
*A dreamlike experience you have while awake is a **daydream**, **fantasy** or **reverie**.*
*Something you see in a dream or daydream is a **vision**.*
*The dreamlike state when you are hypnotised is a **trance**.*
*Something you think you see that is not real is a **hallucination** or **illusion**.*

dreary *adjective*
1 *The newsreader had a very **dreary** voice.*
dull, boring, flat, tedious, unexciting, uninteresting
OPPOSITE lively
2 *When will this **dreary** weather end?*
depressing, dismal, dull, gloomy, cheerless, murky, overcast
OPPOSITE bright, sunny

dress *noun*
1 *What kind of **dress** are you wearing to the party?*
frock, gown
2 *The invitation said to wear casual **dress**.*
clothes, clothing, outfit, costume, garments

WORD WEB

dragon *noun*
*A fearsome **dragon** once lived in these hills.*

SOME WAYS TO DESCRIBE A DRAGON
ancient, fearsome, fiery, fire-breathing, mighty, monstrous, scaly

BODY PARTS A DRAGON MIGHT HAVE
claws, crest, forked tail or tongue, scales, spikes or spines, bat-like wings

A DRAGON'S SCALES MIGHT BE
dazzling, iridescent, patterned, shimmering

A DRAGON'S BREATH MIGHT BE
fiery, flaming, scorching, searing

THINGS A DRAGON MIGHT DO
breathe fire, puff smoke, roar, snort, change shape, fly, swoop

PLACES WHERE A DRAGON MIGHT LIVE
cave, den, lair

dress *verb*
1 *I helped to **dress** my little brother.*
clothe, put clothes on
OPPOSITE undress
2 *A nurse **dressed** my wound.*
bandage, put a dressing on,
bind up

dribble *verb*
1 *Careful, the baby's **dribbling** on your jumper.*
drool
2 *Water **dribbled** out of the hole in the tank.*
drip, trickle, leak, ooze, seep

drift *verb*
1 *The boat **drifted** downstream.*
float, be carried, move slowly
2 *The crowd lost interest and **drifted** away.*
stray, wander, meander, ramble, walk aimlessly
3 *The snow will **drift** in this wind.*
pile up, accumulate, make drifts

drift *noun*
1 *The car was stuck in a snow **drift**.*
bank, heap, mound, pile, ridge
2 *Did you understand the **drift** of the speech?*
gist, main idea, point

drill *verb*
*It took a long time to **drill** through the wall.*
bore, penetrate, pierce

drink *verb*
To drink greedily is to *gulp*, *guzzle* or *swig*.
To drink noisily is to *slurp*.
To drink a small amount at a time is to *sip*.
To drink with the tongue as a cat does is to *lap*.

drip *noun*
*Dad was worried by the **drips** of oil underneath the car.*
spot, dribble, splash, trickle

drip *verb*
*The oil **dripped** on to the garage floor.*
drop, leak, dribble, splash, trickle

drive *verb*
1 *The dog **drove** the sheep through the gate.*
direct, guide, herd
2 *I couldn't **drive** the spade into the hard ground.*
push, thrust, hammer, plunge, ram
3 *When can I learn to **drive** a car?*
control, handle, manage
4 *Lack of money **drove** him to steal.*
force, compel, oblige
to drive someone out
*The invading soldiers **drove** the people **out**.*
eject, expel, throw out
To drive people out of their homes is to *evict* them.

To drive people out of their country is to *banish* or *exile* them.

drive *noun*
1 *We went for a **drive** in the country.*
ride, trip, journey, outing, excursion, jaunt
2 *Have you got the **drive** to succeed?*
ambition, determination, keenness, motivation, energy, zeal

droop *verb*
*Plants tend to **droop** in dry weather.*
sag, wilt, bend, flop, be limp

drop *noun*
1 *Large **drops** of rain began to fall.*
drip, droplet, spot, bead, blob
2 *Could I have another **drop** of milk in my tea?*
dash, small quantity
3 *We expect a **drop** in the price of fruit in the summer.*
decrease, reduction, cut
4 *There's a **drop** of two metres on the other side of the wall.*
fall, descent, plunge

drop *verb*
1 *The hawk **dropped** on to its prey.*
descend, dive, plunge, swoop
2 *I **dropped** to the ground exhausted.*
collapse, fall, sink, subside, slump, tumble
3 *Why did you **drop** me from the team?*
omit, eliminate, exclude, leave out
4 *They **dropped** the plan for a new bypass.*
abandon, discard, reject, give up, scrap

drown *verb*
*The music from upstairs **drowned** our conversation.*
overwhelm, overpower, drown out

drowsy *adjective*
*If you feel **drowsy**, why not go to bed?*
sleepy, tired, weary

drug *noun*
*A new **drug** has been discovered for back pain.*
medicine, remedy, treatment
A drug which relieves pain is an *analgesic* or *painkiller*.
A drug which calms you down is a *sedative* or *tranquilliser*.
Drugs which make you more active are *stimulants*.

dry *adjective*
1 *Nothing will grow in this **dry** soil.*
arid, parched, moistureless, waterless, dehydrated, desiccated, barren
A common simile is *as dry as a bone*.
OPPOSITE wet

2 *He gave rather a **dry** speech.*
dull, boring, dreary, tedious, uninteresting
OPPOSITE interesting
3 *I can't understand his **dry** sense of humour.*
ironic, wry, witty, subtle

duck *verb*
*Oliver **ducked** to avoid the snowball.*
bend down, bob down, crouch, stoop

dull *adjective*
1 *I don't like **dull** colours.*
dim, dingy, drab, dreary, dismal, faded, gloomy, sombre, subdued
OPPOSITE bright, colourful
2 *The sky was **dull** that day.*
cloudy, overcast, grey, sunless, murky
OPPOSITE clear
3 *I heard a **dull** thud from upstairs.*
indistinct, muffled, muted
OPPOSITE distinct
4 *He's rather a **dull** student.*
stupid, slow, unintelligent, dim, unimaginative, dense, obtuse
(*informal*) thick
OPPOSITE clever
5 *The play was so **dull** that I fell asleep.*
boring, dry, monotonous, tedious, uninteresting, unexciting, lacklustre
A common simile is *as dull as ditchwater*.
OPPOSITE interesting

dumb *adjective*
1 *The spectators were struck **dumb** with amazement.*
If you do not speak, you are *mute* or *silent*.
If you cannot speak because you are surprised, confused, or embarrassed, you are *speechless* or *tongue-tied*.
If you find it hard to express yourself, you are *inarticulate*.
2 (*informal*) *He's too **dumb** to understand.*
stupid, unintelligent, dim, slow, dense, obtuse
(*informal*) thick

dump *verb*
1 *I decided to **dump** some of my old toys.*
get rid of, throw away, throw out, discard, dispose of, scrap
2 *Just **dump** your things in the bedroom.*
put down, set down, deposit, place, drop, throw down, tip

dusk *noun*
*Bats begin to emerge at **dusk**.*
twilight, nightfall, sunset, sundown
OPPOSITE dawn

duty *noun*
1 *I have a **duty** to help my parents.*
responsibility, obligation

a b c d e f g h i j k l m n o p q r s t u v w x y z

2 *I carried out my* **duties** *conscientiously.*
job, task, assignment, chore
3 *The government has increased the* **duty** *on petrol.*
charge, tax

dwindle *verb*
Our enthusiasm **dwindled** *as the day went on.*
become less, diminish, decline, decrease, lessen, subside, wane, weaken
OPPOSITE increase

dynamic *adjective*
The team has a new, **dynamic** *captain.*
energetic, lively, enthusiastic, vigorous, active, forceful, powerful
OPPOSITE apathetic

eager *adjective*
He is always **eager** *to help.*
keen, enthusiastic, desperate, anxious
OPPOSITE unenthusiastic

early *adjective*
1 *The bus was* **early** *today.*
ahead of time, ahead of schedule
OPPOSITE late
2 *The* **early** *computers were huge machines.*
first, old, primitive, ancient
OPPOSITE recent, new

earth *noun*
The **earth** *was so dry that many plants died.*
ground, land, soil
Rich, fertile earth is **loam**.
The top layer of fertile earth is **topsoil**.
Rich earth consisting of decayed plants is **humus**.
A heavy, sticky kind of earth is **clay**.

easy *adjective*
1 *Tonight's homework is really* **easy**.
undemanding, effortless, light
An informal word for an easy task is a **doddle**.
2 *The instructions were* **easy** *to understand.*
simple, straightforward, clear, plain, elementary
A common simile is **as easy as ABC**.
3 *Our cat has an* **easy** *life.*
carefree, comfortable, peaceful, relaxed, leisurely, restful, tranquil, untroubled
OPPOSITE difficult

eat *verb*
Hannah was **eating** *a cheese sandwich.*
consume, devour
(*informal*) scoff
When cattle eat grass they are **grazing**.
A person who eats a large amount is said to **eat like a horse**.
I was so hungry, I **wolfed down** *a whole pizza.*
bolt down, gobble, gulp, guzzle, gorge, polish off, wolf down
Rabbits like to **chomp** *raw carrots.*
chomp, crunch, gnash, gnaw, munch, slurp
Do you have any biscuits we could **nibble**?
nibble, peck, pick at or pick away at, taste
Mr Hogg was **savouring** *a sausage roll.*
relish, savour, tuck into
The guests will be **dining** *in the great hall.*
banquet, dine, feast

eccentric *adjective*
What is the reason for his **eccentric** *behaviour?*
odd, peculiar, strange, weird, abnormal, unusual, curious, unconventional, unorthodox, quirky, zany
(*informal*) way-out, dotty
OPPOSITE conventional, orthodox

echo *verb*
1 *The sound* **echoed** *across the valley.*
resound, reverberate
2 *'He's gone home.' 'Gone home?' she* **echoed**.
repeat, imitate, mimic

ecstatic *adjective*
Samantha was feeling **ecstatic** *about her party.*
elated, delighted, overjoyed, gleeful, joyful, blissful, rapturous, euphoric, exultant, delirious, fervent, frenzied

edge *noun*
The edge of a cliff or other steep place is the **brink**.

The edge of a cup or other container is the **brim** or **rim**.
The line round the edge of a circle is the **circumference**.
The line round the edge of any other shape is its **outline**.
The distance round the edge of an area is the **perimeter**.
The stones along the edge of a road are the **kerb**.
Grass along the edge of a road is the **verge**.
The space down the edge of a page is the **margin**.
The space round the edge of a picture is a **border**.
Something that fits round the edge of a picture is a **frame**.
The edge of a garment is the **hem**.
An edge with threads or hair hanging loosely down is a **fringe**.
The edge of a crowd also is the **fringe** of the crowd.
The area round the edge of a city is the **outskirts** or **suburbs**.
The edge of a cricket field is the **boundary**.
The edge of a football pitch is the **touchline**.

edge *verb*
1 *We* **edged** *away from the lion's den.*
creep, inch, move stealthily, steal, slink
2 *Her bonnet was* **edged** *with black lace.*
trim, hem

edgy *adjective*
Horses become **edgy** *during thunderstorms.*
nervous, restless, anxious, agitated, excitable, tense, jumpy, fidgety
(*informal*) uptight, jittery
OPPOSITE calm

educate *verb*
The job of a school is to **educate** *young people.*
teach, train, inform, instruct, tutor

eerie *adjective*
I heard some **eerie** *sounds in the night.*
strange, weird, uncanny, mysterious, frightening, creepy, ghostly, sinister, unearthly, unnatural
(*informal*) scary, spooky

effect *noun*
1 *The* **effect** *of eating too much was that I became fat!*
result, consequence, outcome, sequel, upshot
2 *Does this music have any* **effect** *on you?*
impact, influence
3 *The lighting gives an* **effect** *of warmth.*
feeling, impression, sense, illusion

efficient *adjective*
1 An **efficient** worker can do the job in an hour.
effective, competent, able, capable, proficient
2 Dad tried to work out an **efficient** way of heating our house.
economic, productive

effort *noun*
1 A lot of **effort** went into making the film.
work, trouble, exertion, industry, labour, toil
2 She congratulated us on a good **effort**.
attempt, try, endeavour, go, shot

elaborate *adjective*
The plot of the book is so **elaborate** that I got lost halfway through.
complicated, complex, detailed, intricate, involved, convoluted
OPPOSITE simple

elect *verb*
We **elected** a new captain.
vote for, appoint

elegant *adjective*
She always wears **elegant** clothes.
graceful, stylish, fashionable, chic, smart, tasteful, sophisticated
OPPOSITE inelegant

eliminate *verb*
The government wants to **eliminate** crime.
get rid of, put an end to
To be eliminated from a competition is to be **knocked out**.

embarrass *verb*
Will it **embarrass** you if I tell people our secret?
humiliate, distress, mortify, make you blush

embarrassed *adjective*
Don't feel **embarrassed**—it happens to everyone!
humiliated, ashamed, awkward, uncomfortable, bashful, distressed, flustered, mortified, self-conscious

embrace *verb*
1 The mother gorilla **embraced** her baby.
hug, clasp, cuddle, hold
2 She's always ready to **embrace** new ideas.
welcome, accept, adopt, take on

embrace

emerge *verb*
He didn't **emerge** from his bedroom until ten o'clock.
appear, come out

emergency *noun*
Try to keep calm in an **emergency**.
crisis, serious situation, danger, difficulty

emotional *adjective*
1 He made an **emotional** farewell speech.
moving, touching
2 The music for the love scenes was very **emotional**.
romantic, sentimental
3 She's a very **emotional** woman.
passionate, intense

emphasise *verb*
She **emphasised** the important points.
highlight, stress, focus on, dwell on, underline

empty *adjective*
1 Please put the **empty** milk bottles outside the door.
OPPOSITE full
2 The house next to ours has been **empty** for weeks.
unoccupied, uninhabited, vacant, deserted
OPPOSITE occupied
3 After we put up our display, there was still some **empty** space on the wall.
blank, bare, clear, unused

empty *verb*
1 **Empty** the dirty water into the sink.
drain, pour out
OPPOSITE fill
2 The building **emptied** when the fire alarm went off.
clear, evacuate, vacate
3 Did you **empty** all the shopping out of the trolley?
remove, unload

enchanting *adjective*
The ballet dancers were **enchanting**.
delightful, charming, appealing, attractive, bewitching, spellbinding

enchantment *noun*
1 The forest had an air of **enchantment**.
magic, wonder, delight, pleasure
2 The witch recited an **enchantment**.
spell, incantation

encourage *verb*
1 We went to the match to **encourage** our team.
inspire, support, motivate, cheer, spur on, egg on

2 The poster **encourages** people to eat healthily.
persuade, urge
3 Is advertising likely to **encourage** sales?
increase, boost, stimulate, further, promote, help, aid

encouraging *adjective*
The results of the tests were **encouraging**.
hopeful, positive, promising, cheering, reassuring, optimistic, favourable

end *noun*
1 The fence marks the **end** of the garden.
boundary, limit
2 The **end** of the film was the most exciting part.
ending, finish, close, conclusion, culmination
The last part of a show or piece of music is the **finale**.
A section added at the end of a letter is a **postscript**.
A section added at the end of a story is an **epilogue**.
3 I was tired by the time we got to the **end** of the journey.
termination, destination
4 We arrived late and found ourselves at the **end** of the queue.
back, rear, tail
5 What **end** did you have in view when you started?
aim, purpose, intention, objective, plan, outcome, result

end *verb*
1 The meeting should **end** in time for lunch.
finish, complete, conclude, break off, halt (*informal*) round off
2 When did they **end** public executions?
abolish, do away with, get rid of, put an end to, discontinue, eliminate
3 The festival **ended** with a show of fireworks.
close, come to an end, stop, cease, terminate, culminate, wind up

ending *noun*
The **ending** of the film was the most exciting part.
end, finish, close, conclusion, culmination, last part
The ending of a show or piece of music is the **finale**.

endless *adjective*
1 Teachers need **endless** patience.
unending, limitless, infinite, inexhaustible, unlimited
2 There's an **endless** procession of cars along the main road.
continual, continuous, constant, incessant, interminable, perpetual, unbroken, uninterrupted, everlasting, ceaseless

a b c d e f g h i j k l m n o p q r s t u v w x y z

endure *verb*
1 *She had to* **endure** *a lot of pain.*
bear, stand, suffer, cope with, experience, go through, put up with, tolerate, undergo
2 *These traditions have* **endured** *for centuries.*
survive, continue, last, persist, carry on, keep going

enemy *noun*
They used to be friends but now they are bitter **enemies**.
opponent, adversary, foe, rival
OPPOSITE friend, ally

energetic *adjective*
1 *She's a very* **energetic** *person.*
dynamic, spirited, enthusiastic, animated, active, zestful
OPPOSITE inactive, lethargic
2 *It was a very* **energetic** *exercise routine.*
lively, vigorous, brisk, fast, quick moving, strenuous
OPPOSITE slow-paced, sluggish

energy *noun*
1 *The dancers had tremendous* **energy**.
liveliness, spirit, vitality, vigour, life, drive, zest, verve, enthusiasm, dynamism
(*informal*) get-up-and-go, zip
OPPOSITE lethargy
2 *Wind power is a renewable source of* **energy**.
power, fuel

enjoy *verb*
I really **enjoyed** *the film.*
like, love, get pleasure from, be pleased by, admire, appreciate

enjoyable *adjective*
It was an **enjoyable** *party.*
pleasant, agreeable, delightful, entertaining, amusing
OPPOSITE unpleasant

enlarge *verb*
The zoo is going to **enlarge** *the lion enclosure.*
expand, extend, develop, make bigger
To make something wider is to **broaden** or **widen** it.
To make something longer is to **extend**, **lengthen** or **stretch** it.
To make something seem larger is to **magnify** it.
OPPOSITE reduce

enormous *adjective*
Enormous *waves battered the ship.*
huge, gigantic, immense, colossal, massive, monstrous, monumental, mountainous, towering, tremendous, vast
(*informal*) ginormous, humungous
OPPOSITE small

enough *adjective*
Is there **enough** *food for ten people?*
sufficient, adequate, ample

enquire *verb*
to enquire about
I **enquired about** *train times to Bristol.*
ask for, get information about, request, investigate

enter *verb*
1 *Silence fell as I* **entered** *the room.*
come in, walk in
To enter a place without permission is to **invade** it.
OPPOSITE leave
2 *The arrow* **entered** *his shoulder.*
go into, penetrate, pierce
3 *Can I* **enter** *my name on the list?*
insert, record, register, put down, set down, sign, write, inscribe
OPPOSITE cancel
4 *Our class decided to* **enter** *the competition.*
take part in, enrol in, sign up for, go in for, join in, participate in, volunteer for
OPPOSITE withdraw from

entertain *verb*
1 *The storyteller* **entertained** *us with scary ghost stories.*
amuse, divert, keep amused, make you laugh, please, cheer up
OPPOSITE bore
2 *You can* **entertain** *friends in the private dining room.*
receive, welcome, cater for, give hospitality to

entertainment *noun*
Our hosts had arranged some **entertainment** *for us.*
amusements, recreation, diversions, enjoyment, fun, pastimes

enthusiasm *noun*
1 *The young athletes showed plenty of* **enthusiasm**.
keenness, ambition, commitment, drive, zeal, zest
OPPOSITE apathy
2 *Collecting fossils is one of my* **enthusiasms**.
interest, passion, pastime, hobby, craze, diversion, fad

enthusiastic *adjective*
1 *He's an* **enthusiastic** *supporter of our local team.*
keen, passionate, avid, devoted, energetic, fervent, zealous
2 *The audience burst into* **enthusiastic** *applause.*
eager, excited, lively, vigorous, exuberant, hearty

entire *adjective*
Donald spent the **entire** *evening watching television.*
complete, whole, total, full

entirely *adverb*
I'm not **entirely** *sure that I agree with you.*
completely, absolutely, wholly, totally, utterly, fully, perfectly, quite

energy

entrance noun
1 *Please pay at the **entrance**.*
entry, way in, access, door, gate
When you go through the entrance to
a building, you cross the **threshold**.
2 *I'll meet you in the **entrance**.*
entrance hall, foyer, lobby, porch
3 *Her sudden **entrance** took
everyone by surprise.*
entry, arrival, appearance

entrance verb
*The crowd were **entranced** by the
fireworks display.*
charm, delight, please, enchant

envious adjective
*He was **envious** of his brother's
success.*
jealous, resentful

environment noun
*Animals should live in their natural
environment, not in cages.*
habitat, surroundings, setting,
conditions, situation
the environment
*We must do all we can to protect
the environment.*
the natural world, nature, the earth,
the world

envy noun
*I didn't feel any **envy**, even when I
saw how rich she was.*
jealousy, resentment, bitterness

envy verb
*The evil queen **envied** Snow White's
beauty.*
be jealous of, begrudge, grudge, resent

episode noun
1 *I paid for the broken window, and I
want to forget the whole **episode**.*
event, incident, experience
2 *I missed last night's **episode** of
'Dr Who'.*
instalment, part

equal adjective
1 *Give everyone an **equal** amount.*
equivalent, identical, matching,
similar, corresponding, fair
2 *The scores were **equal** at half-time.*
even, level, the same, square
To make the scores equal is to
equalise.

equipment noun
*The shed is full of gardening
equipment.*
apparatus, gear, kit, tackle, tools,
implements, instruments, materials,
machinery, paraphernalia, things
Computing equipment is **hardware**.

erase verb
*I **erased** the writing on the blackboard.*
delete, remove, rub out, wipe out, get
rid of

erode verb
*The flood water **eroded** the river bank.*
wear away, eat away, destroy

errand noun
*I went on an **errand** to the corner shop.*
job, task, assignment, trip, journey

error noun
1 *The accident was the result of an
error by the driver.*
mistake, fault, lapse, blunder
2 *I think there is an **error** in your
argument.*
flaw, inaccuracy, misunderstanding,
inconsistency
The error of leaving something out is
an **omission** or **oversight**.

escape verb
1 *Why did you let him **escape**?*
get away, get out, run away, break
free, break out
(*informal*) give you the slip
A performer who escapes from
chains, etc., is an **escape artist**
or **escapologist**.
2 *She always **escapes** the nasty jobs.*
avoid, get out of, evade, dodge, shirk

escape noun
1 *The prisoner's **escape** was filmed
by security cameras.*
getaway, breakout, flight
2 *The explosion was caused by an
escape of gas.*
leak, leakage, seepage

essential adjective
*Fruit and vegetables are an **essential**
part of our diet.*
important, necessary, basic, vital,
principal, fundamental, chief, crucial,
indispensable

establish verb
1 *He plans to **establish** a new
business.*
set up, start, begin, create, found,
initiate, institute, introduce, launch,
originate
2 *The police have not managed to
establish his guilt.*
prove, show to be true, confirm, verify

estimate verb
*The builders **estimate** that the work
will take four months.*
calculate, assess, work out, compute,
count up, evaluate, judge, reckon,
think out

eternal adjective
1 *The magic fountain was said to
give **eternal** youth.*
everlasting, infinite, lasting,
unending, timeless
Beings with eternal life are said to be
immortal.
2 *I'm sick of your
eternal quarrelling!*
constant, continual,
never-ending, non-stop,
persistent, perpetual,
endless, ceaseless,
incessant, unceasing

even adjective
1 *You need an **even** surface for
ice skating.*
level, flat, smooth, straight
OPPOSITE uneven
2 *The runners kept up an **even** pace.*
regular, steady, unvarying,
rhythmical, monotonous
OPPOSITE irregular
3 *Mr Lee has an **even** temper.*
calm, cool, placid, unexcitable
OPPOSITE excitable
4 *The scores were **even** at half time.*
equal, level, matching, identical, the
same, square
OPPOSITE different
5 *2, 4 and 6 are **even** numbers.*
OPPOSITE odd

evening noun
*Towards **evening** it clouded over and
began to rain.*
dusk, nightfall, sundown, sunset,
twilight

event noun
1 *Her autobiography describes the
main **events** of her life.*
happening, incident, occurrence
2 *There was an **event** to mark the
launch of the new film.*
function, occasion, ceremony,
entertainment, party, reception
3 *The World Cup is an important
event for football fans.*
competition, contest, fixture, match,
engagement, meeting, game,
tournament

eventually adverb
*The journey took ages, but
eventually we arrived safely.*
finally, at last, in the end, ultimately

evidence noun
*This piece of paper is **evidence** that
he is lying.*
proof, confirmation
Evidence that someone accused of a
crime was not there when the crime
was committed is an **alibi**.
Evidence given in a law court is
a **testimony**.
To give evidence in court is to **testify**.

evil adjective
1 *The charm was used to keep away
evil spirits.*
malevolent, fiendish, diabolical
2 *Who would do such an **evil** deed?*
wicked, immoral, cruel, sinful,
villainous, malicious, foul, hateful,
vile
OPPOSITE good

evil noun
1 *The good witch tried to fight
against **evil**.*
wickedness, badness,
wrongdoing, sin, immorality,
villainy, malevolence, malice

2 *They had to endure the **evils** of famine and drought.*
disaster, misfortune, suffering, pain, affliction, curse

exact *adjective*
1 *I gave the police an **exact** account of what happened.*
accurate, precise, correct, true, faithful, detailed, meticulous, strict
2 *Is this an **exact** copy of the original document?*
identical, perfect, indistinguishable
OPPOSITE inaccurate

exaggerate *verb*
*He tends to **exaggerate** his problems.*
magnify, inflate, overdo, make too much of
OPPOSITE minimise

examination *noun*
1 *The results of the **examinations** will be announced next month.*
test, assessment
(*informal*) exam
2 *The judge made a thorough **examination** of the facts.*
investigation, inspection, study, analysis, survey, review, appraisal
3 *He was sent to hospital for an **examination**.*
check-up
A medical examination of a dead person is a ***post-mortem**.

examine *verb*
1 *The judge **examined** the evidence.*
inspect, study, investigate, analyse, look closely at, pore over, scrutinise, probe, survey, review, weigh up, sift
2 *They were **examined** on their knowledge of history.*
question, interrogate, quiz
To examine someone rigorously is to ***grill** them.

example *noun*
1 *Give me an **example** of what you mean.*
instance, illustration, sample, specimen, case
2 *She's an **example** to us all.*
model, ideal

excellent *adjective*
*That's an **excellent** idea!*
first-class, first-rate, outstanding, exceptional, remarkable, tremendous, wonderful, superb, great, fine, marvellous, superior, superlative, top-notch
(*informal*) brilliant, fantastic, terrific, fabulous, sensational, super
OPPOSITE bad, awful, second-rate

exceptional *adjective*
*It is **exceptional** to have such cold weather in June.*
unusual, extraordinary, uncommon, unexpected, amazing, rare, odd,

peculiar, strange, surprising, special, abnormal, phenomenal, unheard-of, bizarre
OPPOSITE normal, usual

exchange *verb*
*The shop will **exchange** faulty goods.*
change, replace
To exchange goods for other goods without using money is to ***barter**.
To exchange an old thing for part of the cost of a new one is to ***trade it in**.
To exchange things with your friends is to ***swap** or ***swop** them.
To exchange players for other players in football, etc., is to ***substitute** them.

excited *adjective*
*On Christmas Eve, my little brother was too **excited** to sleep.*
agitated, lively, enthusiastic, exuberant, thrilled, elated, eager, animated
OPPOSITE calm

excitement *noun*
*I could hardly bear the **excitement**!*
suspense, tension, drama, thrill

exciting *adjective*
*The last minutes of the match were the most **exciting** of all!*
dramatic, eventful, thrilling, gripping, sensational, stirring, rousing, stimulating, electrifying
OPPOSITE dull, boring

exclude *verb*
1 *Adults are **excluded** from joining our club.*
ban, bar, prohibit, keep out, banish, reject
2 *She had to **exclude** dairy products from her diet.*
leave out, omit

excuse *noun*
*What is your **excuse** for being so late?*
reason, explanation, defence, justification

excuse *verb*
*I can't **excuse** his bad behaviour.*
forgive, overlook, pardon
OPPOSITE punish
to be excused something
*May I **be excused** swimming?*
be exempt from, be let off, be released from

exercise *noun*
1 ***Exercise** helps to keep you fit.*
physical activity, working out, keep fit, training
2 *Doing **exercises** will improve your guitar playing.*
practice, training, drill

exercise *verb*
1 *If you **exercise** regularly, you will keep fit.*
keep fit, train, exert yourself
2 *I sometimes **exercise** our neighbour's dog.*
take for a walk, take out, walk
3 *We must **exercise** patience.*
show, use, apply, display, employ

exhausted *adjective*
*After a hard race, we lay **exhausted** on the grass.*
tired, weary, worn out, fatigued, breathless, gasping, panting
(*informal*) all in, done in, bushed, zonked

exhausting *adjective*
*Digging the garden is **exhausting** work.*
tiring, demanding, hard, laborious, strenuous, difficult, gruelling, wearisome
OPPOSITE easy

exhibition *noun*
*We went to see an **exhibition** of paintings by Picasso.*
display, show

expand *verb*
*Their computer business is **expanding** rapidly.*
increase, enlarge, extend, build up, develop, make bigger
To become larger is to ***grow** or ***swell**.
To become wider is to ***broaden**, ***thicken** or ***widen**.
To become longer is to ***extend**, ***lengthen** or ***stretch**.
OPPOSITE contract, reduce

expect *verb*
1 *I **expect** that it will rain today.*
anticipate, imagine, forecast, predict, foresee, prophesy
2 *She **expects** me to do everything for her!*
require, want, count on, insist on, demand
3 *I **expect** they missed the bus.*
believe, imagine, guess, suppose, presume, assume, think

expedition *noun*
An expedition into unknown territory is an ***exploration**.
An expedition to carry out a special task is a ***mission**.
An expedition to find something is a ***quest**.
An expedition to worship at a holy place is a ***pilgrimage**.
An expedition to see or hunt wild animals is a ***safari**.

expel *verb*
1 *A fan **expels** the stale air and fumes.*
send out, force out

2 *He was **expelled** from school.*
dismiss, ban, remove, throw out, send away
To expel someone from their home is to *eject* or *evict* them.
To expel someone from their country is to *banish* or *exile* them.
To expel evil spirits is to *exorcise* them.

experience *noun*
1 *Have you had any **experience** of singing in a choir?*
practice, involvement, participation
2 *I had an unusual **experience** today.*
happening, event, occurrence, incident
An exciting experience is an *adventure*.
An unpleasant experience is an *ordeal*.

expert *noun*
*He's an **expert** at chess.*
specialist, authority, genius, wizard (*informal*) dab hand, whizz

expert *adjective*
*Only an **expert** sailor could cross the ocean.*
brilliant, capable, clever, competent, experienced, knowledgeable, professional, proficient, qualified, skilful, skilled, specialised, trained
OPPOSITE amateur, unskilful

explain *verb*
1 *The doctor **explained** the procedure carefully.*
make clear, give an explanation of, clarify, describe
2 *Can you **explain** your strange behaviour?*
give reasons for, account for, excuse, make excuses for, justify

explode *verb*
1 *The firework **exploded** with a bang.*
blow up, make an explosion, go off, burst, shatter
2 *The slightest movement might **explode** the bomb.*
detonate, set off

explore *verb*
1 *The spacecraft will **explore** the solar system.*
search, survey, travel through, probe
2 *We must **explore** all the possibilities.*
examine, inspect, investigate, look into, research, analyse, scrutinise

WORD WEB

explorer *noun*
*The **explorers** were looking for the legendary Lost City.*
traveller, voyager, discoverer, wanderer

THINGS AN EXPLORER MIGHT FIND
catacombs, cave, cavern, chest, hieroglyphics, inscription, labyrinth, maze, mummy, parchment, pyramid, riddle, sarcophagus, seal, secret passage, skeleton, stone tablet, temple, tomb, treasure, tunnel, underground chamber

THINGS AN EXPLORER MIGHT USE OR CARRY
binoculars, chart, compass, machete, map, penknife, rope, rucksack, telescope, tent, torch, water bottle

explosion *noun*
*The **explosion** rattled the windows.*
blast, bang
An explosion from a volcano is an *eruption*.
An explosion of laughter is an *outburst*.
The sound of a gun going off is a *report*.

WORD WEB

expression *noun*
EXPRESSIONS YOU MIGHT SEE ON A FACE
beam, frown, glare, glower, grimace, grin, laugh, leer, long face, poker-face, pout, scowl, smile, smirk, sneer, wide-eyed look, wince, yawn

1 *'Tickled pink' is a colloquial **expression**.*
phrase, saying, term, wording
An expression that people use too much is a *cliché*.
2 *Did you see her **expression** when I told her the news?*
look, appearance, countenance, face

extra *adjective*
1 *There is an **extra** charge for taking your bike on the train.*
additional, further, added, supplementary, excess
2 *There is **extra** food in the kitchen if you need it.*
more, spare, surplus, reserve

extraordinary *adjective*
*The astronauts saw many **extraordinary** sights.*
amazing, astonishing, remarkable, outstanding, exceptional, incredible, fantastic, marvellous, miraculous, phenomenal, rare, special, strange, surprising, unheard of, unusual, weird, wonderful, abnormal, curious
OPPOSITE ordinary

extreme *adjective*
1 *Polar bears can withstand **extreme** cold.*
great, intense, severe, acute, excessive
2 *She lives on the **extreme** edge of the town.*
farthest, furthest

a b c d e f g h i j k l m n o p q r s t u v w x y z

fabric noun
This **fabric** will make a lovely dress for my doll.
cloth, material, stuff
A plural word is **textiles**.

fabulous adjective
1 (informal) We had a **fabulous** time at the party.
excellent, first-class, marvellous, outstanding, superb, tremendous, wonderful
(informal) brilliant, fantastic, smashing
2 Dragons are **fabulous** creatures.
fictitious, imaginary, legendary, mythical

face noun
1 We saw the anger in the witch's **face**.
expression, features, look, countenance
2 The **face** of the clock had been smashed.
front

3 A cube has six **faces**.
side, surface

face verb
1 Stand and **face** your partner.
be opposite to, look towards
2 The astronauts had to **face** many dangers.
cope with, deal with, face up to, stand up to, tackle, meet, encounter, confront
OPPOSITE avoid

fact noun
It is a **fact** that dodos are now extinct.
reality, truth, certainty
OPPOSITE fiction
the facts
The detective considered **the facts** in the case.
details, particulars, information, data
Facts which are useful in trying to prove something are **evidence**.
Facts expressed as numbers are **statistics**.

factual adjective
Anne Frank wrote a **factual** account of her life during the war.
real, true, truthful, accurate, authentic, faithful, genuine, objective, reliable
A film or story based on a person's life is **biographical**.

A film or story based on history is **historical**.
A film telling you about real events is a **documentary**.
OPPOSITE made-up, fictional

fade verb
1 Sunlight has **faded** the curtains.
make paler, bleach, blanch, whiten, dim
OPPOSITE brighten
2 Those flowers will **fade** in a few days.
wither, wilt, droop, flag, shrivel
OPPOSITE flourish
3 Gradually, the light began to **fade**.
weaken, decline, diminish, dwindle, fail, wane, disappear, melt away, vanish
OPPOSITE increase

fail verb
1 Their plan to steal the crown jewels **failed** miserably.
be unsuccessful, go wrong, fall through, founder, come to grief, miscarry
(informal) flop, bomb
OPPOSITE succeed
2 The rocket engine **failed** before take-off.
break down, cut out, give up, stop working

✎ **WRITING TIPS**

face noun
You can use these words to describe a **face**.

TO DESCRIBE ITS SHAPE
flat, long, oval, round, rounded; lantern-jawed, square-jawed

TO DESCRIBE ITS FEATURES
chiselled, chubby, craggy, delicate, fine, gaunt, haggard, hollow, pinched, prominent, puffy, skeletal, sunken
Their faces were **gaunt** and **pinched** from hunger.

TO DESCRIBE ITS SKIN OR COLOUR
clear, dark, fair, flushed, freckled, fresh, glowing, healthy, rosy, ruddy, tanned; ashen, grey, leaden, pale, pallid, pasty, sallow, sickly, unhealthy, wan; flabby, saggy, shrivelled, weather-beaten, wizened, wrinkled, wrinkly; disfigured, pimply, pock-marked, scarred, spotty
The old witch was **wizened** like a prune.

TO DESCRIBE THE LOOK ON A FACE
cheeky, cheerful, radiant, sunny; grave, grim, serious; sulky, sullen, surly; blank, deadpan, faceless, impassive, unmoving, vacant The guard stared ahead, his face **unmoving**.

You can use these words to describe **eyes**:
beady, bulbous, bulging, deep-set, glassy, heavy-lidded, hooded, protuberant, saucer-like, sunken, cloudy, misty, moist, piercing, steely, tearful, watery The monster had a single **bulging** red eye.

You can use these words to describe a **nose**:
beak-like, bulbous, button, classical or Roman, crooked, pointed, snub, upturned The troll had **bushy** eyebrows and a red, **bulbous** nose.

3 *By late afternoon, the light had begun to* **fail**.
weaken, decline, diminish, dwindle, fade, get worse, deteriorate
OPPOSITE improve
4 *The professor* **failed** *to warn us of the danger.*
neglect, forget, omit
OPPOSITE remember
5 *I hope I don't* **fail** *my violin exam.*
OPPOSITE pass

failure noun
1 *The storm caused a power* **failure**.
breakdown, fault, malfuction, crash, loss, collapse, stoppage
2 *Their attempt to reach the North Pole was a* **failure**.
defeat, disappointment, disaster, fiasco
(informal) flop, wash-out
OPPOSITE success

faint adjective
1 *The details in the photograph are very* **faint**.
faded, dim, unclear, indistinct, vague, blurred, hazy, pale, shadowy, misty
OPPOSITE clear, distinct
2 *There was a* **faint** *smell of burning in the air.*
delicate, slight
OPPOSITE strong
3 *We heard a* **faint** *cry for help.*
weak, low, muffled, distant, hushed, muted, soft, thin
OPPOSITE loud
4 *Gordon was so hungry that he felt* **faint**.
dizzy, giddy, light-headed, unsteady, weak, exhausted, feeble
(informal) woozy

faint verb
The explorers nearly **fainted** *from exhaustion.*
become unconscious, collapse, pass out, black out
(old use) swoon

fair adjective
1 *I think the referee made a* **fair** *decision.*
just, proper, right, fair-minded, honest, honourable, impartial, unbiased, unprejudiced, disinterested
OPPOSITE unfair
2 *The twins both have* **fair** *hair.*
blond or blonde, light, golden, yellow
OPPOSITE dark
3 *Our team has a* **fair** *chance of winning the cup.*
reasonable, moderate, average, acceptable, adequate, satisfactory, passable, respectable, tolerable
4 *The weather should be* **fair** *today.*
dry, fine, sunny, bright, clear, cloudless, pleasant, favourable

fair noun
1 *My sister won a teddy at the* **fair**.
fairground, funfair, carnival, fête, gala

2 *Our school is holding a book* **fair** *next week.*
show, exhibition, display, market, bazaar

fairly adverb
1 *The competition will be judged* **fairly**.
honestly, properly, justly, impartially
2 *The ground is still* **fairly** *wet. I'm* **fairly** *certain that we are heading north.*
quite, rather, somewhat, slightly, moderately, up to a point, reasonably, tolerably
(informal) pretty

WORD WEB

fairy noun

THINGS A FAIRY MIGHT HAVE OR USE
fairy dust, lantern, wand, wings

A FAIRY'S WINGS OR CLOTHES MIGHT BE
diaphonous, feathery, glittering, glowing, gossamer, lustrous, sheer, sparkling, translucent, transparent

PLACES WHERE A FAIRY MIGHT LIVE
dell, glen, magic forest or tree, glade, mound, toadstool

SOME CREATURES LIKE FAIRIES
brownie, elf, imp, leprechaun, nymph, pixie, sprite

faithful adjective
My dog, Scruffy, is my **faithful** *friend.*
loyal, devoted, reliable, trustworthy, dependable, firm, constant, close
OPPOSITE unfaithful

fake noun
That's not a real Roman coin—it's a **fake**.
copy, imitation, reproduction, replica, forgery
(informal) phoney
An event which fakes a real event is a **hoax**, **sham**, or **simulation**.
A person who pretends to be another person is an **impostor**.

fake verb
The spy tried to **fake** *a foreign accent.*
imitate, copy, pretend, put on, reproduce, simulate
To fake someone's signature is to **forge** it.

fall verb
1 *The acrobat* **fell** *off a ladder and broke his leg.*
tumble, topple, crash down, pitch, plunge
2 *Snow was beginning to* **fall** *quite thickly.*
drop, come down, descend, rain down, plummet

3 *The level of the river had* **fallen** *since March.*
go down, subside, recede, sink, ebb
4 *The temperature in the cave* **fell** *to below freezing.*
go down, become lower, decrease, decline, lessen, diminish, dwindle
to fall in
The roof of the cabin **fell in** *during the storm.*
cave in, collapse, give way
to fall out
The twins are always **falling out** *with each other.*
argue, disagree, quarrel, squabble, bicker

fall noun
1 *Ellen had a* **fall** *and cut her knee.*
tumble
2 *We noticed a sharp* **fall** *in the temperature.*
drop, lowering
OPPOSITE rise
3 *There has been a* **fall** *in the price of coffee.*
decrease, reduction, decline
OPPOSITE increase
4 *This is a story about the* **fall** *of Troy.*
defeat, surrender

false adjective
1 *They gave us* **false** *information about the treasure.*
wrong, incorrect, untrue, inaccurate, mistaken, erroneous, faulty, invalid, misleading, deceptive
OPPOSITE correct
2 *The spy was travelling with a* **false** *passport.*
fake, bogus, sham, counterfeit, forged
OPPOSITE genuine, authentic
3 *Mrs Gummidge put in her* **false** *teeth.*
artificial, imitation
OPPOSITE real, natural
4 *The Black Knight turned out to be a* **false** *ally.*
unfaithful, disloyal, unreliable, untrustworthy, deceitful, dishonest, treacherous
OPPOSITE faithful, loyal

familiar adjective
1 *Seagulls are a* **familiar** *sight on the beach.*
common, everyday, normal, ordinary, usual, regular, customary, frequent, mundane, routine
OPPOSITE rare
2 *It seems a bit* **familiar** *to call her by her first name.*
informal, friendly, intimate, relaxed, close
OPPOSITE formal, unfriendly
to be familiar with something
Are you **familiar with** *the rules of chess?*
be acquainted with, be aware of, know

WORD WEB

family *noun*
*Some members of my **family** live in New Zealand.*
relations, relatives
An old-fashioned term for your family is your **kin**.
The official term for your closest relative is **next of kin**.
A group of related Scottish families is a **clan**.
A succession of people from the same powerful family is a **dynasty**.
In certain societies, a group of families living together is a **tribe**.
A single stage in a family is a **generation**.
The line of ancestors from which a family is descended is its **ancestry**.
A diagram showing how people in your family are related is a **family tree**.
The study of family history is **genealogy**.
A family of young birds is a **brood**.
A family of kittens or puppies is a **litter**.

MEMBERS OF A FAMILY MAY INCLUDE
adopted child, aunt, brother, child, cousin, daughter, father, foster-child, foster-parent, grandchild, grandparent, guardian, husband, mother, nephew, niece, parent, sister, son, spouse, step-child, step-parent, uncle, ward, wife

family

famous *adjective*
*Pele was a very **famous** football player.*
well-known, celebrated, renowned, acclaimed, notable, prominent, distinguished, eminent
To be famous for doing something bad is to be **notorious**.
OPPOSITE unknown, obscure

fan *noun*
*I used to be a **fan** of jazz music.*
enthusiast, admirer, devotee, follower, supporter

fanatic *noun*
*My brother is a rugby **fanatic**.*
enthusiast, addict, devotee
(*informal*) freak, nut

fancy *adjective*
*Alice bought a **fancy** hat for her friend's wedding.*
elaborate, decorative, ornamental, ornate
OPPOSITE plain

fancy *verb*
1 *What do you **fancy** to eat?*
feel like, want, wish for, desire, prefer
2 *I **fancied** I heard a noise downstairs.*
imagine, think, believe, suppose

fantastic *adjective*
1 *The story is full of **fantastic** creatures.*
fanciful, extraordinary, strange, odd, weird, outlandish, far-fetched, incredible, imaginative
OPPOSITE realistic
2 (*informal*) *We had a **fantastic** time at camp.*
excellent, first-class, outstanding, superb, wonderful, tremendous, marvellous
(*informal*) brilliant, fabulous, smashing

fantasy *noun*
*Rosie had a **fantasy** about being a mermaid.*
dream, daydream, delusion, fancy

far *adjective*
1 *The castle stood in the **far** north of the country.*
distant, faraway, remote
2 *The ferry took us to the **far** side of the river.*
opposite, other

fascinate *verb*
*We were **fascinated** by the inventor's workshop.*
interest (in), engross, captivate, enthrall, absorb, beguile, entrance, attract, charm, enchant, delight
OPPOSITE bore

fashion *noun*
1 *The Martians behaved in a peculiar **fashion**.*
way, manner
2 *Zoe dresses according to the latest **fashion**.*
trend, vogue, craze, fad, style, look

fashionable *adjective*
*Megan has a **fashionable** new hairstyle.*
stylish, chic, up-to-date, popular, elegant, smart
(*informal*) trendy, hip, in
OPPOSITE unfashionable, out-of-date

fast *adjective*
*The robber made a **fast** exit when he heard us coming.*
quick, rapid, speedy, swift, brisk, hasty, hurried, high-speed, headlong, breakneck
(*informal*) nippy
Something which goes faster than sound is **supersonic**.
A common simile is **as fast as lightning**.
OPPOSITE slow, unhurried

WORD WEB

farm *noun*
The formal word for farming is **agriculture**.
A farm which uses no artificial fertilisers or chemicals is an **organic farm**.
A very small farm is a **smallholding**.
A small farm growing fruit and vegetables is a **market garden**.
A small farm in Scotland is a **croft**.
A large cattle farm in America is a **ranch**.

combine harvester

fast *adverb*
1 *Mr Toad was driving too **fast** in his motor car.*
quickly, speedily, swiftly, rapidly, briskly
2 *The boat was stuck **fast** on the rocks.*
firmly, securely, tightly
3 *Be quiet! The baby is **fast** asleep.*
deeply, sound, completely

fasten *verb*
1 *They **fastened** their ropes to the rock face.*
tie, fix, attach, connect, join, link, bind, hitch, clamp, pin, clip, tack, stick

FARM BUILDINGS
barn, byre or cowshed, dairy, farmhouse, granary, milking parlour, outhouse, pigsty, stable

OTHER PARTS OF A FARM
barnyard or farmyard, cattle pen, fields, haystack, meadow, paddock, pasture, rick, sheep fold, silo

ITEMS OF FARM EQUIPMENT
baler, combine harvester, cultivator, drill, harrow, harvester, mower, planter, plough, tractor, trailer

PEOPLE WHO WORK ON A FARM
agricultural worker, (old use) dairymaid, farmer, farm labourer, ploughman, shepherd, stockbreeder, tractor driver

SOME FARM ANIMALS
bull, bullock, chicken or hen, cow, duck, goat, goose, horse, pig, sheep, turkey
Birds kept on a farm are *poultry*.
Animals kept for milk or beef are *cattle*.
Farm animals in general are *livestock*.
Birds kept on a farm are *poultry*.
Animals kept for milk or beef are *cattle*.
Farm animals in general are *livestock*.

tractor

To fasten a boat is to *anchor* or *moor* it.
To fasten an animal is to *tether* it.
2 They *fastened* the gate with a heavy chain.
secure, seal, lock, bolt, make fast

fat adjective
1 You'll get *fat* if you eat too many crisps!
overweight, obese, chubby, plump, podgy, dumpy, flabby, portly, stout, round, rotund
2 The witch opened a big, *fat* book of spells.
thick, bulky, chunky, weighty, substantial
OPPOSITE thin

fatal adjective
1 The knight delivered a *fatal* wound to his enemy.
deadly, lethal, mortal
A fatal illness is an *incurable* or *terminal* illness.
2 Leaving the door unlocked was a *fatal* mistake.
disastrous, catastrophic, dreadful, calamitous

fate noun
1 The shipwrecked crew were in the hands of *fate*.
fortune, destiny, providence, chance, luck
2 The prisoner met with a terrible *fate*.
death, end

fault noun
1 This DVD has a *fault* in it.
defect, flaw, malfunction, snag, problem, weakness
2 It was my *fault* that we missed our bus.
responsibility, liability

faulty adjective
The TV was *faulty*, so we took it back to the shop.
broken, not working, defective, out of order, unusable, damaged
OPPOSITE perfect

favour noun
1 I asked my friend to do me a *favour*.
good deed, good turn, kindness, service, courtesy
2 The captain's plan found *favour* with most of the crew.
approval, support, liking, goodwill
to be in favour of something
We're all *in favour of* longer holidays.
agree to, approve of, support, like the idea of

favourite adjective
What is your *favourite* book?
best-loved, preferred, treasured, dearest, special, top

a
b
c
d
e
f
g
h
i
j
k
l
m
n
o
p
q
r
s
t
u
v
w
x
y
z

fear *noun*
*When Garth heard the monster, he trembled with **fear**.*
fright, terror, horror, alarm, panic, dread, anxiety, apprehension, trepidation
A formal word for a special type of fear is **phobia**.
A fear of open spaces is **agoraphobia**.
A fear of spiders is **arachnophobia**.
A fear of enclosed spaces is **claustrophobia**.
A fear or dislike of foreigners is **xenophobia**.
OPPOSITE courage

fear *verb*
1 *My sister **fears** snakes and spiders.*
be frightened of, be afraid of, be scared of, dread
2 *I **fear** we may be too late.*
suspect, expect, anticipate

fearless *adjective*
*The **fearless** explorers entered the dark cave.*
brave, courageous, daring, heroic, valiant, intrepid, plucky
OPPOSITE cowardly

feast *noun*
*The king held a great **feast** to celebrate his birthday.*
banquet, dinner
(*informal*) spread

feat *noun*
*The trapeze artists performed many daring **feats**.*
act, action, deed, exploit, achievement, performance

feather *noun*
A large feather is a **plume**.
All the feathers on a bird are its **plumage**.
Soft, fluffy feathers are **down**.
A feather used as a pen is a **quill**.

feature *noun*
1 *The room has several unusual **features**.*
characteristic, detail, point, aspect, quality, peculiarity, trait, facet
A person's features are their **face**.
2 *There was a **feature** about our school in the newspaper.*
article, report, story, item, piece

feeble *adjective*
1 *The elderly knight looked tired and **feeble**.*
weak, frail, infirm, delicate, poorly, sickly, puny, weary, weedy
OPPOSITE strong, powerful
2 *I made a **feeble** attempt to stop the ball. Do you expect me to believe that **feeble** excuse?*
weak, poor, ineffective, inadequate, unconvincing,
tame, flimsy, lame

feed *verb*
*We have enough sandwiches to **feed** six people.*
provide for, cater for, give food to, nourish
to feed on
*The leopard was **feeding on** its prey.*
eat, consume, devour

feel *verb*
1 *I **felt** the llama's soft, woolly fur.*
touch, caress, stroke, fondle
2 *It **feels** colder today.*
appear, seem, strike you as
3 *Older people tend to **feel** the cold.*
notice, be aware of, be conscious of, experience, suffer from
4 *I **feel** that it's time we made a start.*
think, believe, consider
to feel like
*Do you **feel like** going for a walk?*
fancy, want, wish for, desire

feel *noun*
*I love the **feel** of warm sand between my toes.*
feeling, sensation, touch

feeling *noun*
1 *The cat had lost all **feeling** in its paw.*
sense of touch, sensation, sensitivity
2 *I didn't mean to hurt your **feelings**.*
emotion, passion, sentiment
3 *I have a **feeling** that something is wrong.*
suspicion, notion, inkling, hunch, idea, impression, fancy, intuition

fence *noun*
*The mansion was surrounded by a tall **fence**.*
railing, barrier, wall, paling, stockade, hedge

ferocious *adjective*
*The mansion was guarded by a **ferocious** dog.*
fierce, fearsome, savage, wild, vicious, violent, bloodthirsty, brutal
OPPOSITE tame

fertile *adjective*
*The surrounding countryside was green and **fertile**.*
fruitful, productive, rich, fecund
OPPOSITE barren, sterile

festival *noun*
*The town holds a **festival** every summer.*
carnival, fiesta, fête, gala, fair, celebration, jamboree
A celebration of a special anniversary is a **jubilee**.

fetch *verb*
1 *I **fetched** the shopping from the car.*
get, bring, carry, collect, transfer, transport, convey, pick up, retrieve, obtain
2 *If we sell our car, how much will it **fetch**?*
make, raise, sell for, go for, bring in, earn

feud *noun*
*There has been a **feud** between our families for years.*
quarrel, dispute, conflict, hostility, enmity, rivalry, strife, antagonism
A feud that lasts a long time is a **vendetta**.

feverish *adjective*
1 *I felt **feverish** with the cold.*
When you are feverish you are **hot** and **shivery**.
With a bad fever you may become **delirious**.
2 *There was **feverish** activity in the kitchen.*
frenzied, frantic, frenetic, excited, agitated, hectic, busy, hurried, impatient, restless

fictional *adjective*
*Harry Potter is a **fictional** character.*
imaginary, made-up, invented, fanciful
OPPOSITE factual, real

fiddle *verb*
1 *Who's been **fiddling** with the DVD player?*
tinker, meddle, tamper, play about, mess about, twiddle
2 (*informal*) *Mr Filch had been **fiddling** the bank account for years.*
falsify, alter, rig
(*informal*) cook the books

fidget *verb*
*I begin to **fidget** when I'm bored.*
be restless, fiddle about, play about, mess about

field *noun*
1 *Cattle were grazing in the **field**.*
meadow, pasture
A small field for horses is a **paddock**.
An area of grass in a village is a **green**.
2 *The **field** is too wet to play football.*
ground, pitch, playing field
3 *Electronics is not my **field**.*
special interest, speciality, area of study

fierce *adjective*
1 *The travellers were killed in a **fierce** attack by armed bandits.*
vicious, ferocious, savage, brutal, violent, wild, cruel, merciless, ruthless, pitiless
2 *Our team will face **fierce** opposition in the final.*
strong, keen, eager, aggressive, competitive, passionate, relentless
3 *The explorers braved the **fierce** heat of the desert sun.*
blazing, intense, raging

fiery *adjective*
1 *It's best to avoid the **fiery** heat of the midday sun.*
blazing, burning, hot, intense, fierce, raging, flaming, red-hot, glowing
2 *My great aunt has always had a **fiery** temper.*
violent, passionate, excitable, angry, furious

fight *noun*
1 *The warriors faced each other for a **fight** to the death.*
Fighting is **combat** or **hostilities**.
A fight between armies is a **battle**.
A minor unplanned battle is a **skirmish**.
A series of battles is a **campaign** or **war**.
A minor fight is a **brawl**, **scrap**, **scuffle** or **tussle**.
A fight arranged between two people is a **duel**.
2 *We support the **fight** to save the rainforest.*
campaign, crusade, struggle

fight *verb*
1 *Two seagulls were **fighting** over a scrap of bread.*
have a fight, scrap, scuffle, exchange blows, come to blows
2 *The two countries **fought** each other in the war.*
do battle with, wage war with, attack
Fighting with swords is **fencing**.
Fighting with fists is **boxing**.
Fighting in which you try to throw your opponent to the ground is **wrestling**.
Fighting sports such as karate and judo are **martial arts**.
3 *We will **fight** the decision to close our local library.*
protest against, oppose, resist, make a stand against, campaign against

figure *noun*
1 *Please write the **figure** '8' on the board.*
number, numeral, digit, integer
2 *Ballet dancers need to have a good **figure**.*
body, build, form, shape
3 *Inside the temple were several clay **figures**.*
statue, carving, sculpture

figure *verb*
*Donald Duck **figures** in cartoons.*
appear, feature, take part
to figure out
*We couldn't **figure out** what the riddle meant.*
work out, make out, understand, see

fill *verb*
1 *Dad **filled** the trolley with shopping.*
load, pack, stuff, cram, top up
To fill a tyre with air is to **inflate** it.
OPPOSITE empty
2 *What can I use to **fill** this hole?*
close up, plug, seal, block up, stop up
3 *Sightseers **filled** the streets.*
crowd, jam, block, obstruct
(*informal*) bung up

film *noun*
1 *There is a good **film** on TV tonight.*
movie, picture, video, DVD
A long film is a **feature film**.
A short excerpt from a film is a **clip**.
A script for a film is a **screenplay** and a writer of screenplays is a **screenwriter**.
A well-known film actor is a **film star**.
A theatre where films are shown is a **cinema**, **picture house** or (*American*) **movie theatre**.
2 *There was a **film** of oil on the water.*
coat, coating, layer, covering, sheet, skin
A large patch of oil floating on water is a **slick**.

filthy *adjective*
*Those trainers are **filthy**!*
dirty, mucky, messy, grimy, grubby, muddy, soiled, stained
OPPOSITE clean

final *adjective*
1 *The **final** moments of the match were very tense.*
last, closing, concluding
OPPOSITE opening
2 *What was the **final** result?*
eventual, ultimate

finally *adverb*
*I've **finally** managed to finish my book.*
eventually, at last, in the end

find *verb*
1 *Did you **find** any fossils on the beach?*
come across, discover, see, spot, locate, encounter, stumble across, unearth
2 *The children never **found** the secret door again.*
trace, track down, recover, retrieve
OPPOSITE lose
3 *Did the doctor **find** what was wrong?*
detect, identify, diagnose, ascertain
4 *You will **find** that building a tree house is hard work.*
become aware, realise, learn, recognise, notice, observe

fine *adjective*
1 *The young musicians gave a **fine** performance.*
excellent, first-class, superb, good, splendid, admirable, commendable
OPPOSITE bad
2 *As the weather was **fine**, we took a picnic.*
sunny, fair, bright, clear, cloudless, pleasant
OPPOSITE dull
3 *Spiders spin very **fine** thread for their webs.*
delicate, fragile, thin, flimsy, slender, slim
OPPOSITE thick
4 *The desert dunes were made of **fine** sand.*
dusty, powdery
OPPOSITE coarse

finish *verb*
1 *When are you likely to **finish** your homework?*
complete, reach the end of, cease, round off
2 *The film should **finish** around nine o'clock.*
end, stop, conclude, terminate
(*informal*) wind up
3 *I've already **finished** my bag of crisps.*
consume, use up, get through, exhaust
(*informal*) polish off
OPPOSITE start

a b c d e f g h i j k l m n o p q r s t u v w x y z

finish noun
*We stayed to watch the parade until the **finish**.*
end, close, conclusion, completion, result, termination
OPPOSITE start

fire noun
*The campers toasted marshmallows in the **fire**.*
blaze, flames, burning, combustion
A very big hot fire is an **inferno**.
An open fire out of doors is a **bonfire**.
An enclosed fire which produces great heat is a **furnace**.
An enclosed fire for cooking food is an **oven**.
An enclosed fire for making pottery is a **kiln**.
A team of people whose job is to put out fires is a **fire brigade**.
A member of a fire brigade is a **firefighter**.

fire verb
1 *The soldier aimed his rifle and **fired** two shots.*
shoot, discharge, let off, set off
To fire a missile is to **launch** it.
2 (informal) *Miss Stark **fired** her assistant for being late for work.*
dismiss, sack

firm noun
*Mr Perkins owns a **firm** that makes biscuits.*
company, business, organisation, enterprise

firm adjective
1 *The surface of the planet was dry and **firm**.*
hard, solid, dense, compact, rigid, set
OPPOSITE soft
2 *Make sure the knots in the rope are **firm**.*
secure, tight, strong, stable, fixed, sturdy, steady
3 *Zelda had a **firm** belief in the power of magic.*
definite, certain, sure, decided, determined, resolute, unshakeable, unwavering
OPPOSITE unsure
4 *The two girls have become **firm** friends.*
close, devoted, faithful, loyal, constant, dependable, reliable

first adjective
1 *The **first** inhabitants of the area were Picts.*
earliest, original
2 *The **first** thing to do in an emergency is to keep calm.*
principal, key, main, fundamental, basic, chief

fit adjective
1 *Cinderella's gown was **fit** for a princess.*
suitable, appropriate, fitting, right, good enough, worthy (of)
OPPOSITE unsuitable
2 *I walk to school every day to keep **fit**.*
healthy, well, strong, robust
(old use) hale and hearty
A common simile is **as fit as a fiddle**.
OPPOSITE unhealthy
3 *After a long ride, the horses were **fit** to collapse.*
ready, liable, likely, about

fit verb
1 *We need to **fit** a new lock on the door.*
install, put in place, position
2 *This key doesn't **fit** the lock. He **fits** the description of the wanted criminal.*
match, correspond to, go together with, tally with
3 *Her speech perfectly **fitted** the occasion.*
be suitable for, be appropriate to, suit

fix verb
1 *The soldier **fixed** a bayonet to the end of his rifle.*
fasten, attach, connect, join, link
2 *We **fixed** the tent poles in the ground.*
set, secure, make firm, stabilise
3 *Let's **fix** a time for the party.*
decide on, agree on, set, arrange, settle, determine, specify, finalise
4 (informal) *Dad says he can **fix** my bike.*
repair, mend, sort, put right

fix noun
(informal) *Can you help me? I'm in a **fix**.*
difficulty, mess, predicament, plight
(informal) jam, hole

fizzy adjective
*Could I have a bottle of **fizzy** water, please?*
sparkling, bubbly, effervescent, gassy, foaming
OPPOSITE still

flag noun
*The street was decorated with **flags** for the carnival.*
banner, pennant, streamer
The flag of a regiment is its **colours** or **standard**.
A flag flown on a ship is an **ensign**.
Decorative strips of small flags are **bunting**.

flap verb
*The sail **flapped** in the wind.*
flutter, sway, swing, wave about, thrash about

flash verb
*We saw a light **flash** from an upstairs window.*
shine, beam, blaze, flare, glare, gleam, glint, flicker, glimmer, sparkle

flash noun
*There were **flashes** of lightning in the sky.*
blaze, flare, beam, ray, shaft, burst, gleam, glint, flicker, glimmer, sparkle

flat adjective
1 *You need a **flat** surface to write on.*
even, level, smooth, plane
A common simile is **as flat as a pancake**.
OPPOSITE uneven
2 *I lay **flat** on the ground.*
horizontal, outstretched, spread out
To be lying face downwards is to be **prone**.
To be lying face upwards is to be **supine**.
OPPOSITE upright
3 *The robot spoke in a **flat**, electronic voice.*
dull, boring, lifeless, uninteresting, monotonous, tedious
OPPOSITE lively
4 *The front tyre of my bike was **flat**.*
deflated, punctured
OPPOSITE inflated
5 *Our request met with a **flat** refusal.*
outright, straight, positive, absolute, total, utter, point-blank

flatten verb
1 *We **flattened** the crumpled map on the desk.*
smooth, press, roll out, iron out
2 *The earthquake **flattened** several buildings.*
demolish, destroy, knock down, pull down, level
3 *The young plants were **flattened** by the rain.*
squash, crush, trample

flavour noun
1 *I don't like the **flavour** of raw onions.*
taste, tang
2 *Which **flavour** of ice cream do you like best?*
kind, sort, variety

flexible adjective
1 *I need a pair of trainers with **flexible** soles.*
bendable, supple, pliable, bendy, elastic, springy
OPPOSITE rigid, inflexible
2 *My working hours are very **flexible**.*
adjustable, adaptable, variable, open
OPPOSITE fixed

flicker *verb*
*The candlelight **flickered** in the draught.*
twinkle, glimmer, waver, flutter, blink, shimmer

flimsy *adjective*
1 *The kite was so **flimsy** that it broke apart.*
fragile, delicate, frail, brittle, weak, wobbly, shaky, rickety
OPPOSITE sturdy, robust
2 *The fairy wore a dress of the **flimsiest** silk.*
thin, fine, light, lightweight, floaty

flinch *verb*
*He **flinched** as an arrow flew past his head.*
back off, draw back, falter, recoil, shrink back, start, wince

fling *verb*
*I **flung** a stone into the pond.*
throw, cast, sling, toss, hurl, pitch (*informal*) chuck, bung

float *verb*
*We watched the twigs **float** gently down the river.*
sail, drift, glide, slip, slide, waft

flood *noun*
1 *The **flood** of water swept away the bridge.*
deluge, inundation, rush, torrent, spate
2 *The restaurant has received a **flood** of complaints.*
succession, barrage, storm, volley

flood *verb*
1 *The river burst its banks and **flooded** the valley.*
drown, swamp, inundate, submerge, immerse, engulf
2 *We have been **flooded** with entries for our competition.*
overwhelm, swamp, besiege

flop *verb*
1 *I was so tired that I just **flopped** on to my bed.*
collapse, drop, fall, slump
2 *The plants will **flop** if you don't water them.*
dangle, droop, hang down, sag, wilt
3 (*informal*) *The first film **flopped**, but the sequel was a big hit.*
be unsuccessful, fail, founder, fall flat

floppy *adjective*
*The dog had long, **floppy** ears.*
droopy, limp, saggy, soft
OPPOSITE stiff, rigid

flow *verb*
*The rain water **flowed** along the gutter.*
run, stream, pour, glide
To flow slowly is to *dribble*, *drip*, *ooze*, *seep* or *trickle*.
To flow fast is to *cascade*, *gush* or *sweep*.

flood

To flow with sudden force is to *spurt* or *squirt*.
To flow over the edge of something is to *overflow* or *spill*.
When blood flows from a wound, it *bleeds*.
When the tide flows out, it *ebbs*.

flow *noun*
1 *It's hard work rowing against the **flow**.*
current, tide, drift
2 *There was a steady **flow** of water into the pond.*
stream, flood, cascade, gush, rush, spate

fluffy *adjective*
*Four **fluffy** ducklings were swimming in the pond.*
feathery, downy, furry, fuzzy, hairy, woolly, shaggy, soft

flush *verb*
*Rory **flushed** with embarrassment.*
blush, go red, colour, redden, burn

flustered *adjective*
*I get **flustered** when I have to read in assembly.*
confused, upset, bothered, agitated, unsettled, ruffled
(*informal*) rattled
OPPOSITE calm

flutter *verb*
*A moth **fluttered** about the light bulb.*
flap, beat, flicker, quiver, tremble, vibrate

foam *noun*
*The bath water was covered with pinkish **foam**.*
bubbles, froth, suds, lather
Foam made by sea water is *surf* or *spume*.

foam *verb*
*The mixture in the cauldron **foamed** and gurgled.*
froth, bubble, fizz, boil, seethe, ferment, lather

fog *noun*
*The top of the mountain was covered with **fog**.*
Thin fog is *haze* or *mist*.
A thick mixture of fog and smoke is *smog*.

fold *verb*
***Fold** the paper along the dotted line.*
bend, double over, crease, pleat

fold *noun*
*She smoothed the soft **folds** of her dress.*
crease, furrow, layer
A fold which is pressed into a garment is a *pleat*.

follow *verb*
1 *Why does thunder always **follow** lightning?*
come after, succeed, replace
OPPOSITE precede
2 *I think that car is **following** us!*
go after, chase, pursue, track, trail, tail, stalk, hunt, shadow
3 ***Follow** this path until you reach the river.*
go along, keep to
4 *I **followed** the instructions on the packet.*
carry out, comply with, heed, obey, observe
5 *Which football team do you **follow**?*
be a fan of, support
6 *We found it hard to **follow** what the creature was saying.*
understand, comprehend, grasp, take in, catch

fond *adjective*
1 *Mrs Walker gave her pet poodle a **fond** kiss.*
loving, tender, affectionate
2 *Anna had a **fond** hope that she would become a film star.*
foolish, silly, unrealistic, fanciful
to be fond of
*I'm very **fond** of chocolate cake.*
be keen on, be partial to, like, love

a
b
c
d
e
f
g
h
i
j
k
l
m
n
o
p
q
r
s
t
u
v
w
x
y
z

food
see panel below

fool *noun*
*Only a **fool** would believe that ridiculous story.*
idiot, dope, ass, clown, halfwit, moron, dimwit, dunce, simpleton, blockhead, buffoon, clot, dunderhead, imbecile, (*informal*) twit, chump, nitwit, nincompoop

fool *verb*
*The spy **fooled** everyone with his disguises.*
deceive, trick, mislead, hoax, dupe, hoodwink
(*informal*) con, kid, have you on, take you in, pull the wool over your eyes

to fool about or **around**
*We were told not to **fool about** in the swimming pool.*
play about, mess about, misbehave

foolish *adjective*
*It would be **foolish** to stand too close to the lions.*
stupid, silly, idiotic, senseless, ridiculous, nonsensical, unwise, ill-advised, half-witted, unintelligent, absurd, crazy, mad, hare-brained
(*informal*) daft
OPPOSITE sensible

foot *noun*
1 *Rhona walked on the sand in her bare **feet**.*
The foot of an animal that has claws is a ***paw***.

The foot of a cow, deer or horse is a ***hoof***.
A pig's foot is a ***trotter***.
A bird's feet are its ***claws***.
The feet of a bird of prey are its ***talons***.
2 *We set up camp at the **foot** of the mountain.*
base, bottom

football
see panel below

forbidden *adjective*
*Skateboarding is **forbidden** in the playground.*
banned, barred, prohibited, disallowed, outlawed
OPPOSITE allowed

force *noun*
1 *The firefighters had to use **force** to open the door.*
strength, power, might, muscle, vigour, effort, energy
2 *The **force** of the explosion broke all the windows.*
impact, effect, shock, intensity
3 *The soldiers are part of a peace-keeping **force**.*
group, unit, team, corps, army, troops

WORD WEB

food *noun*
*The banquet table was laid out with all kinds of **food**.*
foodstuffs, rations, provisions, refreshments, eatables, nourishment, nutrition
(*informal*) grub, nosh
The food that you normally eat or choose to eat is your ***diet***.
A diet which includes no meat is a ***vegetarian*** diet.
A diet which includes no animal products is a ***vegan*** diet.
Food which includes fish or shellfish is ***seafood***.
Foods made from milk, butter, cheese or eggs are ***dairy foods***.
Food for farm animals is ***fodder***.

SOME TYPES OF SEAFOOD
bloater, bream, caviare, cod, crab, eel, haddock, halibut, herring, kipper, lobster, mackerel, monkfish, mussels, oysters, pilchard, plaice, prawn, salmon, sardine, scampi, sea bass, shrimp, sole, sprat, trout, tuna, whelks, whitebait, whiting

SOME DAIRY FOODS
butter, cheese, cream, curds, custard, eggs, ice cream, milk, yoghurt

FOODS MADE FROM FLOUR OR CEREALS
batter, biscuits, bread, bun, cornflakes, cracker, crispbread, muesli, noodles, oatcake, pancake, pastry, popcorn, porridge, ricecake, roll, scone, toast

SOME PREPARED DISHES OF FOOD
balti, bhaji, broth, casserole, chilli, chips, chop suey, chow mein, curry, dhal, fritters, goulash, houmous, hotpot, omelette, pakora, panini, pasta, pie, pizza, quiche, samosa, sandwich, soufflé, soup, stew, stir-fry, sushi

SOME PUDDINGS AND OTHER SWEET FOODS
brownie, cake, chocolate, flan, gateau, honey, jam, jelly, marmalade, marzipan, meringue, mousse, muffin, sponge, steamed pudding, sugar, tart, treacle, trifle

SOME FLAVOURINGS AND SAUCES FOR FOOD
chilli, chutney, French dressing, garlic, gravy, herbs, ketchup, mayonnaise, mustard, pepper, pickle, salsa, salt, spice, vinegar

Things like salt and pepper which you add to food are ***condiments*** or ***seasoning***.

WORD WEB

football *noun*
Football is also known as ***soccer***.
Someone who plays football is a ***footballer***.
Football is played on a ***field*** or ***pitch*** in a ***ground***, ***park*** or ***stadium***.

MEMBERS OF A FOOTBALL TEAM
captain, defender, fullback, forward, goalkeeper or (*informal*) goalie, midfielder, striker, substitute, sweeper, winger

referee

force *verb*

1 *The slaves were **forced** to work in the mines.*
compel, make, order, require, oblige, pressurise, coerce
2 *The king **forced** a new law upon the country.*
impose, inflict
3 *The firefighters had to **force** the door.*
break open, burst open, prise open, smash, wrench
(*informal*) yank

foreign *adjective*

1 *Lots of **foreign** tourists visit Edinburgh in the summer.*
overseas, international
OPPOSITE native, domestic
2 *I like travelling to **foreign** countries.*
overseas, distant, faraway, exotic, remote, far-flung

forever *adverb*

*Timmy is **forever** complaining about something.*
constantly, continually, always, perpetually

forgery *noun*

*One of these paintings is a **forgery**.*
fake, copy, imitation, reproduction, replica
(*informal*) phoney

forget *verb*

1 *I **forgot** my toothbrush when I packed my suitcase.*
leave out, leave behind, overlook
2 *I **forgot** to switch off the computer.*
omit, neglect, fail

forgive *verb*

*Please **forgive** me for being so rude.*
excuse, pardon, let off, overlook, spare

form *noun*

1 *I made out the **form** of a man through the mist.*
shape, figure, outline, silhouette
2 *Ice is a **form** of water.*
kind, sort, type, variety
3 *My brother moves up into a higher **form** next term.*
class, year, grade, set

form *verb*

1 *The sculptor **formed** the clay into the shape of a bird.*
shape, mould, model, fashion, work, cast

2 *My friends and I have **formed** a chess club.*
set up, establish, found, create, start
3 *Icicles had **formed** on the roof of the cave.*
appear, develop, grow, emerge, take shape

formal *adjective*

1 *I was invited to the **formal** opening of the museum.*
official, ceremonial
2 *The letter was written in a very **formal** style.*
correct, proper, conventional, dignified, solemn
OPPOSITE informal, casual

fortune *noun*

1 *By good **fortune**, I stumbled across a secret doorway.*
chance, luck, accident, fate
2 *The millionairess left her **fortune** to charity.*
wealth, riches, possessions, property, assets, estate
(*informal*) millions

foul *adjective*

1 *The knight fainted at the **foul** smell of the dragon's breath.*
disgusting, revolting, repulsive, vile, rotten, stinking, offensive, unpleasant, loathsome, nasty, horrible
OPPOSITE pleasant
2 *The walls and floor of the dungeon were **foul**.*
dirty, unclean, filthy, mucky, messy
OPPOSITE clean, pure
3 *The player was sent off for using **foul** language.*
rude, offensive, insulting, abusive, improper, indecent, obscene

fragile *adjective*

*Fossil dinosaur bones are very **fragile**.*
breakable, delicate, frail, brittle, easily damaged, weak
OPPOSITE strong

frail *adjective*

1 *My grandad felt **frail** after his illness.*
weak, infirm, feeble
2 *That step-ladder looks a bit **frail**.*
flimsy, fragile, delicate, rickety, unsound
OPPOSITE strong, robust

frantic *adjective*

1 *I was **frantic** with worry when our kitten got lost.*
beside yourself, fraught, desperate, distraught, hysterical, worked up, berserk
2 *There was **frantic** activity on the day of the wedding.*
excited, hectic, frenzied, feverish, wild, mad

footballer

OTHER PEOPLE INVOLVED IN FOOTBALL
ballboy or ballgirl, coach, linesman, manager, referee

SOME MOVES A FOOTBALLER MIGHT MAKE
chip, dribble, dummy, header, kick, mazy run, miss, pass, score, shot, tackle, volley

SOME OTHER TERMS USED IN FOOTBALL
corner, crossbar, deflection, dugout, equaliser, extra time, final whistle, foul, free kick, goal, goalposts, half-time, kick-off, net, offside, penalty, penalty shootout, red or yellow card, sending off, throw-in

boots

corner flag

football

a b c d e f g h i j k l m n o p q r s t u v w x y z

fraud noun
1 *The bank manager was found guilty of* **fraud***.*
deceit, deception, dishonesty, swindling, cheating
2 *The prize draw was just a* **fraud**—*no one won anything.*
swindle, trick, hoax, pretence, sham (*informal*) con, scam (*informal*) con man, phoney

free adjective
1 *You are* **free** *to wander anywhere in the building.*
able, allowed, permitted, at liberty
OPPOSITE restricted
2 *After ten years in jail, the prisoners were* **free** *at last.*
freed, liberated, released, emancipated, at large, on the loose
A common simile is **as free as a bird**.
OPPOSITE imprisoned, enslaved
3 *I got a* **free** *drink with my sandwich.*
complimentary, free of charge, gratis, on the house
4 *Are you* **free** *this weekend?*
available, unoccupied
OPPOSITE busy, occupied
5 *The bathroom is* **free** *now.*
available, unoccupied, vacant, empty
OPPOSITE engaged

free verb
1 *The soldiers* **freed** *the prisoners of war.*
release, liberate, set free, deliver
To free slaves is to **emancipate** them.
To free prisoners by paying money to the captors is to **ransom** them.
OPPOSITE imprison
2 *We* **freed** *the dogs and let them run about.*
loose, turn loose, let go, untie, unchain
OPPOSITE confine

freedom noun
The animals have a lot of **freedom** *in the safari park.*
liberty, independence

freeze verb
1 *Water begins to* **freeze** *at 0°C.*
become ice, ice over, harden, solidify
2 *If you* **freeze** *food, you can store it for a long time.*
deep-freeze, chill, refrigerate

freezing adjective
It's **freezing** *cold outside in winter.*
chilly, frosty, icy, wintry, raw, bitter

frequent adjective
1 *I send* **frequent** *email messages to my friends.*
numerous, constant, continual, recurring, recurrent, repeated, countless
OPPOSITE infrequent

2 *Badgers are* **frequent** *visitors to the garden.*
regular, habitual, common, familiar, persistent
OPPOSITE rare

fresh adjective
1 *This pudding is made with* **fresh** *fruit.*
natural, raw, unprocessed
2 *The shop bakes* **fresh** *bread every day.*
new
OPPOSITE old, stale
3 *Sally went outside to get some* **fresh** *air.*
clean, cool, crisp, refreshing
OPPOSITE stuffy
4 *Have you put* **fresh** *sheets on the bed?*
new, clean, laundered, washed
OPPOSITE dirty
5 *Having a shower makes me feel nice and* **fresh***.*
refreshed, revived, restored, invigorated
6 *We need some* **fresh** *ideas for our magazine.*
new, original, different, novel, innovative
OPPOSITE old

friend noun
I am inviting four **friends** *to my birthday party.*
companion, comrade (*informal*) mate, pal, buddy, chum
A friend you play games with is a **playmate**.
A friend you work with or live with is your **partner**.
A friend you write to but don't normally meet is a **penfriend**.
A friend you know only slightly is an **acquaintance**.
OPPOSITE enemy

friendly adjective
1 *Our neighbour's pet dog is very* **friendly***.*
affectionate, loving, good-natured, likeable, amiable, approachable, kind-hearted, kindly, amicable, genial, sociable, outgoing, sympathetic
2 *Those two are very* **friendly** *with each other.*
close, familiar, intimate (*informal*) pally, chummy
3 *I like this cafe—it has a very* **friendly** *atmosphere.*
warm, welcoming, hospitable, cordial, neighbourly

fright noun
1 *The girl jumped up in* **fright** *and began to scream.*
fear, terror, alarm, horror, panic, dread

2 *The explosion gave us an awful* **fright***!*
scare, shock, surprise, start, turn, jolt

frighten verb
Sorry—I didn't mean to **frighten** *you.*
scare, terrify, startle, alarm, shock, panic, petrify

frightened adjective
Mia always felt **frightened** *in the dark.*
afraid, scared, terrified, alarmed, fearful, panicky, petrified

frightening adjective
The ghost story she told was quite **frightening***.*
terrifying, horrifying, scary, alarming, nightmarish, chilling, spine-chilling, hair-raising, bloodcurdling, chilling, eerie, sinister, fearsome
(*informal*) creepy, spooky

frisky adjective
The new lion cubs in the zoo are very **frisky***.*
playful, lively, high-spirited, sprightly

frivolous adjective
Don't waste my time asking **frivolous** *questions.*
foolish, silly, ridiculous, shallow, superficial, pointless, unimportant, trivial, petty

front noun
1 *We stood at the* **front** *of the queue.*
head, start, beginning, lead, top
2 *The* **front** *of the house was painted white.*
face, facing, frontage, facade
The front of a ship is the **bow** or **prow**.
The front of a picture is the **foreground**.

front adjective
1 *The* **front** *runners came into sight round the corner.*
first, leading, most advanced
OPPOSITE back
2 *The horse had injured one of its* **front** *legs.*
fore
OPPOSITE back, rear, hind

frosty adjective
1 *It was a clear,* **frosty** *night.*
cold, crisp, icy, freezing, wintry
2 *The shopkeeper gave us a* **frosty** *stare.*
unfriendly, unwelcoming, cold, cool, stony

frown noun
On Christmas Eve, Scrooge had a **frown** *on his face.*
scowl, glare, grimace, glower, black look

WORD WEB

fruit *noun*
SOME COMMON VARIETIES OF FRUIT
apple, apricot, avocado, banana,
bilberry, blackberry or bramble,
blackcurrant, blueberry, cherry, coconut,
cranberry, damson, date, fig, gooseberry,
grape, guava, kiwi fruit, loganberry, lychee, mango, melon,
nectarine, pawpaw or papaya, peach, pear, pineapple, plum,
pomegranate, quince, raspberry, redcurrant, rosehip, sloe,
strawberry, tomato

CITRUS FRUITS
clementine, grapefruit, kumquat, lemon, lime, mandarin,
orange, satsuma, tangerine

DRIED FRUITS
currant, prune, raisin, sultana

Rhubarb is not a fruit, although it is often eaten like
one. A person who sells fruit and
vegetables is a **greengrocer**.

frown *verb*
*The witch **frowned** when her spell
didn't work.*
scowl, glare, grimace, glower, knit
your brow, look sullen

fruit *noun see panel above*

frustrate *verb*
1 *It was **frustrating** to have to wait
in the long queue.*
exasperate, discourage, dispirit,
irritate
2 *Our plan for the day was
frustrated by the weather.*
block, foil, thwart, defeat, check,
hinder, prevent

full *adjective*
1 *My suitcase is **full** to the brim.*
filled, loaded, topped up
OPPOSITE empty
2 *The shopping centre was **full** on
Saturday.*
busy, crowded, jammed, packed,
crammed, congested
OPPOSITE empty
3 *The detective gave a **full** account
of his findings.*
complete, detailed, exhaustive
comprehensive, thorough,
OPPOSITE incomplete
4 *The horses were galloping at **full**
speed.*
top, maximum, greatest, highest
OPPOSITE minimum

fun *noun*
*We had great **fun** at the beach on our
holiday.*
amusement, diversion, enjoyment,
entertainment, games, jokes,
laughter, merriment, play, pleasure,
recreation, sport
to make fun of someone
*It was cruel to **make fun of** her when
she fell over.*
jeer at, laugh at, mock, ridicule,
taunt, tease

funny *adjective*
1 *There are some very **funny** jokes
in the film.*
amusing, humorous, comic, comical,
hilarious, witty, entertaining,
diverting
(*informal*) hysterical, priceless
OPPOSITE serious
2 *There's a **funny** smell in here.*
strange, odd, peculiar, curious,
puzzling, weird, queer, bizarre

furious *adjective*
*The manager was **furious** when his
team lost.*
angry, mad, enraged, infuriated,
incensed, livid, fuming, raging,
seething

furry *adjective*
*A small, **furry** creature was curled
inside the box.*
hairy, fleecy, woolly, fuzzy, downy,
feathery

fuss *noun*
*There was a lot of **fuss** when the
queen arrived.*
bother, commotion, excitement,
trouble, hullabaloo

fuss *verb*
*Please don't **fuss**!*
worry, fret, bother, get worked
up

fussy *adjective*
1 *Our cat is **fussy** about her food.*
finicky, hard to please, particular
(*informal*) choosy, picky
An informal name for a fussy person
is a **fusspot**.
2 *I don't like clothes with **fussy**
designs.*
fancy, elaborate, ornate, florid

future *noun*
*She has a bright **future** as a tennis
player.*
outlook, prospects
OPPOSITE past

fuzzy *adjective*
1 *The TV picture has gone **fuzzy**.*
blurred, bleary, unfocused, unclear,
indistinct, hazy, cloudy
OPPOSITE clear
2 *Mia was wearing a **fuzzy**
cardigan.*
fluffy, frizzy, furry, woolly,
fleecy

G g

gadget noun
This torch is a handy little **gadget**.
tool, instrument, implement, device, contraption, gizmo

game noun
1 My favourite **game** is hide-and-seek.
amusement, pastime, sport, activity, recreation
2 The big **game** is on this Saturday.
match, contest, competition, tournament

cards

chess

gang noun
1 The sea was swarming with **gangs** of pirates.
group, band, crowd, pack, set, mob
2 A **gang** of workmen dug a hole in the road.
team, unit, crew, squad, party

gap noun
1 The animals escaped through a **gap** in the fence.
opening, space, hole, breach, break, crack, rift
2 She returned to work after a **gap** of two years.
break, interval, interruption, pause, lull

gate noun
People waited at the **gate** to be let in.
gateway, doorway, entrance, portal

gather verb
1 A crowd **gathered** to watch the performers.
assemble, collect, come together, congregate
OPPOSITE disperse
2 The captain **gathered** her team to give them a talk.
bring together, round up, muster
3 We **gathered** daisies to make into chains.
pick, pluck, collect, harvest

4 I **gather** that you've been on holiday.
understand, hear, learn, believe

general adjective
1 There was a **general** air of gloom about the abbey.
widespread, extensive, broad, sweeping, overall, prevalent
2 I've only got a **general** idea of where we are.
rough, approximate, indefinite, vague, loose

generous adjective
1 It was **generous** of you to give me your seat.
unselfish, charitable, kind-hearted
OPPOSITE selfish
2 We each got a **generous** helping of ice cream.
ample, large, lavish, plentiful
OPPOSITE meagre

genius noun
Nila is a **genius** at maths.
expert, master, mastermind, wizard, ace

gentle adjective
1 The vet is very **gentle** with sick animals.
kind, tender, good-tempered, humane
2 Grasses swayed in the **gentle** breeze.
light, slight, mild, soft, faint
OPPOSITE strong
3 There is a **gentle** slope to the top of the hill.
slight, gradual, easy
OPPOSITE steep

genuine adjective
1 Is that a **genuine** diamond?
real, actual, true, authentic
OPPOSITE fake
2 Your friend seems like a very **genuine** person.
honest, sincere, frank, earnest
OPPOSITE false

gesture noun
She opened her arms in a **gesture** of welcome.
sign, signal, motion, movement

get verb
1 We're **getting** a goldfish for our class.
acquire, obtain, buy, purchase
2 Can you **get** me another blanket, please?
bring, fetch, collect, pick up, retrieve
3 Cara **got** a medal for swimming.
receive, gain, earn, win, achieve
4 What time did you **get** home?
arrive at, reach, come to
OPPOSITE leave

5 It was starting to **get** dark outside.
become, grow, turn
6 I **got** a stomach bug on holiday last year.
catch, develop, pick up, come down with
7 You'll never **get** Oscar to eat celery.
persuade, urge, influence, coax
8 I don't **get** the point of that film.
understand, follow, comprehend, grasp
to get out of
My brother **got out of** doing the washing up.
avoid, evade, shirk
to get over
He hasn't **got over** the accident yet.
get better from, recover from, shake off, survive

ghastly adjective
The boy's face turned a **ghastly** shade of green.
appalling, awful, dreadful, frightful, grim, grisly, horrible, horrifying, shocking, monstrous, terrible

★ WORD WEB

ghost noun
Meldrop House was haunted by several **ghosts**.
spirit, spectre, phantom, ghoul, apparition, shade, wraith
(informal) spook
A ghost that makes a lot of noise is a **poltergeist**.

A GHOST OR GHOSTLY EXPERIENCE MIGHT BE
bloodcurdling, chilling, grisly, gruesome, hair-raising, macabre, nightmarish, spine-chilling, spine-tingling

THINGS A GHOST MIGHT DO
flit, float, glide, glow, haunt a person or place, hover, lurk, materialise, pass through walls, rattle chains, shimmer, vanish, waft

NOISES A GHOST MIGHT MAKE
cackle, clang, clank, creak, groan, hoot, howl, moan, screech, sigh, sob, wail

PLACES A GHOST MIGHT BE FOUND
catacombs, crypt, haunted house or mansion, graveyard, sepulchre, tomb, vault

OTHER THINGS THAT MIGHT BE IN A HAUNTED HOUSE
bats, candles, cellar, cobwebs, dungeon, gargoyle, mummy, owl, secret door or passage, skeleton, skull, trap door, turret

ghostly *adjective*
*The candlelight cast **ghostly** shadows on the wall.*
spectral, phantom, ghoulish, unearthly, eerie, sinister, uncanny
(*informal*) spooky, creepy

giant *adjective*
*A **giant** tree towered above us.*
gigantic, huge, enormous, massive, immense, mammoth, colossal, monstrous
OPPOSITE tiny

giddy *adjective*
*I felt **giddy** when I stood at the edge of the cliff.*
dizzy, faint, unsteady

gift *noun*
1 *I received some nice **gifts** on my birthday.*
present
2 *Elsa has a **gift** for music.*
talent, ability, flair, knack, genius

gigantic *adjective*
*The dragon reared its **gigantic** head.*
huge, giant, enormous, massive, colossal, immense, mammoth, monstrous
(*informal*) whopping, humungous
OPPOSITE tiny

giggle *verb*
*Ailsa and I couldn't stop **giggling**.*
snigger, titter, chuckle, laugh

girl *noun*
A synonym used in some parts of Britain is *lass*.
Old-fashioned words are *damsel*, *maid* and *maiden*.

give *verb*
1 *Santa Claus **gave** each child a present.*
deal out, distribute, issue, supply, offer, present, hand over, pass, award
2 *Will you **give** something to our collection for charity?*
contribute, donate
3 *The giant **gave** a loud sneeze.*
utter, emit, let out
4 *We are **giving** a concert at the end of term.*
present, put on, lay on, organise, arrange

5 *Will this branch **give** if I sit on it?*
collapse, give way, bend, break, buckle
to give in
*The boxer **gave in** after a long fight.*
surrender, yield, submit, quit
to give up
*He **gave up** trying to start the car.*
abandon, stop, cease, quit

glad *adjective*
*I'm **glad** to hear that you're feeling better.*
pleased, happy, delighted, thrilled
OPPOSITE sad

glance *verb*
*The bus driver **glanced** quickly at his watch.*
look quickly, peek, peep, glimpse

glare *verb*
*The troll **glared** at us from under his bushy eyebrows.*
stare, frown, scowl, glower

glare *noun*
1 *The **glare** of the lights dazzled me.*
dazzle, blaze, brightness, brilliance
2 *Miss Frump silenced the children with an angry **glare**.*
stare, scowl, glower, frown, nasty look

gleam *noun*
*I saw a **gleam** of moonlight between the clouds.*
glimmer, glint, flash, ray, shaft

gleam *verb*
*The lights **gleamed** on the water.*
glimmer, glint, glisten, shimmer, shine

glide *verb*
*The boat **glided** gently across the lake.*
move smoothly, slide, slip, drift, float, coast

glimmer *verb*
*The city lights **glimmered** in the distance.*
gleam, glint, glow, glisten, shimmer, flicker, blink

glimpse *verb*
*I **glimpsed** a deer running through the forest.*
catch sight of, spot, spy, sight

glimmer

glimpse *noun*
*We caught a **glimpse** of a whale in the sea.*
peek, peep, glance, sighting, view

glint *verb*
*Sunlight **glinted** on the windows.*
flash, glitter, sparkle, twinkle

glisten *verb*
*The pavement **glistened** with frost.*
gleam, shine, glint, shimmer, glimmer

glitter *verb*
*The jewels **glittered** under the bright lights.*
sparkle, twinkle, shimmer, glimmer, glint, glisten, flash, shine

gloat *verb*
*He was **gloating** about winning the poetry prize.*
boast, brag, crow, show off

global *adjective*
*The Internet is a **global** network of computers.*
worldwide, international, universal

gloom *noun*
1 *We could hardly see in the **gloom** of the cave.*
darkness, dimness, shade, shadow, murk
The gloomy light late in the evening is *dusk* or *twilight*.
2 *There was an air of **gloom** in the abandoned tower.*
depression, sadness, unhappiness, melancholy, misery, despair

gloomy *adjective*
1 *It was cold and **gloomy** in the cellar.*
dark, dingy, dim, dismal, dreary, sombre, cheerless, murky, shadowy
OPPOSITE bright
2 *Eeyore was feeling **gloomy** again.*
depressed, sad, unhappy, glum, miserable, melancholy, low, downcast, dejected
(*informal*) down in the dumps
OPPOSITE cheerful

a b c d e f **g** h i j k l m n o p q r s t u v w x y z

glorious *adjective*
*Look at that **glorious** sunset!*
magnificent, splendid, stunning, spectacular, superb, wonderful, marvellous

glossy *adjective*
*The bear had a thick, **glossy** coat of black fur.*
shiny, sleek, silky, shining, gleaming, lustrous
OPPOSITE dull

glow *noun*
*The soft **glow** of burning candles lit the room.*
brightness, shine, gleam, radiance

glow *verb*
*The embers of the bonfire were still **glowing**.*
shine, gleam, burn
Something that glows in the dark is **luminous** or **phosphorescent**.

glum *adjective*
*Why are you looking so **glum**?*
depressed, sad, unhappy, gloomy, miserable, melancholy, low, downcast, dejected
OPPOSITE cheerful

gnarled *adjective*
*The branches of the tree were **gnarled** with age.*
bent, twisted, crooked, distorted, knobbly, knotty

gnaw *verb*
*The wolves **gnawed** at a pile of bones.*
chew, bite, nibble, munch

go *verb*
1 *A carriage was **going** slowly along the road.*
move, progress, proceed
2 *My granny has always wanted to **go** to China.*
travel, journey
3 *Some of the guests had already **gone**.*
leave, depart, get away, withdraw
4 *By morning, the ice had all **gone**.*
disappear, vanish
5 *The canal **goes** all the way from Inverness to Fort William.*
extend, lead, reach, stretch, run
6 *The mountaineer's face **went** blue with cold.*
become, turn, grow
7 *Is that old grandfather clock still **going**?*
function, operate, work, run
8 *Cups and saucers **go** on the bottom shelf.*
belong, be kept, be placed
9 *Time **goes** slowly when you're stuck indoors.*
pass, go by, elapse
to go back
*Sarah has **gone back** to the house.*
return, retreat, retrace your steps

to go off
1 *A bomb **went off** nearby.*
explode, blow up, detonate
2 *The milk will **go off** if it's not in the fridge.*
turn sour, go bad, rot
to go on
1 *What's **going on** over there?*
happen, occur, take place
2 *Please **go on** with your story.*
carry on, continue, keep going, proceed

go *noun*
*Would you like to have a **go** on my computer?*
try, turn, chance, opportunity
(*informal*) shot, bash, stab

goal *noun*
*The **goal** of the society is to protect wildlife.*
aim, ambition, intention, object, objective, purpose, target

gobble *verb*
*Ladybirds love to **gobble** greenfly.*
guzzle, gulp, bolt, devour

good *adjective*
see panel opposite
*That is a really **good** idea!*
excellent, fine, lovely, nice, wonderful
(*informal*) fantastic, great, super, cool
OPPOSITE bad

gorgeous *adjective*
*The gardens look **gorgeous** in the summer.*
beautiful, glorious, dazzling, stunning, splendid, superb, glamorous, handsome

gossip *verb*
*Two neighbours were **gossiping** over the fence.*
chatter, tell tales
(*informal*) natter

gossip *noun*
1 *Don't believe all the **gossip** you hear.*
chatter, rumour, hearsay, scandal
(*informal*) tittle-tattle
2 *Our next-door neighbour is a dreadful **gossip**.*
busybody, chatterbox, telltale, scandalmonger

govern *verb*
*The ancient Romans **governed** a vast empire.*
rule, run, administer, direct, command, manage, be in charge of

grab *verb*
*The cowboy **grabbed** the reins of the runaway horse.*
seize, grasp, catch, clutch, grip, get hold of, snatch

graceful *adjective*
*The gymnast made a **graceful** landing.*
elegant, beautiful, stylish, smooth, flowing, agile, nimble
OPPOSITE clumsy, graceless

grade *noun*
*My sister has reached the top **grade** in judo.*
class, standard, level, stage, rank, degree

gradual *adjective*
*There's been a **gradual** change in the weather.*
steady, slow, gentle, moderate, regular, even
OPPOSITE sudden

gnarled

grand *adjective*
1 *The wedding was a grand occasion.*
magnificent, splendid, stately, impressive, big, great, important, imposing
2 (*informal*) *Keep going—you're doing a grand job!*
excellent, fine, good, first-class

grapple *verb*
The guard grappled with the thief, but he got away.
struggle, wrestle, fight, tussle

grasp *verb*
1 *The climber grasped the rope.*
clutch, grab, grip, seize, catch, snatch, take hold of, hang on to
2 *The ideas were quite difficult to grasp.*
understand, comprehend, follow, take in

grateful *adjective*
I'm grateful for your help.
thankful, appreciative, obliged, indebted
OPPOSITE ungrateful

grave *adjective*
1 *They looked grave when they heard the news.*
grim, sad, serious, thoughtful
OPPOSITE cheerful

2 *She made a grave mistake.*
crucial, important, serious, vital
OPPOSITE trivial

graze *verb*
I grazed my knee falling off my bike.
scrape, cut, scratch, scuff

great *adjective*
1 *The inventor had made a great discovery.*
important, significant, major, leading, noteworthy
OPPOSITE insignificant, minor
2 *Mozart was a great composer.*
famous, notable, celebrated, eminent, distinguished, outstanding, brilliant
3 *Their voices echoed round the great hall.*
big, huge, large, enormous, vast, immense, gigantic, extensive, cavernous
OPPOSITE small
4 *Beth took great care over her knitting.*
considerable, extreme, exact
OPPOSITE little
5 (*informal*) *That is a great idea!*
very good, excellent, marvellous, outstanding, superb, tremendous, wonderful

(*informal*) brilliant, fantastic, super, smashing, terrific
OPPOSITE bad, awful

greed *noun*
The king wanted more gold to satisfy his greed.
avarice, selfishness, hunger, craving, gluttony

greedy *adjective*
1 *The boys were so greedy that they ate all the cakes.*
gluttonous
(*informal*) piggish
A common simile is *as greedy as a pig*.
2 *Mr Skimp is very greedy with his money.*
selfish, miserly, tight-fisted, grasping

greet *verb*
My aunt greeted us with a friendly wave.
welcome, hail, receive, salute

grey *adjective*
1 *The old wizard had a bushy grey beard.*
silver, silvery, grizzly, hoary, whitish
2 *The mother's face was grey with worry.*
ashen, pale, leaden, wan
3 *The day began cold and grey.*
dull, cloudy, overcast

grief *noun*
He couldn't hide his grief at his friend's death.
sorrow, sadness, mourning, anguish, unhappiness, distress, heartache
OPPOSITE joy

grieve *verb*
The family is still grieving over her death.
mourn, lament, sorrow, weep
OPPOSITE rejoice

grim *adjective*
1 *The judge wore a grim expression on his face.*
stern, severe, harsh, bad-tempered, sullen
OPPOSITE cheerful
2 *The detective made the grim discovery of the body.*
unpleasant, horrible, dreadful, terrible, hideous, shocking, gruesome, grisly
OPPOSITE pleasant

grimy *adjective*
Don't wipe those grimy feet on the carpet!
dirty, filthy, grubby, mucky, soiled
OPPOSITE clean

grin *noun, verb*
Mark arrived with a silly grin on his face.
smile, beam, smirk
A large grin is a *broad*, *wide* or *cheesy* grin.

! OVERUSED WORDS

good *adjective*
Try to vary the words you use for **good**. Here are some other words you could use.

FOR A GOOD PERSON
honest, worthy, honourable, moral, decent, virtuous, noble, kind, humane, charitable, merciful *The virtuous knight defeated the evil queen.*
OPPOSITE evil, wicked
A good character in a story or film is a **hero** or **heroine** or (*informal*) **goody**.

FOR GOOD BEHAVIOUR
well-behaved, obedient, angelic, exemplary *The twins are surprisingly well-behaved.*
A common simile is *as good as gold*.
OPPOSITE naughty, disobedient

FOR A GOOD FRIEND
true, loyal, loving, reliable, trusty, trustworthy *My dog, Rusty, is a loyal companion.*

FOR A GOOD FEELING OR GOOD MOOD
happy, cheerful, light-hearted, positive, contented *Mr Fox was in a cheerful mood after his tea.*

FOR A GOOD EXPERIENCE OR GOOD NEWS
pleasant, enjoyable, delightful, agreeable, pleasing

OPPOSITE unpleasant, disagreeable
The girls had an enjoyable time at the party. The letter contained some pleasing news.

FOR A GOOD PERFORMER OR GOOD WORK
capable, skilful, clever, able, talented, competent, commendable, sound *My friend, Chris, is a talented dancer.*
OPPOSITE poor, awful

FOR GOOD FOOD OR A GOOD MEAL
delicious, healthy, nourishing, nutritious, tasty, well-cooked, wholesome, substantial, hearty *The crew ate a hearty breakfast together.*

FOR A GOOD EXCUSE OR GOOD REASON
acceptable, valid, proper, satisfactory, legitimate *I hope you have a valid excuse for being late.*
OPPOSITE poor, unacceptable

FOR GOOD TIMING
convenient, suitable, fortunate, appropriate, opportune *Is this a convenient time for a chat?*
OPPOSITE inconvenient, unsuitable

FOR GOOD WEATHER
fine, favourable *We are hoping for fine weather tomorrow.*
OPPOSITE harsh, adverse

grind verb
1 *Grind the spices into a fine powder.*
crush, pound, powder, pulverise, mill
2 *This tool is used for grinding knives.*
sharpen, file, hone, whet

grip verb
1 *Grip the handle tightly.*
grasp, seize, clutch, clasp, hold
2 *The audience was gripped by the film.*
fascinate, engross, absorb, enthrall

grisly adjective
We found the grisly remains of a dead sheep.
gruesome, gory, ghastly, hideous, nasty, revolting, sickening

groan verb
The wounded soldier groaned with pain.
cry out, moan, sigh, wail

gross adjective
1 *That is a gross exaggeration!*
extreme, glaring, obvious, sheer, blatant, outright
2 *Most ogres have gross table manners.*
offensive, rude, coarse, vulgar

ground noun
1 *I planted some seeds in the ground.*
earth, soil, land
2 *The ground was too wet to play on.*
field, pitch, park, stadium, arena

group noun
1 *Japan consists of a group of islands.*
collection, set, batch, cluster, clump
2 *A group of children was waiting at the bus stop.*
crowd, bunch, gathering, band, body, gang

grow

3 *The book group meets once a month.*
club, society, association, circle
4 *We sorted the fossils into different groups.*
category, class, type, kind, sort

grow verb
1 *I've grown an inch taller since last summer.*
get bigger, put on growth, spring up, sprout
2 *The number of children in the school has grown.*
increase, develop, enlarge, expand, build up
OPPOSITE decrease
3 *Our neighbour grows orchids in her greenhouse.*
cultivate, produce, raise, farm
4 *It is growing dark outside.*
become, get, turn

growth noun
There's been a growth of interest in golf for kids.
increase, rise, spread, expansion, development, enlargement

grubby adjective
My hands were grubby from working in the garden.
dirty, filthy, grimy, messy, mucky, soiled
OPPOSITE clean

gruesome adjective
The battlefield was a gruesome sight.
grisly, gory, ghastly, hideous, monstrous, revolting, sickening, appalling, dreadful, frightful, shocking, abominable

gruff adjective
The ogre spoke in a gruff voice.
harsh, rough, hoarse, husky, throaty

grumble verb
You're always grumbling about the weather!
complain, moan, groan, protest, whine, gripe

grumpy adjective
Marge was grumpy because she had a headache.
bad-tempered, cross, irritable, testy, tetchy, cantankerous
(*informal*) grouchy
OPPOSITE good-humoured

guard verb
The cave was guarded by a one-eyed giant.
protect, defend, stand guard over, patrol, safeguard, shield, watch over

guard noun
A guard was on duty at the gate.
sentry, sentinel, warder, lookout, watchman

guess verb
1 *There was a prize for guessing the weight of the cake.*
estimate, judge, work out, gauge, predict, reckon
2 *I guess you must be tired after your journey.*
suppose, imagine, expect, assume, think

guest noun
We are having guests for tea on Sunday.
visitor, caller, company

guide noun
1 *Our guide showed us around the zoo.*
courier, escort, leader, chaperon
2 *We bought a useful guide to the city.*
guidebook, handbook, manual

guide verb
The explorers used the stars to guide them at night.
direct, lead, steer, conduct, escort, show the way

guilty adjective
1 *The prisoner was found guilty of the crime.*
responsible, to blame, at fault, in the wrong, liable
OPPOSITE innocent
2 *You have a guilty look on your face!*
ashamed, guilt-ridden, remorseful, sorry, conscience-stricken, repentant, shamefaced, sheepish
OPPOSITE unrepentant

gulp verb
Peter gulped down the cake in one go.
swallow, bolt, gobble, guzzle, devour

gush noun
There was a gush of water from the pipe.
rush, stream, torrent, rush, cascade, flood, jet, spout, spurt

gush verb
Water gushed from the broken pipe.
rush, stream, flow, pour, flood, spout, spurt, squirt

guzzle verb
The seagulls guzzled all the bread.
gobble, gulp, bolt, devour

habit noun
1 *It's her **habit** to go for a walk each morning.*
custom, practice, routine, rule
2 *My dog has a **habit** of scratching his ear.*
mannerism, way, tendency, inclination, quirk

haggard adjective
*The warriors looked **haggard** after the battle.*
drawn, gaunt, thin, pinched, wasted, shrunken, wan
OPPOSITE healthy

haggle verb
*The men **haggled** over the price of the gems.*
bargain, negotiate, argue, wrangle

✎ **WRITING TIPS**

hair noun
You can use these words to describe **hair**.

TO DESCRIBE ITS COLOUR
auburn, blond (male) or blonde (female), brunette, carroty, dark, fair, flaxen, ginger, grey, grizzled, hoary, mousy, platinum blonde, raven, red, silver

TO DESCRIBE HOW IT LOOKS OR FEELS
bushy, coarse, curly, dishevelled, fine, frizzy, glossy, greasy, lank, limp, ringletted, shaggy, shiny, silky, spiky, straggly, straight, stringy, tangled, thick, tousled, tuggy, unkempt, wavy, windswept, wispy *The elderly knight had a **grizzled**, **straggly** beard.*

---

hairy adjective
*Mammoths were like elephants with thick **hairy** coats.*
shaggy, bushy, bristly, woolly, fleecy, furry, fuzzy, long-haired, hirsute

hall noun
1 *The **hall** was full for the concert.*
assembly hall, auditorium, concert hall, theatre
2 *You can use the coat stand in the **hall**.*
entrance hall, hallway, lobby, foyer

halt verb
1 *The car **halted** at the red light.*
stop, come to a halt, draw up, pull up, wait

2 *A traffic jam **halted** the traffic.*
stop, check, obstruct
3 *Work **halted** when the whistle went.*
end, cease, terminate, break off
OPPOSITE start, go

hand verb
*The postman **handed** me several letters.*
give, pass, present, offer, deliver

handle verb
1 *Please don't **handle** the exhibits.*
touch, feel, hold, stroke, fondle, finger, grasp
2 *The referee **handled** the game well.*
manage, control, conduct, deal with, cope with, tackle

handsome adjective
1 *Prince Charming was very **handsome**.*
attractive, good-looking, nice-looking, gorgeous, (*informal*) dishy
OPPOSITE ugly, unattractive
2 *They sold their house for a **handsome** profit.*
big, large, substantial, sizeable
OPPOSITE slight

handy adjective
1 *This **handy** gadget is for peeling potatoes.*
useful, helpful, convenient, practical
OPPOSITE awkward
2 *I always keep my umbrella **handy**.*
accessible, available, close at hand, nearby, ready
OPPOSITE inaccessible

hang verb
1 *A monkey was **hanging** from the tree branch.*
dangle, be suspended, swing, sway
2 *The dog had hair **hanging** down over his eyes.*
droop, drape, flop, trail, cascade
3 *I **hung** the picture on the wall.*
fix, attach, fasten, stick, peg
4 *Smoke **hung** in the air.*
float, hover, drift, linger, cling
to hang about or **around**
*Don't **hang about**, we'll miss the bus.*
delay, dawdle, linger, loiter
to hang on
(*informal*) *Try to **hang on** a bit longer.*
carry on, continue, stay, remain, persist, keep going, persevere
to hang on to something
1 *Hang on to the rope.*
hold, grip, grasp
2 *Hang on to your bus ticket.*
keep, retain, save

happiness noun
*The bride's face glowed with **happiness**.*
joy, joyfulness, delight, jubilation, pleasure, contentment, gladness, cheerfulness, merriment, ecstasy, bliss
OPPOSITE sorrow

happy adjective
1 *The girls look really **happy** in the photograph.*
cheerful, joyful, jolly, merry, light-hearted, contented, gleeful, delighted
OPPOSITE unhappy, sad
2 *Sandy was **happy** when she won first prize.*
thrilled, ecstatic, elated, overjoyed (*informal*) over the moon, thrilled to bits, tickled pink
3 *They spent a **happy** summer on the island.*
enjoyable, joyous, glorious, blissful, heavenly, idyllic

harbour noun
*Several yachts were tied up in the **harbour**.*
port, dock, mooring, quay, pier, wharf

hard adjective
1 *The ground was **hard** and covered with frost.*
solid, firm, dense, compact, rigid, stiff
OPPOSITE soft
2 *The climber gave the rope a **hard** pull.*
strong, forceful, heavy, powerful, violent
OPPOSITE light
3 *Digging the tunnel was **hard** work.*
tough, gruelling, strenuous, tiring, exhausting, laborious, backbreaking
OPPOSITE easy
4 *None of us could solve the **hard** riddle.*
difficult, complicated, complex, intricate, perplexing, puzzling, baffling, knotty, thorny
OPPOSITE simple

hard adverb
1 *Ros is working **hard** at learning French.*
strenuously, energetically, diligently, keenly, intently
2 *It has been raining **hard** all afternoon.*
heavily, steadily
(*informal*) cats and dogs

hardly adverb
*I could **hardly** see in the fog.*
barely, scarcely, only just, with difficulty

harm verb
1 *His captors didn't **harm** him.*
hurt, injure, ill-treat, wound

a
b
c
d
e
f
g
h
i
j
k
l
m
n
o
p
q
r
s
t
u
v
w
x
y
z

2 *Too much direct sunlight may* **harm** *this plant.*
damage, spoil, ruin

harm *noun*
I didn't mean to cause him any **harm**.
damage, hurt, injury, pain
OPPOSITE benefit

harmful *adjective*
Junk food can be **harmful** *to your health.*
damaging, dangerous, destructive, injurious, unhealthy
OPPOSITE harmless, beneficial

harmless *adjective*
1 *You can drink the potion—it is quite* **harmless**.
safe, non-toxic, innocuous
OPPOSITE harmful, dangerous
2 *It was just a bit of* **harmless** *fun.*
innocent, inoffensive

harsh *adjective*
1 *The trumpet sounded loud and* **harsh**.
rough, rasping, grating, jarring, shrill, raucous
OPPOSITE soft, gentle
2 *We blinked in the* **harsh** *light.*
bright, brilliant, dazzling, glaring
OPPOSITE soft, subdued
3 *The rescue team braved the* **harsh** *weather.*
severe, strict, cruel, hard, tough, bleak
OPPOSITE mild
4 *The coach had some* **harsh** *words to say.*
strong, sharp, unkind, unfriendly

hasty *adjective*
1 *The robbers made a* **hasty** *exit.*
fast, hurried, quick, sudden, swift, rapid, speedy
OPPOSITE slow
2 *The king regretted his* **hasty** *decision.*
rash, reckless, impatient, foolhardy, thoughtless
OPPOSITE careful

hate *verb*
1 *Eddie* **hates** *broccoli and peas.*
dislike, detest, despise, loathe
2 *I* **hate** *to bother you.*
be sorry, be reluctant, regret

have *verb*
1 *I* **have** *my own CD player.*
own, possess
2 *Our house* **has** *three bedrooms.*
consist of, comprise, include, incorporate
3 *We are* **having** *a barbecue at the weekend.*
hold, organise, provide, host, throw
4 *Dad* **had** *trouble finding a place to park.*
experience, go through, meet with, run into, face, suffer

5 *The girls* **had** *a great time at the party.*
experience, enjoy
6 *The BBC has* **had** *lots of email messages.*
receive, get, be given, be sent
7 *Sharon* **had** *the last toffee.*
take, consume, eat
8 *One of the giraffes has* **had** *a baby.*
give birth to, bear, produce
9 *I* **have** *to be home by six o'clock.*
must, need to, ought to, should

hazy *adjective*
1 *The things in the distance were rather* **hazy**.
blurred, misty, unclear, dim, faint
2 *He's only got a* **hazy** *knowledge of history.*
uncertain, vague

head *noun*
1 *My dad hit his* **head** *on the attic ceiling.*
skull, crown
(*informal*) nut
2 *Can you add up these figures in your* **head**?
brain, mind, intellect, intelligence
3 *There is a new* **head** *of the music department.*
chief, leader, manager, director, controller
(*informal*) boss
4 *The girls waited at the* **head** *of the queue.*
front, lead, top
OPPOSITE back, rear

head *verb*
The professor was chosen to **head** *the expedition.*
lead, be in charge of, direct, command, manage, oversee, supervise
to head for
At the end of the day we **headed** *for home.*
go towards, make for, aim for

heal *verb*
1 *It took two months for my leg to* **heal** *properly.*
get better, mend, recover
2 *Part of a vet's job is to* **heal** *sick animals.*
cure, make better, treat, restore

health *noun*
The puppies are in excellent **health**.
condition, fitness, shape, strength, vigour, wellbeing

healthy *adjective*
1 *Neil has always been a* **healthy** *child.*
well, fit, strong, sturdy, vigorous, robust
(*informal*) in good shape
OPPOSITE ill
2 *Porridge makes a very* **healthy** *breakfast.*
health-giving, wholesome, invigorating
OPPOSITE unhealthy

heap *noun*
There was an untidy **heap** *of clothes on the floor.*
mound, pile, stack, mountain, collection, mass

heap *verb*
We **heaped** *up all the rubbish in the corner.*
pile, stack, collect, bank, mass

hear *verb*
1 *Did you* **hear** *what she said?*
catch, listen to, make out, pick up, overhear, pay attention to
A sound that you can hear is **audible**.
A sound that you cannot hear is **inaudible**.
2 *Have you* **heard** *the news?*
be told, discover, find out, learn, gather

heart *noun*
1 *Have you no* **heart**?
compassion, feeling, sympathy, tenderness, affection, humanity, kindness, love
2 *The hotel is located right in the* **heart** *of the city.*
centre, middle, hub
3 *They tried to get to the* **heart** *of the problem.*
core, essence

heat *noun*
1 *The cat basked in the* **heat** *of the fire.*
warmth, hotness, glow
2 *Last summer, the* **heat** *made me feel ill.*
hot weather, high temperatures, closeness
A long period of hot weather is a **heatwave**.

heave *verb*
The men **heaved** *the sacks on to a lorry.*
haul, drag, pull, draw, tow, tug, hoist, lug, lift, raise, throw

heavy *adjective*
1 *The box was too* **heavy** *for me to lift.*
weighty, massive, dense, bulky
2 *Digging the garden is* **heavy** *work.*
hard, tough, gruelling, back-breaking, strenuous
3 *This book makes* **heavy** *reading.*
serious, intense, demanding
4 *The rain has caused* **heavy** *flooding.*
severe, extreme, torrential
5 *Both sides suffered* **heavy** *losses in the battle.*
large, substantial, considerable
6 *A* **heavy** *mist hung over the landscape.*
dense, thick

hectic *adjective*
The days before the wedding were **hectic**.
busy, frantic, feverish, frenzied, chaotic, (*informal*) manic
OPPOSITE quiet, leisurely

help *noun*
1 *Thank you for your* **help**.
aid, assistance, support, guidance, cooperation, advice
OPPOSITE hindrance
2 *Would a torch be of any* **help** *to you?*
use, benefit

help *verb*
1 *Could you please* **help** *me with my luggage?*
aid, assist, cooperate with (*informal*) give a hand to
2 *The Red Cross is an organisation that* **helps** *people in need.*
be helpful to, support, serve, stand by
3 *This medicine will* **help** *your cough.*
make better, cure, ease, relieve, improve
OPPOSITE aggravate, worsen
4 *I can't* **help** *coughing.*
stop, avoid, prevent, refrain from

helpful *adjective*
1 *The staff were friendly and* **helpful**.
obliging, cooperative, kind, considerate, thoughtful, sympathetic
OPPOSITE unhelpful
2 *The shop assistant gave us some* **helpful** *advice.*
useful, valuable, worthwhile, beneficial, profitable
OPPOSITE worthless

helpless *adjective*
Kittens are born blind and **helpless**.
powerless, weak, feeble, dependent, defenceless, vulnerable
OPPOSITE independent, strong

heroic *adjective*
The firefighters made a **heroic** *effort to put out the blaze.*
bold, brave, courageous, daring, fearless, noble, selfless, valiant
OPPOSITE cowardly

hesitate *verb*
I **hesitated** *for a moment before ringing the doorbell.*
pause, delay, wait, hold back, dither, falter, waver
(*informal*) think twice

hidden *adjective*
1 *The giant kept his gold* **hidden** *in a wooden chest.*
concealed, out of sight, unseen, invisible, covered, disguised
OPPOSITE visible
2 *There's a* **hidden** *message in the riddle.*
secret, mysterious, obscure, coded, cryptic
OPPOSITE obvious

hide *verb*
1 *Quick!—someone's coming—we'd better* **hide**.
go into hiding, take cover, take refuge, keep out of sight, lie low, go to ground
2 *They* **hid** *the jewels in a secret drawer.*
conceal, secrete, bury
(*informal*) stash
OPPOSITE expose
3 *The clouds* **hid** *the sun.*
blot out, cover, screen, shroud, veil, mask
OPPOSITE uncover
4 *I tried to* **hide** *my feelings.*
disguise, keep secret, suppress, camouflage, cloak
OPPOSITE show

hide

hideous *adjective*
The troll had a **hideous** *grin on his face.*
repulsive, revolting, ugly, grotesque, monstrous, ghastly, gruesome, horrible, appalling, dreadful, frightful
OPPOSITE beautiful

high *adjective*
1 *The castle was surrounded by a* **high** *wall.*
tall, towering, elevated, lofty
OPPOSITE low
2 *Sir Grinalot was a knight of* **high** *rank and status.*
senior, top, leading, important, prominent, powerful
OPPOSITE low, junior
3 *House prices are very* **high** *at the moment.*
expensive, dear, costly, excessive
OPPOSITE low
4 *A* **high** *wind was blowing.*
strong, powerful, forceful, extreme
OPPOSITE gentle
5 *The pixie spoke in a* **high** *squeaky voice.*
high-pitched, sharp, shrill, piercing
A high singing voice is **soprano** or **treble**.
OPPOSITE deep

hilarious *adjective*
The boys thought the cartoon was **hilarious**.
funny, amusing, comical
(*informal*) hysterical

hill *noun*
1 *From the top of this* **hill** *you can see for miles.*
mount, peak, ridge
A small hill is a **hillock** or **mound**.
The top of a hill is the **summit**.
2 *Jenny pushed her bike up the steep* **hill**.
slope, rise, incline, ascent, gradient

hinder *verb*
The snowstorm **hindered** *the rescue attempt.*
hamper, hold up, obstruct, impede, slow down, stand in the way of, restrict, handicap
OPPOSITE help

hint *noun*
1 *I don't know the answer—can you give me a* **hint**?
clue, indication, sign, suggestion, inkling
2 *The magazine offers handy* **hints** *for decorating.*
tip, pointer

hint *verb*
Mum **hinted** *that we might be getting a puppy.*
give a hint, suggest, imply, indicate

hit *noun*
1 *Matt got a nasty* **hit** *on the head.*
bump, blow, bang, knock, whack
A hit with your fist is a **punch**.
A hit with your open hand is a **slap** or **smack**.
A hit with a bat or club is a **drive**, **stroke** or **swipe**.
2 *Their new album was an instant* **hit**.
success, triumph
(*informal*) winner

hit *verb*
1 *Auntie Flo* **hit** *the burglar on the head with her umbrella.*
strike, knock, bang, bash, thump, bump, crack, rap, slam, swipe, slog, cuff
(*informal*) whack, wham, wallop, sock, clout, clobber, belt, biff
(*old use*) smite
To hit with your fist is to **punch**.
To hit with the palm of your hand is to **slap** or **smack**.
To punish someone by hitting them is to **beat** them.
To hit someone with a stick is to **club** them.
To hit your toe on something is to **stub** it.
To kill an insect by hitting it is to **swat** it.
To hit something repeatedly is to **batter**, **buffet** or **pound** it.

a
b
c
d
e
f
g
h
i
j
k
l
m
n
o
p
q
r
s
t
u
v
w
x
y
z

To hit something gently is to **tap** it.
2 *The drought has **hit** many farms in the area.*
affect, damage, harm, hurt

hoard noun
*Hamish keeps a **hoard** of sweets in his desk.*
cache, store, stock, supply, pile, stockpile
A hoard of treasure is a **treasure trove**.

hoard verb
*Squirrels **hoard** nuts for the winter.*
store, collect, gather, save, put by, pile up, stockpile
(*informal*) stash away

hoard

hoarse adjective
*Mr Barker's voice was **hoarse** from shouting.*
rough, harsh, husky, croaky, throaty, gruff, rasping, gravelly

hobby noun
*My favourite **hobby** is snorkelling.*
pastime, pursuit, interest, activity, recreation

hold verb
1 *Please **hold** the dog's lead.*
clasp, grasp, grip, cling to, hang on to, clutch, seize
2 *Can I **hold** the baby?*
embrace, hug, cradle
3 *They **held** the suspect until the police arrived.*
confine, detain, keep
4 *Will the ladder **hold** my weight?*
bear, support, carry, take
5 *If our luck **holds**, we could reach the final.*
continue, last, carry on, persist, stay
6 *She **holds** strong opinions.*
believe in, maintain, stick to
to hold out
1 *The robot **held out** one of his arms.*
extend, reach out, stick out, stretch out
2 *Our supplies won't **hold out** much longer.*
keep going, last, carry on, continue, endure
to hold something up
1 *Please **hold up** your hand.*
lift, put up, raise
2 *The accident **held up** the traffic.*
delay, hinder, slow down

hole noun
1 *The meteor created a massive **hole** in the ground.*
pit, hollow, crater, dent, depression, cavity, chasm, abyss
2 *The rabbits escaped through a **hole** in the fence.*
gap, opening, breach, break, cut, slit, gash, split, tear, vent

hollow adjective
*Tennis balls are **hollow**.*
empty, unfilled
OPPOSITE solid

hollow noun
*The ball rolled into a **hollow** in the ground.*
dip, dent, depression, hole, pit, crater
A hollow between two hills is a **valley**.

holy adjective
1 *The pilgrims knelt to pray in the **holy** shrine.*
sacred, blessed, revered
2 *The pilgrims were **holy** people.*
religious, spiritual, devout, pious, godly, saintly

home noun
*The hurricane forced people to flee their **homes**.*
house, residence, dwelling, abode, lodging
A home for the sick is a **convalescent home** or **nursing home**.
A place where a bird or animal lives is its **habitat**.

honest adjective
1 *He's an **honest** boy, so he gave the money back.*
good, honourable, law-abiding, moral, trustworthy, upright, virtuous
OPPOSITE dishonest
2 *Please give me your **honest** opinion.*
sincere, genuine, truthful, direct, frank, candid, plain, straightforward, unbiased
OPPOSITE insincere

honour noun
1 *Her success brought **honour** to the school.*
credit, good reputation, good name, respect, praise, acclaim
2 *It's an **honour** to meet you.*
privilege, distinction

honour verb
*The winners were **honoured** at a special ceremony.*
praise, celebrate, salute, give credit to, pay tribute to, glorify

honourable adjective
1 *The knight was an **honourable** man.*
good, honest, sincere, noble, principled, moral, righteous, trustworthy, upright, virtuous, worthy, decent, fair, trusty
2 *It was an **honourable** thing to do.*
noble, admirable, praiseworthy, decent

hop verb
*The goblins **hopped** about in excitement.*
jump, leap, skip, spring, prance, caper, bound, dance

hope verb
*I **hope** to see you again soon.*
wish, trust, expect, look forward

hope noun
1 *Her dearest **hope** was to see her family again.*
ambition, dream, desire, wish
2 *There's **hope** of better weather tomorrow.*
prospect, expectation, likelihood

hopeful adjective
1 *I am feeling **hopeful** about tomorrow's match.*
optimistic, confident, positive, expectant
OPPOSITE pessimistic
2 *The future is beginning to look more **hopeful**.*
promising, encouraging, favourable, reassuring
OPPOSITE discouraging

hopeless adjective
1 *The shipwrecked crew were in a **hopeless** situation.*
desperate, wretched, beyond hope
OPPOSITE hopeful
2 *I'm **hopeless** at ice-skating.*
bad, poor, incompetent
(*informal*) useless, rubbish
OPPOSITE good, competent

horrible adjective
*What a **horrible** smell!*
awful, terrible, dreadful, appalling, unpleasant, disagreeable, offensive, objectionable, disgusting, repulsive, revolting, horrendous, horrid, nasty, hateful, odious, loathsome, beastly, ghastly
OPPOSITE pleasant

horrific adjective
*The film has some **horrific** scenes of battle.*
horrifying, terrifying, shocking, gruesome, dreadful, appalling, ghastly, hideous, atrocious, grisly, sickening

horrify verb
We were **horrified** by the sight of the monster.
appal, shock, terrify, scare, frighten, alarm, sicken, disgust

horror noun
1 Ingrid screamed in **horror** when she saw the snake.
terror, fear, fright, alarm, dread
2 The film depicts the full **horror** of war.
awfulness, hideousness, gruesomeness, ghastliness, frightfulness

hostile adjective
The warriors shook their weapons in a **hostile** manner.
aggressive, antagonistic, unfriendly, unwelcoming, warlike, malevolent
OPPOSITE friendly

hot adjective
1 The weather has been **hot** this summer.
warm, balmy, blazing, roasting, scorching, blistering, sweltering, stifling
OPPOSITE cold, cool
2 Careful—the soup's really **hot**.
burning, boiling, baking hot, piping hot, scalding, searing, sizzling, steaming
OPPOSITE cold, cool
3 I like curry, but only if it's not too **hot**.
spicy, peppery, fiery
OPPOSITE mild
4 My sister, Diana, has a **hot** temper.
fierce, fiery, violent, passionate, raging, angry, intense
OPPOSITE calm, mild

WORD WEB

house noun
WORDS FOR THE PLACE YOU LIVE IN
abode, dwelling, home, lodging, quarters, residence

BUILDINGS WHERE PEOPLE LIVE
apartment, bungalow, chalet, cottage, council house, croft, detached house, farmhouse, flat, hovel, hut, igloo, lodge, manor, manse, mansion, rectory, semi-detached house, shack, shanty, tenement, terraced house, thatched house, vicarage, villa

hover verb
1 A flock of seagulls **hovered** overhead.
fly, flutter, float, hang, drift
2 He **hovered** outside the room, afraid to knock.
linger, pause, wait about, hesitate, dally, loiter, dither
(informal) hang about

hover

howl verb
1 The injured boy **howled** in pain.
cry, yell, scream, yelp, shriek, wail
2 They heard wolves **howling** in the night.
bay, yowl

huddle verb
The penguins **huddled** together to get warm.
crowd, gather, flock, cluster, squeeze, pack, nestle, cuddle, snuggle
OPPOSITE scatter

hug verb
Ellie was **hugging** her favourite teddy bear.
cuddle, clasp, embrace, cling to, hold close, squeeze

huge adjective
Elephants are **huge** animals.
enormous, gigantic, massive, colossal, giant, immense, vast, mighty, mammoth, monumental, hulking, great, big, large
(informal) whopping, ginormous, humungous
OPPOSITE small, little, tiny

hum verb
We heard insects **humming** in the air.
buzz, drone, murmur, purr, whirr

humble adjective
1 The gentle giant was both **humble** and kind.
modest, meek, unassuming, polite, respectful, submissive
OPPOSITE proud
2 Hansel and Gretel lived in a **humble** cottage.
simple, modest, plain, ordinary, commonplace, lowly
OPPOSITE grand

humid adjective
I don't like this **humid** weather.
muggy, clammy, close, sticky, steamy, sweaty
OPPOSITE fresh

humiliate verb
He **humiliated** her in front of her friends.
embarrass, disgrace, shame, make ashamed, humble, crush, degrade
(informal) put you in your place, take you down a peg

humour noun
1 I liked the **humour** in the film.
comedy, wit, amusement, jokes

2 The ogre was in a very bad **humour**.
mood, temper, disposition, frame of mind, spirits

hunger noun
After a week without food, the crew were faint with **hunger**.
lack of food, starvation, famine
Bad health caused by not having enough food is **malnutrition**.

hungry adjective
Our dog always seems to be **hungry**.
starving, famished, ravenous
(informal) peckish

hunt noun
Police have begun the **hunt** for clues.
search, quest, chase, pursuit (of)

hunt verb
1 Some Native Americans tribes used to **hunt** buffalo.
chase, pursue, track, trail, hound, stalk
An animal which hunts other animals for food is a **predator**.
2 I **hunted** in the attic for our old photos.
search, seek, look, rummage, ferret, root around

hurry verb
1 If you want to catch the bus, you'd better **hurry**.
be quick, hasten, make speed
(informal) get a move on, step on it
OPPOSITE dawdle
2 Alice saw the White Rabbit **hurrying** past.
rush, dash, fly, speed, hurtle, scurry
OPPOSITE amble, stroll

hurt verb
1 Be careful not to **hurt** yourself with the scissors.
harm, injure, damage, wound, maim
To hurt someone deliberately is to **torment** or **torture** them.
2 My feet **hurt**.
be sore, be painful, ache, throb, sting, smart
3 Your letter **hurt** me deeply.
upset, distress, offend, grieve

hurtful adjective
That was a very **hurtful** remark.
upsetting, unkind, cruel, mean, painful, spiteful, nasty

hut noun
The walkers came across a **hut** in the forest.
shed, shack, cabin, den, shelter, shanty, hovel

hysterical adjective
1 The fans became **hysterical** when the band appeared.
crazy, frenzied, mad, delirious, raving, wild, uncontrollable
2 (informal) We laughed at the **hysterical** jokes in the film.
hilarious, funny, amusing, comical

a b c d e f g h i j k l m n o p q r s t u v w x y z

ice hockey

WORD WEB

ice noun
WAYS TO DESCRIBE ICE
brittle, cracked, frozen solid, glacial, glassy, gleaming, glinting, hard, packed, slippery or (informal) slippy, smooth, treacherous

THINGS YOU MIGHT DO ON ICE
glide, skate, skid, slide, slip, slither

SPORTS THAT ARE PLAYED ON ICE
curling, figure skating, ice skating, ice hockey, speed skating

Ice sports are played on an **ice rink**.

icy adjective
1 You need to dress warmly in **icy** weather.
cold, freezing, frosty, wintry, arctic, bitter, biting
2 **Icy** roads are dangerous.
frozen, slippery, glacial, glassy (informal) slippy

idea noun
1 I've got a great **idea**!
plan, scheme, proposal, suggestion, inspiration
2 She has some funny **ideas** about life.
belief, notion, opinion, view, theory, concept, conception, hypothesis
3 What's the main **idea** of this poem?
point, meaning, intention, thought
4 Give me an **idea** of what you are planning.
clue, hint, inkling, impression

ideal adjective
It's **ideal** weather for a picnic.
perfect, excellent, the best, faultless, suitable

identical adjective
The twins were wearing **identical** clothes.
matching, similar, alike, indistinguishable
OPPOSITE different

identify verb
1 The police asked if I could **identify** the thief.
recognise, name, distinguish, pick out, single out

2 The doctor couldn't **identify** what was wrong.
diagnose, discover, spot (informal) put a name to

idiotic adjective
That was an **idiotic** thing to do.
stupid, silly, foolish, unwise, senseless, ridiculous, half-witted, unintelligent, crazy, mad, hare-brained (informal) daft
OPPOSITE sensible

idle adjective
1 The ogre was an **idle**, foul-smelling creature.
lazy, indolent, slothful, work-shy
OPPOSITE hard-working
2 The computers lay **idle** all week.
inactive, unused, inoperative
OPPOSITE busy, active

idol noun
1 The floor of the temple was littered with broken **idols**.
god, deity, image, statue
2 He was a pop **idol** of the fifties.
star, celebrity, icon, pin-up, favourite

ignorant adjective
Trolls are often described as **ignorant** creatures.
uneducated, simple, stupid

ignore verb
Ignoring the weather, Lynn went for a walk.
disregard, take no notice of, overlook, neglect, spurn, snub
(informal) turn a blind eye to

ill adjective
1 I missed school for a week when I was **ill**.
sick, unwell, poorly, sickly, ailing, infirm, unfit, indisposed, diseased, infected, nauseous, queasy, off colour, peaky
(informal) under the weather
OPPOSITE healthy, well
2 Did the plants suffer **ill** effects in the frost?
bad, harmful, adverse, damaging
OPPOSITE good

illegal adjective
Stealing is **illegal**.
unlawful, against the law, banned, prohibited, criminal, forbidden, wrong
OPPOSITE legal

illustrate verb
1 I used some photos to **illustrate** my story.
depict, picture, portray
2 The accident **illustrates** the importance of road safety.
show, demonstrate, make clear

illustration noun
1 I like cookery books with lots of **illustrations**.
picture, photograph, drawing, sketch, diagram
2 I'll give you an **illustration** of what I mean.
example, instance, demonstration, specimen

image noun
1 The film contained frightening **images** of war.
picture, portrayal, depiction, representation
2 The temple contained **images** of the gods.
figure, idol, statue, carving
3 You can see your **image** in the mirror.
reflection, likeness

imaginary adjective
The story takes place in an **imaginary** universe.
imagined, non-existent, unreal, made up, invented, fanciful, fictitious, fictional
OPPOSITE real

imagination noun
Use your **imagination** to draw an alien spaceship.
creativity, inventiveness, ingenuity, inspiration, originality, vision, artistry, fancy

imaginative adjective
Roald Dahl wrote highly **imaginative** stories.
creative, inventive, inspired, original, artistic, fanciful, ingenious, clever
OPPOSITE unimaginative, dull

imagine verb
1 **Imagine** what it would be like to visit Mars.
picture, visualise, pretend, think up, dream up, fancy, conjure up
2 I **imagine** you'd like something to eat.
suppose, assume, presume, believe, guess

imitate verb
Parrots can **imitate** the human voice.
copy, reproduce, mimic, mirror, echo, simulate, impersonate, follow, match
(informal) send up, take off

imitation noun
This is an **imitation** of a Viking helmet.
copy, replica, reproduction, duplicate
An imitation made to deceive someone is a **fake** or a **forgery**.

immediate adjective
1 Please can I have an **immediate** reply.
instant, instantaneous, prompt, speedy, swift, urgent, quick, direct
(informal) snappy
OPPOSITE slow

2 *Are you friends with your*
immediate *neighbours?*
closest, nearest, adjacent, next
OPPOSITE distant

immediately *adverb*
You must fetch a doctor **immediately**!
at once, now, straight away, right
away, instantly, promptly, directly

immense *adjective*
The giant wiggled one of his
immense *toes.*
huge, great, massive, enormous,
colossal, vast, giant, gigantic,
mighty, mammoth, monumental
(*informal*) whopping, ginormous,
humungous
OPPOSITE tiny

immoral *adjective*
It would be **immoral** *to steal the money.*
wrong, wicked, bad, sinful, dishonest,
corrupt
OPPOSITE moral, right

immortal *adjective*
The ancient Greeks believed their
gods were **immortal**.
undying, ageless, eternal, everlasting
OPPOSITE mortal

impact *noun*
1 *The crater was caused by the*
impact *of a meteor.*
crash, collision, smash, blow, bump,
bang, knock, jolt
2 *Computers have a big* **impact**
on our lives.
effect, influence

impatient *adjective*
1 *As time went on, Henry grew more*
and more **impatient**.
restless, agitated, anxious, fidgety,
irritable, snappy, testy, jumpy, edgy
OPPOSITE patient
2 *The crowd were* **impatient** *for the*
show to begin.
anxious, eager, in a hurry, keen
(*informal*) itching

important *adjective*
1 *The World Cup is an* **important**
sporting event.
major, significant, big, central,
momentous, outstanding, historic
2 *I have some* **important** *business*
to attend to.
serious, urgent, pressing, weighty,
vital, essential, crucial
3 *The prime minister is an*
important *person.*
prominent, powerful, influential,
notable, eminent, distinguished

impossible *adjective*
We used to think that space travel
was **impossible**.
impractical, unthinkable, unrealistic,
unachievable, unworkable, out of the
question
OPPOSITE possible

impact

impress *verb*
Frank **impressed** *the coach with his*
football skills.
make an impression on, influence,
leave its mark on, stick in your mind

impression *noun*
1 *I had the* **impression** *that*
something was wrong.
feeling, idea, sense, notion,
suspicion, hunch
2 *The film made a big* **impression**
on them.
effect, impact, influence, mark
3 *My sister does a good* **impression**
of the Queen.
imitation, impersonation
(*informal*) send-up

impressive *adjective*
The film includes some **impressive**
special effects.
striking, effective, powerful, remarkable,
spectacular, exciting, inspiring
OPPOSITE unimpressive, uninspiring

imprison *verb*
The thief was **imprisoned** *for two years.*
send to prison, jail, lock up,
incarcerate, confine, detain
(*informal*) put away, send down, put
under lock and key
OPPOSITE liberate

improve *verb*
1 *Her work* **improved** *this term.*
get better, advance, progress,
develop, move on
OPPOSITE deteriorate
2 *Has he* **improved** *since his illness?*
get better, recover, recuperate, pick
up, rally, revive
OPPOSITE get worse
3 *How can I* **improve** *this story?*
make better, enhance, refine, amend,
revise, correct, upgrade

improvement *noun*
1 *Your handwriting shows signs of*
improvement.
getting better, advance, progress,
development, recovery, upturn

2 *The author made some*
improvements *to the book.*
amendment, correction, revision,
modification, enhancement

impulsive *adjective*
She regretted her **impulsive** *decision*
to dye her hair.
hasty, rash, reckless, sudden,
spontaneous, thoughtless,
unthinking, impetuous
OPPOSITE deliberate

inaccurate *adjective*
That spelling of my surname is
inaccurate.
wrong, incorrect, mistaken, false,
inexact, untrue
OPPOSITE accurate

inadequate *adjective*
They had brought an **inadequate**
supply of matches.
insufficient, not enough, limited,
scarce, scanty, meagre
OPPOSITE adequate

incident *noun*
There was an amusing **incident**
at school this morning.
event, happening, occurrence,
episode, affair

include *verb*
Does the cost **include** *postage*
and packing?
contain, incorporate, comprise,
involve, take in, allow for, take into
account, cover
OPPOSITE exclude

inconsiderate *adjective*
It's **inconsiderate** *to play the radio*
so loudly.
selfish, unthinking, thoughtless, rude,
insensitive, tactless, unkind, uncaring
OPPOSITE considerate

inconvenient *adjective*
The guests arrived at an
inconvenient *moment.*
awkward, difficult, unsuitable,
unfortunate, untimely, inopportune
OPPOSITE convenient

a
b
c
d
e
f
g
h
i
j
k
l
m
n
o
p
q
r
s
t
u
v
w
x
y
z

A B C D E F G H I J K L M N O P Q R S T U V W X Y Z

increase *verb*
1 *They've **increased** the size of the tennis courts.*
make bigger, enlarge, expand, develop, add to, widen, broaden
2 *She **increased** the cooking time in the recipe.*
extend, lengthen, prolong
3 *The police **increased** their efforts to find the murderer.*
intensify, step up
4 *Will you be **increasing** the bus fares?*
put up, raise
5 *Can you **increase** the volume of the TV?*
turn up, amplify, boost
6 *The number of cars on the roads continues to **increase**.*
grow, mount, go up, rise, soar, build up, escalate, multiply

incredible *adjective*
1 *Do you expect us to believe that **incredible** story?*
unbelievable, unlikely, improbable, far-fetched, absurd, implausible
OPPOSITE credible
2 *The Forth Bridge is an **incredible** feat of engineering.*
extraordinary, amazing, astounding, magnificent, marvellous, spectacular

independent *adjective*
1 *My granny is a very **independent** person.*
free, liberated, self-sufficient, self-reliant
OPPOSITE dependent
2 *Luxembourg is an **independent** country.*
autonomous, self-governing
3 *We need an **independent** opinion on the matter.*
impartial, neutral, objective, unbiased
OPPOSITE biased

indifferent *adjective*
1 *I felt **indifferent** as I watched the game.*
uninterested, detached, uncaring, unenthusiastic, unmoved, uninvolved, unconcerned
OPPOSITE enthusiastic
2 *The food in the restaurant was **indifferent**.*
mediocre, ordinary, unexciting, average
OPPOSITE excellent

indignant *adjective*
*The player was **indignant** when he was sent off.*
annoyed, angry, cross, affronted, offended, outraged, piqued

indirect *adjective*
*The bus took an **indirect** route into town.*
roundabout, winding, meandering, rambling, zigzag
OPPOSITE direct

individual *adjective*
*Her singing has an **individual** style.*
characteristic, distinct, distinctive, special, unique, personal, singular

inevitable *adjective*
*If it rains, it is **inevitable** that the pitch will get wet.*
certain, sure, definite, unavoidable, inescapable

infect *verb*
*A virus may have **infected** the water supply.*
contaminate, pollute, poison

infection *noun*
*The **infection** spread rapidly.*
disease, virus, contagion, contamination

infectious *adjective*
*Chickenpox is highly **infectious**.*
contagious, catching

inferior *adjective*
1 *The clothes were of **inferior** quality.*
poor, bad, second-rate, mediocre, cheap, shoddy
2 *Officers can give orders to those of **inferior** rank.*
lesser, lower, junior, subordinate

infinite *adjective*
*You need **infinite** patience to train a puppy.*
endless, limitless, unlimited, boundless, never-ending, unending, inexhaustible
OPPOSITE finite

influence *noun*
*Rock music had a big **influence** on her life.*
effect, impact, power, dominance, guidance, authority, control

influence *verb*
*The money he was offered **influenced** his decision.*
affect, have an effect on, direct, guide, control, motivate

inform *verb*
*Please **inform** us if you move house.*
tell, let you know, notify, advise

informal *adjective*
1 *The party will be a very **informal** event.*
casual, relaxed, easygoing, friendly, homely, natural
2 *Emails are usually written in an **informal** style.*
colloquial, familiar, chatty, personal

information *noun*
*There is more **information** on our website.*
details, particulars, facts, data, advice, guidance, knowledge, (*informal*) info

inhabit *verb*
*People **inhabited** the caves thousands of years ago.*
live in, occupy, dwell in, reside in, populate, settle in

initiative *noun*
*You must use your **initiative** on the treasure hunt.*
resourcefulness, inventiveness, originality, enterprise

injure *verb*
*Was anyone **injured** in the accident?*
hurt, harm, wound
To injure someone causing permanent damage is to **maim** them.

innocent *adjective*
1 *The jury found the man **innocent**.*
guiltless, blameless, free from blame
OPPOSITE guilty
2 *Baby tigers look so **innocent**.*
angelic, harmless, faultless, virtuous, pure, simple, inexperienced, naïve
OPPOSITE wicked

inquire *verb*
to inquire into
*Detectives are **inquiring into** the robbery.*
look into, investigate, examine, explore

insane *adjective*
1 *It was rumoured that the king had gone **insane**.*
mentally ill, mad, crazy, deranged, demented, disturbed, unhinged, (*informal*) off your head, out of your mind
OPPOSITE sane
2 *It would be **insane** to swim in the sea in January!*
crazy, mad, daft, senseless, stupid, foolish, idiotic
OPPOSITE sensible, wise

⭐ WORD WEB

insect *noun*
SOME TYPES OF INSECT
ant, aphid, bee, beetle, bluebottle, bumble-bee, butterfly, cicada, cockroach, crane fly or daddy-long-legs, cricket, dragonfly, earwig, firefly, flea, fly, glow-worm, gnat, grasshopper, greenfly, hornet, horsefly, ladybird, locust, louse, mantis, mayfly, midge, mosquito, moth, stick insect, termite, tsetse fly, wasp, weevil

LIFE STAGES OF SOME INSECTS
caterpillar, chrysalis, grub, larva, maggot, pupa

PARTS OF INSECTS' BODIES
head, thorax, abdomen, antennae, legs, wings

SOME CREATURES SIMILAR TO INSECTS
centipede, earthworm, mite, slug, spider, woodlouse, worm

insensitive adjective
I'm sorry if my comments were **insensitive**.
thoughtless, tactless, unfeeling, uncaring, unsympathetic, callous
OPPOSITE sensitive

inside noun
The **inside** of the nest was lined with feathers.
interior, inner surface, centre, core, heart, middle
OPPOSITE outside

insignificant adjective
The author made a few **insignificant** changes.
unimportant, minor, trivial, negligible, slight, meaningless
OPPOSITE significant

insincere adjective
The butler welcomed us with an **insincere** smile.
false, pretended, hypocritical, dishonest, deceitful, deceptive, lying
(informal) two-faced
OPPOSITE sincere

insist verb
Griselda **insisted** that she was not a witch.
declare, state, assert, maintain, stress, emphasise, swear, vow, claim
to insist on
The magician **insisted on** silence before he began.
demand, require

inspect verb
They **inspected** the damage done by the storm.
check, examine, investigate, look over, study, survey, scrutinise

inspire verb
The crowd **inspired** the team to play well.
motivate, prompt, stimulate, encourage, stir, arouse, spur on

instant adjective
Gardeners don't expect **instant** results.
immediate, quick, rapid, fast, prompt, snappy, speedy, swift, direct

instant noun
The shooting star was gone in an **instant**.
moment, second, split second, flash
(informal) tick, jiffy

instinct noun
The detective always followed his own **instincts**.
impulse, inclination, intuition, hunch, feeling, urge

instruct verb
1 All the staff are **instructed** in first aid.
teach, train, coach, tutor
2 The police officer **instructed** the cars to wait.
tell, order, direct, command

instructions plural noun
Please follow the **instructions** carefully.
directions, guidelines, orders, commands

instrument noun
Dentists use special **instruments** to check your teeth.
tool, implement, utensil, appliance, device, gadget, contraption

insult verb
He was **insulted** not to be invited to the wedding.
offend, outrage, be rude to, hurt, injure, slight, snub

insult noun
It is considered an **insult** to refuse a gift.
rudeness, offence, affront, slight, slur, snub

insulting adjective
She made an **insulting** comment about my clothes.
offensive, rude, impolite, derogatory, scornful
OPPOSITE complimentary

intelligent adjective
The aliens from Planet Zog are highly **intelligent**.
clever, bright, smart, quick, sharp, perceptive, shrewd, able, brilliant, rational, thinking
(informal) brainy
OPPOSITE unintelligent, stupid

intense adjective
1 I felt a sudden, **intense** pain in my chest.
extreme, acute, severe, sharp, great, strong, violent
OPPOSITE slight, mild
2 The contest aroused **intense** feelings.
deep, passionate, powerful, strong, profound
OPPOSITE mild

interest verb
Politics doesn't **interest** me at all.
appeal to, stimulate, attract, capture your imagination, excite, fascinate, absorb
OPPOSITE bore

interest noun
1 The dog showed no **interest** in the bone.
curiosity, attention, concern, involvement
2 The information was of no **interest** to anyone.
importance, significance, consequence, value

3 My **interests** include judo and playing the trombone.
hobby, pastime, pursuit, activity, diversion

interesting adjective
Everyone wanted to hear about our **interesting** adventures.
fascinating, absorbing, enthralling, intriguing, engrossing, stimulating, riveting, gripping, entertaining diverting
OPPOSITE boring, dull

interfere verb
to interfere in
Don't **interfere in** other people's affairs.
intervene in, intrude in, meddle in, pry into, encroach on, butt in on
to interfere with
The bad weather **interfered with** our plans.
hamper, hinder, get in the way of, obstruct

international adjective
Interpol is an **international** police organisation.
global, worldwide, intercontinental

interrupt verb
1 Please don't **interrupt** while I am speaking.
intervene, interject, break in, butt in, cut in
2 Heavy rain **interrupted** the tennis match.
stop, suspend, disrupt, break off, cut short

interruption noun
He wrote for an hour without any **interruption**.
break, pause, stop, gap, halt, disruption, suspension

interval noun
1 There will be a short **interval** after the first act.
break, pause, wait, delay, lapse, lull
Another word for an interval in a play or film is **interlude** or **intermission**.
An interval in a meeting is a **recess**.

a b c d e f g h i j k l m n o p q r s t u v w x y z

An interval when you take a rest is a **breather** or **breathing space**.
2 There were signs at regular **intervals** along the road.
space, gap, distance

interview verb
He **interviewed** the author about her new book.
question, talk to, interrogate, examine

intimate adjective
1 They have been **intimate** friends for years.
close, cherished, dear, friendly, informal
OPPOSITE distant
2 The newspaper printed **intimate** details about her life.
personal, private, confidential, secret

intriguing adjective
The results of the experiment are **intriguing**.
interesting, attractive, fascinating, captivating, beguiling

introduce verb
1 Let me **introduce** you to my friend.
present, make known
2 The director stood up to **introduce** the film.
give an introduction to, announce, lead into
3 They are **introducing** a new bus service next year.
set up, start, begin, create, establish, initiate, bring in

introduction noun
Something which happens as an introduction to a bigger event is a **prelude**.
An introduction to a book is a **preface**.
An introduction to a play is a **prologue**.
A piece played as an introduction to a concert or opera is an **overture**.

invade verb
The Vikings **invaded** many parts of Europe.
attack, enter, occupy, overrun, march into, raid

invent verb
James Dewar **invented** the thermos flask.
create, devise, think up, conceive, design, originate

inventor noun
James Dewar was the **inventor** of the thermos flask.
creator, designer, originator, discoverer

investigate verb
Police are **investigating** the cause of the accident.
examine, explore, inquire into, look into, study, consider, follow up, probe, research, scrutinise
(informal) go into

investigation noun
An **investigation** showed how the accident happened.
examination, inquiry, inspection, study, review, survey

invisible adjective
The wizard was **invisible** when he wore his magic cloak.
out of sight, unseen, unnoticed, hidden, concealed, covered, obscured, camouflaged, disguised, undetectable, unnoticeable, inconspicuous
OPPOSITE visible

invite verb
Our neighbours **invited** us round for tea.
ask, request your company, welcome, summon

involve verb
1 My job **involves** a lot of travel.
include, comprise, require, demand, necessitate, mean
2 Protecting the environment **involves** us all.
affect, concern, interest, touch

involved adjective
1 The film has a long and **involved** plot.
complex, complicated, elaborate, intricate, confusing, difficult, convoluted
OPPOSITE simple
2 Are you **involved** in the theatre?
concerned, participating, engaged, caught up, mixed up

irregular adjective
1 The bricks were arranged in an **irregular** pattern.
varying, erratic, haphazard, random, unpredictable, fitful
OPPOSITE regular
2 It is highly **irregular** to eat pizza with a spoon!
abnormal, unusual, exceptional, unconventional, improper
OPPOSITE normal

irresponsible adjective
It's **irresponsible** to drive too fast.
reckless, rash, thoughtless, inconsiderate, uncaring, unthinking, negligent
OPPOSITE responsible

irritable adjective
After a bad night, he woke in an **irritable** mood.
bad-tempered, grumpy, short-tempered, cross, impatient, snappy, touchy, testy, prickly, peevish
(informal) stroppy, shirty
OPPOSITE good-humoured, cheerful

irritate verb
The noise from next door began to **irritate** me.
annoy, bother, exasperate, anger, provoke, madden, vex
(informal) get on your nerves, bug

isolated adjective
They sheltered in an **isolated** cave in the mountains.
remote, out-of-the-way, secluded, outlying, inaccessible, cut off, deserted
OPPOSITE accessible

issue verb
1 They **issued** blankets to the refugees.
give out, distribute, supply
2 They have **issued** a new set of stamps.
bring out, put out, produce, publish, release, circulate, print
3 Green smoke **issued** from the dragon's nostrils.
come out, emerge, appear, flow out, gush, erupt

issue noun
1 The new **issue** of the magazine comes out this week.
edition, number, instalment, copy
2 They print stories about local **issues** in the magazine.
matter, subject, topic, affair, concern, question, problem

itch noun
1 I had an annoying **itch** on my foot.
tickle, tingling, prickle
2 Olga had a great **itch** to travel.
desire, longing, urge, wish, yearning, ache, impulse

item noun
1 I bought a few **items** in the jumble sale.
thing, object, article
2 There was an **item** about our school in the paper.
article, piece, report, feature

jab *verb*
*A passer-by **jabbed** me in the ribs.*
poke, prod, elbow, nudge, stab, thrust

jagged *adjective*
*This dinosaur had **jagged** teeth.*
rough, uneven, ragged, spiky,
toothed, serrated
OPPOSITE smooth

jam *noun*
1 *We got stuck in a **jam** on the
motorway.*
traffic jam, hold-up, tailback,
blockage
2 (*informal*) *I'm in a bit of a **jam**.*
difficulty, mess, predicament, plight
(*informal*) fix, tight corner

jam *verb*
1 *Someone had **jammed** the door
open.*
prop, wedge, stick
2 *The roads are **jammed** at rush
hour.*
block, clog, obstruct, congest
(*informal*) bung up
3 *I **jammed** my things into a
backpack.*
cram, pack, stuff, squeeze, squash,
crush, ram, crowd

jangle *verb*
*Silver bracelets **jangled** on her wrists.*
jingle, chink, clink, tinkle

jealous *adjective*
*Cinderella's sisters were **jealous**
of her beauty.*
envious, resentful, grudging

jeer *verb*
*Some of the audience whistled and
jeered.*
boo, hiss, sneer, taunt, mock, scoff,
ridicule
OPPOSITE cheer

jerk *verb*
*The rider **jerked** on the horse's reins.*
pull, tug, yank, pluck, wrench, tweak

jerky *adjective*
*The stagecoach drew to a **jerky** halt.*
jolting, jumpy, shaky, bouncy,
bumpy, uneven
OPPOSITE steady

jet *noun*
*A **jet** of water shot high in the
air.*
spout, spurt, squirt, gush, stream,
fountain

jingle *verb*
*Some coins **jingled** in his back
pocket.*
jangle, chink, clink, tinkle

job *noun*
1 *My sister wants a **job** as a TV reporter.*
post, position, profession, occupation,
employment, trade, work, career
The job you particularly want to do is
your **mission** or **vocation**.
2 *Whose **job** is it to do the washing-
up?*
duty, task, assignment, chore, errand

jog *verb*
1 *He **jogs** round the park every
morning.*
go jogging, run, trot
2 *A boy sitting next to me **jogged**
my elbow.*
nudge, prod, jolt, knock, bump, jar,
jostle
3 *The photograph may **jog** her
memory.*
prompt, stir, arouse, set off, stimulate

join *verb*
1 *Our families **joined** together to
buy the present.*
combine, come together, merge,
unite, amalgamate
OPPOSITE separate
2 *Join one piece of rope to the other.*
connect, fasten, attach, fix, link, put
together, tack on
OPPOSITE detach
3 *The two roads **join** here.*
meet, merge, converge
OPPOSITE divide
4 *I **joined** the crowd going into the
cinema.*
follow, go with, tag along with
OPPOSITE leave
5 *We have **joined** a local sports club.*
become a member of, enrol in, sign
up for
To join the army is to **enlist**.
OPPOSITE leave, resign from

join *noun*
*If you look hard, you can still see
the **join**.*
joint, connection, link, mend, seam

joint *adjective*
*The preparation of the meal was a
joint effort.*
combined, shared, common,
communal, cooperative, united,
collective, mutual
OPPOSITE individual

joke *noun*
*Do you know any good **jokes**?*
jest, quip, crack, witticism, wisecrack
(*informal*) gag

joke *verb*
*Those two are always laughing and
joking.*
jest, clown, have a laugh, make jokes

jolly *adjective*
*We had a **jolly** time on holiday.*
cheerful, merry, happy, joyful,
pleasant, enjoyable
OPPOSITE gloomy

jolt *verb*
*The car **jolted** over the bumps in the
road.*
jerk, jog, bump, bounce, shake,
shudder

journey *noun*
*On their **journey**, the astronauts will
pass the Moon.*
voyage, trip, expedition, travels, tour,
route

joy *noun*
*I remember the sheer **joy** of scoring
a goal!*
happiness, joyfulness, delight,
cheerfulness, gladness, mirth, glee,
jubilation, gaiety, rejoicing, bliss,
ecstasy, elation
OPPOSITE sorrow

joyful *adjective*
*The wedding was a **joyful** occasion.*
happy, cheerful, merry, joyous, jolly,
jovial, good-humoured
OPPOSITE sad

judge *verb*
1 *The umpire **judged** that the ball
was out.*
rule, decide, decree, adjudicate
2 *Who's **judging** the flower show
this year?*
decide on, assess, evaluate, appraise
3 *He **judged** the coin to be about
1000 years old.*
reckon, suppose, consider, gauge,
guess, estimate

judgement *noun*
1 *What is the **judgement** of the
court?*
decision, finding, ruling, verdict,
decree
2 *His comments show a lack of
judgement.*
wisdom, common sense,
understanding, discrimination
3 *In my **judgement**, you're making
a big mistake.*
opinion, view, belief, assessment,
estimate

jumble *noun*
*There was a **jumble** of clothes on the
floor.*
mess, muddle, clutter, chaos,
confusion, disorder

jumble *verb*
*Please don't **jumble** the pages.*
muddle, mix up, mess up,
disorganise, shuffle
OPPOSITE arrange

jump *verb*
1 *Suddenly a rabbit **jumped** in front
of us.*
leap, spring, bound, bounce, hop
When a cat jumps it **pounces**.
2 *All the horses **jumped** the first
hurdle.*
leap over, vault, clear

a
b
c
d
e
f
g
h
i
j
k
l
m
n
o
p
q
r
s
t
u
v
w
x
y
z

A

3 *The loud bang made them all jump.*
start, flinch, jolt

jump *noun*
With a jump, the grasshopper landed on the leaf.
leap, spring, bound, vault, hop

junk *noun*
The garage is full of old junk.
rubbish, clutter, garbage, jumble, trash, waste, scrap, odds and ends

just *adjective*
It was a just punishment, considering the crime.
fair, fitting, appropriate, deserved, proper, reasonable, justified
OPPOSITE unjust, unfair

Kk

keen *adjective*
1 *Rhona is a keen hockey player.*
enthusiastic, eager, fervent, avid, devoted, committed, motivated
A common simile is **as keen as mustard**.
OPPOSITE unenthusiastic
2 *A carving knife should have a keen edge.*
sharp, razor-sharp, cutting
OPPOSITE blunt
3 *Owls must have keen eyesight.*
sharp, acute, piercing
OPPOSITE poor
4 *A keen wind was blowing from the east.*
bitter, cold, icy, penetrating
OPPOSITE mild

keep *verb*
1 *Let's keep the rest of the cake for later.*
save, conserve, preserve, retain, hang on to, hold on to, guard, store
2 *Please keep still.*
stay, remain
3 *A man in the audience kept coughing.*
persist in, go on, carry on, continue
4 *You're late. What kept you?*
delay, detain, hold up, keep waiting
5 *Where do you keep the knives and forks?*
store, house, put, stow
6 *Will the milk keep until tomorrow?*
last, be usable, stay good
7 *It costs money to keep a pet.*
support, maintain, provide for, pay for
to keep something up
Keep up the good work!
carry on, continue, maintain

key *noun*
Have you found the key to the riddle?
answer, solution, explanation, clue

kick *noun*
1 *He gave the television a kick.*
hit, boot, blow
2 *(informal) Some people might get a kick out of crossing the Atlantic in an old bath.*
thrill, excitement, (informal) buzz

kick *verb*
1 *Merv kicked the ball out.*
boot, hit, drive, send, punt, heel
2 *(informal) I kicked my bad habit.*
give up, quit, break, abandon, cease, desist from

kidnap *verb*
In the story, a boy is kidnapped by bandits.
abduct, capture, seize, carry off, snatch

kill *verb*
A person was killed in the explosion.
(informal) bump off, do away with (old use) slay
To kill someone deliberately is to **murder** them.
To kill large numbers of people is to **massacre** or **slaughter** them.
To kill someone as a punishment is to **execute** them or **put them to death**.
To kill someone for political reasons is to **assassinate** them.

kind *noun*
What kind of music do you like to play?
sort, type, variety, style, category, class, set

kind *adjective*
It was very kind of you to help me.
kind-hearted, caring, good-natured, kindly, affectionate, warm, genial, loving, sweet, gentle, lenient, amiable, friendly, generous, sympathetic, thoughtful, obliging, considerate, understanding, compassionate, unselfish, giving, gracious, merciful, benevolent, charitable, humane, neighbourly
OPPOSITE unkind

kit *noun*
I've forgotten my games kit.
gear, outfit, equipment, paraphernalia, tools, tackle

knack *noun*
George has a knack for taking photographs.
skill, talent, gift, flair

★ **WORD WEB**

knight *noun*
THINGS A MEDIEVAL KNIGHT MIGHT WEAR OR CARRY
armour, baldric (leather belt), coat of arms, falcon or hawk, lance, mace (metal club), pennant, shield, surcoat, sword, tabard, tunic

A fight between knights on horseback was a *joust*.
A series of sporting contests between knights was a *tournament*.
A boy training to be a knight was first a *page* and then a *squire*.
An expedition made by a knight was a *quest*.

knock *verb*
I knocked my head as I came out of the car.
bump, bang, hit, strike, thump
(*informal*) bash

knot *verb*
The sailors knotted the two ropes together.
tie, bind, fasten, join, entwine, lash
OPPOSITE untie

know *verb*
1 *Do you know how to mend a puncture?*
understand, have knowledge of, comprehend
2 *As soon as she saw the unicorn, she knew what it was.*
recognise, realise, appreciate, be aware of
3 *Do you know Stewart well?*
be acquainted with, be familiar with, be a friend of

knowledge *noun*
1 *She has a good knowledge of Italian.*
understanding, grasp, command, familiarity (with)
2 *An encyclopedia contains a lot of knowledge.*
information, data, facts, learning, know-how, wisdom, scholarship

label *noun*
The washing instructions are on the label.
tag, ticket, sticker

lack *noun*
The judge dismissed the case because of a lack of evidence.
absence, shortage, scarcity, want
A general lack of food is a famine.
A general lack of water is a drought.
OPPOSITE abundance

lack *verb*
The game lacked excitement.
be short of, be without, want, need, require, miss

lag *verb*
One runner was lagging behind the others.
straggle, trail, fall behind, drop behind, dawdle, linger, loiter

lake *noun*
We rowed across the lake.
pond, pool
(*Scottish*) loch
A salt-water lake is a lagoon.

A lake used to supply water is a reservoir.

land *noun*
1 *The castle is surrounded by several acres of land.*
grounds, estate, property
2 *The land here is good for growing strawberries.*
ground, soil, earth
3 *China is a land with an ancient history.*
country, nation, state, region, territory

land *verb*
1 *The plane landed exactly on time.*
touch down, arrive
OPPOSITE take off
2 *The ship will land at Dover.*
dock, berth, come ashore
3 *How did these papers land on my desk?*
arrive, turn up, end up, wind up, settle

landscape *noun*
We sat on the hill and admired the landscape.
countryside, scenery, view, scene, outlook, prospect

lap *noun*
1 *My cat, Snowy, likes to sit on my lap.*
knees, thighs
2 *The cars were on the last lap of the race.*
circuit, round, loop

large *adjective*
1 *Elephants are large animals.*
big, huge, enormous, colossal, giant, gigantic, immense, great, massive, bulky, heavy, hefty, weighty, mighty, towering
(*informal*) whopping, ginormous
2 *The cook gave me a large helping of pudding.*
ample, generous, plentiful, abundant, lavish
3 *Is this room large enough for dancing in?*
spacious, roomy, sizeable
4 *The gales caused damage over a large area.*
wide, broad, extensive, widespread, vast
5 *The meeting was attended by a large number of people.*
considerable, substantial

last *adjective*
1 *Z is the last letter of the alphabet.*
final, closing, concluding, terminating, ultimate
OPPOSITE first
2 *Did you see the last Harry Potter film?*
latest, most recent
OPPOSITE next

last *noun*
at last
The holidays are here at last!
finally, eventually, in the end

late *adjective*
1 *The bus is late.*
delayed, overdue
OPPOSITE early, punctual, on time
2 *Mr Pettigrew showed us a portrait of his late wife.*
dead, deceased, departed, former

lately *adverb*
There has been a lot of snow lately.
recently, latterly, of late

later *adverb*
I'm busy now, but I'll phone you later.
afterwards, in a while, subsequently, next

laugh *verb*
1 *The children laughed when the clown fell over.*
chuckle, chortle, giggle, titter, burst out laughing, roar or scream with laughter, roll or fall about laughing, guffaw
(*informal*) have hysterics, be in stitches
2 *It's rude to laugh at his way of singing.*
make fun of, mock, ridicule, scoff at, tease, deride

laughter *noun*
We heard bursts of laughter coming from the kitchen.
laughing, amusement, hilarity, mirth, merriment

lavish *adjective*
The king put on a lavish feast for his birthday.
generous, extravagant, sumptuous, luxurious, opulent, grand, abundant, copious, plentiful, bountiful
OPPOSITE meagre, paltry

law *noun*
A law passed by parliament is an act.
A proposed law to be discussed by parliament is a bill.
The laws of a game are regulations or rules.
A regulation which must be obeyed is a commandment, decree, edict or order.

lay *verb*
1 *He laid the parchment carefully on his desk.*
put down, set down, place, position, spread, deposit, leave
2 *Please lay the table for dinner.*
set out, arrange

layer *noun*
1 *The walls needed two layers of paint.*
coat, coating, covering, thickness, film, sheet, skin

a b c d e f g h i j k l m n o p q r s t u v w x y z

2 *You can see various* **layers** *of rock in the cliff.*
seam, stratum

laze *verb*
We spent the day **lazing** *in the garden.*
be lazy, idle, loaf, lounge, lie about, relax, loll

lazy *adjective*
My **lazy** *little brother stayed in bed all day!*
idle, inactive, lethargic, slack, slothful, indolent
An informal name for a lazy person is **lazybones**.

lead *verb*
1 *The rescuers* **led** *the climbers to safety.*
guide, conduct, escort, usher, steer, pilot, shepherd
OPPOSITE follow
2 *Dr Martez will* **lead** *the expedition to Peru.*
be in charge of, direct, command, head, manage, supervise
3 *The British cyclist* **led** *from the start of the race.*
be in front, be in the lead, head the field
4 *The animals in the zoo* **lead** *a peaceful life.*
have, pass, spend, experience

lead *noun*
1 *The team followed the captain's* **lead**.
example, guidance, leadership, direction
2 *The Australian swimmer is in the* **lead**.
first place, front position
3 *Don't trip over the electrical* **lead**.
cable, flex, wire

leader *noun*
The **leader** *of the pirates was Captain Cutlass.*
head, chief, commander, ruler, captain, director, principal
(informal) boss
The leader of a group of wrongdoers is the **ringleader**.

leak *verb*
1 *The juice had* **leaked** *all over my schoolbag.*
escape, drip, seep, ooze, trickle
2 *Details of a secret plan were* **leaked** *to the newspaper.*
reveal, disclose, make known, pass on, give away, let out

lean *verb*
1 *I* **leaned** *against the wall.*
recline, rest, prop yourself, support yourself
2 *The yacht* **leaned** *to one side in the wind.*
slope, tilt, tip, incline, slant, list, bank

leap *verb*
The dog **leaped** *in the air to catch the ball.*
jump, spring, bound, vault

learn *verb*
1 *We are* **learning** *about the Vikings this term.*
discover, find out, gather, grasp, pick up
2 *I've got to* **learn** *the words of this song.*
learn by heart, memorise, master

learner *noun*
This swimming class is for **learners** *only.*
beginner, starter, novice
Someone learning things at school or college is a **pupil** or **student**.
Someone learning a trade is an **apprentice** or **trainee**.

leave *verb*
1 *Do you have to* **leave** *now?*
go, go away, depart, withdraw, take your leave, go out, set off, say goodbye
(informal) take off, disappear
OPPOSITE arrive
2 *The doctor* **left** *the room in a hurry.*
exit, go out of, depart from, quit, vacate
OPPOSITE enter
3 *Don't* **leave** *me here on my own!*
abandon, desert, forsake
4 *The crew* **left** *the sinking ship.*
evacuate, get out of
5 *My sister has* **left** *her job at the bank.*
give up, quit, resign from
(informal) walk out of
6 **Leave** *the milk bottles by the front door.*
place, position, put down, set down, deposit
7 *Lady Bigwig* **left** *all her money to charity.*
bequeath, hand down, will, endow

lecture *noun*
1 *There is a* **lecture** *about dinosaurs at the museum today.*
talk, lesson, speech, address
2 *The teacher gave us a* **lecture** *on how to behave.*
reprimand, warning
(informal) telling off

ledge *noun*
The climbers rested on a **ledge** *of rock.*
shelf, projection
A ledge under a window is a **windowsill**.

leg *noun*
1 *Boris fell and bruised his* **leg**.
For parts of your body, see **body**.
2 *The rowers completed the first* **leg** *of the race.*
part, stage, section, phase, stretch

legal *adjective*
Is it **legal** *to park here on Sundays?*
lawful, legitimate, permissible, permitted, allowed
OPPOSITE illegal

legend *noun*
I like reading **legends** *about ancient heroes.*
myth, story, folk tale, fairy tale, fable, tradition

leisure *noun*
Grandad has plenty of **leisure** *since he retired.*
free time, spare time, relaxation, recreation, rest

lend *verb*
Can you **lend** *me some money until the weekend?*
loan, advance, let you have
OPPOSITE borrow

length *noun*
1 *My heart sank when I saw the* **length** *of the queue.*
extent, size
2 *We only had to wait a short* **length** *of time.*
space, period, stretch

lengthen *verb*
1 *Is it possible to* **lengthen** *these curtains?*
extend, make longer, increase, stretch
2 *The days* **lengthen** *in spring.*
draw out, get longer, stretch out

lenient *adjective*
The teacher was **lenient** *and let us off.*
easygoing, soft-hearted, tolerant, forgiving, indulgent, kind, merciful
OPPOSITE strict

lesson *noun*
My piano **lesson** *is on Friday afternoon.*
class, period, tutorial, instruction

let *verb*
1 *Abby's parents **let** her go to the party.*
allow, give permission to, permit, consent to, agree to
OPPOSITE forbid
2 *Our friends are **letting** their house for the summer.*
lease, rent out, hire out

lethal *adjective*
*This bottle contains a **lethal** potion.*
deadly, fatal, mortal, poisonous

level *adjective*
1 *You need a **level** field for playing rounders.*
even, flat, horizontal, smooth
OPPOSITE uneven
2 *At half-time the scores were **level**.*
equal, even, the same, matching
(*informal*) neck-and-neck

level *noun*
1 *The water had reached a high **level**.*
height
2 *The lift takes you up to the sixth **level**.*
floor, storey, tier
3 *What **level** have you reached in judo?*
grade, standard, stage, rank, degree

lid *noun*
*Can you help me get the **lid** off this jar?*
cap, cover, covering, top

lie *noun*
*He accused the newspaper of printing **lies**.*
deceit, falsehood, dishonesty
(*informal*) fib
OPPOSITE truth

lie *verb*
1 *It's twelve o'clock and he's still **lying** in bed!*
recline, stretch out, lounge, sprawl, rest
To lie face down is to be **prone**.
To lie face upwards is to be **supine**.
2 *The castle **lies** in a valley.*
be sited, be situated, be located, be found
3 *I don't trust her—I think she's **lying**.*
deceive someone, bluff
(*informal*) fib

life *noun*
1 *My hamster, Fluffy, leads a very easy **life**.*
existence, being, way of life
2 *Our **lives** depended on finding water.*
survival
3 *You seem to be full of **life** today!*
energy, liveliness, vigour, vitality, spirit, sprightliness, animation
4 *I'm reading a **life** of Elvis Presley.*
life story, autobiography, biography

lift *verb*
1 *The removal men **lifted** the piano carefully.*
pick up, raise, elevate, pull up, hoist
2 *The plane **lifted** off the ground.*
rise, ascend, soar

✏ **WRITING TIPS**

light

light *noun*
You can use these words to describe **light**.
TO DESCRIBE *HOW LIGHT APPEARS*
bright, brilliant, harsh, luminous, lustrous, strong; diffused, dim, muted, soft, warm

LIGHT MAY:
beam, blaze, dazzle, flash, flicker, glare, gleam, glimmer, glint, glisten, glitter, glow, shimmer, shine, sparkle, twinkle

light *adjective*
1 *The artist worked in a **light** and airy studio.*
bright, well-lit, illuminated
OPPOSITE dim, gloomy
2 *She was wearing **light** blue jeans.*
pale
OPPOSITE dark
3 *The parcel looks big, but it is quite **light**.*
lightweight, portable, weightless, slight
A common simile is **as light as a feather**.
OPPOSITE heavy
4 *A **light** wind rippled the surface of the water.*
gentle, faint, slight
OPPOSITE strong
5 *We had a **light** meal before we went out.*
small, modest, simple, insubstantial
OPPOSITE heavy, substantial

light *verb*
1 *We **lit** the candles on my birthday cake.*
ignite, kindle, set alight, set fire to, switch on
OPPOSITE extinguish
2 *The fireworks **lit** the sky.*
light up, brighten, illuminate, shed light on, shine on
OPPOSITE darken

like *verb*
1 *Lauren **likes** her new puppy more than anything.*
admire, adore, be attached to, be fond of, care for, cherish, esteem, hold dear, love
(*informal*) have a soft spot for
2 *Alex **likes** chocolate cake very much. What sort of films do you **like**?*
appreciate, be interested in, be keen on, be partial to, delight in, enjoy, prefer, relish
OPPOSITE dislike

likely *adjective*
*It's **likely** that the shop will be closed tomorrow.*
probable, expected, anticipated, predictable, foreseeable
OPPOSITE unlikely

limit *noun*
1 *There is a **limit** of twenty pupils for this class.*
maximum, restriction, threshold, ceiling, cut-off point
A limit on time is a **deadline** or **time limit**.
2 *The fence marks the **limit** of the school grounds.*
border, boundary, edge, perimeter, frontier

limit *verb*
*I had to **limit** the invitations to my party.*
put a limit on, restrict, control, ration

limp *adjective*
*The leaves on the plant are looking **limp**.*
drooping, floppy, sagging, wilting, soft, flabby, slack
OPPOSITE rigid

line *noun*
1 *I drew a pencil **line** across the page.*
stroke, rule, underline, stripe, streak, band, bar, dash
A line that is cut into a surface is a **groove**, **score** or **scratch**.
A line on a person's skin is a **wrinkle**.
A deep groove or wrinkle is a **furrow**.
A line on fabric is a **crease**
2 *There was a long **line** of people waiting at the bus stop.*
queue, row, file, column, rank, procession, chain
A line of police officers forming a barrier is a **cordon**.
A line of schoolchildren walking in pairs is a **crocodile**.
3 *The clothes were drying on the washing **line**.*
cord, rope, string, thread, wire, cable, flex, lead

a b c d e f g h i j k l m n o p q r s t u v w x y z

linger verb
1 *The smell of burning wood lingered in the air.*
continue, remain, stay, last, persist
OPPOSITE disappear
2 *Don't linger outside in this cold weather.*
hang about, wait about, loiter, dawdle, dally, delay
OPPOSITE hurry

link noun
The two schools have close links with each other.
relationship, association, connection, bond, tie

link verb
They linked the trailer to the tractor.
attach, connect, fasten, join, couple
OPPOSITE separate

list noun
A list of people's names is a *roll* or *register*.
A list of people who have tasks to do is a *rota*.
A list of books in the library or of goods for sale is a *catalogue*.
A list of topics mentioned in a book is an *index*.
A list of things to choose from is a *menu*.
A list of things to do or remember is a *checklist*.

list verb
I helped to list the books in the library.
record, write down, catalogue, index, register

listen verb
to listen to something
The spy listened carefully to the instructions.
pay attention to, take notice of, attend to, heed
To listen secretly to a private conversation is to *eavesdrop*.

litter noun
The street was covered with litter.
rubbish, waste, refuse, garbage, junk, clutter, mess, odds and ends

little adjective
1 *The camera is so little it will fit in your pocket.*
compact, mini, miniature, minute, petite, small, tiny
(*informal*) teeny (*Scottish*) wee
OPPOSITE big, large
2 *My granny lived in India when she was little.*
small, young
OPPOSITE big, old

live adjective
The fishermen caught a live octopus in their nets.
alive, living, breathing
OPPOSITE dead

live verb
Will these plants live through the winter?
stay alive, survive, exist, flourish, last, continue, remain
OPPOSITE die

lively adjective
1 *The toddlers were in a lively mood.*
active, energetic, animated, spirited, boisterous, excited, vivacious, sprightly, frisky, chirpy, perky
OPPOSITE inactive
2 *The city centre is always lively at night.*
busy, bustling, crowded, exciting, buzzing
OPPOSITE quiet, dead

living adjective
1 *Miss Millicent had no living relatives.*
alive
OPPOSITE dead
2 *There are no dinosaurs still living.*
existing, surviving
OPPOSITE extinct

living noun
1 *He makes a living from painting.*
income, livelihood
2 *What does she do for a living?*
job, occupation, profession, trade, career

load noun
1 *Camels can carry heavy loads.*
burden, weight
2 *The lorry delivered its load to the supermarket.*
cargo, consignment, goods, freight

load verb
1 *We loaded the suitcases into the car.*
pack, pile, heap, stow
2 *He arrived loaded with shopping bags.*
weigh down, burden, saddle

loathe verb
My brother loathes the colour pink.
hate, detest, dislike, despise
OPPOSITE love, adore

local adjective
Our local shop delivers newspapers.
neighbourhood, nearby, neighbouring

lock noun
1 *There was a heavy lock on the lid of the chest.*
fastening, clasp, padlock, bolt, latch
2 *The princess cut a lock from her hair.*
tress, curl, tuft

lock verb
Make sure you lock the door when you go out.
fasten, secure, bolt, close, shut, seal

logical adjective
The robot always gave a logical answer.
rational, reasonable, sensible, sound, valid, intelligent, clear, lucid, methodical, systematic
OPPOSITE illogical

lone adjective
A lone rider galloped past.
single, solitary, unaccompanied, isolated

lonely adjective
1 *Cara felt lonely while her friends were away.*
alone, friendless, lonesome, solitary, abandoned, neglected, forlorn, forsaken
2 *The climbers sheltered in a lonely hut.*
deserted, isolated, remote, secluded, out-of-the-way

long adjective
It seemed a long time before the bus came.
lengthy, prolonged, extended, extensive, long-lasting
OPPOSITE short

long verb
to long for something
I'm longing for a drink.
yearn for, crave, want, wish for, desire, fancy, hunger for, pine for, hanker after, itch for
(*informal*) be dying for

look verb
1 *If you look carefully, you'll see an owl in the tree.*
watch, observe, view, regard, keep your eyes open
2 *My pet snake looks a bit hungry.*
appear, seem
3 *The secret agent looked at her watch.*
glance, glimpse, peek, peep

little

4 *The fossil hunters **looked** at the rocks.*
stare, peer, study, scrutinise, examine, inspect, take a good look at
5 *The grumpy knight **looked** at his servant.*
glare, glower, grimace, frown, scowl
To look steadily is to **gaze**.
To look quickly is to **glance, glimpse, peek** or **peep**.
To look in amazement is to **gape**.
To look over a wide area is to **scan** or **survey** it.

look *noun*
1 *Did you have a **look** at what she was wearing?*
glance, glimpse, peep, sight, view
2 *The guard had an unfriendly **look**.*
appearance, bearing, manner, air, expression, face

loop *noun*
*Make a **loop** in the string and then tie a knot.*
coil, hoop, circle, ring, noose, bend, curl, kink, twist

loop *verb*
*The cowboy **looped** the reins round a fence post.*
coil, wind, curl, bend, turn, twist

loose *adjective*
1 *Some of the cobbles on the road are **loose**.*
insecure, unfixed, movable, unsteady, shaky, wobbly
OPPOSITE firm, secure
2 *The fire was started by a **loose** wire.*
disconnected, unattached, detached
3 *These jeans are **loose** around the waist.*
slack, baggy, roomy, loose-fitting
OPPOSITE tight
4 *The chickens wander **loose** about the farm.*
free, at large, at liberty, on the loose, unconfined, unrestricted
OPPOSITE confined

loot *noun*
*The thieves buried their **loot** in a safe place.*
haul, plunder, takings

loot *verb*
*Rioters **looted** the shops.*
raid, ransack, rob, steal from, pillage, plunder

lose *verb*
1 *Debbie has **lost** one of her gloves.*
be unable to find, mislay, misplace
OPPOSITE find
2 *Unfortunately, we **lost** the game on Saturday.*
be defeated, get beaten, suffer a defeat
OPPOSITE win

lot *noun*
*We are having another **lot** of visitors this weekend.*
group, batch, set, crowd, collection

a lot of
*My brother needs **a lot of** help with his spelling.*
a large amount of, a good or great deal of, plenty of

lots of
*There are **lots of** toys to choose from in the shop.*
a great number of, many, numerous, plenty (of)
(*informal*) loads of, tons of, masses of, oodles of, hundreds of

loud *adjective*
*The whole house was kept awake by the **loud** music.*
noisy, blaring, booming, deafening, rowdy, resounding, thunderous, penetrating, piercing
A noise which is loud enough to hear is **audible**.
OPPOSITE quiet, soft

love *noun*
*She often mentions her **love** of the outdoors.*
liking, passion, fondness, affection, devotion, admiration, adoration
(*informal*) soft spot (for)

love *verb*
1 *They **love** each other and want to get married.*
be in love with, care for, adore, cherish, hold dear, treasure, worship, idolise
A relationship between two people who love each other is a **romance**.
2 *My friend, Dot, **loves** knitting.*
like, have a passion for, be fond of, be partial to, enjoy

lovely *adjective*
1 *Jemma is a **lovely** girl.*
charming, delightful, lovable, likeable, dear, sweet, enchanting, endearing
2 *It's a **lovely** day for a bicycle trip.*
fine, glorious
3 *The girls had an **lovely** time camping.*
pleasant, pleasing, enjoyable
OPPOSITE nasty
4 *The roses look **lovely** in that vase.*
appealing, attractive, beautiful, pretty

low *adjective*
1 *The garden is surrounded by a **low** wall.*
short, shallow, sunken
2 *They were soldiers of **low** rank in the army.*
junior, inferior, lowly, modest, humble
3 *We spoke in **low** whispers.*
quiet, soft, muted, subdued, muffled
4 *The tuba plays **low** notes.*
bass, deep
OPPOSITE high

lower *verb*
1 *The supermarket **lowered** its prices.*
reduce, cut, bring down, decrease, lessen
(*informal*) slash
2 *Please **lower** the volume of your radio.*
quieten, turn down
3 *At the end of the Olympic Games, they **lower** the flag.*
take down, let down, dip

loyal *adjective*
*Sir Valiant had always been a **loyal** knight.*
true, trusty, faithful, steadfast, reliable, dependable, devoted, constant, sincere
OPPOSITE disloyal

luck *noun*
1 *He found the secret entrance by **luck**.*
accident, chance, coincidence, fluke, fate, destiny
2 *She had a bit of **luck** today.*
good fortune, success

lucky *adjective*
1 *I got the right answer by a **lucky** guess.*
accidental, chance, unintentional, unplanned
2 *Some **lucky** person won a million pounds.*
fortunate, favoured, successful

luggage *noun*
*The **luggage** can go in the boot of the car.*
baggage, cases, suitcases, bags

lump *noun*
1 ***Lumps** of sticky clay stuck to his boots.*
chunk, piece, cluster, clump, wad, mass, hunk, wedge, block
A round lump of something is a **ball**.
A lump of gold is a **nugget**.
A lump of earth is a **clod**.
A lump of blood is a **clot**.
2 *I could feel a **lump** where I'd bumped my head.*
bump, swelling, bulge, protrusion

a b c d e f g h i j k l m n o p q r s t u v w x y z

lunge verb
*Robin **lunged** at the sheriff with his sword.*
thrust, charge, rush, dive, pounce, throw yourself

lurch verb
1 *The bus passengers **lurched** from side to side.*
reel, sway, rock, stagger, stumble, totter
2 *The ship **lurched** as the waves pounded it.*
pitch, roll, heave, lean, list

lure verb
*Spiders **lure** insects into their webs.*
attract, entice, tempt, coax, draw, invite, persuade
Something used to lure an animal into a trap is **bait**.

lurk verb
*The jaguar **lurked** in wait for its prey.*
skulk, loiter, prowl, crouch, hide, lie in wait, lie low

lush adjective
*Rainforests have **lush** vegetation.*
rich, dense, thick, rampant, abundant

luxurious adjective
*The dress was trimmed with **luxurious** lace.*
grand, lavish, lush, rich, expensive, costly, deluxe, plush, magnificent, splendid, sumptuous
OPPOSITE simple, austere

luxury noun
*The millionaire lived a life of **luxury**.*
affluence, wealth, richness, splendour, comfort, ease
OPPOSITE poverty

Mm

machine noun
*Do you know how this **machine** works?*
apparatus, appliance, device, engine, contraption

mad adjective
1 *You must be **mad** to go out on a day like this.*
crazy, daft, insane, senseless, stupid, foolish, idiotic
(*informal*) out of your mind, potty, nuts
OPPOSITE sensible, wise
2 *The emperor was **mad** with rage.*
angry, furious, beside yourself, frenzied, hysterical
3 (*informal*) *Sandra is **mad** about horses.*
enthusiastic, fanatical, passionate

magazine noun
*I bought a **magazine** to read on the train.*
journal, periodical, paper, comic

magic adjective
1 *My uncle taught me some **magic** tricks.*
conjuring
2 *The castle was surrounded by a **magic** spell.*
magical, supernatural

🕸 WORD WEB

magic noun
Do you believe in magic?
sorcery, witchcraft, wizardry, spells, charms, enchantments

PEOPLE WHO USE MAGIC
enchanter or enchantress, magician, sorceror or sorceress, warlock, witch, wizard

THINGS WHICH A SORCEROR MIGHT DO
bewitch, enchant, cast or undo a spell, become invisible or vanish, brew a potion, put a curse on you

THINGS WHICH A SORCEROR MIGHT HAVE OR USE
apprentice, cauldron, charm, elixir, magic potion, magic spell or incantation, talisman, wand

magician noun
1 *The **magician** pulled a scarf out of his hat.*
conjuror
2 *King Arthur was helped by the **magician**, Merlin.*
sorcerer, witch, wizard

magnificent adjective
1 *The mountain scenery was **magnificent**.*
beautiful, glorious, splendid, spectacular, impressive, majestic
2 *The film star lived in a **magnificent** house.*
grand, imposing, stately
(*informal*) posh
3 *That was a **magnificent** meal!*
excellent, first-class, marvellous, superb
(*informal*) fabulous, fantastic

magnify verb
*Objects are **magnified** through binoculars.*
enlarge, make larger
(*informal*) blow up
OPPOSITE reduce, minimise

main adjective
1 *What was the **main** point of the story?*
central, chief, most important, basic, essential, fundamental, primary, predominant
2 *This is the **main** shopping area in the town.*
major, principal, biggest, foremost, largest, leading, prime
OPPOSITE minor, unimportant

mainly adverb
*Chimpanzees eat **mainly** fruit and vegetables.*
largely, mostly, chiefly, principally, predominantly, primarily

maintain verb
1 *The referee tried to **maintain** order.*
keep, preserve
2 *A team of gardeners **maintain** the grounds.*
look after, take care of, keep in order
3 *He still **maintains** that he's innocent.*
claim, declare, assert, insist, state, contend

major adjective
1 *There are delays on all the **major** roads into the city.*
chief, principal, primary, leading
2 *Writing her first novel was a **major** achievement.*
big, great, considerable, significant, important
OPPOSITE minor

make verb
1 *We **made** a shelter out of leaves and branches.*
build, construct, assemble, put together, produce, manufacture
2 *Those two are always **making** trouble.*
cause, bring about, give rise to, provoke

3 *They **made** me captain.*
appoint, elect, nominate
4 *They've **made** the attic into a games room.*
change, turn, convert, modify, transform, alter
5 *She'll **make** a good actress when she's older.*
become, grow into, turn into, change into
6 *We can't **make** her go if she doesn't want to.*
force, compel, order
7 *He **made** a lot of money last year.*
gain, get, obtain, acquire, receive, earn, win
8 *The ship finally **made** land.*
reach, arrive at, get to, get as far as
9 *What time do you **make** it?*
calculate, estimate, reckon
10 *2 and 2 **make** 4.*
add up to, come to, total
11 *I'll **make** you an offer for your old bike.*
propose, suggest
12 *Have you **made** your bed this morning?*
arrange, tidy

to make someone or **something out**
*I can't **make out** why everything went wrong.*
understand, work out, comprehend, fathom, make sense of

to make up
*I **made up** a new flavour of ice cream.*
create, invent, think up, concoct

make noun
*What **make** of computer do you have?*
brand, model, label

man noun
A polite word for a man is **gentleman**.
Informal words are **bloke**, **chap**, **fellow** and **guy**.
A married man is a **husband**.
A man who has children is a **father**.
An unmarried man is a **bachelor**.
A man whose wife has died is a **widower**.
A man on his wedding day is a **bridegroom**.
A man who is engaged to be married is a **fiancé**.
Words for a young man are **boy**, **lad** and **youth**.

manage verb
1 *His eldest son **manages** the business now.*
be in charge of, run, direct, lead, control, govern, rule, supervise, oversee, preside over

2 *I can't **manage** any more work this week.*
cope with, deal with, take on, carry out
3 *We'll have to **manage** without the car.*
cope, make do, get along, get by

manner noun
1 *They did the work in an efficient **manner**.*
way, style, fashion, method
2 *I was put off by her frosty **manner**.*
behaviour, conduct, attitude, disposition, air, look, bearing
manners
*Trolls have no **manners** at all!*
politeness, courtesy, graces

manufacture verb
*The factory **manufactures** pine furniture.*
make, build, assemble, fabricate

many adjective
*I've been on an aeroplane **many** times.*
a lot of, plenty of, numerous, frequent, countless, innumerable, untold
(*informal*) umpteen, lots of
OPPOSITE few

map noun
*The travel agent gave us a free **map** of Paris.*
chart, diagram, plan
A book of maps is an **atlas**.
A person who draws maps is a **cartographer**.

march verb
*The brass band **marched** down the High Street.*
parade, file, troop, stride, pace

mark noun
1 *There were muddy paw **marks** all over the kitchen floor.*
spot, stain, blemish, blotch, blot, smear, smudge, streak
A mark left by a pen or pencil is a **scribble**.
A mark left by fingers is a **fingermark**.
A mark on your skin that you are born with is a **birthmark**.
2 *They stood in silence as a **mark** of respect.*
sign, token, indication, symbol, emblem
3 *What **mark** did you get in the spelling test?*
score, grade

mark verb
1 *Please be careful not to **mark** the photographs.*
stain, smudge, dirty, blot
2 *The teacher had a pile of essays to **mark**.*
correct, grade, assess

marry verb
*In what year did your grandparents **marry**?*
get married, wed
(*informal*) tie the knot, get hitched
A couple who have promised to marry are **engaged** to each other.
A man who is engaged to be married is a **fiancé** and the woman he is engaged to is his **fiancée**.

marsh noun
*Wading birds are found in coastal **marshes**.*
swamp, bog, wetland, marshland, fen

marvel verb
to marvel at
*The crowd **marvelled at** the juggler's skill.*
admire, wonder at, be amazed by, be astonished by

marvellous adjective
1 *The professor showed us his **marvellous** inventions.*
amazing, remarkable, extraordinary, incredible, miraculous, astonishing, phenomenal
OPPOSITE ordinary
2 *We had a **marvellous** day at the zoo.*
excellent, superb, tremendous, wonderful, splendid
(*informal*) brilliant, fantastic, terrific, super, smashing
OPPOSITE bad, awful

mash verb
***Mash** the potatoes until they're smooth.*
crush, pound, pulp, smash, squash
To make something into powder is to **grind** or **pulverise** it.

mask verb
*The entrance was **masked** by an overhanging tree.*
conceal, hide, cover, obscure, screen, veil, shroud, camouflage

mass noun
*She sifted through the **mass** of papers on her desk.*
heap, pile, mound, stack, collection, quantity, accumulation
(*informal*) load

master noun
1 *We played a game in which I was **master** of the castle.*
lord, ruler, governor, chief
2 *Sherlock Holmes was a **master** of disguises.*
expert (at), genius, ace, wizard

master verb
1 *Have you **mastered** chess yet?*
grasp, learn, understand
(*informal*) get the hang of, get to grips with

a b c d e f g h i j k l m n o p q r s t u v w x y z

2 *I've managed to **master** my fear of heights.*
overcome, conquer, defeat, triumph over, get the better of, control, curb, subdue, tame

match *noun*
*The semi-final was a really exciting **match**.*
game, contest, competition, fixture, tournament, tie

match *verb*
*Does this tie **match** my shirt?*
go with, suit, fit with, blend with, tone in with
OPPOSITE contrast with

material *noun*
1 *I'm collecting **material** for the school magazine.*
information, facts, data, ideas, notes
2 *The cleaning **materials** are in the cupboard.*
stuff, substances, things
3 *The kite is made of lightweight **material**.*
cloth, fabric

matter *noun*
1 *The manager will deal with this **matter**.*
affair, concern, issue, business, situation, incident, subject, topic, thing
2 *Peat consists mainly of plant **matter**.*
material, stuff, substance
3 *What's the **matter** with the car?*
problem, difficulty, trouble, worry

matter *verb*
*Will it **matter** if I'm late?*
be important, count, make a difference

mature *adjective*
1 *The zoo has two **mature** gorillas.*
adult, fully grown, well developed
OPPOSITE young
2 *He acts very **mature** for his age.*
grown-up, responsible, sensible
OPPOSITE immature, childish

mean *adjective*
1 *Scrooge was too **mean** to buy any presents.*
selfish, miserly, uncharitable
(*informal*) stingy, tight-fisted, penny-pinching
OPPOSITE generous
2 *That was a **mean** trick to play.*
unkind, unpleasant, nasty, spiteful, vicious, cruel, malicious
OPPOSITE kind

mean *verb*
1 *A red traffic light **means** that cars have to stop.*
indicate, signify, denote, express, imply, convey, communicate, stand for, symbolise
2 *I **mean** to get better at swimming this year.*
intend, plan, aim, propose, want

meaning *noun*
*What is the **meaning** of this riddle?*
sense, significance, explanation, interpretation, definition

measure *verb*
***Measure** the height of the wall.*
calculate, gauge, assess, survey
To measure the weight of something is to **weigh** it.

measure *noun*
*They are taking **measures** to improve the park.*
step, action, course, procedure, means

medium *adjective*
*The man was of **medium** height.*
average, middle, middling, standard, moderate, normal

meek *adjective*
*Koalas look **meek**, but they have fierce claws.*
gentle, mild, tame, submissive, modest, docile, quiet, humble
OPPOSITE aggressive

meet *verb*
1 *I **met** an old friend at the party.*
come across, encounter, run into, see
(*informal*) bump into
2 *My parents **met** me at the station.*
greet, pick up, welcome
3 *We're **meeting** outside the cinema at eight.*
gather, assemble, collect, muster, rally
4 *The two roads **meet** here.*
come together, merge, connect, join, cross, intersect

meeting *noun*
*The bandits held a **meeting** to discuss their plan.*
gathering, assembly, council, forum, congress, conference
A large outdoor public meeting is a **rally**.
A formal meeting with a king or queen is an **audience**.

melt *verb*
*The ice began to **melt** in the sun.*
thaw, soften, unfreeze
To melt frozen food is to **defrost** it.
To melt ore to get metal from it is to **smelt** it.
Rock or metal that has melted through great heat is **molten**.
OPPOSITE freeze

mend *verb*
*Workmen were **mending** the pavement.*
fix, repair, put right, restore, renovate, patch

mention *verb*
1 *Please don't **mention** the idea to anyone.*
refer to, speak about, touch on, hint at

2 *You **mentioned** that you spoke Japanese.*
say, remark, reveal, disclose
(*informal*) let out
3 *The director **mentioned** all the cast.*
name, acknowledge, list

mercy *noun*
*The evil queen showed no **mercy**.*
compassion, humanity, sympathy, pity, leniency, kindness, charity
OPPOSITE cruelty

merge *verb*
1 *They plan to **merge** the two schools.*
join together, combine, integrate, put together, unite, amalgamate
2 *Two streams **merge** here to form a river.*
come together, converge, join, meet
OPPOSITE separate

merry *adjective*
*The postman was whistling a **merry** tune.*
cheerful, happy, jolly, bright, joyful, light-hearted, lively, spirited
OPPOSITE gloomy

mess *noun*
1 *Please clear up this **mess**.*
muddle, untidiness, chaos, disorder, confusion, clutter, jumble, litter, dirt
(*informal*) shambles
2 *Zoe made a **mess** of her audition.*
disaster, botch
(*informal*) hash

mess *verb*
to mess about
*We spent the day **messing about** on the beach.*
play about, fool around, lounge about
(*informal*) muck about
to mess things up
*I hope you haven't **messed up** my room.*
confuse, mix up, muddle, jumble, make a mess of, tangle
to mess something up
*I think I **messed up** my interview.*
bungle, botch
(*informal*) make a hash of

message noun
*Did you get my **message**?*
note, letter, text, email

messy adjective
*My bedroom is really **messy**!*
muddled, untidy, disorderly, chaotic, dirty, filthy, grubby, mucky
(*informal*) higgledy-piggledy
OPPOSITE neat

method noun
*My granny has a secret **method** for making jam.*
technique, way, procedure, process
A specially skilful method for doing something is a **knack**.

middle adjective
*The **middle** lane is reserved for buses.*
central, inner, inside, midway

middle noun
*A scarecrow stood in the **middle** of the field.*
centre, core, heart, midpoint
The middle of a wheel is the **hub**.
The middle part of an atom or cell is the **nucleus**.

mighty adjective
*The dragon let out a **mighty** roar.*
powerful, forceful, vigorous, ferocious, violent, great, enormous, hefty
OPPOSITE weak

mild adjective
1 *He's a **mild** person who never complains.*
amiable, docile, easygoing, gentle, good-tempered, harmless, kind, lenient, merciful, placid, soft-hearted
2 *The weather has been **mild** for this time of year.*
pleasant, warm, temperate
OPPOSITE severe

mind noun
1 *Her **mind** was as sharp as ever.*
brain, intelligence, intellect, head, sense, understanding, wits, judgement, mental powers, reasoning
2 *Are you sure you won't change your **mind**?*
wishes, intention, fancy, inclination, opinion, outlook, point of view

mind verb
1 *Will you **mind** my bag for a minute?*
guard, look after, watch, care for
(*informal*) keep an eye on
2 *Mind the step.*
look out for, watch out for, beware of, pay attention to, heed, note
3 *They won't **mind** if I'm late.*
bother, care, worry, be upset, take offence, object, disapprove

mingle verb
*The secret agent **mingled** with the crowd.*
mix in, circulate, blend, combine, merge, fuse

miniature adjective
*A piccolo looks like a **miniature** flute.*
tiny, minute, diminutive, small-scale, baby, mini

minor adjective
*I only had a **minor** part in the play.*
small, unimportant, insignificant, inferior, subordinate, trivial, petty
OPPOSITE major

minute adjective
*You can hardly see the **minute** crack.*
tiny, minuscule, microscopic, negligible
OPPOSITE large

miraculous adjective
*The patient made a **miraculous** recovery.*
amazing, astonishing, astounding, extraordinary, incredible, marvellous, unbelievable, wonderful, mysterious, inexplicable

misbehave verb
*My puppy has been **misbehaving** again!*
behave badly, be naughty, be disobedient, get up to mischief
OPPOSITE behave

miserable adjective
1 *You look **miserable**—what's the matter?*
sad, unhappy, sorrowful, gloomy, glum, downhearted, despondent, dejected, depressed, melancholy, mournful, tearful
OPPOSITE cheerful, happy
2 *The poor animals lived in **miserable** conditions.*
distressing, uncomfortable, wretched, pitiful, pathetic, squalid
OPPOSITE comfortable

misery noun
*The slaves must have led a life of **misery**.*
sadness, sorrow, unhappiness, grief, distress, despair, anguish, wretchedness, suffering, torment, heartache, depression
OPPOSITE happiness

misfortune noun
*I heard about her family's **misfortune**.*
bad luck, trouble, hardship, adversity, affliction, setback, mishap
OPPOSITE good luck

misleading adjective
*The directions he gave were quite **misleading**.*
confusing, unreliable, deceptive, ambiguous, unclear

miss verb
1 *I **missed** the bus.*
be too late for
2 *The arrow **missed** the target.*
fall short of, go wide of
3 *If we leave now, we should **miss** the traffic.*
avoid
4 *I **missed** dad when he was in hospital.*
long for, yearn for, pine for
to miss something out
*I **missed out** the boring bits of the story.*
leave out, omit, ignore, overlook, skip

mission noun
1 *Her **mission** in life was to help those in need.*
aim, purpose, objective, task, job, campaign
2 *The astronauts are on a **mission** to Mars.*
expedition, journey, voyage, exploration

mist noun
*We drove slowly through the **mist**.*
fog, haze, cloud, drizzle

mistake noun
*This piece of writing is full of **mistakes**.*
error, inaccuracy, blunder, slip, slip-up, lapse
A spelling mistake is a **misspelling**.
A mistake where something is left out is an **omission**.
A mistake in a printed book is a **misprint**.

misty adjective
1 *If it's **misty** outside, take a torch.*
foggy, hazy
2 *I can't see through the **misty** window.*
steamy, cloudy, smoky, opaque

mix verb
Mix the ingredients in a bowl.
combine, blend, mingle
to mix something up
*Please don't **mix up** my DVDs.*
muddle, jumble, confuse
To mix up playing cards is to **shuffle** them.

mixed adjective
*Add a teaspoon of **mixed** herbs.*
assorted, various, different, miscellaneous
OPPOSITE separate

mixture noun
1 *Put the cake **mixture** in a baking tin.*
mix, blend, combination
A mixture of metals is an **alloy**.
A mixture of two different species of plant or animal is a **hybrid**.

a b c d e f g h i j k l m n o p q r s t u v w x y z

2 *There's an odd* **mixture** *of things in the drawer.*
assortment, collection, variety, jumble
A confused mixture is a **mishmash**.

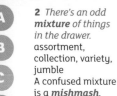

moan *verb*
1 *The wounded warrior* **moaned** *in pain.*
cry, groan, sigh, wail, howl, whimper
2 *Ned's always* **moaning** *about the food.*
complain, grumble, grouse, whine (*informal*) whinge

mob *noun*
An angry **mob** *stormed the gates of the castle.*
crowd, horde, throng, mass, rabble, gang, pack, herd, bunch

mock *verb*
It was mean of them to **mock** *his singing.*
jeer at, laugh at, make fun of, scoff at, sneer at, ridicule, scorn, deride (*informal*) take the mickey out of

monster

model *noun*
1 *I'm building a* **model** *of a space rocket.*
copy, replica, toy
2 *This is the latest* **model** *of skateboard.*
design, type, version
3 *She's a* **model** *of good behaviour.*
example, ideal

moderate *adjective*
Her first book was a **moderate** *success.*
average, fair, modest, medium, reasonable, passable, tolerable
OPPOSITE exceptional

modern *adjective*
1 *All the equipment in their kitchen was* **modern**.
up to date, contemporary, advanced, the latest
OPPOSITE out of date
2 *She always dresses in* **modern** *clothes.*
fashionable, stylish, modish (*informal*) trendy, hip
OPPOSITE old-fashioned

modest *adjective*
1 *He's very* **modest** *about his success.*
humble, quiet, reserved, shy, bashful, coy
OPPOSITE conceited
2 *There has been a* **modest** *increase in sales.*
moderate, reasonable, average, medium

moist *adjective*
1 *The walls of the dungeon were* **moist**.
damp, wet, watery, clammy, dank
2 *Tropical plants grow well in a* **moist** *atmosphere.*
humid, muggy, steamy, rainy

moisture *noun*
There is still a lot of **moisture** *on the ground.*
wetness, dampness, damp, dew, condensation, humidity

moment *noun*
1 *I'll be ready in a* **moment**.
minute, second, instant, flash (*informal*) jiffy, tick
2 *It was a great* **moment** *in the history of space travel.*
time, occasion, period

money *noun*
How much **money** *do you have with you?*
cash, currency, funds, finance (*informal*) dough, dosh
A large amount of money is a **fortune**, **riches** or **wealth**.

monster *noun*
A sea **monster** *reared its head above the waves.*
beast, giant, ogre, brute

monstrous *adjective*
1 *The town was engulfed by a* **monstrous** *wave.*
huge, gigantic, enormous, immense, massive, colossal, great, hulking, mighty, towering, vast
2 *The nation was shocked by the* **monstrous** *crime.*
horrifying, shocking, wicked, evil, hideous, horrible, terrible, atrocious, dreadful, gruesome, outrageous, scandalous

mood *noun*
What sort of **mood** *is he in today?*
temper, humour, state of mind, disposition

moody *adjective*
She's been **moody** *and withdrawn for weeks.*
sulky, sullen, grumpy, bad-tempered, temperamental, touchy, miserable, gloomy, glum
OPPOSITE cheerful

WORD WEB

moon *noun*
FORMS IN WHICH WE SEE THE MOON
crescent moon, full moon, new moon; moonbeam, moonlight

THINGS YOU MIGHT FIND OR DO ON THE MOON
crater, moon dust, moon rock, moonscape, moonwalk

A word meaning 'to do with the Moon' is **lunar**.

moral *noun*
The **moral** *of this story is that crime doesn't pay.*
lesson, message, meaning

more *adjective*
The soup needs **more** *pepper.*
extra, further, added, additional
OPPOSITE less

mostly *adverb*
I spend my money **mostly** *on books and music.*
mainly, largely, chiefly, primarily, generally, usually, normally, typically, principally, predominantly

motive *noun*
The police can find no **motive** *for the crime.*
cause, motivation, reason, purpose, grounds

mould *verb*
The sculptor **moulded** *the figures from clay.*
shape, form, fashion, model, cast

mouldy *adjective*
All I found in the fridge was some **mouldy** *cheese.*
rotten, rotting, decaying, musty, damp

mound *noun*
1 *Her desk was covered with* **mounds** *of paper.*
heap, pile, stack, mass
2 *There used to be a castle on top of that* **mound**.
hill, hillock, rise, hump
An ancient mound of earth over a grave is a **barrow**.

mountain *noun*
see panel opposite

mourn *verb*
He was still **mourning** *the loss of his friend.*
grieve for, lament for

move *noun*
1 *Don't make a* **move**!
movement
2 *The spy was watching their every* **move**.
action, step, deed, manoeuvre
3 *Is it my* **move** *next?*
turn, go, chance, opportunity

move *verb*
to move from one place to another
carry, remove, transfer, transport, shift
*They **shifted** the piano into the front room.*
to move from a position
go, leave, depart, quit, budge
*The camel stared and refused to **budge**.*
to move restlessly
toss, turn, stir, twist, shake, fidget, twitch, flap
*Please stop **twitching** in your seat.*
to move from side to side
sway, swing, wave, wag, wiggle
*The knight **swung** a sword above his helmet.*
to move along
travel, walk, proceed
*Few people **travel** on these roads after dark.*
to move along quickly
hurry, dash, race, run, rush, hasten, hurtle, career, fly, speed, sweep, shoot, zoom
*A boy went **careering** past on a scooter.*
to move along slowly
amble, stroll, saunter, dawdle, crawl, drift
*Gerald the tortoise **sauntered** down the path.*
to move towards something
advance, approach, come, proceed, progress
*The lookout saw a pirate ship **approaching**.*
to move back or move away
back, retreat, reverse, withdraw

WORD WEB

mountain *noun*
The top of a mountain is the **peak** or **summit.**
A line of mountains is a **range.**
A long, narrow mountain is a **ridge.**
A mountain with a hole at the top caused by an eruption is a **volcano.**
An area of land with many mountains is said to be **mountainous.**

THINGS YOU MIGHT SEE ON OR NEAR A MOUNTAIN
avalanche, boulder, cave, cliff, crag, crevice, glacier, gorge, ledge, mountain pass, mountain stream, precipice, rocks, slope, valley or *(Scottish)* glen

SOME WORDS TO DESCRIBE A MOUNTAIN
barren, craggy, forbidding, jagged, lofty, massive, misty, rocky, rugged, snow-capped, soaring, towering, treacherous

*The serpent **retreated**, hissing, into its lair.*
to move downwards
drop, descend, fall, sink, swoop
*A pair of vultures **swooped** down from the sky.*
to move upwards
rise, ascend, climb, mount, soar, arise
*A hot-air balloon **mounted** into the air.*

movement *noun*
1 *The robot made a sudden, jerky **movement**.*
motion, move, action, gesture
2 *She was involved in the peace **movement**.*
organisation, group, party, campaign

moving *adjective*
*The story was so **moving** that I started to cry.*
emotional, inspiring, stirring, touching
(informal) tear-jerking

muck *noun*
*They cleared the **muck** out of the stable.*
dirt, filth, grime, mud, sludge, dung, manure

mud *noun*
*The tractor left a trail of **mud** on the road.*
dirt, muck, mire, sludge, clay, soil

muddle *noun*
1 *There was a **muddle** over the date of the party.*
confusion, misunderstanding
(informal) mix-up
2 *There was a **muddle** of clothes on the floor.*
jumble, mess, tangle

muddle *verb*
1 *Who **muddled** the papers on my desk?*
mix up, mess up, disorder, jumble up, shuffle, tangle
OPPOSITE tidy
2 *They got **muddled** and took the wrong turning.*
confuse, bewilder, puzzle, perplex

muffled *adjective*
*They heard **muffled** voices from the next room.*
faint, indistinct, unclear, muted, deadened

OPPOSITE clear

muggy *adjective*
*The weather is often **muggy** before a storm.*
humid, close, clammy, sticky, moist, damp, oppressive
OPPOSITE fresh

mumble *verb*
*We couldn't hear the actor as he was **mumbling**.*
mutter, talk indistinctly

munch *verb*
*Kim sat **munching** popcorn all through the film.*
chew, crunch

murky *adjective*
*A creature loomed out of the **murky** waters of the loch.*
dark, clouded, cloudy, dim, dull, dingy, gloomy, grey, foggy, misty
OPPOSITE clear

murmur *verb*
*We heard voices **murmuring** in the room above.*
mutter, mumble, whisper

music *noun*
see panel on following page

musical *adjective*
*Helena has a very **musical** voice.*
tuneful, melodic, melodious, harmonious, sweet-sounding

musty *adjective*
*There was a **musty** smell in the cellar.*
damp, dank, mouldy, stale, stuffy, airless
OPPOSITE fresh

mutter *verb*
*The goblin sat **muttering** to himself in the corner.*
mumble, murmur, whisper

mysterious *adjective*
*They uncovered a **mysterious** sign on the wall.*
strange, puzzling, baffling, mystifying, perplexing, obscure, unexplained, incomprehensible, inexplicable, curious, weird

mystery *noun*
*What really happened was a **mystery**.*
puzzle, riddle, secret

WORD WEB

music *noun*

VARIOUS KINDS OF MUSIC
blues, classical music, country and western, dance music, disco music, folk music, gospel, hip hop, jazz, orchestral music, pop music, punk, ragtime, rap, reggae, rock, soul, swing

TYPES OF MUSICAL COMPOSITION
anthem, ballad, carol, concerto, folk song, fugue, hymn, lullaby, march, melody, musical, opera, operetta, sonata, song, symphony, tune

FAMILIES OF MUSICAL INSTRUMENTS
brass, keyboard, percussion, strings, woodwind

STRINGED INSTRUMENTS THAT CAN BE PLAYED WITH A BOW
cello, double bass, viola, violin or fiddle

STRINGED INSTRUMENTS PLAYED BY PLUCKING OR STRUMMING
banjo, cittern, guitar, harp, lute, lyre, mandolin, sitar, ukulele, zither

BRASS INSTRUMENTS
bugle, cornet, euphonium, flugelhorn, French horn, trombone, trumpet, tuba

OTHER INSTRUMENTS PLAYED BY BLOWING
bagpipes, bassoon, clarinet, cor anglais, flute, harmonica or mouth organ, oboe, piccolo, recorder, saxophone

guitar

KEYBOARD INSTRUMENTS
accordion, harmonium, harpsichord, keyboard, organ, piano, synthesiser

PERCUSSION INSTRUMENTS
bass drum, bongo drum, castanets, cymbals, drum, glockenspiel, gong, kettledrum, maracas, marimba, rattle, snare drum, tabor, tambour, tambourine, timpani, tom-tom, triangle, tubular bells, vibraphone, xylophone

PEOPLE WHO PLAY VARIOUS INSTRUMENTS
bugler, cellist, clarinettist, drummer, fiddler, flautist, guitarist, harpist, lutenist, oboist, organist, percussionist, pianist, piper, timpanist, trombonist, trumpeter, violinist

SOME OTHER MUSICIANS
accompanist, composer, conductor, instrumentalist, singer, vocalist

saxophone

GROUPS OF MUSICIANS
band, choir or chorus, duet or duo, ensemble, group, orchestra, quartet, quintet, trio

TERMS USED IN MUSIC
chord, counterpoint, discord, harmony, melody, note, octave, pitch, rhythm, scale, semitone, tempo, theme, tone, tune

NAMES OF NOTES AND SIGNS IN WRITTEN MUSIC
clef, crotchet, flat, key signature, minim, natural, quaver, semibreve, semiquaver, sharp, stave, time signature

violin

accordion

drums

nag *verb*
*He was always **nagging** her to work harder.*
badger, pester, scold

naked *adjective*
*He walked **naked** into the bathroom.*
bare, nude, unclothed, undressed
OPPOSITE clothed

name *noun*
The official names you have are your **first names** or **forenames**, and **surname**.
Names a Christian is given at baptism are **Christian names**.
A false name is an **alias**.
A name people use instead of your real name is a **nickname**.
A false name an author uses is a **pen name** or **pseudonym**.
The name of a book or film is its **title**.

name *verb*
*The zoo **named** the new lion cubs, Kiara and Kovu.*
call
To name someone at the ceremony of baptism is to **baptise** or **christen** them.

nap *noun*
*Granny always takes a **nap** on Sunday afternoons.*
rest, sleep, doze, lie-down, siesta
(*informal*) snooze, forty winks

narrow *adjective*
*The rabbit squeezed through a **narrow** opening in the fence.*
thin, slender, slim
OPPOSITE wide

nasty *adjective*
*1 Ogres have a thoroughly **nasty** temper.*
unkind, unpleasant, unfriendly, disagreeable, objectionable, odious, mean, malicious, cruel, spiteful, vicious
*2 A **nasty** smell wafted from the laboratory.*
unpleasant, offensive, disgusting, repulsive, revolting, horrible, foul, rotten, sickening
OPPOSITE agreeable, pleasant
*3 The weather suddenly turned **nasty**.*
unpleasant, rough, stormy, squally

national *adjective*
*The programme will be broadcast on **national** television.*
nationwide
OPPOSITE local

natural *adjective*
*1 Karen has a **natural** gift for music.*
born, inborn, instinctive, intuitive, native
*2 It's only **natural** to be nervous before an exam.*
normal, common, understandable, reasonable, predictable
OPPOSITE unnatural

nature *noun*
*1 I like TV programmes about **nature**.*
natural history, wildlife
*2 The old sheepdog has a very kind **nature**.*
character, disposition, personality, manner
*3 I collect coins, medals and things of that **nature**.*
kind, sort, type, description, variety

naughty *adjective*
*The puppies were quite **naughty** when they were young.*
bad, badly behaved, disobedient, mischievous, uncontrollable, unmanageable, troublesome, unruly
OPPOSITE well behaved

near *adjective*
*1 We get on well with our **near** neighbours.*
next-door, nearby, close, adjacent, surrounding
*2 My birthday is **near**.*
approaching, coming
(*informal*) round the corner
*3 We send cards to all our **near** relatives.*
close, dear, familiar, intimate
OPPOSITE distant

nearly *adverb*
*Thank goodness, it's **nearly** dinner time!*
almost, practically, virtually, just about, approaching

neat *adjective*
*1 Please leave the room as **neat** as possible.*
clean, orderly, tidy, uncluttered, immaculate
(*informal*) spick and span
*2 Craig always looks **neat** in his school uniform.*
smart, elegant, spruce, trim
*3 Her handwriting is very **neat**.*
precise, skilful, well-formed
OPPOSITE untidy

necessary *adjective*
*The recipe lists all the **necessary** ingredients.*
essential, required, needed, needful, compulsory, obligatory, unavoidable
OPPOSITE unnecessary

need *noun*
*There's a **need** for more shops in our area.*
call, demand, requirement

need *verb*
*1 I **need** a pound coin for the locker.*
require, want, be short of, lack
*2 The charity **needs** our support.*
depend on, rely on

neglect *verb*
*She's been **neglecting** her work.*
forget, ignore, overlook, abandon, disregard, pay no attention to, shirk

nervous *adjective*
*She always feels **nervous** before an exam.*
anxious, worried, apprehensive, concerned, uneasy, fearful, edgy, fraught, tense, troubled
(*informal*) uptight, jittery
OPPOSITE calm

neutral *adjective*
*A referee has to be **neutral**.*
impartial, unbiased, unprejudiced, even-handed
OPPOSITE biased, prejudiced

new *adjective*
*1 Start on a **new** sheet of paper.*
clean, fresh, unused, brand-new
Something new and unused is **in mint condition**.
*2 They went to the motor show to see the **new** models.*
latest, current, modern, recent, up-to-date
*3 They've found a **new** bug in the computer program.*
additional, extra, unexpected, unfamiliar
*4 Haven't you got any **new** ideas?*
fresh, original, novel, innovative, creative, different
OPPOSITE old

news *noun*
*What's the latest **news**?*
information, word, report, bulletin
(*old use*) tidings

next *adjective*
*1 He lives in the house **next** to the chip shop.*
adjacent, closest, nearest
OPPOSITE distant
*2 If you miss this bus, you can catch the **next** one.*
following, subsequent
OPPOSITE previous

nice *adjective*
see panel on following page
*1 That's not a very **nice** thing to say!*
pleasant, agreeable
OPPOSITE nasty
*2 There is a **nice** distinction between borrowing and stealing.*
delicate, fine, precise, subtle

night *noun*
*Badgers usually come out at **night**.*
night-time, dark
Animals which are active at night are **nocturnal** animals.

a b c d e f g h i j k l m n o p q r s t u v w x y z

A B C D E F G H I J K L M N **O** P Q R S T U V W X Y Z

nice *adjective*
Try to vary the words you use for
nice. Here are some other words
you could use.

FOR A *NICE PERSON*
good, kind, friendly, helpful,
generous, likeable, amiable,
charming, polite, genial *Our
singing teacher is very **likeable**.*
FOR A *NICE EXPERIENCE*
delightful, enjoyable, wonderful,
marvellous, splendid *Did you have
an **enjoyable** time in France?*
FOR SOMETHING THAT *LOOKS NICE*
beautiful, attractive, pleasing,
lovely *There is an **attractive** view
from the upstairs window.*
FOR A *NICE SMELL*
agreeable, fragrant, sweet-
smelling *The **fragrant** scent of
lavender filled the garden.*
FOR *NICE FOOD*
delicious, tasty, appetising,
satisfying *They serve **tasty**
sandwiches in the cafe.*
FOR *NICE WEATHER*
fine, sunny, warm *The weather
has been **fine** all week.*

noble *adjective*
1 *The knight belonged to an ancient
noble family.*
aristocratic, high-born, upper-class
2 *The rescuers were congratulated
for their **noble** efforts.*
brave, heroic, courageous,
honourable, worthy, virtuous,
gallant
OPPOSITE cowardly, unworthy

nod *verb*
*Simon **nodded** his head in
agreement.*
bob, bow, dip, lower

noise *noun*
*Where is that dreadful **noise** coming
from?*
din, racket, row, uproar, commotion,
tumult, hullabaloo, pandemonium

noisy *adjective*
1 *The people next door were playing
noisy music.*
loud, blaring, booming, deafening,
ear-splitting, thunderous
2 *The children are very **noisy** this
morning.*
rowdy, raucous, chattering,
talkative

nonsense *noun*
*Stop talking **nonsense**!*
rubbish, drivel, balderdash, piffle,
gibberish, claptrap, gobbledegook
(*informal*) rot, tripe, twaddle

normal *adjective*
1 *He had a **normal** kind of day
at work.*
average, common, customary,
familiar, habitual, ordinary,
predictable, regular, routine,
standard, typical, unsurprising, usual
2 *No **normal** person would sleep on
a bed of nails.*
healthy, rational, reasonable, sane
OPPOSITE abnormal

nosy *adjective (informal)*
*Stop being so **nosy** and asking all
these questions!*
inquisitive, curious, prying, snooping,
intrusive
An informal name for a nosy person
is a **nosy parker**.

note *noun*
1 *I sent a **note** thanking him for
the present.*
message, letter, communication
2 *There was a **note** of anger in her
voice.*
sound, tone, feeling, quality
note *verb*
1 *The detective **noted** the address
on a scrap of paper.*
jot down, make a note of, write down,
record, scribble
2 *Did you **note** what she was
wearing?*
notice, see, take note of, pay
attention to, heed, mark, observe

nothing *noun*
*Four minus four equals **nothing**.*
nought, zero
In cricket a score of nothing is a
duck; in tennis it is **love**, and in
football it is **nil**.

notice *noun*
*Someone put up a **notice** about the
meeting.*
sign, advertisement, placard, poster,
warning
to take notice of something
*They **took** no **notice of** the warning.*
heed, pay attention to
notice *verb*
1 *Did you **notice** what he was
wearing?*
note, see, take note of, pay attention
to, heed, mark, observe
2 *I **noticed** a funny smell in the room.*
become aware of, detect

now *adverb*
1 *My cousins are **now** living in
Melbourne.*
at present, at the moment, currently,
nowadays
2 *I'll give them a ring **now**.*
immediately, at once, straight away,
without delay, instantly

nudge *verb*
*She **nudged** me with her elbow.*
poke, prod, shove, bump, jog, jolt

nuisance *noun*
*The traffic noise is a real **nuisance**.*
annoyance, irritation, inconvenience,
bother, menace, pest, drawback

numb *adjective*
*My toes are **numb** with cold.*
unfeeling, deadened, frozen,
insensitive, paralysed
OPPOSITE sensitive

number *noun*
1 *Add the **numbers** together to get
the answer.*
figure, numeral
Any of the numbers from 0 to 9 is a
digit.
A negative or positive whole number
is an **integer**.
An amount used in measuring or
counting is a **unit**.
2 *A large **number** of people applied
for the job.*
amount, quantity, collection, crowd
3 *The band played some well-known
numbers.*
song, piece, tune

obedient *adjective*
*The dog seems very **obedient**.*
well-behaved, disciplined,
manageable, dutiful, docile
OPPOSITE disobedient

obey *verb*
1 *The dog **obeyed** his owner's
commands.*
follow, carry out, execute, implement,
observe, adhere to, heed
2 *The soldiers **obeyed** without
question.*
do what you are told, take orders, be
obedient, conform
OPPOSITE disobey

object *noun*
1 *We saw some strange **objects** in
the museum.*
article, item, thing
2 *What is the **object** of this exercise?*
point, purpose, aim, goal, intention,
objective
object *verb*
to object to something
*Several residents have **objected to**
the plan.*
complain about, be opposed to,
disapprove of, take exception to,
protest against
OPPOSITE accept, agree to

observant adjective
If you're observant, you might see a fox tonight.
alert, attentive, sharp-eyed, vigilant, watchful
OPPOSITE inattentive

observation noun
1 *They took him to hospital for observation.*
study, watching, scrutiny
2 *The detective made an interesting observation.*
comment, remark, statement

observe verb
1 *Astronomers observed the eclipse last night.*
watch, look at, view, study
2 *I have observed a change in his behaviour.*
notice, note, see, detect, spot, discern, perceive, witness
3 *It's important to observe the rules.*
follow, abide by, adhere to, heed, keep to, obey
4 *My friend observed that I had grown taller.*
mention, say, comment, remark, declare

obsession noun
Football is Frank's obsession.
passion, fixation, addiction, mania

obstacle noun
1 *They drove around the obstacles in the road.*
obstruction, barrier, barricade
2 *His age proved to be an obstacle.*
problem, difficulty, hindrance, hurdle, snag, catch

obvious adjective
1 *It was silly to make so many obvious mistakes.*
glaring, noticeable, pronounced
2 *The castle is an obvious landmark.*
conspicuous, notable, prominent, visible
OPPOSITE inconspicuous
3 *It was obvious that the woman was a spy.*
clear, evident, apparent, plain, undeniable, unmistakable
OPPOSITE hidden

occasion noun
1 *I've been to Italy on several occasions.*
time, moment, instance, opportunity, chance
2 *The wedding was a happy occasion.*
affair, event, happening, incident, occurrence

occasional adjective
The weather forecast said there would be occasional showers.
intermittent, odd, scattered, irregular, infrequent
OPPOSITE frequent, regular

occasionally adverb
The dragon occasionally lifted its head and roared.
sometimes, now and again, once in a while, every so often
OPPOSITE frequently, often

occupation noun
1 *He's not happy with his present occupation.*
job, post, employment, profession, trade, work
2 *Vita's favourite occupation is reading.*
activity, hobby, pastime, pursuit

occupy verb
1 *They occupy the house next door.*
live in, reside in, dwell in, inhabit
2 *The rebel army occupied the town.*
capture, seize, take over, conquer, invade

occur verb
1 *She told us what had occurred.*
happen, take place, come about, arise
2 *The disease only occurs in certain plants.*
develop, crop up, turn up

odd adjective
1 *Her behaviour seemed very odd.*
strange, unusual, abnormal, peculiar, curious, puzzling, queer, unconventional, eccentric, funny, weird
OPPOSITE normal
2 *He could only find a couple of odd socks.*
left over, single, spare
3 *He does odd jobs to earn money.*
occasional, casual, irregular, various

offend verb
I hope my letter didn't offend you.
give or cause offence to, insult, upset, hurt your feelings, anger, displease, annoy, affront, disgust, vex

offensive adjective
1 *The gas produces an offensive smell.*
unpleasant, repellent, disgusting, revolting, nasty
OPPOSITE pleasant
2 *He apologised for his offensive remarks.*
insulting, impolite, rude, abusive

offer verb
1 *A reward was offered for the capture of the outlaws.*
propose, put forward, suggest, make available
2 *He offered to help with the washing-up.*
volunteer

offer noun
Their offer of help was gratefully received.
proposal, suggestion

often adverb
It often rains in April.
frequently, regularly, repeatedly, time after time, many times, again and again, constantly

old adjective
1 *The old Norman church is to be restored.*
ancient, historic, original
2 *I put on old jeans to do some gardening.*
worn, scruffy, shabby, threadbare
OPPOSITE new
3 *The museum has a display of old computers.*
old-fashioned, out of date, antiquated, early, obsolete
Things which are valuable because they are old are **antique**.
OPPOSITE up to date, current, modern

old-fashioned adjective
That hairstyle is quite old-fashioned now.
out of date, outdated, outmoded, antiquated
OPPOSITE modern, up to date

omit verb
1 *His article was omitted from the magazine.*
exclude, leave out, miss out, cut, eliminate, overlook, skip
2 *Don't omit to turn off the lights.*
forget, fail, neglect

ooze verb
The filling started to ooze out my sandwich.
leak, seep, escape, dribble, drip

open adjective
1 *The puppy escaped through the open door.*
unlocked, unfastened, ajar, gaping
OPPOSITE closed
2 *The jam jar had been left open.*
uncovered, unsealed
3 *There is a view of open country from the back window.*
clear, unrestricted, unenclosed, extensive
OPPOSITE enclosed
4 *He was open about what he had done wrong.*
frank, honest, sincere, straightforward, candid
OPPOSITE deceitful
5 *The captain faced open rebellion from the crew.*
unconcealed, undisguised, obvious, plain
OPPOSITE concealed

a
b
c
d
e
f
g
h
i
j
k
l
m
n
o
p
q
r
s
t
u
v
w
x
y
z

open verb
1 *Please open the door.*
unfasten, unlock, unbolt
2 *I can't wait to open my birthday presents!*
undo, unwrap, untie, unseal
To open an umbrella is to **unfurl** it.
To open a wine bottle is to **uncork** it.
To open a map is to **unfold** or **unroll** it.
3 *The jumble sale opens at 10 a.m.*
begin, start, commence
(*informal*) get going

opening noun
1 *The sheep got out through an opening in the fence.*
gap, hole, breach, break, split
2 *The film has a very dramatic opening.*
beginning, start, commencement
3 *We are invited to the opening of the new sports centre.*
launch, initiation

opinion noun
What was your honest opinion of the film?
view, judgement, impression, belief, attitude, point of view, thought, conclusion, assessment, notion, feeling, idea

opportunity noun
1 *There were few opportunities to relax.*
chance, occasion, moment, time
2 *The job offers a good opportunity for a keen young person.*
opening
(*informal*) break

oppose verb
Many people opposed the building of the new road.
object to, disapprove of, be against, be hostile towards, argue against, fight against, attack, resist
OPPOSITE support, defend

opposite adjective
1 *They have opposite views about politics.*
contrasting, conflicting, contradictory, opposed, opposing, different, contrary
OPPOSITE similar
2 *My friend lives on the opposite side of the road.*
facing

opposite noun
She says one thing and does the opposite.
contrary, reverse, converse

optimistic adjective
She's optimistic about her chances of success.
hopeful, positive, confident, expectant, cheerful, buoyant
OPPOSITE pessimistic

ordeal noun
The shipwrecked sailor told us about his ordeal.
suffering, troubles, trial, anguish, torture, nightmare

order noun
1 *The captain gave the order to abandon ship.*
command, instruction, direction
2 *I've put in an order for the new book.*
request, demand, reservation, booking
3 *The police restored order after the riot.*
peace, calm, control, quiet, harmony, law and order
4 *The books are arranged in alphabetical order.*
arrangement, sequence, series, succession
5 *She keeps her bike in good order.*
condition, state

order verb
1 *She ordered them to be quiet.*
command, instruct, require, tell
2 *He ordered the new magazine.*
request, reserve, apply for, book

ordinary adjective
1 *It was just an ordinary sort of day.*
normal, typical, usual, customary, habitual, everyday
2 *This is more than just an ordinary robot.*
standard, average, common, conventional, regular
3 *It was a very ordinary game.*
mediocre, unexceptional, run-of-the-mill, routine

organise verb
1 *It took her ages to organise the party.*
coordinate, plan, make arrangements for, see to, set up, run
2 *The librarian has to organise the books in the library.*
arrange, put in order, classify, sort out, tidy up

original adjective
1 *The settlers drove out the original inhabitants.*
earliest, first, initial, native, aboriginal
2 *The story was very original.*
inventive, new, novel, creative, fresh, imaginative, unusual, unconventional
3 *Is that an original work of art or a copy?*
genuine, real, authentic, unique

ornament noun
A few ornaments will make the room more attractive.
decoration, adornment, trinket, bauble

outrageous adjective
1 *The behaviour of the trolls was outrageous.*
disgraceful, scandalous, shocking, atrocious, appalling, monstrous, shameful
2 *They charge outrageous prices at that shop.*
excessive, unreasonable

outside adjective
Lookouts were stationed on the outside wall of the castle.
exterior, external, outer

outside noun
Insects have their skeletons on the outside of their bodies.
exterior, shell, surface
OPPOSITE inside

outstanding adjective
1 *She will be an outstanding tennis player in a few years.*
excellent, exceptional, superb, extraordinary, superlative, brilliant, great, fine, distinguished, celebrated, remarkable, superior, striking, notable
OPPOSITE ordinary
2 *There are still some outstanding bills to pay.*
overdue, unpaid, owing

overcome verb
He managed to overcome his fear of flying.
conquer, defeat, master, get the better of

overpowering adjective
I felt an overpowering urge to giggle.
overwhelming, powerful, strong, compelling, irresistible, uncontrollable

overtake verb
We overtook the car in front.
pass, leave behind, pull ahead of, outstrip

own verb
It was the first bike she had owned.
be the owner of, have, possess
to own up to
No one owned up to breaking the window.
confess to, admit to, tell the truth about
(*informal*)
come clean about

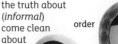

order

pace noun
1 *Move forward two **paces**.*
step, stride
2 *The front runner set a fast **pace**.*
rate, speed
A formal word is **velocity**.

pack noun
*There were four candles in each **pack**.*
package, packet, bundle,
bale

pack verb
1 *She **packed** her suitcase and called a taxi.*
fill, load up
2 *I forgot to **pack** my hairdryer.*
stow away, wrap up
3 *They tried to **pack** too many passengers on to the train.*
cram, crowd, squeeze, stuff, jam, wedge

page noun
1 *Several **pages** have been torn out of this book.*
sheet, leaf
2 *He wrote two **pages** of notes.*
side

pain noun
*Dirk felt a sudden jabbing **pain** in his foot.*
anguish, suffering
A dull pain is an **ache** or **soreness**.
Severe pain is **agony**, **torment** or **torture**.
A slight pain is **discomfort**.
A slight pain which doesn't last long is a **twinge**.
A sudden pain is a **pang** or **stab**.
Pain in your head is a **headache**.
Pain in your teeth is **toothache**.

painful adjective
1 *My shoulder is still really **painful**.*
sore, aching, tender, hurting, smarting, stinging, throbbing
2 *The conversation brought back many **painful** memories.*
unpleasant, upsetting, distressing, disagreeable, traumatic

paint verb
1 *The bedroom walls were **painted** green.*
colour, decorate
2 *Samantha **painted** the flowers in bright colours.*
depict, portray, represent

painting noun
A picture painted on a wall is a **fresco** or a **mural**.
A picture painted by a famous artist of the past is an **old master**.

pair noun
A pair of people who go out together are a **couple**.
Two people who sing or play music together are a **duet**.
Two people who work together are **partners** or a **partnership**.
Two babies born together are **twins**.

pale adjective
1 *Are you all right? You're looking a little **pale**.*
white, pallid, pasty, wan, ashen, sallow, anaemic
To go pale with fear is to **blanch**.
OPPOSITE ruddy, flushed
2 *That shade of pink is too **pale**.*
light, pastel, faded, faint, dim, bleached, colourless
OPPOSITE bright

panic noun
*People fled the streets in **panic**.*
alarm, fright, terror, frenzy, hysteria

panic verb
*If a fire starts, don't **panic**!*
be alarmed, take fright, become hysterical
(*informal*) lose your head, get in a flap
To panic is also to be **panic-stricken**.

pant verb
*Some of the runners were **panting** by the last lap.*
breathe quickly, gasp, wheeze, puff

paper noun
1 *She started her diary on a fresh sheet of **paper**.*
A piece of paper is a **leaf** or a **sheet**.
2 *The doctor had some important **papers** to sign.*
document, deed, certificate
3 *The story made the front page of the local **paper**.*
newspaper, journal
(*informal*) rag

parade noun
*A circus **parade** passed along the street.*
procession, march, spectacle, show, display
A parade of vehicles or people or horseback is a **cavalcade**.
A parade of people in costume is a **pageant**.

parcel noun
*The postman delivered a bulky **parcel**.*
package, packet

pardon verb
*The king decided to **pardon** the prisoners.*
release, free, set free, let off, spare, excuse, forgive
To pardon someone who is condemned to death is to **reprieve** them.

part noun
1 *All the **parts** of the engine are now working properly.*
bit, component, constituent
2 *I only saw the first **part** of the programme.*
section, piece, portion, element
3 *Which **part** of the business do they own?*
branch, department, division
4 *Granny lives in another **part** of the town.*
area, district, region, neighbourhood, sector
5 *He's just right to act the **part** of Peter Pan.*
character, role

part verb
1 *It was the first time she'd been **parted** from her parents.*
separate, divide, remove
OPPOSITE join
2 *They exchanged a final kiss before **parting**.*
go away, leave, depart, say goodbye
OPPOSITE meet

mural

particular adjective
1 *The tickets must be used on a particular day.*
specific, certain, distinct, definite, exact
2 *She took particular care not to damage the parcel.*
special, exceptional, unusual, extreme, marked, notable
3 *The cat's very particular about his food.*
fussy, finicky, hard to please (*informal*) choosy, picky

partner noun
The two women have been business partners for years.
colleague, associate, ally
In marriage, your partner is your *spouse* or your *husband* or *wife*.
An animal's partner is its *mate*.

party noun
1 *We had a class party at the end of term.*
celebration, festivity, function, gathering, reception
(*informal*) get-together, do
2 *A party of tourists was going round the museum.*
group, band, crowd, gang

pass verb
1 *We watched the parade as it passed.*
go by, move past
2 *She tried to pass the car in front.*
overtake, go ahead of
3 *We passed over the bridge.*
go, advance, proceed, progress
4 *Could you pass me the sugar, please?*
hand, give, deliver, offer, present
5 *Do you think you will pass your music exam?*
be successful in, get through, succeed in
6 *How did you pass the time on holiday?*
spend, use, occupy, fill, while away
7 *Three years passed before we met again.*
go by, elapse
8 *The pain will soon pass.*
go away, come to an end, disappear, fade

pass noun
We had a pass to get into the concert for free.
permit, licence, ticket

passage noun
1 *A secret passage led from the chamber to the outside.*
passageway, corridor, tunnel
2 *The guards forced a passage through the crowd.*
path, route, way
3 *Our homework is to choose a favourite passage from a book.*
episode, excerpt, extract, piece, quotation, section

4 *He hadn't changed, despite the passage of time.*
passing, progress, advance

passion noun
1 *'Romeo and Juliet' is a story of youthful passion.*
love, emotion
2 *She has a passion for sports.*
enthusiasm, eagerness, appetite, desire, craving, urge, zest, thirst, mania

passionate adjective
1 *The captain gave a passionate speech before the battle.*
emotional, intense, moving, heartfelt
OPPOSITE unemotional
2 *He is a passionate follower of football.*
eager, keen, avid, enthusiastic, fanatical, fervent
OPPOSITE apathetic

past noun
In the past, things were different.
past times, old days, olden days, days gone by
The study of what happened in the past is *history*.
The things and ideas that have come down to us from the past are our *heritage* or *traditions*.
OPPOSITE future

past adjective
Things were very different in past centuries.
earlier, former, previous, old
OPPOSITE future

pat verb
Andy patted the Shetland pony on the head.
tap, touch, stroke, pet
To touch something quickly and lightly is to *dab* it.
To stroke someone with an open hand is to *caress* them.

patch verb
I need some material to patch my jeans.
mend, repair
Another way to mend holes in clothes is to *darn* them or *stitch* them up.

path noun
Please keep to the path as you walk through the gardens.
pathway, track, trail, footpath, walk, walkway, lane
A path for horse-riding is a *bridleway*.
A path by the side of a road is a *pavement*.
A path above a beach is an *esplanade* or *promenade*.
A path along a canal is a *towpath*.
A path between buildings is an *alley*.

pathetic adjective
1 *The abandoned kittens were a pathetic sight.*
moving, touching, pitiful, distressing, heartbreaking, sad, sorry
2 *The goalie made a pathetic attempt to stop the ball.*
hopeless, useless, weak, feeble, inadequate, incompetent

patience noun
She waited with great patience for an hour.
calmness, tolerance, self-control, endurance, restraint, perseverance, persistence, resignation
OPPOSITE impatience

patient adjective
1 *The nurse was very patient with the children.*
calm, composed, even-tempered, easygoing, tolerant, lenient, mild, quiet, uncomplaining, resigned, long-suffering
2 *It took hours of patient work to restore the painting.*
persevering, persistent, unhurried, untiring, steady, determined
OPPOSITE impatient

pause noun
There was a pause while the singers got their breath back.
break, gap, halt, rest, lull, stop, wait, interruption, stoppage
A pause in the middle of a performance is an *interlude* or *interval*.
A pause in the middle of a cinema film is an *intermission*.

pause verb
1 *The stranger paused at the door before knocking.*
hesitate, wait, delay, hang back
2 *The cyclists paused to let the others catch up.*
halt, stop, rest, take a break, break off

pay verb
1 *How much did you pay for your new bike?*
spend, give out, hand over
(*informal*) fork out
2 *Who's going to pay the bill?*
pay off, repay, settle, clear, refund
3 *They had to pay for all the damage they caused.*
compensate, pay back
4 *I'll make you pay for this!*
suffer

pay noun
We should get an increase in pay next year.
wages, salary, income, earnings
A payment you get for doing a single job is a *fee*.

peace noun
1 *After the war there was a period of peace.*
agreement, harmony, friendliness
2 *She enjoys the peace of the countryside.*
calmness, peacefulness, quiet, tranquillity, stillness, serenity, silence

peaceful adjective
They enjoyed a peaceful day fishing.
calm, quiet, relaxing, tranquil, restful, serene, undisturbed, untroubled, gentle, placid, soothing, still
OPPOSITE noisy, troubled

peak noun
1 *The peak of the mountain was covered in snow.*
summit, cap, crest, crown, pinnacle, top, tip, point
2 *She is at the peak of her career as an athlete.*
top, height, highest point, climax

peculiar adjective
1 *What's that peculiar smell?*
strange, unusual, odd, curious, extraordinary, abnormal, funny, weird, bizarre
OPPOSITE ordinary
2 *He recognised her peculiar way of writing.*
characteristic, distinctive, individual, particular, personal, special, unique, identifiable

people plural noun
1 *How many people are you inviting?*
persons, individuals
People as opposed to animals are **humans** or **human beings** or **mankind**.
2 *The government is elected by the people of the country.*
population, citizens, the public, society, nation, race

perceptive adjective
It was very perceptive of you to spot my mistake.
observant, clever, sharp, shrewd, quick, alert
OPPOSITE unobservant

perfect adjective
1 *Each petal on the flower was perfect.*
faultless, flawless, ideal, intact, undamaged, complete, whole
2 *The dress is a perfect fit.*
exact, faithful, precise, accurate, correct
OPPOSITE imperfect
3 *I received a letter from a perfect stranger.*
complete, total, absolute, utter

perform verb
1 *Is this your first time performing on stage?*
act, appear, play, dance, sing
2 *The children performed a play about Cinderella.*
present, stage, produce, put on
3 *Soldiers are expected to perform their duty.*
do, carry out, execute, fulfil
To perform a crime is to **commit** a crime.

performance noun
1 *Tonight's performance is already sold out.*
show, production, presentation
2 *He congratulated the players on their outstanding performance.*
effort, work, endeavour, exertion, behaviour, conduct

permanent adjective
1 *Sugar can do permanent damage to your teeth.*
lasting, long-lasting, long-term, everlasting, enduring
2 *Traffic noise is a permanent problem in the city centre.*
never-ending, perpetual, persistent, chronic, perennial
3 *She has been offered a permanent job in the firm.*
stable, steady, fixed, lifelong

permission noun
They had the teacher's permission to leave.
consent, agreement, approval
(*informal*) go-ahead

permit verb
The council doesn't permit fishing in the lake.
allow, consent to, give permission for, authorise, license, grant, tolerate, admit

permit noun
You need a permit to fish in the river.
licence, pass, ticket

persecute verb
People were persecuted for their religious beliefs.
oppress, discriminate against, harass, intimidate, bully, terrorise, torment

persevere verb
The rescuers persevered despite the bad weather.
continue, carry on, keep going, persist
(*informal*) keep at it, stick at it
OPPOSITE give up

person noun
Not a single person has replied to my email.
individual, human being, character, soul

personal adjective
1 *The book is based on the writer's personal experience.*
own, individual, particular
2 *The contents of the letter are personal.*
confidential, private, secret, intimate

personality noun
Like all ogres, he has an ugly personality.
character, nature, disposition, temperament, make-up

persuade verb
I persuaded my friend to join the choir.
convince, coax, induce
To persuade someone to do something is also to **talk them into** doing it.
OPPOSITE dissuade

persuasive adjective
She used some very persuasive arguments.
convincing, effective, sound, strong, forceful, compelling, valid
OPPOSITE unconvincing

pessimistic adjective
The players are pessimistic about their chances of winning.
negative, unhopeful, gloomy, despairing, resigned, cynical
OPPOSITE optimistic

pester verb
Please don't pester me while I'm busy!
annoy, bother, trouble, harass, badger, hound, nag
(*informal*) bug

petrified adjective
Jack stood petrified as the monster lumbered towards him.
terrified, horrified, terror-struck, paralysed, frozen

phase noun
Going to school is the start of a new phase in your life.
period, time, stage, step

phone verb
I'll phone you later this evening.
telephone, call, ring, dial

photograph noun
I put my holiday photographs in an album.
photo, snap or snapshot, shot
The photographs you get when a film is processed are **prints**.
A photograph on the original film from which a print is made is a **negative**.
A photograph for projecting on to a screen is a **slide** or **transparency**.

pick verb
1 *They've picked the players for the hockey team.*
choose, select, decide on, settle on, opt for, single out
2 *Irene picked some flowers from the garden.*
gather, collect, cut
3 *I picked an apple off the tree.*
pluck, pull off, take

a b c d e f g h i j k l m n o p q r s t u v w x y z

to pick up
1 *He was too weak to **pick up** the box.*
lift, raise, hoist
2 *I'll **pick up** some milk on the way home.*
get, collect, fetch

picture noun
1 *There's a **picture** of a pyramid in this book.*
illustration, image, print
A picture which represents a particular person is a ***portrait***.
A picture which represents the artist himself or herself is a ***self-portrait***.
A picture which represents a group of objects is a ***still life***.
A picture which represents a country scene is a ***landscape***.

Pictures on a computer are ***graphics***.
2 *Mum took some **pictures** of us building a sandcastle.*
photograph, snapshot, snap

picture verb
1 *The girl is **pictured** against a background of flowers.*
depict, illustrate, represent, show, portray
2 *Can you **picture** what the world will be like in 100 years?*
imagine, visualise

piece noun
1 *They collected **pieces** of wood to build a raft.*
bar, block, length, stick, chunk, lump, hunk, bit, chip, fragment, particle, scrap, shred
2 *I've only got two **pieces** of chocolate left.*

bit, portion, part, section, segment, share, slice
3 *I've lost one of the **pieces** of the jigsaw.*
part, element, unit, component, constituent
4 *There's a **piece** about our school in the local paper.*
article, item, report, feature

pierce verb
*The arrow had **pierced** the knight's armour.*
enter, go through, make a hole in, penetrate, bore through
To pierce a hole through paper is to ***punch*** a hole or ***perforate*** it.
To pierce a hole in a tyre is to ***puncture*** it.
To pierce someone with a spike is to ***impale*** or ***spear*** them.

WORD WEB

pirate noun
*The ship was overrun by bloodthirsty **pirates**.*
buccaneer, marauder

THINGS YOU MIGHT FIND ON A PIRATE SHIP
barrels, cabin, crow's nest, deck, hammock, lantern, mast, plank, pirate flag, rigging, sail, treasure chest, wheel

telescope

A pirate flag is a ***Jolly Roger*** or ***skull-and-crossbones***.
A pirate ship might sail on the ***high seas*** or the ***Spanish Main***.

PEOPLE YOU MIGHT FIND ON A PIRATE SHIP
cabin boy or girl, captain, captives, cook, crew, first mate, lookout, stowaway

PIRATE TREASURE MIGHT CONTAIN
doubloons or ducats, gold bullion, pieces of eight
Goods or treasure seized by pirates is ***booty***.

WEAPONS A PIRATE MIGHT USE
cannon, cutlass, dagger, gunpowder, musket, pistol

OTHER THINGS A PIRATE MIGHT WEAR OR CARRY
bandanna or kerchief, bottle of rum, breeches, cocked hat, earrings, eye patch, hook, parrot or cockatoo, pigtail, sea chart, spyglass or telescope, treasure map, wooden leg or peg leg

SOME WORDS TO DESCRIBE A PIRATE
barbaric, black-hearted, bloodthirsty, cut-throat, daring, dastardly, fearless, heartless, lawless, merciless, murderous, pitiless, ruthless, savage, swashbuckling, vengeful, vicious, villainous

hat

parrot

dagger

musket

Jolly Roger

treasure map

treasure

pile noun
1 *Where did this **pile** of rubbish come from?*
heap, mound, mountain, stack, hoard, mass, quantity, collection, assortment
2 *I've still got **piles** of homework to do.*
plenty, a lot, a great deal
(*informal*) lots, masses

pile verb
Pile everything in the corner and we'll sort it out later.
heap, stack, collect, gather, assemble, hoard
to pile up
*The bills are beginning to **pile up**.*
build up, mount up, accumulate

pillar noun
*The roof was supported by tall **pillars**.*
column, pier, post, prop, support

pinch verb
1 *The baby **pinched** my arm and wouldn't let go.*
nip, squeeze, press, tweak, grip
2 (*informal*) *Who **pinched** my calculator?*
steal, take, snatch, pilfer
(*informal*) nick, swipe, make off with

pipe noun
*The water flows away along this **pipe**.*
tube
A pipe used for watering the garden is a ***hose***.
A pipe in the street which supplies water for fighting fires is a ***hydrant***.
A pipe which carries oil, etc., over long distances is a ***pipeline***.
The system of water pipes in a house is the ***plumbing***.

pirate noun
see panel on previous page

pity noun
*The pirates showed no **pity** towards the captives.*
mercy, compassion, sympathy, humanity, kindness, concern, feeling
OPPOSITE cruelty
a pity
*It's **a pity** that you have to leave so early.*
a shame, unfortunate, bad luck

pity verb
*We **pitied** anyone who was caught up in the storm.*
feel sorry for, feel for, sympathise with, take pity on

place noun
1 *This is a good **place** to park.*
site, venue, spot, location, position, situation
2 *They are looking for a quiet **place** to live.*

area, district, locality, neighbourhood, region, vicinity
3 *Save me a **place** on the bus.*
seat, space

place verb
1 *The hotel is **placed** next to the beach.*
locate, situate, position, station
2 *You can **place** your coats on the bed.*
put down, set down, leave, deposit, lay
(*informal*) dump, plonk

plain adjective
1 *The furniture in the room was very **plain**.*
simple, modest, basic, unelaborate
OPPOSITE elaborate
2 *Some people say she looks **plain** compared with her sister.*
unattractive, ordinary
OPPOSITE attractive
3 *It is **plain** to me that you are not interested.*
clear, evident, obvious, apparent, unmistakable
OPPOSITE unclear
4 *She told us what she thought in very **plain** terms.*
direct, frank, blunt, outspoken, honest, sincere, straightforward
5 *We need to wear a **plain** t-shirt for sports.*
unpatterned, self-coloured

plan noun
1 *The captain explained her **plan** to the rest of the team.*
idea, proposal, scheme, strategy, project, suggestion, proposition
A plan to do something bad is a ***plot***.
2 *They looked at the **plans** for the new sports centre.*
design, diagram, chart, map, drawing, blueprint

plan verb
1 *The outlaws **planned** an attack upon the sheriff.*
scheme, design, devise, work out, formulate, prepare, organise
To plan to do something bad is to ***plot***.
2 *What do you **plan** to do next?*
aim, intend, propose, mean

planet noun
*The new space probe will travel to far-off **planets**.*
world

THE PLANETS OF THE SOLAR SYSTEM (IN ORDER FROM THE SUN) ARE
Mercury, Venus, Earth, Mars, Jupiter, Saturn, Uranus, Neptune.

The path followed by a planet is its ***orbit***.
Minor planets orbiting the sun are ***asteroids***.

Something which orbits a planet is a ***satellite***.

The earth's large satellite is the ***Moon***.

WRITING TIPS

You can use these words to describe an **alien planet**
Earth-like, gaseous, inhospitable, uninhabitable

TO DESCRIBE ITS *SURFACE*
barren, desolate, dusty, frozen, icy, molten, rocky, volcanic

TO DESCRIBE ITS *ATMOSPHERE OR AIR*
airless, noxious, poisonous, thin, unbreathable

play noun
1 *There was a good **play** on TV last night.*
drama, performance, production
2 *It is important to balance work and **play**.*
playing, recreation, amusement, fun, games, sport

play verb
1 *The children went out to **play**.*
amuse yourself, have fun, romp about
2 *Do you like **playing** basketball?*
take part in, participate in, compete in

3 We are **playing** the home team next week.
compete against, oppose, challenge, take on
4 Mira **played** the piano at the school concert.
perform on
5 My sister **played** Goldilocks in the school **play**.
act, take the part of, portray, represent

playful adjective
The kittens were in a **playful** mood.
lively, spirited, frisky, mischievous, roguish, impish, joking, teasing
OPPOSITE serious

plead verb
to plead with
The children **pleaded with** the witch to let them go.
beg, entreat, implore, appeal to, ask, request, petition

pleasant adjective
1 The owner of the shop is always **pleasant** to us.
kind, friendly, likeable, charming, amiable, amicable, cheerful, genial, good-natured, good-humoured, approachable, hospitable, welcoming
2 We spent a very **pleasant** evening playing cards.
pleasing, enjoyable, agreeable, delightful, lovely, entertaining

pleased adjective
Why do you look so **pleased** today?
contented, delighted, elated, glad, grateful, happy, satisfied, thankful, thrilled
OPPOSITE annoyed

pleasure noun
1 Mrs Ramsay gets a lot of **pleasure** from her garden.
delight, enjoyment, happiness, joy, satisfaction, comfort, contentment, gladness
Very great pleasure is **bliss** or **ecstasy**.
2 He talked about the **pleasures** of living in the country.
joy, comfort, delight

plenty noun
Don't buy any milk—there's **plenty** in the fridge.
a lot, a large amount, an abundance, a profusion
A lot more than you need is a **glut** or **surplus**.
OPPOSITE scarcity
plenty of
We've still got **plenty of** time.
a lot of, lots of, ample, abundant
(informal) loads of, masses of, tons of

plot noun
1 Guy Fawkes was part of a **plot** against the government.
conspiracy, scheme, secret plan

2 It was hard to follow the **plot** of the film.
story, storyline, narrative, thread
3 They bought a **plot** of ground to build a new house.
area, piece, lot, patch
A plot of ground for growing flowers or vegetables is an **allotment**.
A large plot of land is a **tract** of land.

plot verb
1 The gang were **plotting** a daring bank raid.
plan, devise, concoct, hatch
(informal) cook up
2 They were accused of **plotting** against the queen.
conspire, intrigue, scheme

plump adjective
The goblin was short and **plump**, with pointy ears.
chubby, dumpy, fat, tubby, podgy, round, stout, portly
OPPOSITE skinny

plunge verb
1 One by one, the girls **plunged** into the pool.
dive, jump, leap, throw yourself
2 As the wind died down, the kite **plunged** to the ground.
drop, fall, pitch, tumble, plummet, swoop
3 I **plunged** my hand in the cold water.
dip, lower, sink, immerse, submerge
4 Finn **plunged** his spear into the dragon's throat.
thrust, stab, push, stick, shove, force

point noun
1 Be careful—that knife has a very sharp **point**.
tip, end, spike, prong
2 The stars looked like **points** of light in the sky.
dot, spot, speck, fleck
3 He marked on the map the exact **point** where the treasure lay.
location, place, position, site
4 At that **point** the rain started to come down.
moment, instant, time
5 I agree with your last **point**.
idea, argument, thought
6 His sense of humour is one of his good **points**.
characteristic, feature, attribute
7 There is no **point** in phoning at this hour.
purpose, reason, aim, object, use, usefulness
8 I think I missed the **point** of that film.
meaning, essence, core, gist

point verb
1 She **pointed** the way.
draw attention to, indicate, point out, show, signal
2 Can you **point** me in the right direction for the station?
aim, direct, guide, lead, steer

pointless adjective
It's **pointless** to argue with him— he's so stubborn.
useless, futile, vain
OPPOSITE worthwhile

poisonous adjective
Some of those mushrooms may be **poisonous**.
toxic, venomous, deadly, lethal

poke verb
Someone **poked** me in the back with an umbrella.
prod, dig, jab, stab, thrust
to poke out
The kitten's head was **poking out** of the basket.
stick out, project, protrude

pole noun
Four **poles** marked the corners of the field.
post, bar, rod, stick, shaft
A pole that you use when walking or as a weapon is a **staff**.
A pole for a flag to fly from is a **flagpole**.
A pole to support sails on a boat or ship is a **mast** or **spar**.
A pole with a pointed end to stick in the ground is a **stake**.
Poles which a circus entertainer walks on are **stilts**.

polish verb
Beeswax is used to **polish** furniture.
rub down, shine, buff, burnish, wax

polish noun
The silverware had been cleaned to give it a good **polish**.
shine, sheen, gloss, lustre, sparkle, brightness, glaze, finish

polite adjective
My aunt is always **polite** to visitors.
courteous, well-mannered, respectful, civil, well-behaved, gracious, gentlemanly or ladylike, chivalrous, gallant
OPPOSITE rude, impolite

pollute verb
The river has been **polluted** by chemicals.
contaminate, infect, poison

poor adjective
1 You can't afford luxuries if you're **poor**.
impoverished, poverty-stricken, penniless, needy, badly off, hard-up
OPPOSITE rich

point

2 *His handwriting is very **poor**.*
bad, inferior, inadequate,
incompetent, unsatisfactory, shoddy,
weak, worthless
OPPOSITE good, superior
3 *They pitied the **poor** animals
standing in the rain.*
unlucky, unfortunate, pitiful,
wretched
OPPOSITE lucky

popular *adjective*
1 *Disney has made a lot of **popular**
children's films.*
well-liked, well-loved, celebrated,
favourite
OPPOSITE unpopular
2 *Rollerblades are very **popular** just
now.*
fashionable, widespread, current, in
demand
(*informal*) trendy
OPPOSITE unpopular

port *noun*
*A large cruise ship sailed into
the **port**.*
harbour, dock, anchorage
A harbour for yachts and pleasure
boats is a *marina*.

portrait *noun*
*There's a **portrait** of the Queen on
every stamp.*
picture, image, likeness,
representation
A portrait which shows a side view of
someone is a *profile*.
A portrait which shows just the
outline of someone is a *silhouette*.
A portrait which exaggerates some
aspect of a person is a *caricature*.

portrait

posh *adjective* (*informal*)
*We went to a **posh** restaurant for a
treat.*
smart, stylish, high-class, elegant,
fashionable, up-market, luxurious,
luxury, deluxe, plush
(*informal*) classy, swanky, swish,
snazzy

position *noun*
1 *Mark the **position** on the map.*
location, place, point, spot, site,
whereabouts
2 *He shifted his **position** to avoid
getting cramp.*
pose, posture, stance
3 *Losing all her money put her in
a difficult **position**.*
situation, state, condition,
circumstances
4 *A referee should adopt a neutral
position.*
opinion, attitude, outlook, view
5 *Being a head teacher is an
important **position**.*
job, post, appointment, function

positive *adjective*
1 *The detective was **positive** that the
cook was lying.*
certain, sure, convinced, assured,
confident
OPPOSITE uncertain
2 *Miss Andrews made some **positive**
comments on my singing.*
helpful, useful, worthwhile,
beneficial, constructive
OPPOSITE negative

possible *adjective*
1 *Is it **possible** that life exists on
other planets?*
likely, probable, conceivable, credible
2 *It wasn't **possible** to shift the
piano.*
feasible, practicable, practical

post *noun*
1 *The farmer put up some **posts** for
a new fence.*
pole, pillar, shaft, stake, support, prop
2 *The **post** was delivered late.*
mail, letters, delivery
3 *Are you thinking of applying for
the **post**?*
job, position, situation, appointment,
vacancy

post *verb*
1 *Did you **post** those letters?*
mail, send, dispatch
2 *The names of the winners will be
posted on the noticeboard.*
display, put up, announce,
advertise

postpone *verb*
*They **postponed** the match because
of bad weather.*
put off, defer, delay
To stop a game or meeting that
you intend to start again later is to
adjourn or *suspend* it.

potion *noun*
*A magic **potion** was brewing in the
wizard's cauldron.*
drug, medicine, mixture

potion

pounce *verb*
to pounce on
*The cat **pounced on** the mouse.*
jump on, leap on, spring on, swoop
down on, lunge at, ambush, attack

pour *verb*
1 *Water **poured** through the hole.*
flow, run, gush, stream, spill, spout
2 *I **poured** some milk into my cup.*
tip, serve

power *noun*
1 *They were amazed by the **power** of
the robot.*
strength, force, might, energy
2 *The storyteller has the **power** to
enthral an audience.*
skill, talent, ability, competence
3 *A policeman has the **power** to
arrest someone.*
authority, right
4 *The empress had **power** over
all the people.*
authority, command, control,
dominance, domination

powerful *adjective*
1 *Sir Joustalot was the most
powerful knight in the
kingdom.*
influential, leading, commanding,
dominant, high-powered
2 *The wrestler had a **powerful**
punch.*
strong, forceful, hard, mighty,
vigorous, formidable, potent
3 *He used some **powerful**
arguments.*
strong, convincing, effective,
persuasive, impressive

practical *adjective*
1 *I'll ask Katie what to do—she is
always very **practical**.*
down-to-earth, matter-of-fact,
sensible, level-headed
OPPOSITE impractical
2 *The robbers' plan was not very
practical.*
workable, realistic, sensible, feasible,
viable, achievable
OPPOSITE impractical
3 *Do you have any **practical**
experience of childminding?*
real, actual, hands-on
OPPOSITE theoretical

practice noun
1 *We have extra football **practice** this week.*
training, exercises, preparation, rehearsal, drill
2 *Is it the **practice** amongst ogres to eat grubs for breakfast?*
custom, habit, convention, routine
in practice
*What will the plan involve **in practice**?*
in effect, in reality, actually, really

practise verb
1 *My piano teacher asked me to **practise** for longer.*
do exercises, rehearse, train, drill
To practise just before the start of a performance is to ***warm up***.
2 *My sister wants to **practise** veterinary medicine.*
do, perform, carry out, put into practice, follow, pursue

praise verb
*The critics **praised** the actress for her outstanding performance.*
commend, congratulate, applaud, admire, compliment, pay tribute to
(*informal*) rave about
OPPOSITE criticise

praise noun
*She received a lot of **praise** for her painting.*
approval, admiration, compliments, congratulations, applause

prance verb
*Milly started **prancing** about in a silly way.*
dance, skip, hop, leap, romp, cavort, caper, frolic, gambol

precious adjective
1 *Her most **precious** possession was an old photograph.*
treasured, cherished, valued, prized, dearest, beloved
2 *The throne glittered with **precious** gems and gold.*
valuable, costly, expensive, priceless
OPPOSITE worthless

precise adjective
1 *Can you tell me the **precise** time, please?*
exact, accurate, correct, true, right
OPPOSITE rough
2 *The map gave **precise** directions for finding the treasure.*
careful, detailed, specific, particular, definite
OPPOSITE vague

predict verb
*You can't **predict** what may happen in the future.*
forecast, foresee, foretell, prophesy

prefer verb
*Would you **prefer** juice or lemonade?*
rather have, go for, opt for, plump for, choose, fancy

prejudice noun
*The school has a policy against racial **prejudice**.*
bias, discrimination, intolerance, narrow-mindedness, bigotry
Prejudice against other races is ***racism***.
Prejudice against other nations is ***xenophobia***.
Prejudice against the other sex is ***sexism***.
OPPOSITE fairness, tolerance

prepare verb
*The museum staff are **preparing** for the new exhibition.*
get ready, make arrangements for, organise, plan, set up
To prepare for a play is to ***rehearse***.
To prepare to take part in a sport is to ***train***.

present adjective
1 *Is everyone **present**?*
here, in attendance, at hand
2 *Who is the **present** world chess champion?*
current, existing

present noun
*What would you like for your birthday **present**?*
gift (*informal*) prezzie

present verb
1 *The head **presents** the prizes on sports day.*
award, hand over
2 *Our class is **presenting** a play about the Vikings.*
put on, perform, stage, mount
3 *Dr Smart **presented** her amazing invention to the world.*
put forward, show, display, exhibit, make known

press verb
1 ***Press** the fruit through a sieve to get rid of the seeds.*
push, force, squeeze, squash, crush, shove, cram, compress
2 *She **pressed** her blouse for the party.*
iron, flatten, smooth
3 *Our friends **pressed** us to stay a bit longer.*
beg, urge, entreat, implore

press noun
1 *We read about the competition in the **press**.*
newspapers, magazines
2 *The **press** came to the opening of the new arts centre.*
journalists, reporters, the media

pressure noun
1 *The nurse applied **pressure** to the wound.*
force, compression, squeezing, weight, load
2 *In the final, the home team were under a lot of **pressure**.*
stress, strain, tension

presume verb
*I **presume** you'd like something to eat.*
assume, take it, imagine, suppose, think, believe, guess

pretend verb
*She's not really crying—she's only **pretending**.*
put on an act, bluff, fake, sham, pose (*informal*) kid, put it on

pretend adjective
*That's not a real spider—it's just a **pretend** one!*
fake, false, artificial, made-up
OPPOSITE real

pretty adjective
*The doll was dressed in a **pretty** blue outfit.*
attractive, beautiful, lovely, nice, pleasing, charming, dainty, picturesque, quaint
(*informal*) cute
A common simile is ***as pretty as a picture***.
OPPOSITE ugly

prevent verb
1 *The driver could do nothing to **prevent** the accident.*
stop, avert, avoid, head off
2 *The police **prevented** an attempted bank raid.*
block, foil, frustrate, thwart
3 *There's not much you can do to **prevent** colds.*
stave off, ward off

price noun
*What is the **price** of a return ticket to Sydney?*
cost, amount, figure, expense, payment, sum, charge, rate
The price you pay for a journey on public transport is a ***fare***.
The price you pay to send a letter is the ***postage***.
The price you pay to use a private road, bridge or tunnel is a ***toll***.

priceless adjective
*The museum contained many **priceless** antiques.*
precious, rare, valuable, costly, expensive, dear

prick verb
*Jamie burst the balloon by **pricking** it with a pin.*
pierce, puncture, stab, jab, perforate

prickly adjective
*Holly leaves are very **prickly**.*
spiky, spiny, thorny, bristly, sharp, scratchy

pride noun
1 *Mr Dodds takes great* **pride** *in his garden.*
satisfaction, pleasure, delight
2 *The medal winner was a source of great* **pride** *to his family.*
self-esteem, self-respect, dignity, honour
3 **Pride** *comes before a fall.*
arrogance, conceit, bigheadedness, vanity, snobbery
OPPOSITE humility

prim adjective
Aunt Jemima is always very **prim** *and proper.*
prudish, strait-laced, formal, demure

prisoner noun
The **prisoner** *tried to escape from jail.*
convict, captive, inmate
A person who is held prisoner until some demand is met is a **hostage**.

private adjective
1 *Everything I write in my diary is* **private**.
secret, confidential, personal, intimate
Secret official documents are **classified** documents.
2 *Can we go somewhere a little more* **private**?
quiet, secluded, hidden, concealed

prize noun
Our team won first **prize** *in the relay race.*
award, reward, trophy
Money that you win as a prize is your **winnings**.
Prize money that keeps increasing until someone wins it is a **jackpot**.

prize verb
Chrissie **prized** *her grandmother's ring above all else.*
treasure, value, cherish, hold dear, esteem, revere
OPPOSITE dislike

probable adjective
A burst pipe was the most **probable** *cause of the flood.*
likely, feasible, possible, predictable, expected
OPPOSITE improbable

problem noun
1 *Our maths teacher set us a difficult* **problem**.
puzzle, question
(*informal*) brainteaser, poser
2 *I'm having a* **problem** *with my computer.*
difficulty, trouble, snag, worry
(*informal*) headache

procession noun
The **procession** *made its way slowly down the hill.*
parade, march, column, line

prod verb
Someone **prodded** *me in the back with an umbrella.*
poke, dig, jab, nudge, push

production noun
1 **Production** *at the factory has increased this year.*
output
2 *We went to see a* **production** *of 'The Sound of Music'.*
performance, show

programme noun
1 *We worked out a* **programme** *for sports day.*
plan, schedule, timetable
A list of things to be done at a meeting is an **agenda**.
2 *There was a really good* **programme** *on TV last night.*
broadcast, show, production, transmission

progress noun
1 *I traced their* **progress** *on the map.*
journey, route, movement, travels
2 *I'm not making much* **progress** *learning Dutch.*
advance, development, growth, improvement, headway
An important piece of progress is a **breakthrough**.

progress verb
Work on the new building is **progressing** *well.*
proceed, advance, move forward, make progress, make headway, continue, develop, improve
(*informal*) come along

prohibit verb
Skateboarding is **prohibited** *in the school grounds.*
ban, forbid, outlaw, rule out, veto
OPPOSITE permit, allow

project noun
1 *We did a history* **project** *on the Victorians.*
activity, task, assignment, piece of research
2 *There is a* **project** *to create a bird sanctuary in the area.*
plan, proposal, scheme

project verb
1 *A narrow ledge* **projects** *from the cliff.*
extend, protrude, stick out, jut out, overhang

2 *The lighthouse* **projects** *a beam of light.*
cast, shine, throw out

promise noun
1 *We had* **promises** *of help from many people.*
assurance, pledge, guarantee, commitment, vow, oath, word of honour
2 *That young pianist shows* **promise**.
potential, talent

promise verb
Dad **promised** *that we'd go camping this summer.*
assure someone, give your word, guarantee, swear, take an oath, vow

promote verb
1 *Gareth has been* **promoted** *to captain.*
move up, advance, upgrade, elevate
2 *The singer is here to* **promote** *her new CD.*
advertise, publicise, market, push, sell (*informal*) plug
3 *The school is trying to* **promote** *healthy eating.*
encourage, foster, advocate, back, support

prompt adjective
I received a **prompt** *reply to my email.*
punctual, quick, rapid, swift, immediate, instant
OPPOSITE delayed

prompt verb
Having a dog **prompted** *her to take more exercise.*
cause, lead, induce, motivate, stimulate, encourage, provoke

proof noun
There is no **proof** *that he is a secret agent.*
evidence, confirmation

proper adjective
1 *The nurse showed them the* **proper** *way to tie a bandage.*
correct, right, accurate, precise, true, genuine
OPPOSITE wrong, incorrect
2 *It's only* **proper** *that he should pay for the broken window.*
fair, just, fitting, appropriate, deserved, suitable
OPPOSITE inappropriate
3 *It's not* **proper** *to speak with your mouth full.*
decent, respectable, tasteful
OPPOSITE rude

property noun
1 *This office deals with lost* **property**.
belongings, possessions, goods

a b c d e f g h i j k l m n o p q r s t u v w x y z

2 *The website lists **property** that is for sale in the city.*
buildings, houses, land, premises
3 *Many herbs have healing **properties**.*
quality, characteristic, feature, attribute, trait

protect *verb*
1 *A sentry was posted outside to **protect** the palace.*
defend, guard, safeguard, keep safe, secure
2 *I wore a hat to **protect** myself from the sun.*
shield, shade, screen, insulate

protest *noun*
1 *There were **protests** at the plan to close the cinema.*
complaint, objection
A general protest is an **outcry**.
2 *Some streets will be closed for a **protest** in the city centre.*
demonstration, march, rally
(*informal*) demo

protest *verb*
*We wrote a letter **protesting** about the closure of the cinema.*
complain, make a protest, object (to), take exception (to), express disapproval (of)

proud *adjective*
1 *Jennie's father was very **proud** when she passed her music exam.*
delighted (with), pleased (with)
A common simile is **as proud as a peacock**.
2 *He's too **proud** to mix with the likes of us!*
conceited, big-headed, arrogant, vain, haughty, self-important, snobbish, superior
(*informal*) stuck-up
OPPOSITE humble

prove *verb*
*The evidence will **prove** that he is innocent.*
confirm, demonstrate, establish, verify
OPPOSITE disprove

provide *verb*
1 *We'll **provide** the juice if you bring the sandwiches.*
bring, contribute, arrange for, lay on
To provide food and drink for people is to **cater** for them.
2 *The ski centre can **provide** you with boots and skis.*
supply, equip, furnish

provoke *verb*
1 *Don't do anything to **provoke** the lions!*
annoy, irritate, anger, incense, infuriate, exasperate, tease, taunt, goad
(*informal*) wind up
OPPOSITE pacify

2 *The referee's decision **provoked** anger from the crowd.*
arouse, produce, prompt, cause, generate, induce, stimulate, spark off, stir up, whip up

prowl *verb*
*Guard dogs **prowled** about the grounds of the palace.*
roam, slink, sneak, creep, steal

public *adjective*
1 *The **public** entrance is at the front of the gallery.*
common, communal, general, open, shared
OPPOSITE private
2 *The name of the author is now **public** knowledge.*
well-known, acknowledged, published, open, general, universal
OPPOSITE secret

publish *verb*
1 *The magazine is **published** every week.*
issue, print, produce, bring out, release, circulate
2 *When will they **publish** the results?*
announce, declare, disclose, make known, make public, report, reveal
To publish information on radio or TV is to **broadcast** it.

pudding *noun*
*Do you want any **pudding**?*
dessert, sweet
(*informal*) afters

puff *noun*
1 *A **puff** of wind caught his hat.*
gust, breath, flurry
2 *A **puff** of smoke rose from the chimney.*
cloud, whiff

puff *verb*
1 *The dragon **puffed** green smoke from its nostrils.*
blow out, send out, emit, belch
2 *By the end of the race I was **puffing**.*
breathe heavily, pant, gasp, wheeze
3 *The sails **puffed** out as the wind rose.*
become inflated, billow, swell

pull *verb*
1 *She **pulled** her chair nearer to the desk.*
drag, draw, haul, lug, trail, tow
OPPOSITE push
2 *Be careful—you nearly **pulled** my arm off!*
tug, rip, wrench, jerk, pluck

prowl

to pull out
1 *The dentist **pulled out** one of his teeth.*
extract, take out, remove
2 *He had to **pull out** of the race.*
back out, withdraw, retire
to pull up
*The bus **pulled up** at the traffic lights.*
draw up, stop, halt

pump *verb*
*The fire brigade **pumped** water out of the cellar.*
drain, draw off, empty
To move liquid from a higher container to a lower one through a tube is to **siphon** it.

punch *verb*
1 *Mrs Rafferty **punched** the robber on the nose.*
jab, poke, prod, thump
2 ***Punch** a hole through the card.*
bore, pierce

punish *verb*
*Those responsible for the crime will be **punished**.*
penalise, discipline, chastise

pupil *noun*
*There are 33 **pupils** in our class.*
schoolchild, student, learner, scholar
Someone who follows a great teacher is a **disciple**.

pure *adjective*
1 *The bracelet is made of **pure** gold.*
authentic, genuine, real
2 *He was talking **pure** nonsense.*
complete, absolute, utter, sheer, total
3 *All our dishes are made from **pure** ingredients.*
natural, wholesome
4 *They swam in the **pure**, clear water of the lake.*
clean, fresh, unpolluted
OPPOSITE impure

purpose *noun*
1 *Have you got a particular* **purpose** *in mind?*
intention, aim, end, goal, target, objective, outcome, result
2 *What's the* **purpose** *of your invention?*
point, use, usefulness, value

push *verb*
1 *We* **pushed** *our way through the crowd.*
shove, thrust, force, propel, barge, elbow, jostle
OPPOSITE pull
2 *Pete* **pushed** *his things into a bag.*
pack, press, cram, crush, compress, ram, squash, squeeze
3 *They* **pushed** *him to work even harder.*
pressurise, press, drive, urge, compel, bully
(*informal*) lean on

put *verb*
1 *You can* **put** *your schoolbags in the corner.*
place, set down, leave, deposit, dump, stand
2 *The dog* **put** *its head on my lap.*
lay, lean, rest
3 *I'll* **put** *some pictures on the wall.*
attach, fasten, fix, hang
4 *Where are they planning to* **put** *the car park?*
locate, situate
5 *I'm not sure of the best way to* **put** *this.*
express, word, phrase, say, state
to put someone off
The colour of the food **put** *me* **off** *eating.*
deter, discourage, distract
to put something off
They **put off** *their journey because of the fog.*
delay, postpone, defer
to put something out
The firefighters quickly **put out** *the blaze.*
extinguish, quench, smother
to put something up
1 *It doesn't take long to* **put up** *the tent.*
set up, construct, erect
2 *I'm going to buy a new bike before they* **put up** *the price.*
increase, raise

to put up with something
I don't know how you **put up with** *that noise.*
bear, stand, tolerate, endure

puzzle *noun*
Has anyone managed to solve the **puzzle***?*
question, mystery, riddle, conundrum, problem
(*informal*) brainteaser, poser

puzzle *verb*
1 *Phil was* **puzzled** *by the mysterious message.*
confuse, baffle, bewilder, bemuse, mystify, perplex, fox
2 *We* **puzzled** *over the problem for hours.*
ponder, think, meditate, worry, brood

puzzled *adjective*
Why are you looking so **puzzled***?*
confused, baffled, bewildered, mystified, perplexed

quaint *adjective*
They stayed in a **quaint** *thatched cottage.*
charming, picturesque, sweet, old-fashioned, old-world

quake *verb*
The ground **quaked** *with the thud of the giant's footsteps.*
shake, shudder, tremble, quiver, shiver, vibrate, rock, sway, wobble

quality *noun*
1 *We only use ingredients of the highest* **quality***.*
grade, class, standard
2 *The most obvious* **quality** *of rubber is that it stretches.*
characteristic, feature, property, attribute, trait

quantity *noun*
1 *She receives a huge* **quantity** *of fan mail every week.*
amount, mass, volume, bulk, weight
(*informal*) load

quay

2 *We recycled a large* **quantity** *of empty bottles.*
number
When you add up numbers, you get a **sum** or **total**.

quarrel *noun*
We have **quarrels***, but really we are good friends.*
argument, disagreement, dispute, difference of opinion, row, squabble, clash, tiff
Continuous quarrelling is **strife**.
A long-lasting quarrel is a **feud** or **vendetta**.
A quarrel in which people become violent is a **brawl** or **fight**.

quarrel *verb*
The twins **quarrelled** *over who should sit in the front.*
disagree, argue, row, squabble, bicker, clash, fight, fall out
to quarrel with something
I can't **quarrel with** *your decision.*
disagree with, object to, take exception to, oppose

quay *noun*
The ship unloaded its cargo on to the **quay***.*
dock, harbour, pier, wharf, jetty, landing stage

quest *noun*
The knights set out on a **quest** *to find the enchanted tower.*
search, hunt, expedition, mission

question *noun*
1 *Does anyone have any* **questions***?*
enquiry, query, problem
A question which someone sets as a puzzle is a **brain-teaser** or **conundrum** or **riddle**.
A series of questions asked as a game is a **quiz**.
A set of questions which someone asks to get information is a **questionnaire** or **survey**.

a
b
c
d
e
f
g
h
i
j
k
l
m
n
o
p
q
r
s
t
u
v
w
x
y
z

queue

2 *There's some* **question** *over the player's fitness.*
uncertainty, doubt, argument, debate, dispute

question *verb*
1 *The detective decided to* **question** *the suspect.*
ask, examine, interview, quiz, interrogate
To question someone intensively is to **grill** them.
2 *He* **questioned** *the referee's decision.*
challenge, dispute, argue over, quarrel with, object to, query

queue *noun*
There was a **queue** *of people outside the cinema.*
line, file, column, string
A long queue of traffic on a road is a **tailback**.

queue *verb*
Please **queue** *at the door.*
line up, form a queue

quick *adjective*
1 *You'd better be* **quick**—*the bus leaves in 10 minutes.*
fast, swift, rapid, speedy, hasty
(*informal*) nippy
A common simile is **as quick as a flash**.
OPPOSITE slow
2 *Do you mind if I make a* **quick** *phone call?*
short, brief, momentary, immediate, instant, prompt, snappy
OPPOSITE long, lengthy
3 *She's very* **quick** *at mental arithmetic.*
bright, clever, sharp, acute, alert
(*informal*) on the ball
OPPOSITE slow

quiet *adjective*
1 *The deserted house was still and* **quiet**.
silent, noiseless, soundless
A common simile is **as quiet as a mouse**.
OPPOSITE noisy
2 *The children spoke in* **quiet** *whispers.*
hushed, low, soft
Something that is so quiet that you can't hear it is **inaudible**.
OPPOSITE loud
3 *Amy has always been a* **quiet** *child.*
shy, reserved, subdued, placid, uncommunicative, retiring, withdrawn
OPPOSITE talkative
4 *We found a* **quiet** *place for a picnic.*
peaceful, secluded, isolated, restful, tranquil, calm, serene
OPPOSITE busy

quite *adverb*
Take care how you use **quite**, as the two senses are almost opposites.
1 *The two puppies have* **quite** *different personalities.*
completely, totally, utterly, entirely, absolutely, wholly
2 *They played* **quite** *well, but far from their best.*
fairly, reasonably, moderately, rather

quiz *noun*
Our class took part in a general knowledge **quiz**.
test, competition, questionnaire, exam, examination

Rr

race *noun*
1 *We had a* **race** *to see who was the fastest runner.*
competition, contest, chase
A race to decide who will take part in the final is a **heat**.
2 *We belong to different* **races** *but we're all humans.*
nation, people, ethnic group

race *verb*
1 *We* **raced** *each other to the end of the road.*
have a race with, run against, compete with
2 *She had to* **race** *home because she was late.*
run, rush, dash, hurry, sprint, fly, tear, whizz, zoom

racket *noun*
Please stop making that awful **racket**!
noise, row, din, commotion, disturbance, uproar, rumpus

ragged *adjective*
They met a traveller wearing **ragged** *clothes.*
tattered, tatty, threadbare, torn, frayed, patched, ripped, shabby, worn out

raid *noun*
The enemy **raid** *caught them by surprise.*
attack, assault, strike, onslaught, invasion, blitz

raid *verb*
1 *Long ago, Vikings* **raided** *the towns on the coast.*
attack, invade, ransack, plunder, loot, pillage
Someone who raids ships at sea is a **pirate**.
Someone who raids and steals cattle is a **rustler**.
2 *Police* **raided** *the house at dawn.*
descend on, rush, storm, swoop on

rain *noun*   rain
A formal word for rain is **precipitation**.
The rainy season in south and southeast Asia is the **monsoon**.
When there is no rain for a long time you have a **drought**.

raise *verb*
1 **Raise** *your hand if you need help.*
hold up, put up, lift
2 *The box was too heavy for him to* **raise**.
lift, pick up, elevate, hoist, jack up
3 *The Post Office is* **raising** *the price of stamps.*
increase, put up
4 *The runners hope to* **raise** *£1000 for charity.*
collect, gather, take in, make
5 *He* **raised** *some objections to the plan.*
bring up, mention, put forward, present, introduce
6 *The doctor didn't want to* **raise** *their hopes.*
encourage, build up, arouse
7 *It's hard work trying to* **raise** *a family.*
bring up, care for, look after, nurture, rear

ram *verb*
The car skidded and **rammed** *into a lamp-post.*
bump, hit, strike, crash into, collide with, smash into

random *adjective*
They picked a **random** *selection of pupils.*
arbitrary, chance, haphazard, casual, unplanned
OPPOSITE deliberate

range *noun*
1 *There is a* **range** *of mountains to the south.*
chain, line, row, series, string
2 *Supermarkets sell a wide* **range** *of goods.*
variety, assortment, selection, choice, spectrum
3 *The shop caters for all age* **ranges** *from toddlers to teenagers.*
span, scope

range verb
1 Prices **range** from five to twenty euros.
vary, differ, extend, fluctuate
2 Rows of jam jars were **ranged** on the shelf.
arrange, order, lay out, set out, line up
3 Wild deer **range** over the hills.
wander, ramble, roam, rove, stray

rapid adjective
The cyclists set off at a **rapid** pace.
fast, quick, speedy, swift, brisk
OPPOSITE slow

rare adjective
1 These flowers are now very **rare** in the wild.
uncommon, unusual, infrequent, scarce, sparse
OPPOSITE common
2 He has a **rare** ability to make people laugh.
exceptional, remarkable, special

rarely adverb
Our next-door neighbour **rarely** goes out.
seldom, infrequently, hardly ever
OPPOSITE often

rash adjective
Don't make any **rash** promises.
reckless, foolhardy, hasty, hurried, impulsive, unthinking
OPPOSITE careful

rate noun
1 The cyclists were pedalling at a furious **rate**.
pace, speed
2 What's the usual **rate** for washing a car?
charge, cost, fee, payment, price, figure, amount

rate verb
How do you **rate** their chance of winning?
judge, regard, consider, estimate, evaluate

rather adverb
1 It's **rather** chilly today.
quite, fairly, moderately, slightly, somewhat, a bit, a little
2 I'd **rather** not go out tonight.
preferably, sooner

rave verb
1 Connie **raved** about the film she saw last week.
be enthusiastic, talk wildly
2 The head **raved** on about their bad behaviour.
shout, rage, storm, yell, roar

raw adjective
1 **Raw** vegetables are supposed to be good for you.
uncooked
OPPOSITE cooked

2 The factory imports a lot of **raw** materials from abroad.
crude, natural, unprocessed, untreated
OPPOSITE manufactured, processed
3 Her knee felt **raw** after she fell off her bike.
red, rough, sore, tender, inflamed
4 There was a **raw** wind blowing from the east.
bitter, cold, chilly, biting, freezing, piercing

ray noun
A **ray** of light shone into the dark cave.
beam, shaft, stream

reach verb
1 They hoped to **reach** Oxford by lunch time.
arrive at, go as far as, get to, make
2 The appeal fund has **reached** its target.
achieve, attain
3 I'm not tall enough to **reach** the top shelf.
get hold of, grasp, touch
to reach out
Reach out your hands.
extend, hold out, put out, stick out, stretch out

reach noun
1 The shelf was just within his **reach**.
grasp
2 The shops are within easy **reach**.
distance, range

react verb
How did he **react** when he read the letter?
respond, behave, answer, reply

reaction noun
What was her **reaction** when you said you were sorry?
response, answer, reply

read verb
They couldn't **read** the doctor's handwriting.
make out, understand, decipher
To read through something very quickly is to **skim through** it.
To read here and there in a book is to **dip into** it.
To read something intently is to **pore over** it.

ready adjective
1 When will tea be **ready**?
prepared, set, done, available, in place
OPPOSITE not ready
2 He's always **ready** to help.
willing, glad, pleased, happy, keen, eager
OPPOSITE reluctant

real adjective
1 History is about **real** events.
actual, true, factual, verifiable
OPPOSITE fictitious, imaginary
2 The necklace was made from **real** rubies.
authentic, genuine, bona fide, natural
OPPOSITE artificial, fake
3 She doesn't often show her **real** feelings.
true, honest, sincere, genuine, heartfelt
OPPOSITE insincere

realistic adjective
1 The portrait of the artist is very **realistic**.
lifelike, true to life, faithful, convincing, recognisable
2 It's not **realistic** to expect a puppy to be quiet.
feasible, practical, sensible, possible, workable

realise verb
It took him a long time to **realise** what she meant.
understand, appreciate, grasp, comprehend, recognise, see
(informal) catch on to, twig

really adverb
1 Are you **really** going to Peru?
actually, definitely, truly, in fact, certainly, genuinely, honestly
2 I saw a **really** good film last night.
very, extremely, exceptionally

reasonable adjective
1 That's a **reasonable** plan.
sensible, intelligent, rational, logical, sane, sound
OPPOSITE irrational
2 They bought the house for a **reasonable** price.
fair, acceptable, average, moderate, respectable, normal, proper
OPPOSITE excessive

reassure verb
The doctor **reassured** her that the wound was not serious.
calm, comfort, encourage, hearten, give confidence to
OPPOSITE threaten

rebel verb
The king feared that the people would **rebel**.
revolt, rise up
To rebel against the captain of a ship is to **mutiny** and someone who does this is a **mutineer**.
OPPOSITE obey

rebellion noun
The protest soon became a widespread **rebellion**.
revolt, revolution, uprising, resistance
A rebellion on a ship is a **mutiny**.

a
b
c
d
e
f
g
h
i
j
k
l
m
n
o
p
q
r
s
t
u
v
w
x
y
z

recent *adjective*
We watch the news to keep up with ***recent*** *events.*
current, up-to-date, contemporary, new, the latest, fresh

recite *verb*
Zoe ***recited*** *a poem she had written.*
say aloud, read out, narrate

reckless *adjective*
A man has been charged with ***reckless*** *driving.*
careless, irresponsible, mindless, thoughtless, negligent, foolhardy, rash, wild
OPPOSITE careful

reckon *verb*
1 *I tried to* ***reckon*** *how much she owed me.*
calculate, work out, add up, figure out, assess, estimate
2 *Do you* ***reckon*** *it's going to rain?*
think, believe, guess, imagine, feel

recognise *verb*
1 *I didn't* ***recognise*** *her with her new haircut.*
identify, know, distinguish, make out, recall, recollect, remember
2 *He refused to* ***recognise*** *that he was to blame.*
acknowledge, admit, accept, grant, concede, confess, realise

recommend *verb*
1 *The doctor* ***recommended*** *a complete rest.*
advise, counsel, propose, suggest, advocate, prescribe, urge
2 *The restaurant was* ***recommended*** *by a friend of mine.*
approve of, endorse, praise, commend

record *noun*
The zookeepers keep a ***record*** *of the animals' diet.*
account, report
A record of daily events is a *diary* or *journal*.
The record of a voyage at sea or in space is the *log*.

The record of what happened at a meeting is the *minutes*.
A record of people's names is a *register*.
Records consisting of historical documents are *archives*.

record *verb*
1 *The concert is being* ***recorded*** *by the BBC.*
tape, video
2 *She* ***recorded*** *our interview in a notebook.*
write down, note, set down, put down, enter

recover *verb*
1 *It took a long time to* ***recover*** *after my illness.*
get better, heal, improve, recuperate, pick up, mend, come round, pull through, revive, rally
2 *The police have* ***recovered*** *the stolen vehicles.*
get back, retrieve, reclaim, repossess, find, trace

recycle *verb*
You can ***recycle*** *glass by putting it in the bottle bank.*
reuse, reprocess, salvage, use again

red *adjective*
1 *I chose a* ***red*** *ribbon for my doll.*
Something which is rather red is *reddish*.
A common simile is *as red as a beetroot*.
2 *My nose and cheeks were* ***red*** *with cold.*
flushed, glowing, rosy, ruddy, blushing
3 *Her eyes were* ***red*** *from lack of sleep.*
bloodshot, inflamed, red-rimmed
4 *The fairy queen had flaming* ***red*** *hair.*
ginger, auburn, coppery
(*informal*) carroty

recycle

reduce *verb*
She's ***reduced*** *the amount of sugar in her diet.*
decrease, lessen, lower, cut, cut back, slash
To reduce something by half is to *halve* it.
To reduce the width of something is to *narrow* it.
To reduce the length of something is to *shorten* or *trim* it.
To reduce speed is to *decelerate*.
To reduce the strength of a liquid is to *dilute* it.
OPPOSITE increase

refer *verb*
The shop assistant ***referred*** *me to another department.*
hand over, pass on, direct, send
to refer to
1 *Please don't* ***refer to*** *this matter again.*
mention, speak of, make reference to, allude to, bring up
2 *If you can't spell a word,* ***refer to*** *a dictionary.*
look up, consult, go to, turn to

reflect *verb*
1 *Cat's-eyes* ***reflect*** *the light from car headlights.*
send back, throw back, shine back
2 *Their success* ***reflects*** *their hard work.*
show, indicate, demonstrate, exhibit, reveal
to reflect on
We need time to ***reflect on*** *what to do next.*
think about, contemplate, consider, ponder, mull over

refuse *verb*
1 *Why did you* ***refuse*** *my offer of help?*
decline, reject, turn down, say no to
OPPOSITE accept
2 *They were* ***refused*** *permission to enter the building.*
deny, deprive of
OPPOSITE allow

region *noun*
1 *The Arctic and Antarctic are polar* ***regions***.
area, place, land, territory, part of the world
2 *There are two local radio stations serving this* ***region***.
area, district, neighbourhood, locality, vicinity, zone

regret *verb*
She ***regretted*** *her decision to leave Ireland.*
be sorry for, repent, feel sad about

regular *adjective*
1 *Signs are placed at* ***regular*** *intervals along the cycle path.*
evenly spaced, fixed
OPPOSITE irregular, uneven

2 *The drummer kept up a **regular** rhythm.*
constant, consistent, steady, uniform, unvarying
A common simile is **as regular as clockwork**.
OPPOSITE erratic
3 *Is this your **regular** route to school?*
normal, usual, customary, habitual, ordinary, routine
OPPOSITE unusual
4 *Craig is a **regular** customer at the sweet shop.*
frequent, familiar, persistent
OPPOSITE rare, unusual

rehearse *verb*
*We had to **rehearse** the scene again.*
go over, practise, try out

reign *verb*
*Which British monarch **reigned** the longest?*
be king or queen, be on the throne, govern, rule

reject *verb*
1 *At first, she **rejected** their offer of help.*
decline, refuse, turn down, say no to
2 *As we picked the berries, we **rejected** any bad ones.*
discard, get rid of, throw out, scrap

rejoice *verb*
*The people **rejoiced** when the wicked queen died.*
celebrate, delight, be happy, exult
OPPOSITE grieve

relate *verb*
1 *Do you think the two crimes are **related**?*
connect, link, associate
2 *The travellers **related** the story of their adventures.*
tell, narrate, report, describe
relate to
*The letter **relates to** your great grandfather.*
be about, refer to, have to do with, concern

relationship *noun*
1 *There is a **relationship** between your diet and health.*
connection, link, association, bond
The relationship between two numbers is a **ratio**.
2 *The twins have a close **relationship**.*
friendship, attachment, understanding

relax *verb*
1 *I like to **relax** by listening to music.*
unwind, rest, take it easy
2 *This exercise will **relax** your shoulder muscles.*
loosen, ease
OPPOSITE tighten
3 *He **relaxed** his hold on the dog's leash.*
slacken, loosen, ease, lessen, reduce
OPPOSITE tighten

relaxed *adjective*
*They liked the **relaxed** atmosphere of village life.*
informal, casual, carefree, leisurely, easygoing, peaceful, restful, unhurried, calm
(*informal*) laid-back
OPPOSITE tense, stressful

release *verb*
1 *The prisoners were **released** early.*
free, let go, discharge, liberate, set free
To release slaves is to **emancipate** them.
OPPOSITE imprison
2 *The dog was tied up—who **released** him?*
let loose, set loose, unfasten, unleash, untie
3 *The band will **release** their new single in April.*
issue, publish, put out

relevant *adjective*
1 *The detective noted everything that was **relevant** to the case.*
applicable, pertinent, appropriate, suitable, significant, related, connected
2 *Don't interrupt unless your comments are **relevant**.*
to the point

reliable *adjective*
1 *The king summoned his most **reliable** knights.*
faithful, dependable, trustworthy, loyal, constant, devoted, staunch, true
2 *The secret agent always sent **reliable** information.*
dependable, valid, trustworthy, safe, sound, steady, sure

relieve *verb*
*The doctor said the pills would **relieve** the pain.*
ease, help, lessen, diminish, relax, soothe, comfort

religious *adjective*
1 *The choir sang a selection of **religious** music.*
sacred, holy, divine
OPPOSITE secular
2 *My grandparents were very **religious**.*
devout, pious, reverent, spiritual, godly
OPPOSITE ungodly

reluctant *adjective*
*The old woman was **reluctant** to open the door.*
unwilling, hesitant, slow, grudging, half-hearted, resistant
OPPOSITE eager

rely *verb*
*Are you sure that we can **rely** on their help?*
depend on, count on, have confidence in, trust
(*informal*) bank on

remain *verb*
1 *The boys were told to **remain** behind after school.*
stay, wait, linger
(*informal*) hang about
2 *It will **remain** warm and sunny all weekend.*
continue, persist, keep on, carry on
3 *Little **remained** of the house after the fire.*
be left, survive

remains *plural noun*
*They cleared away the **remains** of the picnic.*
remnants, leftovers, leavings, fragments, traces, scraps, debris
The remains at the bottom of a cup are **dregs**.
Remains still standing after a building has collapsed are **ruins**.
Historic remains are **relics**.

remarkable *adjective*
1 *He described his **remarkable** escape from the island.*
amazing, extraordinary, astonishing, memorable, wonderful, incredible, unforgettable, breathtaking
2 *The young violinist shows **remarkable** skill for her age.*
exceptional, notable, noteworthy, striking, outstanding, impressive, phenomenal

remember *verb*
1 *Can you **remember** what she looked like?*
recall, recollect, recognise, place
2 *He was trying to **remember** his lines for the play.*
learn, memorise, keep in mind
OPPOSITE forget
3 *My granny likes to **remember** the old days.*
reminisce about, think back to

remind *verb*
***Remind** me to buy a newspaper.*
prompt, jog your memory
to remind you of something
*What does this tune **remind** you **of**?*
make you think of, take you back to

remote *adjective*
1 *The tour will explore a **remote** part of Brazil.*
distant, faraway, isolated, cut-off, inaccessible, out-of-the-way, unfrequented
OPPOSITE accessible
2 *The chances of us winning are **remote**.*
poor, slender, slight, small, faint, doubtful
OPPOSITE likely

a b c d e f g h i j k l m n o p q r s t u v w x y z

remove verb
1 *Please **remove** your rubbish.*
clear away, take away
2 *The rowdy passengers were **removed** from the bus.*
throw out, turn out, eject, expel
(*informal*) kick out
To remove people from a house where they are living is to **evict** them.
To remove a monarch from the throne is to **depose** him or her.
3 *The author decided to **remove** the last paragraph.*
cut out, delete, erase, get rid of, do away with, eliminate
4 *The dentist **removed** my bad tooth.*
extract, pull out, take out, withdraw
5 *The divers slowly **removed** their wetsuits.*
take off, peel off, strip off, shed, cast off

renew verb
1 *The church roof has been completely **renewed**.*
repair, renovate, restore, replace, rebuild, reconstruct, revamp, refurbish, overhaul
(*informal*) do up
2 *You must **renew** your passport before you go abroad.*
bring up to date, update

repeat verb
1 *The parrot **repeated** everything he said.*
say again, copy, duplicate, reproduce, echo
2 *The actors had to **repeat** the opening scene.*
do again, redo

replace verb
1 *The spy carefully **replaced** the missing document.*
put back, return, restore, reinstate
2 *Who will **replace** the head teacher when she retires?*
follow, succeed, take over from, take the place of
3 *I need to **replace** one of the tyres on my bike.*
change, renew

reply noun
*He has received no **replies** to his email.*
response, answer, reaction, acknowledgement
An angry reply is a **retort**.

reply verb
to reply to
*She took a long time to **reply to** my letter.*
answer, respond to, give a reply to, react to, acknowledge

report verb
1 *The newspapers **reported** what happened.*
give an account of, record, state, describe, announce, publish

2 *We were told to **report** to reception when we arrived.*
present yourself, make yourself known, check in
3 *If you cause any damage, I'll **report** you to the police.*
complain about, inform on, denounce

report noun
*There was a **report** in the paper about the crash.*
account, record, story, article, description

reporter noun
*The film star was being interviewed by a TV **reporter**.*
journalist, correspondent

represent verb
1 *The picture **represents** an ancient legend.*
depict, illustrate, portray, picture, show, describe
2 *A dove is often said to **represent** peace.*
stand for, symbolise
3 *He appointed a lawyer to **represent** him.*
speak for

🕸 WORD WEB

reptile noun
SOME ANIMALS WHICH ARE REPTILES
alligator, chameleon, crocodile, gecko, iguana, lizard, slow-worm, snake, terrapin, tortoise, turtle
A reptile found in myths and legends is the **basilisk**.

repulsive adjective
*We were put off eating by the **repulsive** smell.*
disgusting, revolting, offensive, repellent, disagreeable, foul, repugnant, obnoxious, sickening, hateful, hideous, horrible, loathsome, objectionable, vile
OPPOSITE attractive

reputation noun
*The singer's **reputation** spread throughout the world.*
fame, celebrity, name, renown, eminence, standing, stature

request verb
*She has **requested** a transfer to a different job.*
ask for, appeal for, apply for, beg for, call for, entreat, implore, invite, pray for, seek

request noun
*They have ignored our **request** for help.*
appeal, plea, entreaty, call, cry

crocodile

A request for a job or membership is an **application**.
A request signed by a lot of people is a **petition**.

require verb
1 *They **require** a draw to win the championship.*
need, must have
2 *Visitors are **required** to sign the register.*
instruct, oblige, request, direct, order, command

rescue verb
1 *A helicopter was sent to **rescue** the trapped climbers.*
free, liberate, release, save, set free
To rescue someone by paying money is to **ransom** them.
2 *The divers **rescued** some items from the sunken ship.*
retrieve, recover, salvage

reserve verb
1 *The astronauts had to **reserve** fuel for the return voyage.*
keep, put aside, set aside, save, preserve, retain, hold back
2 *Have you **reserved** your seats on the train?*
book, order, secure

reserve noun
1 *The climbers kept a **reserve** of food in their base camp.*
stock, store, supply, hoard, stockpile
A reserve of money is a **fund** or **savings**.
2 *They put him down as a **reserve** for Saturday's game.*
substitute, standby, stand-in, replacement
Someone who can take the place of an actor is an **understudy**.
3 *The wildlife **reserve** has a new baby rhino.*
reservation, park, preserve, sanctuary

resign verb
*The manager of the football team was forced to **resign**.*
leave, quit, stand down, step down, give in your notice
When a monarch resigns from the throne, he or she **abdicates**.

lizard

tortoise

resist verb
1 *They were too weak to **resist** the sorcerer's magic.*
stand up to, defend yourself against, withstand, defy, oppose, fend off
OPPOSITE yield to, surrender to
2 *I couldn't **resist** having another piece of chocolate.*
avoid, hold back from, refuse
OPPOSITE give in, accept

resources plural noun
1 *The country is rich in natural resources.*
materials, raw materials, reserves
2 *The library has limited **resources** for buying CDs.*
funds, money, capital, assets, means, wealth

respect noun
1 *Her colleagues have the deepest **respect** for her.*
admiration, esteem, regard, reverence, honour
2 *Have some **respect** for other people's feelings.*
consideration, sympathy, thought, concern
3 *In some **respects**, he's a better player than I am.*
way, point, aspect, feature, characteristic, detail, particular

respect verb
1 *Everyone **respects** her for her courage.*
admire, esteem, revere, honour, look up to, value
OPPOSITE scorn, despise
2 *She tried to **respect** the wishes of her dead husband.*
obey, follow, observe, adhere to, comply with
OPPOSITE ignore

respectable adjective
1 *He came from a very **respectable** family.*
decent, honest, upright, honourable, worthy
2 *I finished the race in a **respectable** time.*
reasonable, satisfactory, acceptable, passable, adequate, fair, tolerable

respond verb
to respond to
*He didn't **respond to** my question.*
reply to, answer, react to, acknowledge

response noun
*Did you get a **response** to your letter?*
reply, answer, reaction, acknowledgement
An angry response is a **retort**.

responsible adjective
1 *Parents are legally **responsible** for their children.*
in charge
OPPOSITE not responsible

2 *He's a very **responsible** sort of person.*
reliable, sensible, trustworthy, dependable, conscientious, dutiful, honest
OPPOSITE irresponsible
3 *Looking after people's money is a **responsible** job.*
important, serious
4 *Who is **responsible** for all this mess?*
to blame, guilty (of), at fault

rest noun
1 *The actors had a short **rest** in the middle of the rehearsal.*
break, breather, breathing-space, pause, respite, lie-down, nap
2 *The doctor said the patient needed complete **rest**.*
relaxation, leisure, inactivity, ease, quiet, time off
the rest
*Take a few sweets now, but leave **the rest** for later.*
the remainder, the surplus, the others, the remains

rest verb
1 *I think we should stop and **rest** for a while.*
have a rest, lie down, relax, lounge, have a nap
2 ***Rest** the ladder against the wall.*
lean, prop, stand, place, support

restless adjective
*The animals became **restless** during the storm.*
agitated, nervous, anxious, edgy, fidgety, excitable, jumpy, jittery
OPPOSITE relaxed

result noun
1 *The water shortage is a **result** of a long drought.*
consequence, effect, outcome, sequel (to), upshot
The result of a game is the **score**.
The result of a trial is the **verdict**.
2 *If you multiply 9 by 12, what is the **result**?*
answer, product

result verb
*The bruising on his leg **resulted** from a bad fall.*
come about, develop, emerge, happen, occur, follow, ensue, take place, turn out
to result in
*Severe flooding **resulted in** chaos on the roads.*
cause, bring about, give rise to, lead to, develop into

snake

retreat verb
1 *The army **retreated** to a safe position.*
move back, draw back, fall back, withdraw, retire
To retreat in a shameful way is to **run away** or (informal) **turn tail**.
2 *The snail **retreated** into its shell.*
shrink back, recoil

retrieve verb
*I had to climb the fence to **retrieve** our ball.*
get back, bring back, fetch, recover, rescue, salvage

return verb
1 *We hope to **return** to Paris next summer.*
go back, revisit
2 *My husband **returns** on Friday.*
get back, come back, come home
3 *I **returned** the book to its rightful owner.*
give back, restore
4 *Faulty goods may be **returned** to the shop.*
send back, take back
5 *Please **return** the money I lent you.*
give back, repay, refund
6 *We hoped that the fever would not **return**.*
happen again, recur

reveal verb
1 *The spy refused to **reveal** his real identity.*
declare, disclose, make known, confess, admit, announce, proclaim, publish, tell
2 *She swept aside the curtain to **reveal** a secret door.*
uncover, unveil, expose

revenge noun
*He sought **revenge** for the killing of his brother.*
reprisal, vengeance
to take revenge on someone
*He declared that he would **take revenge on** them all.*
get even with, repay
(informal) get your own back on

review noun
1 *They are carrying out a **review** of after-school clubs.*
study, survey, examination, inspection
2 *We had to write **reviews** of our favourite books.*
report, criticism, appraisal, critique

a b c d e f g h i j k l m n o p q r s t u v w x y z

review *verb*
*The judge began to **review** the evidence.*
examine, go over, study, survey, consider, assess, appraise, evaluate, weigh up

revise *verb*
1 *We **revised** the work we did last term.*
go over, review, study
2 *The new evidence forced me to **revise** my opinion.*
change, modify, alter, reconsider, re-examine
3 *The last chapter has been **revised** by the author.*
correct, amend, edit, rewrite, update

revive *verb*
1 *The patient **revived** slowly after the operation.*
come round, come to, recover, rally, wake up
2 *A cold drink will **revive** you.*
refresh, restore, invigorate, bring back to life, revitalise

revolt *verb*
1 *The people **revolted** against the cruel king.*
rebel, riot, rise up
To revolt on a ship is to **mutiny**.
2 *They were **revolted** by the stench in the dungeon.*
disgust, repel, sicken, nauseate, offend, appal

revolting *adjective*
*What is that **revolting** smell?*
disgusting, foul, horrible, nasty, loathsome, offensive, obnoxious, repulsive, repugnant, sickening, nauseating, vile, unpleasant
OPPOSITE pleasant, attractive

revolution *noun*
1 *The **revolution** brought in a new government.*
rebellion, revolt, uprising
2 *Computers brought about a **revolution** in the way people work.*
change, transformation, shift
3 *We have to understand orbits, **rotations** and **revolutions** of planets.*
rotation, turn, circuit, cycle

revolve *verb*
*She told me her life **revolves** around ponies.*
rotate, turn
To revolve quickly is to **spin** or **whirl**.
To move round something is to **circle** or **orbit** it.

reward *noun*
*There is a **reward** for finding the missing cat.*
prize, bonus, payment, award, decoration
OPPOSITE punishment

reward *verb*
1 *The firefighters were **rewarded** for their bravery.*
honour, decorate
2 *She was generously **rewarded** for her work.*
compensate, repay

rhythm *noun*
*We tapped our feet to the **rhythm** of the music.*
beat, pulse
The speed or type of rhythm of a piece of music is the **tempo**.
The type of rhythm of a piece of poetry is its **metre**.

rich *adjective*
1 *They must be **rich** to live in a castle.*
wealthy, affluent, prosperous, well-off, well-to-do
OPPOSITE poor
2 *The palace was full of **rich** furnishings.*
expensive, costly, luxurious, sumptuous, opulent, lavish, splendid, ornate
3 *The dancer wore a dress of a **rich** red colour.*
deep, strong, vivid, intense

rickety *adjective*
*Take care—that ladder looks **rickety**.*
shaky, unsteady, unstable, wobbly, flimsy
OPPOSITE solid

riddle *noun*
*They had to solve the **riddle** to find the treasure.*
puzzle, mystery, question, conundrum, problem

ride *verb*
*My little brother is learning to **ride** a bike.*
control, handle, manage, steer

ride *noun*
*They took us for a **ride** in their new car.*
drive, run, journey, trip
(*informal*) spin

ridiculous *adjective*
1 *My little sister looked **ridiculous** in high-heeled shoes.*
silly, stupid, foolish, daft, absurd, funny, laughable
2 *That is a **ridiculous** price for a pair of trainers!*
ludicrous, senseless, nonsensical, preposterous, outrageous, absurd, unreasonable, crazy

right *adjective*
1 *Put up your hand if you got the **right** answer.*
correct, accurate, true, exact
OPPOSITE wrong
2 *She was waiting for the **right** moment to tell him.*
proper, appropriate, fitting, suitable, ideal
OPPOSITE wrong

3 *It's not **right** to steal.*
fair, honest, decent, just, honourable, lawful, moral, upright, virtuous, ethical
OPPOSITE wrong

right *noun*
1 *The cafe is on the **right** along the High Street.*
OPPOSITE left
2 *People have the **right** to walk across the common.*
freedom, liberty
3 *You don't have the **right** to tell me what to do.*
authority, power

ring *noun*
1 *The children danced around in a **ring**.*
circle, round, loop, circuit
2 *The wooden barrel had metal **rings** round it.*
band, hoop

ring *verb*
1 *The whole area was **ringed** by a high fence.*
surround, encircle, enclose, circle
2 *The doorbell **rang**.*
chime, peal, toll, jangle, tinkle, sound, buzz
3 ***Ring** me tomorrow evening.*
phone, call, telephone, ring up
(*informal*) give a buzz

riot *noun*
*The police moved in to stop the **riot**.*
commotion, disorder, disturbance, turmoil, uproar, uprising

riot *verb*
*The crowds were **rioting** in the streets.*
run riot, run wild, run amok, rampage, revolt, rise up, rebel

ripe *adjective*
*Some of the plums on the tree are **ripe** now.*
mature, ready to eat
To become ripe is to **ripen**.

rise *verb*
1 *The kite **rose** high into the air.*
climb, mount, fly up, ascend, soar
When a plane rises into the air, it **takes off**.
When a rocket rises into the air, it **lifts off**.
OPPOSITE descend
2 *The outer wall of the castle **rose** before us.*
tower, loom, reach up, stick up
3 *House prices **rose** again last year.*
go up, increase
OPPOSITE fall
4 *The audience **rose** and applauded wildly.*
stand up, get up
OPPOSITE sit

rise noun
There will be a **rise** in temperature over the next few days.
increase, jump
OPPOSITE fall

risk verb
1 If you place a bet, you **risk** losing the money.
chance, dare, gamble, venture
2 The firefighter **risked** his life to save them.
endanger, put at risk, jeopardise, hazard

risk noun
1 All outdoor activities carry an element of **risk**.
danger, hazard, peril
2 The forecast says there's a **risk** of snow.
chance, likelihood, possibility

risky adjective
Cycling on icy roads is **risky**.
dangerous, hazardous, perilous, unsafe
OPPOSITE safe

rival noun
He has no serious **rival** for the championship.
competitor, adversary, challenger, opponent, contender, contestant

river noun
A small river is a **stream** or **rivulet** or (Scottish) **burn**.
A small river which flows into a larger river is a **tributary**.
The place where a river begins is its **source**.
The place where a river goes into the sea is its **mouth**.
A wide river mouth is an **estuary** or (Scottish) **firth**.
The place where the mouth of a river splits before going into the sea is a **delta**.
A river of ice is a **glacier**.

river

roar noun, verb
The dragon lifted its mighty head and **roared**.
bellow, cry, yell, bawl, howl, thunder

rob verb
The thieves planned to **rob** several banks in the city.
steal from, break into, burgle, hold up, raid, loot, ransack, rifle

rock verb
1 I **rocked** the baby's cradle to and fro.
sway, swing
2 The ship **rocked** in the storm.
roll, toss, lurch, pitch, tilt, reel

rod noun
The framework is held together by steel **rods**.
bar, rail, pole, strut, shaft, stick, spoke, staff

role noun
1 Who is playing the lead **role** in the play?
character, part
2 Each player has an important **role** in the team.
job, task, function, position

roll verb
1 The wheels of the carriage began to **roll**.
move round, turn, revolve, rotate, spin, twirl, whirl
2 **Roll** the paper around your finger.
curl, wind, wrap, twist, coil
To roll up a sail on a yacht is to **furl** it.
3 **Roll** the pastry into a large circle.
flatten, level out, smooth
4 The ship **rolled** about in the storm.
pitch, rock, sway, toss, wallow, lurch

romantic adjective
1 The film had a very **romantic** ending.
sentimental, emotional, tender (informal) soppy, mushy
2 The life of an explorer sounds very **romantic**.
exotic, glamorous, exciting

room noun
1 How many **rooms** are there in your house?
An old word for room is **chamber**.
2 Is there **room** in the car for another suitcase?
space, capacity

root noun
We need to get to the **root** of the problem.
origin, source, cause, basis, starting point

rope noun
The sailors threw a **rope** to the men in the water.
cable, cord, line
The ropes that support a ship's mast and sails are the **rigging**.
A rope with a loop at one end used for catching cattle is a **lasso**.

rot verb
The wooden fence had begun to **rot**.
decay, decompose, become rotten, crumble, disintegrate
If metal rots it is said to **corrode**.
If rubber rots it is said to **perish**.
If food rots it is said to **go bad** or **putrefy**.

rotten adjective
1 The window frame is **rotten**.
decayed, decaying, decomposed, crumbling, disintegrating
Rotten metal is **corroded** or **rusty** metal.
OPPOSITE sound
2 The fridge smelled of **rotten** eggs.
bad, mouldy, mouldering, foul, putrid, smelly
OPPOSITE fresh
3 (informal) The weather has been **rotten** all week.
bad, unpleasant, disagreeable, awful, abysmal, dreadful, nasty (informal) lousy
OPPOSITE good

rough adjective
1 A **rough** track led to the farm.
bumpy, uneven, irregular, rocky, stony, rugged, craggy, jagged
OPPOSITE even, smooth
2 The sea was **rough** and the boat lurched from side to side.
stormy, turbulent, heaving
If the sea is rough with small waves it is said to be **choppy**.
OPPOSITE calm
3 The woman wore a **rough** woollen cloak.
coarse, harsh, scratchy, bristly
OPPOSITE soft
4 The prisoners had suffered **rough** treatment.
harsh, severe, cruel, hard, tough, violent
OPPOSITE gentle, mild
5 I had only a **rough** idea of where we were.
approximate, vague, inexact, imprecise, hazy
OPPOSITE exact
6 Our guide made a **rough** sketch of the route.
quick, hasty, crude, basic
OPPOSITE detailed, careful

round adjective
Holly bushes have small **round** berries.
rounded, spherical
A flat round shape is **circular**.

round noun
Our team got through to the second **round** of the competition.
stage, heat, bout, contest, game

round verb
The motorbike **rounded** the corner at top speed.
go round, travel round, turn
to round something off
They **rounded** the evening **off** with some songs.
bring to an end, conclude, end, finish, complete
to round up people or **things**
The captain **rounded up** his players.
assemble, gather, bring together, collect, muster, rally

roar

a
b
c
d
e
f
g
h
i
j
k
l
m
n
o
p
q
r
s
t
u
v
w
x
y
z

routine noun
1 *Brushing my teeth is part of my morning **routine**.*
pattern, procedure, way, custom, habit, practice, order
2 *The ice-skaters practised their new **routine**.*
act, programme, performance, number

row noun
1 *The gardener planted the vegetables in **rows**.* (rhymes with *go*)
column, line, string, series, sequence
A row of people waiting for something is a **queue**.
A row of people walking behind each other is a **file**.
A row of soldiers standing side by side on parade is a **rank**.
2 *The class next door was making a terrible **row**.* (rhymes with *cow*)
noise, racket, din, commotion, disturbance, uproar, rumpus
3 *One of the pirates had a **row** with the captain.* (rhymes with *cow*)
argument, fight, quarrel, squabble, disagreement, dispute

rowdy adjective
*Later in the evening, the party became **rowdy**.*
noisy, unruly, wild, disorderly, boisterous, riotous
OPPOSITE quiet

rub verb
1 *Kathy **rubbed** her sore elbow.*
stroke, knead, massage
2 *I **rubbed** some suncream on my arms.*
spead, smooth, smear, apply (to)
3 *These boots are **rubbing** against my ankles.*
graze, scrape, chafe
4 *She **rubbed** the mirror until it gleamed.*
polish, wipe, shine, buff
to rub something out
*Can you **rub out** those pencil marks?*
erase, wipe out, delete, remove

rubbish noun
1 *Mike took the **rubbish** out to the bin.*
refuse, waste, trash, garbage, junk, litter, scrap
2 *Don't talk **rubbish**!*
nonsense, drivel, balderdash, piffle, gibberish, claptrap, gobbledegook (*informal*), rot, tripe, twaddle

rude adjective
1 *It's very **rude** to talk with your mouth full.*
impolite, discourteous, disrespectful, impertinent, impudent, insolent, offensive, insulting, bad-mannered, ill-bred

To be rude to someone is to **insult** or **snub** them.
To be rude about sacred things is to be **blasphemous** or **irreverent**.
OPPOSITE polite
2 *Some of the jokes in the film are rather **rude**.*
indecent, improper, offensive, coarse, crude
OPPOSITE decent, clean

ruin verb
*The storm had **ruined** the farmer's crops.*
damage, destroy, spoil, wreck, devastate, demolish, lay waste, shatter

ruin noun
*When they lost the match, it was the **ruin** of their dream.*
collapse, failure, breakdown
Financial ruin is **bankruptcy**.
ruins
*Archaeologists have discovered the **ruins** of a Roman fort.*
remains, remnants, fragments

rule noun
1 *Players must stick to the **rules** of the game.*
law, regulation, principle
A set of rules is a **code**.
2 *The country was formerly under French **rule**.*
control, authority, command, power, government, reign

rule verb
1 *The Romans **ruled** a vast empire.*
command, govern, control, direct, lead, manage, run, administer
2 *Queen Victoria continued to **rule** for many years.*
reign, be ruler
3 *The umpire **ruled** that the batsman was out.*
judge, decree, pronounce, decide, determine, find

rumour noun
*There was a **rumour** that the queen was a witch in disguise.*
gossip, hearsay, talk
(*informal*) tittle-tattle

run verb
1 *We **ran** as fast as our legs could carry us.*
race, sprint, dash, tear, bolt, career, speed, hurry, rush, streak, fly, whizz, zoom, scurry, scamper, scoot
To run at a gentle pace is to **jog**.
When a horse runs, it **gallops**, **canters** or **trots**.
2 *Tears **ran** down the mermaid's cheeks.*

stream, flow, pour, gush, flood, cascade, spill, trickle, dribble, leak
3 *That old sewing machine still **runs** well.*
function, operate, work, go, perform
4 *My uncle **runs** a restaurant in Leeds.*
manage, be in charge of, direct, control, supervise, govern, rule
5 *The High Street **runs** through the city centre.*
pass, go, extend, stretch, reach
to run away or **off**
*The thieves **ran off** when they heard footsteps.*
bolt, fly, flee, escape, take off, hurry off (*informal*) make off, clear off, scarper
to run into
1 *Guess who I **ran into** the other day?*
meet, come across, encounter (*informal*) bump into
2 *A cyclist skidded and **ran into** a tree.*
hit, collide with

run noun
1 *She goes for a **run** in the park every morning.*
A fast run is a **dash**, **gallop**, **race** or **sprint**.
A gentle run is a **jog**.
2 *We went for a **run** in the car.*
drive, journey, ride
3 *They've had a **run** of good luck recently.*
sequence, stretch, series

runny adjective
*This custard is too **runny**.*
watery, thin, liquid, fluid
OPPOSITE thick

rush verb
*I **rushed** home with the good news.*
hurry, hasten, race, run, dash, fly, bolt, charge, shoot, speed, sprint, tear, zoom
When cattle or other animals rush along together they **stampede**.

rush noun
1 *We've got plenty of time, so what's the **rush**?*
hurry, haste, urgency
2 *There was a sudden **rush** of water.*
flood, gush, spurt, stream, spate

ruthless adjective
*The pirates launched a **ruthless** attack.*
cruel, brutal, bloodthirsty, barbaric, heartless, pitiless, merciless, callous, ferocious, fierce, savage, vicious, violent
OPPOSITE merciful

runny

A B C D E F G H I J K L M N O P Q R S T U V W X Y Z

sack verb
*The manager threatened to **sack** the whole team.*
dismiss, discharge
(*informal*) fire, give you the sack

sad adjective
*Mia felt **sad** when her best friend moved away.*
unhappy, sorrowful, miserable, depressed, downcast, downhearted, despondent, crestfallen, dismal, gloomy, glum, blue, low, dejected, forlorn, desolate, doleful, wretched, woeful, woebegone, tearful, heartbroken, broken-hearted
If you are sad because you are away from home, you are **homesick**.
OPPOSITE happy

sadden verb
*The news of her friend's illness **saddened** her.*
distress, upset, depress, grieve, disappoint
(*informal*) break your heart
OPPOSITE cheer up

safe adjective
1 *The kitten was found **safe** and well in a neighbour's garden.*
unharmed, unhurt, uninjured, undamaged, sound, intact
(*informal*) in one piece
OPPOSITE hurt, damaged
2 *They felt **safe** indoors as the storm raged outside.*
protected, guarded, defended, secure
OPPOSITE vulnerable
3 *The secret code is in **safe** hands.*
reliable, trustworthy, dependable
4 *Is the tap water **safe** to drink?*
harmless, uncontaminated, innocuous
OPPOSITE dangerous

safety noun
*You must wear a seat belt for your own **safety**.*
protection, security, well-being
OPPOSITE danger

sail verb
*We **sailed** to Norway rather than going by air.*
travel by ship
To have a holiday sailing on a ship is to **cruise**.
To begin a sea voyage is to **put to sea** or **set sail**.

same adjective
the same
1 *Each pirate was given **the same** ration of rum.*
equal, identical, equivalent
2 *Everyone in the choir wore **the same** outfit.*
matching, similar, alike, uniform
3 *Her feelings remain **the same**.*
unaltered, unchanged, constant
OPPOSITE different

sarcastic adjective
*He made a **sarcastic** remark about my hat.*
mocking, satirical, ironical, sneering, taunting

satisfaction noun
*He gets a lot of **satisfaction** from growing vegetables.*
happiness, pleasure, enjoyment, contentment, fulfilment, sense of achievement, pride
OPPOSITE dissatisfaction

satisfactory adjective
*I'm afraid this work is not **satisfactory**.*
acceptable, adequate, passable, good enough, tolerable, competent
(*informal*) all right, up to scratch
OPPOSITE unsatisfactory

satisfy verb
*Nothing **satisfies** him—he's always complaining.*
please, content, make you happy
To satisfy your thirst is to **quench** or **slake** it.
OPPOSITE dissatisfy

savage adjective
1 *The invaders launched a **savage** attack on the town.*
vicious, cruel, barbaric, brutal, bloodthirsty, pitiless, ruthless, merciless, inhuman
OPPOSITE humane
2 *A **savage** beast lived in the cave.*
untamed, wild, ferocious, fierce
OPPOSITE domesticated

save verb
1 *They managed to **save** most of the books from the fire.*
rescue, recover, retrieve, salvage
2 *The knight pledged to **save** the princess from the witch's curse.*
protect, defend, guard, shield, preserve
3 *She **saved** him from making a fool of himself.*
stop, prevent, deter
4 *I **saved** you a piece of cake.*
keep, reserve, set aside, hold on to
5 *If you share a car, then you can **save** petrol.*
be sparing with, conserve, use wisely

say verb
1 *He found it hard to **say** what he meant.*
express, communicate, put into words, convey
2 *I would like to **say** a few words before we start.*
utter, speak, recite, read

Try to vary the words you use for **say**, especially in direct speech. Here are some other words you could use.
TO SAY *LOUDLY*
call, cry, exclaim, bellow, bawl, shout, yell, roar *'Land ahoy!'* **bellowed** the cabin boy.
TO SAY *QUIETLY*
whisper, mumble, mutter *'That woman,'* I **whispered**, *'is a secret agent.'*
TO SAY *STRONGLY*
state, announce, assert, declare, pronounce, insist, maintain, profess *'I never cut my toenails,'* the ogre **declared**.
TO SAY *CASUALLY*
remark, comment, observe, note, mention *'It's very warm for this time of year,'* Mr Lewis **remarked**.
TO SAY *ANGRILY*
snap, snarl, growl, thunder, bark, rasp, rant, rave *'Give me that piece of paper!'* **snapped** Miss Crabbit.
TO SAY *SUDDENLY*
blurt out *'That's just a pretend dinosaur!'* Ben **blurted out**.
TO SAY *UNCLEARLY*
babble, burble, gabble, stammer *The stranger kept **babbling** about hidden treasure.*
TO SAY *IN SURPRISE* OR *ALARM*
gasp, cry, squeal *'The tunnel is sealed! There's no way out!'* **gasped** Alex.
TO SAY *SOMETHING FUNNY*
joke, quip, tease *'Were you singing? I thought it was a cat,'* **teased** my big sister.
TO GIVE AN ORDER
command, demand, order *A voice outside **demanded**, 'Open the door at once!'*
TO ASK A QUESTION
enquire, demand, query *'How do you spell your name?' the judge **enquired**.*
TO GIVE A REPLY
answer, reply, respond, retort *'Certainly not!'* **retorted** Lady Dimsley.
TO MAKE A REQUEST
beg, entreat, implore, plead, urge *The mouse **pleaded**, 'Please let go off my tail!'*
TO MAKE A SUGGESTION
suggest, propose *'Let's make them walk the plank,'* **suggested** Captain Hook.
TO SAY *AGAIN*
repeat, reiterate, echo *The Martians **repeated**, 'Take us to your leader!'*

a b c d e f g h i j k l m n o p q r s t u v w x y z

saying noun
'Many hands make light work' is a common **saying**.
expression, phrase, motto, proverb, catchphrase
An overused saying is a **cliché**.

scan verb
1 The lookout **scanned** the horizon, hoping to see land.
search, study, survey, examine, scrutinise, stare at, eye
2 I **scanned** through some magazines in the waiting room.
skim, glance at, flick through

scandal noun
1 The waste of food after the party was a **scandal**.
disgrace, embarrassment, shame, outrage
2 Some newspapers like to publish the latest **scandal**.
gossip, rumours, dirt

scar noun
The warrior had a **scar** across his forehead.
mark, blemish, wound

scar verb
The injuries he received **scarred** him for life.
mark, disfigure, deface

scarce adjective
Water is very **scarce** in the desert.
hard to find, in short supply, lacking, sparse, scanty, rare, uncommon
(informal) thin on the ground
OPPOSITE plentiful

scarcely adverb
She was so tired that she could **scarcely** walk.
barely, hardly, only just

scare noun
The explosion gave them a nasty **scare**.
fright, shock, alarm

scare verb
My brother tried to **scare** us by making ghost noises.
frighten, terrify, petrify, alarm, startle, panic
OPPOSITE reassure

scared adjective
When she heard the footsteps, Lily was too **scared** to move.
frightened, terrified, petrified, horrified, alarmed, fearful, panicky

scary adjective (informal)
I had to close my eyes at the **scary** bits in the film.
frightening, terrifying, horrifying, alarming, nightmarish, fearsome, chilling, spine-chilling, hair-raising, bloodcurdling, chilling, eerie, sinister

scatter verb
1 She **scattered** the seeds on the ground.
spread, sprinkle, sow, strew, throw about, shower
OPPOSITE collect
2 The animals **scattered** when the children ran towards them.
break up, separate, disperse, disband
OPPOSITE gather

scene noun
1 The police arrived quickly at the **scene** of the crime.
location, position, site, place, situation, spot
2 They were rehearsing a **scene** from the play.
episode, part, section, act
3 I gazed out of the window at the moonlit **scene**.
landscape, scenery, view, sight, outlook, prospect, spectacle, setting, backdrop
4 He didn't want to create a **scene** in the restaurant.
fuss, commotion, disturbance, quarrel, row

scenery noun
We admired the **scenery** from the top of the hill.
landscape, outlook, prospect, scene, view, panorama

scent noun
Rowena loves the **scent** of roses.
smell, fragrance, perfume, aroma

schedule noun
The athletes had a rigorous training **schedule**.
programme, timetable, plan, calendar, diary
A schedule of topics to be discussed at a meeting is an **agenda**.
A schedule of places to be visited on a journey is an **itinerary**.

scheme noun
They worked out a **scheme** to raise some money.
plan, proposal, project, procedure, method, system
scheme verb
The smugglers were **scheming** against each other.
plot, conspire, intrigue

scorch

scold verb
He **scolded** the paper boy for being late.
reprimand, reproach, tell off
(informal) tick off

scorch verb
The dragon's breath **scorched** the wizard's beard.
burn, singe, sear, blacken, char

score noun
We added up each other's **scores**.
marks, points, total
The final score is the **result**.

score verb
1 How many goals did you **score**?
win, get, make, gain, earn
2 Some lines were **scored** into the bark of the tree.
cut, gouge, mark, scrape, scratch

scorn noun
She dismissed my suggestion with **scorn**.
contempt, derision, disrespect, mockery, ridicule
OPPOSITE admiration

scowl verb
The witch **scowled** under her floppy black hat.
frown, glower

scramble verb
1 The smugglers escaped by **scrambling** over the rocks.
clamber, climb, crawl, scrabble
2 The children **scrambled** to get the best seats.
push, jostle, struggle, fight, scuffle

scrap noun
1 They fed the **scraps** of food to the birds.
bit, piece, fragment, morsel, crumb, speck, particle
2 He took a pile of **scrap** to the tip.
rubbish, waste, junk, refuse, litter
Scraps of cloth are **rags** or **shreds**.
3 (informal) There was a **scrap** between the two gangs.
fight, brawl, scuffle, tussle, squabble

scrap verb
The author **scrapped** the last paragraph.
discard, throw away, abandon, cancel, drop, give up
(informal) dump

scrape verb
1 She **scraped** her knee when she fell over.
graze, scratch, scuff
2 I tried to **scrape** the mud off my trainers.
rub, scour, scrub, clean

scratch verb
1 Someone **scratched** the side of the car.
mark, score, scrape, gouge, graze
2 The cat tried to **scratch** her.
claw

scratch noun
Who made this **scratch** on the side of the car?
gash, groove, line, mark, scrape

scream noun, verb
*A woman ran out of the house
screaming. We heard a woman's
scream in the distance.*
shriek, screech, shout, yell, cry, bawl,
howl, wail, squeal, yelp

scribble verb
*He **scribbled** his phone number on a
scrap of paper.*
scrawl, jot down, dash off, write
To scribble a rough drawing,
especially when you are bored, is to
doodle.

scrub verb
*She **scrubbed** the floor clean.*
rub, brush, clean, wash, scour

scruffy adjective
*Magnus wore an old jumper and
scruffy jeans.*
untidy, messy, ragged, tatty,
tattered, worn-out, shabby
OPPOSITE smart

🕷 WORD WEB

sea noun
The very large seas of the world
are called **oceans**.
An area of sea partly enclosed by
land is a **bay** or **gulf**.
A wide inlet of the sea is a **sound**.
A wide inlet where a river joins the
sea is an **estuary**, or in Scotland
a **firth**.
A narrow stretch of water linking
two seas is a **strait**.
The bottom of the sea is the
seabed.
The land near the sea is the **coast**
or the **seashore**.
Creatures that live in the sea are
marine creatures.

THINGS YOU MIGHT SEE ON THE SEA
breaker, iceberg, sea spray, surf,
swell, waves; boat, cruise ship,
ocean liner, yacht

**SOME CREATURES THAT
LIVE IN THE SEA**
dolphin, eel, fish, killer whale,
octopus, porpoise, seahorse,
seal, sea lion, shark, squid,
stingray, turtle, whale

starfish

sculpture noun
*The temple was full of marble
sculptures.*
carving, figure, statue

🕷 WORD WEB

*We explored the **seashore**, looking
for shells and fossils.*
seaside, beach, shore, coast

**THINGS YOU MIGHT SEE ON THE
SEASHORE**
cave, cliff, coral reef, driftwood,
dunes, lighthouse, mudflats,
pebbles, rock pool, rocks, sand,
seashell, seaweed, shingle

**CREATURES THAT LIVE ON THE
SEASHORE**
barnacle, clam, cockle, coral,
crab, cuttlefish, jellyfish, limpet,
mussel, oyster, prawn, razor shell,
sea anemone, sea bird, seagull,
sea urchin, shrimp, sponge,
starfish, whelk

*If it's sunny tomorrow, we might
go to the **seaside**.*
beach, sands, seashore

**THINGS YOU MIGHT SEE AT THE
SEASIDE**
beach huts, funfair, harbour, ice-
cream van, jetty, pier, promenade

*A town where you go to have fun
by the sea is a **seaside resort**.*

**THINGS YOU MIGHT TAKE TO THE
SEASIDE**
beach ball, bucket and spade,
deckchair, fishing net, snorkel,
sunglasses, sunhat, sunshade,
suncream, surfboard, surfsuit,
swimming costume, towel,
windbreak

**THINGS YOU MIGHT DO AT THE
SEASIDE**
ball games, beachcombing,
building sandcastles, collecting
shells, fishing, paddling, scuba
diving, snorkelling, sunbathing,
surfing, swimming, water-skiing,
windsurfing

✏️ WRITING TIPS

You can use these
words to describe the
sea.

crab

TO DESCRIBE A CALM SEA
calm, crystal clear, glassy,
sparkling, tranquil, unruffled

TO DESCRIBE A ROUGH SEA
choppy, raging, rough,
stormy, tempestuous,
turbulent, wild
WAVES ON THE SEA MIGHT
billow, break, crash, heave,
pound, roll, surge, swell,
tumble, wash

lighthouse

seaweed

shell

fish

a b c d e f g h i j k l m n o p q r s t u v w x y z

seal *verb*
*The entrance to the burial chamber
had been **sealed**.*
close, fasten, shut, lock, secure
To seal a leak is to **plug** it or **stop** it.

search *verb*
1 *He was **searching** for the book he
had lost.*
hunt, look, seek
To search for gold or some other
mineral is to **prospect**.
2 *The police **searched** the house but
didn't find anything.*
explore, scour, ransack, rummage
through, comb
3 *Security staff **searched** all the
passengers.*
check, inspect, examine, scrutinise
(*informal*) frisk

search *noun*
*After a long **search**, she found her
keys.*
hunt, look, check
A long journey in search of
something is a **quest**.

season *noun*
*The hotels are full during
the holiday **season**.*
period, time

seat *noun*
*We found two empty
seats at the back of
the cinema.*
chair, place
A long seat for more
than one person is a
bench.
A long wooden seat in a
church is a **pew**.
A seat on a bicycle or
horse is a **saddle**.
A special seat for a king
or queen is a **throne**.

second *adjective*
*Would anyone like
a **second** helping of
pudding?*
another, additional,
extra, further

second *noun*
1 *The magic potion only takes a
second to work.*
instant, moment, flash
(*informal*) jiffy, tick
2 *Inga was **second** in the cross-
country race.*
runner-up

second *verb*
*We need someone to **second** the
proposal.*
back, support

secret *adjective*
1 *The spy managed to get hold of a
secret document.*
confidential, classified, restricted
(*informal*) hush-hush

2 *The detectives are part of a **secret**
operation.*
undercover, covert
3 *The things I write in my diary
are **secret**.*
private, confidential, personal,
intimate
4 *The cook showed us a **secret**
passageway into the castle.*
hidden, concealed, disguised

secretive *adjective*
*Why is she being so **secretive** about
her past?*
uncommunicative, tight-lipped,
reticent, reserved, mysterious, quiet
(*informal*) cagey
OPPOSITE communicative, open

section *noun*
*The website has a special **section**
aimed at children.*
part, division, sector, portion,
segment, bit, fragment
A section of a book is a **chapter**.
A section from a piece of classical
music is a **movement**.
A section taken from a book
or a long piece of music is a
passage.
A section of a journey is a
stage.

seat

secure *adjective*
1 *The ladder was not
very **secure**.*
steady, firm, solid,
fixed, fast, immovable
2 *She is still trying to
find a **secure** job.*
permanent, regular,
steady
3 *They bolted the
doors to make the
castle **secure**.*
safe, guarded,
protected, defended

see *verb*
1 *If you look closely,
you might **see** a
dragonfly.*
catch sight of, spot, notice, observe,
make out, distinguish, note, perceive,
recognise, sight, spy
To see something briefly is to
glimpse it.
To see an accident or some unusual
event is to **witness** it.
2 *Did you **see** the news yesterday?*
watch, look at, view
3 *You may **see** me in my office after
work.*
go to, report to
4 *I didn't expect to **see** you here!*
meet, run into, encounter
(*informal*) bump into
5 *Will we have time to **see** them
on the way home?*
visit, call on, drop in on

6 *I **see** what you mean.*
understand, appreciate, comprehend,
follow, grasp, realise, take in
7 *I find it hard to **see** him in the role
of Peter Pan.*
imagine, picture, visualise
8 *Please **see** that the windows are
shut.*
make sure, make certain, ensure
9 *I'll **see** what I can do.*
think about, consider, ponder, reflect
on, weigh up
10 *I'll **see** you to the door.*
conduct, escort, accompany, guide,
lead, take

seem *verb*
*Everything **seems** to be all right.
She is far more friendly than she
seems.*
appear, look, give the impression of
being

seize *verb*
1 *The climber stretched out to **seize**
the rope.*
grab, catch, snatch, take hold of,
grasp, grip, clutch
2 *The police **seized** the robbers as
they left the bank.*
arrest, capture
(*informal*) collar, nab
To seize someone's property as a
punishment is to **confiscate** it.
To seize someone's power or position
is to **usurp** it.
To seize an aircraft or vehicle during
a journey is to **hijack** it.

seldom *adverb*
*It **seldom** rains in the desert.*
rarely, infrequently
OPPOSITE often

select *verb*
*They had to **select** a new captain.*
choose, pick, decide on, opt for, settle
on, appoint, elect

selection *noun*
*The shop has a wide **selection**
of rollerskates.*
choice, range, variety, assortment

selfish *adjective*
*He's so **selfish** that he kept all the
chocolate to himself.*
greedy, mean, miserly, grasping, self-
centred, thoughtless
OPPOSITE unselfish, generous

sell *verb*
*The corner shop **sells** newspapers
and sweets.*
deal in, trade in, stock, retail
Uncomplimentary synonyms are
peddle and **hawk**.
OPPOSITE buy

send *verb*
1 *I **sent** each of my friends a
postcard.*
post, mail, dispatch

2 *They plan to **send** a rocket to Mars.*
launch, propel, direct, fire, shoot
to send for someone
*I think we should **send for** a doctor.*
call, summon, fetch
to send something out
*The device was **sending out** weird noises.*
emit, issue, give off, discharge

sensational *adjective*
1 *The newspaper printed a **sensational** account of the murder.*
shocking, horrifying, startling, lurid
2 (*informal*) *Did you hear the **sensational** result of yesterday's match?*
amazing, extraordinary, remarkable, fantastic, spectacular, stupendous

sense *noun*
1 *A baby learns about the world through its **senses**.*
Your five senses are **hearing**, **sight**, **smell**, **taste** and **touch**.
2 *A drummer needs to have a good **sense** of rhythm.*
awareness, consciousness, perception, feeling (for)
3 *If you had any **sense** you'd stay at home.*
common sense, intelligence, wisdom, wit, brains
4 *The **sense** of the word is not clear.*
meaning, significance, import
to make sense of something
*They couldn't **make sense of** the garbled message.*
understand, make out, interpret, follow

sense *verb*
1 *He **sensed** that she didn't like him.*
be aware, realise, perceive, feel, guess, notice, suspect
2 *The device **senses** any change of temperature.*
detect, respond to

sensible *adjective*
1 *It would be **sensible** to wait until the weather improves.*
wise, intelligent, shrewd, rational, reasonable, careful, prudent, logical, sane, sound
OPPOSITE stupid
2 *You will need **sensible** shoes for the hiking trip.*
comfortable, practical
OPPOSITE impractical

sensitive *adjective*
1 *She has **sensitive** skin which gets sunburnt.*
delicate, tender, fine, soft
2 *Take care what you say—he's very **sensitive**.*
easily offended, easily upset, touchy
3 *She's very **sensitive** towards other people.*
tactful, considerate, thoughtful, sympathetic, understanding

sentimental *adjective*
1 *He gets **sentimental** looking at old photographs.*
emotional, nostalgic, tearful
2 *I hate **sentimental** messages on birthday cards.*
romantic, tender
(*informal*) soppy, mushy

separate *adjective*
1 *The zoo kept the male lions **separate** from the cubs.*
apart, separated, distinct, independent
OPPOSITE together
2 *They slept in **separate** rooms.*
different, detached, unattached
OPPOSITE attached, joined

separate *verb*
1 *The sheepdog **separated** the sheep from the lambs.*
cut off, divide, fence off, isolate, keep apart, remove, segregate, set apart, take away
To separate something which is connected to something else is to **detach** or **disconnect** it.
To separate things which are tangled together is to **disentangle** them.
OPPOSITE combine, mix
2 *They walked along together until their paths **separated**.*
split, branch, fork
OPPOSITE merge
3 *Her friend's parents have **separated**.*
split up, break up, part company
To end a marriage legally is to **divorce**.

series *noun*
1 *We had to answer a **series** of questions in our exam.*
succession, sequence, string, set, chain, train
2 *Are you watching the new **series** on TV?*
serial

serious *adjective*
1 *His **serious** expression told them something was wrong.*
solemn, sombre, unsmiling, grave, grim
OPPOSITE cheerful
2 *She is writing a **serious** book about global warming.*
learned, intellectual, scholarly
(*informal*) heavy
OPPOSITE light
3 *Are you **serious** about wanting to learn to ski?*
sincere, genuine, in earnest
4 *This hospital ward is for people with **serious** injuries.*
severe, acute, critical, bad, terrible, appalling, dreadful, major, grave
OPPOSITE minor, trivial

servant *noun*
*This part of the house was where the **servants** lived.*
attendant, retainer, helper, domestic, manservant, maid
The chief manservant in a private house is a **butler**.
The servant of a medieval knight was a **page** or **squire**.

serve *verb*
1 *The shopkeeper was busy **serving** customers.*
help, assist, aid
2 *When everyone had sat down they **served** the first course.*
give out, dish up, pass round, distribute

service *noun*
1 *The genie bowed and said he was glad to be of **service**.*
help, assistance, aid, use, usefulness, benefit
2 *Their marriage **service** was held in the local church.*
ceremony, ritual, rite
A service in church is a meeting for **worship**.
3 *Mum says her car needs a **service**.*
a check-over, maintenance, servicing

service *verb*
*The garage **serviced** her car.*
maintain, check, repair, mend, overhaul

set *verb*
1 *The removal men **set** the piano on the floor.*
place, put, stand, position
2 *I helped Dad to **set** the table.*
arrange, lay, set out
3 *Have they **set** a date for the wedding yet?*
appoint, specify, name, decide, determine, choose, fix, establish, settle
4 *The jelly will **set** quicker in the fridge.*
become firm, solidify, harden, stiffen
5 *The sun was just beginning to **set**.*
do down, sink
to set off
1 *The knights **set off** on their quest.*
depart, get going, leave, set out, start out
2 *The burnt toast **set off** the smoke alarm.*
activate, start, trigger
to set something out
*The information is clearly **set out** on the page.*
lay out, arrange, display, present
to set something up
*They're trying to **set up** an after-school club.*
establish, create, start, begin, introduce, organise

a b c d e f g h i j k l m n o p q r s t u v w x y z

set *noun*
1 *There is a **set** of measuring spoons in the drawer.*
collection, batch, kit
2 *Our class painted the **set** for the play.*
scenery, setting

setting *noun*
*The house stood in a rural **setting**.*
surroundings, location, place, position, site, background

settle *verb*
1 *The brothers tried to **settle** their differences.*
resolve, sort out, deal with, end
2 *The cat had just **settled** on the sofa.*
sit down, relax, rest
3 *A robin **settled** on a nearby branch.*
land, alight
4 *The family is planning to **settle** in Canada.*
emigrate (to), move (to), set up home
5 *You can see lots of fish when the mud **settles**.*
sink to the bottom, clear, subside
6 *We'll **settle** the hotel bill in the morning.*
pay, clear, square
to settle on
*Have you **settled on** a date for the wedding?*
agree on, decide on, choose, name, fix

severe *adjective*
1 *The jailer was very **severe** with the prisoners.*
harsh, strict, hard, stern
OPPOSITE lenient
2 *The traffic warden gave him a **severe** look.*
unkind, unsympathetic, disapproving, grim
OPPOSITE kind
3 *Ruby has a **severe** case of chickenpox.*
bad, serious, acute, grave
OPPOSITE mild
4 *The Arctic has a **severe** climate.*
extreme, tough, harsh, hostile
A severe frost is a ***sharp*** frost.
Severe cold is ***intense*** cold.
A severe storm is a ***violent*** storm.

shabby *adjective*
*The witch disguised herself in a **shabby** cloak.*
ragged, scruffy, tattered, worn, worn-out, threadbare, frayed, tatty, seedy, dingy
OPPOSITE smart

shade *noun*
1 *They sat in the **shade** of a chestnut tree.*
shadow
2 *The porch had a **shade** to keep out the sun.*
screen, blind, canopy
A type of umbrella used as a sun shade is a ***parasol***.
3 *The bathroom walls are a pale **shade** of blue.*
hue, tinge, tint, tone, colour
shade *verb*
*Wearing a cap will **shade** your eyes from the sun.*
shield, screen, protect, hide, mask

shadow *noun*
*Her face was deep in **shadow**.*
shade, darkness, gloom
shadow *verb*
*The detective was **shadowing** the suspect.*
follow, pursue, tail, stalk, track, trail

shady *adjective*
1 *They found a **shady** spot under a tree.*
shaded, shadowy, sheltered, dark, sunless
OPPOSITE sunny
2 *He took part in some **shady** business deals.*
dishonest, disreputable, suspicious, dubious, suspect, untrustworthy
(*informal*) fishy, dodgy
OPPOSITE honest

shaggy *adjective*
*Llamas have long **shaggy** coats.*
bushy, woolly, fleecy, hairy, thick

shake *verb*
1 *The hurricane made the whole house **shake**.*
quake, shudder, shiver, rock, sway, totter, wobble, quiver, vibrate, rattle
2 *He was so upset that his voice was **shaking**.*
tremble, quaver
3 *The giant **shook** his fist and growled angrily.*
wave, brandish, flourish, wag, waggle, joggle
4 *They were **shaken** by the terrible news.*
shock, startle, distress, upset, disturb, alarm, frighten

shaky *adjective*
1 *Be careful—the table is rather **shaky**.*
unsteady, wobbly, insecure, rickety, flimsy, weak
2 *He was so nervous that his hands were **shaky**.*
shaking, trembling, quivering
3 *He spoke in a **shaky** voice.*
quavering, faltering, nervous, tremulous
OPPOSITE steady

shame *noun*
*The guilty man hung his head in **shame**.*
disgrace, dishonour, humiliation, embarrassment, guilt
a shame
*It's **a shame** that you can't stay for longer.*
a pity, unfortunate

shape *verb*
*The potter **shaped** the clay into a tall vase.*
form, mould, fashion
To shape something in a mould is to ***cast*** it.

share *noun*
*Each of the pirates got a **share** of rum.*
ration, allowance, portion, quota, helping, division, part
(*informal*) cut
share *verb*
*The robbers **shared** the loot between them.*
divide, split, distribute, allot, allocate, deal out, ration out

shatter *verb*
1 *The ball **shattered** a window.*
break, smash, destroy, wreck
2 *The windscreen **shattered** when a stone hit it.*
break, splinter, disintegrate

shed *noun*
*They kept their lawnmower in the garden **shed**.*
hut, shack, outhouse
shed *verb*
*A lorry **shed** its load on the motorway.*
drop, let fall, spill, scatter

sheer *adjective*
1 *The story he told was **sheer** nonsense.*
complete, total, utter, absolute, pure
2 *Don't try to climb that **sheer** cliff.*
vertical, perpendicular

sheet *noun*
1 *She started her diary on a fresh **sheet** of paper.*
page, leaf, piece
2 *The pond was covered with a thin **sheet** of ice.*
layer, film, covering, surface
3 *The glazier came to fit a new **sheet** of glass.*
panel, pane, plate

shaggy

shelf noun
*She put the books back on the **shelf**.*
ledge, rack
*A shelf above a fireplace is a **mantelpiece**.*

shelter noun
*They reached **shelter** just before the storm broke.*
cover, protection, safety, refuge, sanctuary

shelter verb
1 *The hedge **shelters** the garden from the wind.*
protect, screen, shield, guard, defend, safeguard
2 *We **sheltered** from the rain under the trees.*
hide, take refuge

shield noun
*The trees act as an effective wind **shield**.*
screen, barrier, defence, guard, protection
*The part of a helmet that shields your face is the **visor**.*

shield verb
*The mother bear **shielded** her cubs from danger.*
protect, defend, guard, safeguard, keep safe, shelter

shift verb
1 *I need some help to **shift** the furniture.*
move, rearrange, reposition
2 *It was hard work **shifting** the mud off the tyres.*
remove, dislodge, budge

shine verb
1 *A light **shone** from an upstairs window.*
beam, glow, blaze, glare, gleam
2 *He **shines** his shoes every morning.*
polish, rub, brush

shiny adjective
*She polished the mirror until it was **shiny**.*
shining, bright, gleaming, glistening, glossy, polished, burnished, lustrous
OPPOSITE dull

ship noun
*Ships that travel long distances at sea are **ocean-going** or **seagoing** ships.*
*People who work on ships at sea are **nautical** or **seafaring** people.*

shiver verb
*Ali waited outside, **shivering** with cold.*
tremble, quiver, shake, shudder, quake

shock noun
1 *The news of his death came as a great **shock**.*
blow, surprise, fright, upset

2 *People felt the **shock** of the explosion miles away.*
bang, impact, jolt
3 *The driver involved in the accident was in a state of **shock**.*
distress, trauma

shock verb
*The whole town was **shocked** by the news.*
horrify, appal, startle, alarm, stun, stagger, shake, astonish, astound, surprise, dismay, upset
*A formal synonym is **traumatise**.*

shoot verb
1 *Robin Hood **shot** an arrow into the air.*
fire, discharge, launch, aim
2 *It is now illegal to hunt and **shoot** tigers.*
fire at, hit, open fire on, gun down
3 *They watched the racing cars **shoot** past.*
race, speed, dash, rush, streak, hurtle, fly, whizz, zoom
4 *Part of the film was **shot** in Canada.*
film, photograph

⭐ WORD WEB

shop noun
VARIOUS TYPES OF SHOP
boutique, corner shop, department store, hypermarket, market, shopping arcade, shopping centre, shopping mall, supermarket

SPECIALIST SHOPS
antique shop, baker, bookshop, butcher, cheesemonger, chemist, clothes shop, confectioner, delicatessen, DIY or do-it-yourself shop, fishmonger, florist, garden centre, greengrocer, grocer, haberdasher, health-food shop, ironmonger, jeweller, music shop, newsagent, off-licence, pharmacy, post office, shoe shop or shoemaker, stationer, toyshop, watchmaker

PEOPLE WHO WORK IN SHOPS
cashier, salesman or saleswoman, shop assistant, shopkeeper or storekeeper

short adjective
1 *They live a **short** distance from the shops.*
little, small
OPPOSITE long
2 *It was a very **short** visit.*
brief, quick, fleeting, hasty, temporary
OPPOSITE long
3 *The troll was very **short** and fat.*
small, tiny, little, squat, dumpy, diminutive, petite
OPPOSITE tall

4 *The supply of water was getting **short**.*
low, meagre, scant, limited, inadequate, insufficient
OPPOSITE plentiful
5 *There is no need to be **short** with me!*
abrupt, rude, sharp, curt, impolite, snappy
OPPOSITE patient, polite

shortage noun
*The **shortage** of water is worrying.*
scarcity, deficiency, lack, want, dearth
*A shortage of water is a **drought**.*
*A shortage of food is a **famine**.*

shorten verb
*She had to **shorten** the essay because it was too long.*
cut down, reduce, cut, trim, abbreviate, abridge, condense, compress, curtail
OPPOSITE lengthen

shot noun
1 *I heard a noise like the **shot** of a pistol.*
bang, blast, crack
2 *The striker had an easy **shot** at the goal.*
hit, strike, kick
3 *The photographer took some unusual **shots**.*
photograph, picture, snap, snapshot
4 *(informal) We each had a **shot** at solving the riddle.*
try, go, attempt
(informal) bash

shout verb
*The ogre was **shouting** and stamping with rage.*
call, cry out, bawl, yell, bellow, roar, howl, yelp, scream, screech, shriek
OPPOSITE whisper

shove verb
*A man ran past and **shoved** me to the side.*
push, thrust, force, barge, elbow, jostle, shoulder

shopping

show verb
1 My uncle **showed** us his coin collection.
present, reveal, display, exhibit
2 The photo **shows** my grandparents on holiday.
portray, picture, depict, illustrate, represent
3 The dance tutor **showed** them what to do.
explain to, make clear to, instruct, teach, tell
4 The evidence **shows** that he was right.
prove, demonstrate
5 A nurse **showed** them into the waiting room.
direct, guide, conduct, escort, usher
6 The signpost **shows** the way.
indicate, point out
7 His vest **showed** through his shirt.
be seen, be visible, appear
to show off
Walter is always **showing off**.
boast, brag, crow, gloat, swagger
(informal) blow your own trumpet
A person who shows off is a **show-off**.

show noun
1 There is a **show** of artwork at the end of term.
display, exhibition, presentation
2 There's a good **show** on at the theatre.
performance, production, entertainment

shriek noun, verb
'Quick!' **shrieked** Alice. 'Open the door!'
cry, scream, screech, shout, howl, bawl, squeal, wail, yell

shrill adjective
They heard the **shrill** sound of a whistle.
high, high-pitched, piercing, sharp, screechy
OPPOSITE low, soft

shrink verb
My jeans have **shrunk** in the wash.
become smaller, contract   shrivel
OPPOSITE expand

shrivel verb
The plants **shrivelled** in the heat.
wilt, wither, droop, dry up, wrinkle, shrink

shudder verb
They **shuddered** with fear when they heard the creature roar.
tremble, quake, quiver, shake, shiver

shuffle verb
1 She **shuffled** along the corridor in her slippers.
shamble, scuffle, hobble, scrape
2 Did you remember to **shuffle** the cards?
mix, mix up, jumble

shut verb
Please **shut** the door behind you.
close, fasten, seal, secure, lock, bolt, latch
To shut a door with a bang is to **slam** it.
to shut someone up
He had been **shut up** in a dungeon for five years.
imprison, confine, detain
shut up
(informal) I wish those people behind us would **shut up**!
be quiet, be silent, stop talking, hold your tongue

shy adjective
The little girl was too **shy** to say anything.
bashful, timid, coy, reserved, hesitant, self-conscious, inhibited, modest
OPPOSITE bold

sick adjective
1 Katie is off school because she's **sick**.
ill, unwell, poorly, sickly, ailing, indisposed, off colour, peaky
OPPOSITE healthy
2 The sea was rough and the cabin boy felt **sick**.
nauseous, queasy
to be sick of
I'm **sick of** this miserable weather!
be fed up with, be tired of, have had enough of

side noun
1 A cube has six **sides**.
face, surface
2 The path runs along the **side** of the field.
edge, border, boundary, fringe, perimeter
The side of a page is the **margin**.
The side of a road is the **verge**.
3 I could see both **sides** of the argument.
point of view, view, angle, aspect
4 The football club has a strong **side** this year.
team

sight noun
1 Weasels have sharp **sight** and excellent hearing.
eyesight, vision
2 The woods in autumn are a lovely **sight**.
spectacle, display, show, scene

3 By the third day, the ship was in **sight** of land.
view, range
4 We went to London to see the **sights**.
attraction, landmark

sign noun
1 A **sign** pointed to the exit.
notice, placard, poster, signpost
The sign belonging to a particular business or organisation is a **logo**.
The sign on a particular brand of goods is a **trademark**.
2 The witch gave no **sign** that she was angry.
indication, clue, hint, warning
3 The guard gave us a **sign** to pass through the gates.
signal, gesture, cue, reminder
sign verb
1 Please **sign** your name on the form.
write, inscribe
2 The club **signed** a new player last week.
take on, engage, recruit, enrol

signal noun
The spy waited for the **signal** that all was clear.
sign, indication, prompt, cue
A signal that tells you not to do something is a **warning**.
signal verb
The pilot **signalled** that he was going to descend.
give a sign or signal, gesture, indicate, motion

significant adjective
1 The book describes the **significant** events of last century.
important, major, noteworthy, influential
2 Global warming is having a **significant** effect on wildlife.
noticeable, considerable, perceptible, striking

silence noun
There was **silence** while we sat the exam.
quiet, quietness, hush, stillness, calm, peace
OPPOSITE noise
silence verb
He **silenced** the audience by ringing a gong.
deaden, muffle, quieten, suppress
To silence someone by putting something in or over their mouth is to **gag** them.

silent adjective
1 At night, the desert was cold and **silent**.
quiet, noiseless, soundless, still, hushed
Something you can't hear is **inaudible**.
A common simile is **as silent as the grave**.
OPPOSITE noisy

2 *Morris kept **silent** throughout the meeting.*
quiet, speechless, mute
(*informal*) mum
To be too shy to speak is to be **tongue-tied**.
OPPOSITE talkative

silly *adjective*
*It was **silly** of me to lock myself out of the house.*
foolish, stupid, idiotic, senseless, thoughtless, brainless, unwise, unintelligent, half-witted, hare-brained, scatterbrained
(*informal*) daft
OPPOSITE sensible

similar *adjective*
*The puppies are **similar** in appearance.*
alike, identical, indistinguishable, matching, the same
OPPOSITE dissimilar, different
similar to
*The new book is **similar to** the previous one.*
alike, close to, comparable to
OPPOSITE unlike, different from

similarity *noun*
*It's easy to see the **similarity** between the twins.*
likeness, resemblance
OPPOSITE difference

simple *adjective*
1 *Can you answer this **simple** question?*
easy, elementary, straightforward
OPPOSITE difficult
2 *The help file is written in **simple** language.*
clear, plain, uncomplicated, understandable, intelligible
OPPOSITE complicated
3 *The girl wore a **simple** cotton dress.*
plain, undecorated
OPPOSITE elaborate
4 *He enjoys **simple** pleasures like walking and gardening.*
ordinary, unsophisticated, humble, modest, homely
OPPOSITE sophisticated

sincere *adjective*
*Please accept my **sincere** apologies.*
genuine, honest, true, truthful, real, earnest, wholehearted, frank
OPPOSITE insincere

single *adjective*
1 *We saw a **single** house high on the moors.*
solitary, isolated
When only a single example of something exists, it is **unique**.
2 *Miss Dempster was quite content to stay **single**.*
unmarried
An unmarried man is a **bachelor**.
An unmarried woman is a **spinster**.

sinister *adjective*
*He looked up with a **sinister** smile on his face.*
menacing, threatening, malevolent, evil, disturbing, unsettling, eerie
(*informal*) creepy

sink *verb*
1 *The ship hit the rocks and **sank**.*
go down, become submerged, founder, capsize
To let water into a ship to sink it deliberately is to **scuttle** it.
2 *The sun began to **sink** below the horizon.*
drop, fall, descend, subside, dip
When the sun sinks to the horizon it **sets**.

sit *verb*
1 *Rachel **sat** on the sofa reading a magazine.*
have a seat, settle down, rest, perch
To sit on your heels is to **squat**.
To sit to have your portrait painted is to **pose**.
2 *My brother is **sitting** his driving test next week.*
take
(*informal*) go in for

site *noun*
*This is the **site** of an ancient burial ground.*
location, place, position, situation, setting, plot

situation *noun*
1 *The house is in a pleasant **situation**.*
location, locality, place, position, setting, site, spot
2 *I found myself in an awkward **situation**.*
position, circumstances, condition, state of affairs
A bad situation is a **plight** or **predicament**.

size *noun*
1 *What **size** is the garden?*
dimensions, proportions, area, extent
2 *They were amazed by the sheer **size** of the pyramids.*
scale, magnitude, immensity

sketch *noun*
1 *She drew a quick **sketch** of her cat.*
drawing, picture, outline
A sketch you do while you think of other things is a **doodle**.
2 *The actors performed a comic **sketch**.*
scene, turn, routine

sketch *verb*
*He **sketched** a rough design for the poster*
draw, draft, outline, rough out

skid *verb*
*The postman **skidded** on the icy pavement.*
slide, slip

skilful *adjective*
*Dickens was a **skilful** writer.*
expert, skilled, accomplished, able, capable, talented, brilliant, clever, masterly, deft
If you are skilful at a lot of things, you are **versatile**.
OPPOSITE incompetent

skill *noun*
*It takes a lot of **skill** to build a boat.*
expertise, ability, aptitude, capability, competence, accomplishment, talent, proficiency, deftness

skim *verb*
*The stone **skimmed** across the surface of the pond.*
glide, slide, skid, slip
to skim through
*Luke **skimmed through** the newspaper.*
scan, look through, skip through, flick through

skin *noun*
*The cave people were dressed in animal **skins**.*
coat, fur, hide, pelt
The type of skin you have on your face is your **complexion**.
Skin on fruit or vegetables is **peel** or **rind**.
Skin that might form on top of a liquid is a **coating**, **film** or **membrane**.

skinny *adjective*
*A **skinny** girl in bare feet answered the door.*
thin, lean, bony, gaunt, lanky, scrawny, scraggy
OPPOSITE plump

skip *verb*
1 *The children **skipped** along the pavement.*
hop, jump, leap, bound, caper, dance, prance
2 *I **skipped** the boring bits in the book.*
pass over, miss out, ignore, omit, leave out

slant *verb*
*Her handwriting **slants** backwards.*
lean, slope, tilt, incline, be at an angle

slant *noun*
*The floor of the caravan was at a **slant**.*
slope, angle, tilt, incline, gradient
A slant on a damaged ship is a **list**.
A slanting line joining opposite corners of a square, etc., is a **diagonal**.
A surface slanting up to a higher level is a **ramp**.

slap verb
He **slapped** his hand against his thigh and laughed.
smack, strike, spank, hit, clout
(*informal*) whack

slaughter noun
The battle ended in terrible **slaughter**.
bloodshed, killing, massacre, butchery

sleek adjective
Otters have **sleek** coats.
smooth, glossy, shiny, silky, soft, velvety
OPPOSITE coarse

sleep verb
The baby is **sleeping** in the next room.
be asleep, take a nap, doze
(*informal*) snooze
To go to sleep is to **drop off** or **nod off**.

sleep noun
Mr Khan had a short **sleep** after lunch.
nap, rest, doze, catnap
(*informal*) snooze, forty winks, shut-eye
An afternoon sleep is a *siesta*.
The long sleep some animals have through the winter is *hibernation*.

sleepy adjective
The giant was usually **sleepy** after dinner.
drowsy, tired, weary, heavy-eyed, lethargic, ready to sleep
(*informal*) dopey
OPPOSITE wide awake

slender adjective
1 The ballerina had a **slender** figure.
slim, lean, slight, graceful, trim, svelte
OPPOSITE fat
2 The spider dangled on a **slender** thread.
thin, fine, fragile, delicate
OPPOSITE thick
3 They only had a **slender** chance of winning.
poor, slight, slim, faint, negligible, remote
OPPOSITE good
4 The team won by a **slender** margin.
narrow, small, slim
OPPOSITE wide

slice verb
To slice meat is to **carve** it.

slide verb
I like **sliding** down the chute in the playground.
glide, skid, slip, slither

slight adjective
1 There's a **slight** problem with the computer.
minor, unimportant, insignificant,

slither

negligible, superficial, trifling, trivial
OPPOSITE important
2 The fairy was a **slight** creature, barely two inches tall.
delicate, fragile, frail, slender, slim, small, spare, thin, tiny
OPPOSITE stout

slim adjective
1 A tall, **slim** figure appeared out of the fog.
graceful, lean, slender, spare, thin, trim
OPPOSITE fat
2 Their chances of winning are **slim**.
faint, poor, slight, slender, negligible, remote
OPPOSITE good
3 They won by a **slim** margin.
narrow, small, slender
OPPOSITE wide

slimy adjective
The floor of the tunnel was covered with **slimy** mud.
slippery, slithery, sticky, oozy
(*informal*) gooey, icky

sling verb
Robin Hood **slung** his quiver over his shoulder.
throw, cast, fling, hurl, pitch, heave, toss, lob
(*informal*) chuck

slink verb
The spy **slunk** away without being seen.
slip, sneak, steal, creep, edge, sidle

slip verb
1 The paper boy **slipped** on the ice.
skid, slither, skate
2 The lifeboat **slipped** into the water.
glide, slide
3 Marion **slipped** out while everyone was talking.
sneak, steal, slink, tiptoe, creep, edge, sidle

slippery adjective
Take care—the floor is **slippery**.
slithery, slippy, smooth, glassy
A surface slippery with frost is *icy*.
A surface slippery with grease is *greasy* or *oily*.
A common simile is *as slippery as an eel*.

slit noun
The archers shot arrows through the **slits** in the castle wall.
opening, chink, gap, slot, split, tear, cut

slither verb
The rattlesnake **slithered** through the long grass.
slide, slip, glide, slink, snake

slope verb
The beach **slopes** gently down to the sea.
fall or rise, incline, bank, shelve

slope noun
1 It was hard work pushing my bike up the **slope**.
hill, rise, bank, ramp
An upward slope is an *ascent*.
A downward slope is a *descent*.
2 Rain runs down the roof because of the **slope**.
incline, slant, tilt, gradient

sloppy adjective
1 For breakfast, there was a bowl of steaming, **sloppy** porridge.
runny, slushy, watery, liquid, wet
(*informal*) gloopy
2 His handwriting is very **sloppy**.
untidy, messy, careless, slovenly, slapdash, slipshod

slot noun
To use the phone, put a coin into the **slot**.
slit, chink, hole, opening

slouch verb
Enid sat at her desk, **slouched** over the computer.
hunch, stoop, slump, droop, flop

slow adjective
1 Tortoises move at a **slow** but steady pace.
unhurried, leisurely, gradual, plodding, dawdling, sluggish
2 They took the train to London, followed by a **slow** bus journey.
lengthy, prolonged, drawn-out, tedious
3 The prisoner was **slow** to answer.
hesitant, reluctant, tardy

slow verb
to slow down
Slow down—you're driving too fast!
go slower, brake, reduce speed
OPPOSITE accelerate

sly *adjective*
*The chess player knew several **sly** moves.*
crafty, cunning, artful, clever, wily, tricky, sneaky, devious, furtive, secretive, stealthy, underhand
A common simile is **as sly as a fox**.
OPPOSITE straightforward

smack *verb*
*He **smacked** the other player on the head by accident.*
slap, strike, hit, cuff
(*informal*) whack

small *adjective*
1 *Moles have incredibly **small** eyes and ears.*
little, tiny, minute, compact, miniature, microscopic, minuscule, mini, baby
(*informal*) teeny, titchy, dinky
(*Scottish*) wee
OPPOSITE big, large
2 *A **small** elf was standing on a toadstool.*
little, short, petite, slight, dainty, diminutive
(*informal*) pint-sized
OPPOSITE big, tall, large
3 *For breakfast there was stale bread with a **small** scraping of butter.*
meagre, inadequate, insufficient, paltry, scanty, stingy, skimpy
(*informal*) measly
OPPOSITE large, generous, ample
4 *The writers made some **small** changes to the script.*
minor, unimportant, insignificant, trivial, trifling, negligible
OPPOSITE major, substantial

smart *adjective*
1 *Everyone looked **smart** at the wedding.*
elegant, well-dressed, well-groomed, stylish, spruce, fashionable, chic, neat, trim
To make yourself smart is to **smarten up**.
OPPOSITE scruffy
2 *They booked a table in a very **smart** restaurant.*
fashionable, high-class, exclusive, fancy
(*informal*) posh
3 *The detective made a very **smart** move.*
clever, ingenious, intelligent, shrewd, crafty
OPPOSITE stupid
4 *The cyclists set off at a **smart** pace.*
fast, quick, rapid, speedy, swift, brisk
OPPOSITE slow

smart *verb*
*The smoke from the barbecue made our eyes **smart**.*
hurt, sting, prick, prickle, tingle

smash *verb*
*A vase fell off the table and **smashed** to pieces on the floor.*
break, crush, shatter, crack
When wood smashes it **splinters**.
To smash something completely is to **demolish** or **destroy** or **wreck** it.
to smash into
*A lorry had **smashed into** the side of a bus.*
crash into, collide with, bang into, bump into

smear *verb*
*The chef **smeared** butter over the cooking dish.*
spread, wipe, plaster, rub, dab, smudge, daub

smell *noun*
1 *The air was filled with the **smell** of roses.*
scent, aroma, perfume, fragrance
2 *The **smell** of mouldy cheese was unbearable.*
odour, stench, stink, reek, whiff
(*informal*) pong, niff

smell *verb*
1 *I could **smell** something baking in the oven.*
scent, sniff
(*informal*) get a whiff of
2 *After walking all day, my feet were beginning to **smell**.*
stink, reek
(*informal*) pong

✏️ **WRITING TIPS**

You can use these words to describe **how something smells**.

TO DESCRIBE SOMETHING WHICH SMELLS GOOD
fragrant, aromatic, perfumed, scented, sweet-smelling *The garden was planted with **sweet-smelling** herbs.*

TO DESCRIBE SOMETHING WHICH SMELLS BAD
smelly, stinking, evil-smelling, foul-smelling, musty, odorous, reeking, rotten, fetid, foul
(*informal*) stinky, pongy, whiffy
*The witch stirred the **evil-smelling** brew.*

---

smile *verb*
*The stranger **smiled** and introduced himself.*
grin, beam
To smile in a silly way is to **simper**.
To smile in a self-satisfied way is to **smirk**.
To smile in an insulting way is to **sneer**.

smoke *noun*
*Puffs of green **smoke** came from the dragon's nostrils.*
fumes, gas, steam, vapour
The smoke given out by a car is **exhaust**.
A mixture of smoke and fog is **smog**.

smooth *adjective*
1 *This part of the road is **smooth** and good for cycling.*
flat, even, level
OPPOSITE uneven
2 *In the early morning, the lake was perfectly **smooth**.*
calm, still, unruffled, undisturbed, glassy
OPPOSITE rough
3 *Otters have **smooth** and shiny coats.*
silky, sleek, velvety
OPPOSITE coarse
4 *The journey by train is very quick and **smooth**.*
comfortable, steady
OPPOSITE bumpy
5 *Stir the cake mixture until it is **smooth**.*
creamy, flowing, runny
OPPOSITE lumpy

smooth *verb*
*Charlotte stood up and **smoothed** her dress.*
flatten, level, even out
To smooth cloth you can **iron** or **press** it.
To smooth wood you can **plane** or **sand** it.

smother *verb*
1 *Pythons **smother** their prey to death.*
suffocate, choke, stifle
2 *The pudding was **smothered** with cream.*
cover, coat

smudge *noun*
*There were **smudges** of ink all over the page.*
smear, blot, streak, stain, mark

smudge *verb*
*Don't **smudge** the icing on the cake!*
smear, blur, streak

snap *verb*
1 *A twig **snapped** under one of my boots.*
break, crack
2 *The dog **snapped** at the postman's ankles.*
bite, nip
3 *Mr Baker was in a bad mood and **snapped** at everyone.*
snarl, bark

snatch *verb*
*The thief **snatched** the jewels and ran off.*
grab, seize, grasp, pluck, wrench away, wrest away

a b c d e f g h i j k l m n o p q r s t u v w x y z

sneak verb
*I managed to **sneak** in without anyone seeing.*
slip, steal, creep, slink, tiptoe, sidle, skulk

sneaky adjective
*That was a really **sneaky** trick.*
sly, underhand, cunning, crafty, devious, furtive, untrustworthy
OPPOSITE honest

sneer verb
to sneer at
*He **sneered at** my first attempts to ice-skate.*
make fun of, mock, ridicule, scoff at, jeer at, deride

snobbish adjective
*She's far too **snobbish** to mix with us.*
arrogant, pompous, superior, haughty
(*informal*) stuck-up, snooty, toffee-nosed
OPPOSITE humble

snoop verb
*They caught a man **snooping** round the office.*
sneak, pry, poke, rummage, spy

snub verb
*She **snubbed** the neighbours by not inviting them to the party.*
insult, offend, be rude to, brush off
(*informal*) put down

snug adjective
*Lucy was tucked up **snug** in bed.*
cosy, comfortable, warm, relaxed
(*informal*) comfy
A common simile is *as snug as a bug in a rug*.
OPPOSITE uncomfortable

soak verb
1 *Days of rain had **soaked** the cricket pitch.*
wet thoroughly, drench, saturate
2 *Leave the beans to **soak** in water overnight.*
steep, immerse, submerge

soaking adjective
*My socks are absolutely **soaking**!*
wet through, drenched, dripping, wringing, saturated, sodden, sopping, soggy
Ground that has been soaked by rain is *waterlogged*.

soar verb
*The seagull spread its wings and **soared** into the air.*
climb, rise, ascend, fly, wing

sob verb
*Tina threw herself on the bed, **sobbing** loudly.*
cry, weep, bawl, blubber, shed tears, snivel

soft adjective
1 *The kittens can only eat **soft** food.*
pulpy, spongy, squashy
(*informal*) squidgy
OPPOSITE hard, dry
2 *My head sank into the **soft** pillow.*
supple, pliable, springy, yielding, flexible
OPPOSITE firm, rigid
3 *The rabbit's fur felt very **soft**.*
smooth, silky, sleek, velvety, downy, feathery
OPPOSITE coarse
4 *A **soft** breeze stirred the leaves.*
gentle, light, mild, delicate
OPPOSITE rough, strong
5 *The smugglers spoke in **soft** whispers.*
quiet, low, faint
OPPOSITE loud
6 *It was hard to see clearly in the **soft** light.*
subdued, muted, pale, dim, low
OPPOSITE bright, dazzling
7 *You are being too **soft** with that puppy.*
lenient, easygoing, tolerant, indulgent
OPPOSITE strict, tough

soft

soggy adjective
1 *The pitch was **soggy** after all the rain.*
wet, drenched, soaked, saturated, sodden, waterlogged
2 *The bread in my sandwich had become **soggy**.*
moist, soft, pulpy, squelchy
(*informal*) squidgy

solemn adjective
1 *The butler always had a **solemn** expression on his face.*
serious, grave, sober, sombre, unsmiling, glum
OPPOSITE cheerful
2 *The coronation was a **solemn** occasion.*
formal, dignified, grand, stately, majestic, pompous
OPPOSITE frivolous

solid adjective
1 *A cricket ball is **solid**.*
OPPOSITE hollow
2 *The water turned into **solid** ice.*
hard, firm, dense, compact, rigid, unyielding
A common simile is *as solid as a rock*.
OPPOSITE soft
3 *The bars of the climbing frame are quite **solid**.*
firm, robust, sound, strong, stable, sturdy
OPPOSITE weak, unstable

4 *The crown was made of **solid** gold.*
pure, genuine
5 *He got **solid** support from his team-mates.*
firm, reliable, dependable, united, unanimous
OPPOSITE weak, divided

solve verb
*The professor was trying to **solve** an ancient riddle.*
interpret, explain, answer, work out, find the solution to, unravel, decipher

soothing adjective
*They played **soothing** music.*
calming, relaxing, restful, peaceful, gentle, pleasant

sore adjective
*My feet are still **sore** from the walk.*
painful, aching, hurting, smarting, tender, sensitive, inflamed, raw, red

sorrow noun
1 *He felt great **sorrow** at leaving his children behind.*
sadness, unhappiness, misery, woe, grief, anguish, despair, distress, heartache, heartbreak, melancholy, gloom, depression, desolation, wretchedness
Sorrow because of someone's death is *mourning*.
Sorrow at being away from home is *homesickness*.
OPPOSITE happiness
2 *She expressed her **sorrow** for what she had done.*
regret, remorse, repentance, apologies

sorry adjective
1 *Scott said he was **sorry** for losing my football.*
apologetic, regretful, remorseful, ashamed (of), repentant
OPPOSITE unapologetic
2 *We felt **sorry** for the villagers who had lost their homes.*
sympathetic, pitying, understanding, compassionate
OPPOSITE unsympathetic

sort noun
*What **sort** of music do you like?*
kind, type, variety, form, nature, style, genre, category, order, class
A sort of animal is a *breed* or *species*.

sort verb
*The books are **sorted** according to their subjects.*
arrange, organise, class, group, categorise, classify, divide
OPPOSITE mix
to sort something out
*They managed to **sort out** their disagreement.*
settle, resolve, clear up, cope with, deal with

🕸 WORD WEB

sound noun
We heard the **sound** of footsteps approaching.
noise, tone
A loud, harsh sound is a *din* or *racket*.

SOUNDS MADE BY PEOPLE
bawl, bellow, boo, boom, cackle, chortle, clap, croak, cry, gasp, groan, gurgle, hiccup, hiss, howl, hum, moan, murmur, puff, scream, shout, shriek, sigh, sing, sniff, snore, snort, sob, splutter, stammer, stutter, wail, wheeze, whimper, whine, whisper, whistle, whoop, yell, yodel

SOUNDS MADE BY THINGS
bang, blare, beep, bleep, boom, buzz, chime, chink, chug, clang, clank, clash, clatter, click, clink, clunk, crack, crackle, crash, creak, crunch, ding, drone, drum, fizz, grate, gurgle, jangle, jingle, patter, peal, ping, plop, pop, purr, putter, rattle, ring, rumble, rustle, scrunch, sizzle, slam, snap, squeak, squelch, swish, throb, thud, thunder, tick, ting, tinkle, twang, whirr, whoosh, whistle, whizz, zoom

✏ WRITING TIPS

You can use these words to describe a **sound**.

TO DESCRIBE A *PLEASANT SOUND*
dulcet, harmonious, mellifluous, melodious, sweet *I heard the **sweet** strains of a harp playing.*

TO DESCRIBE AN *UNPLEASANT SOUND*
grating, harsh, jarring, piercing, rasping, raucous, shrill, thin, tinny
*A **raucous** fight was going out outside.*

sound adjective
1 *The walls of the fortress seemed **sound**.*
firm, solid, stable, safe, secure, intact, undamaged
OPPOSITE unsound, unstable
2 *She gave us some **sound** advice.*
good, sensible, wise, reasonable, trustworthy
OPPOSITE unwise
3 *The travellers returned safe and **sound**.*
strong, well, fit, healthy
OPPOSITE weak, unfit

sour adjective
1 *These apples are a bit **sour**.*
tart, bitter, sharp, acid
OPPOSITE sweet
2 *The guard opened the door with a **sour** look on his face.*
cross, bad-tempered, grumpy, disagreeable, peevish

space noun
1 *There wasn't much **space** to move about.*
room, freedom, scope
2 *He peered through the tiny **space** in the curtains.*
gap, hole, opening, break
A space without any air in it is a **vacuum**.
A space of time is an **interval** or **period**.
3 *The astronauts will spend ten days in **space**.*
outer space

🕸 WORD WEB

space noun
Everything that exists in space is the **universe** or **cosmos**.
Distances in space stretch to **infinity**.
Travel to other planets is **interplanetary** travel.
Travel to other stars is **interstellar** travel.
Travel to other galaxies is **intergalactic** travel.
A traveller in space is an **astronaut**.
In stories, beings from other planets are **aliens** or **extraterrestrials**.

NATURAL OBJECTS FOUND IN SPACE
asteroid, black hole, comet, constellation, galaxy, meteor, meteorite, Milky Way, moon, nebula, nova, planet, red dwarf, red giant, shooting star, solar system, star, sun, supernova

WORDS TO DO WITH TRAVEL IN SPACE
blast-off, countdown, launch, mission, orbit, re-entry, rocket, satellite, spacecraft,

spare verb
1 *Can you **spare** any money for a good cause?*
afford, part with, give, provide, do without
2 *Gretel begged the witch to **spare** her brother.*
show mercy to, pardon, reprieve, let off, release, free

spare adjective
1 *The **spare** tyre is in the boot.*
additional, extra, reserve, standby
2 *Have you any **spare** change?*
leftover, surplus, odd, remaining, unused, unwanted

spark noun
*There was a **spark** of light as he struck the match.*
flash, gleam, glint, flicker, sparkle

satellite

spaceship, space shuttle, space station, spacesuit, spacewalk

A robot spacecraft is a **probe**.
A vehicle which can travel on the surface of a planet is a **buggy** or **rover**.

THINGS YOU MIGHT FIND ON A SPACESHIP
booster rocket, bridge, cargo bay, capsule, computer, docking bay, fuel tank, heat shield, instrument panel, life-support system, module, pod, solar panel

THINGS A SPACESHIP MIGHT DO
blast off, burn up, drift off-course, land, lift off, malfunction, orbit, re-enter the earth's atmosphere, splash down, touch down

shuttle

meteor

a b c d e f g h i j k l m n o p q r s t u

sparkle verb
*The diamond ring **sparkled** in the sunlight.*
glitter, glisten, glint, twinkle

speak verb
*The robot opened its mouth and began to **speak**.*
communicate, express yourself, say something, talk, utter

special adjective
1 *Are you keeping the champagne for a **special** occasion?*
important, significant, memorable, noteworthy, momentous, exceptional, extraordinary, out-of-the-ordinary
OPPOSITE ordinary
2 *My granny has her own **special** way of making porridge.*
unique, individual, characteristic, distinctive, different, peculiar
3 *You need a **special** camera to film underwater.*
particular, specific, proper, specialised

speck noun
*She brushed a **speck** of dust from her shoes.*
bit, dot, spot, fleck, grain, particle, trace, mark

spectacle noun
*The fireworks for Diwali will be a great **spectacle**.*
display, show, performance, exhibition, extravaganza

spectacular adjective
1 *The acrobats gave a **spectacular** performance.*
dramatic, exciting, impressive, thrilling, magnificent, sensational
2 *The tulips are **spectacular** at this time of year.*
eye-catching, showy, splendid, breathtaking, colourful

spectator noun
*The spectators at a show are the **audience**.*
*The spectators at a football match are the **crowd**.*
*A person watching TV is a **viewer**.*
*If you see an accident or a crime you are an **eyewitness** or **witness**.*
*If you just happen to see something going on you are a **bystander** or **onlooker**.*

speech noun
1 *His **speech** was slurred and he looked tired.*
speaking, talking, articulation, pronunciation
2 *She was invited to give an after-dinner **speech**.*
talk, address, lecture, oration
*A talk in church is a **sermon**.*
*Speech between actors in a play is **dialogue**.*

A speech delivered by a single actor is a **monologue**.

speed noun
1 *Could a spaceship travel faster than the **speed** of light?*
pace, rate
*A formal synonym is **velocity**.*
*The speed of a piece of music is its **tempo**.*
*To increase speed is to **accelerate**.*
*To reduce speed is to **decelerate**.*
2 *They finished clearing up with amazing **speed**.*
quickness, rapidity, swiftness
OPPOSITE slowness

speed verb
*The skiers **sped** down the mountain.*
race, rush, dash, dart, hurry, hurtle, career, fly, streak, tear, shoot, zoom, zip

spell noun
1 *A magic **spell** had turned the knight into a toad.*
charm, incantation
Making magic spells is **sorcery**, **witchcraft** or **wizardry**.
2 *We're hoping for a **spell** of dry weather.*
period, interval, time, stretch, run

spend verb
1 *Have you **spent** all your pocket money already?*
pay out, use up, get through, exhaust
(informal) fork out, shell out
To spend money unwisely is to **fritter** or **squander** it.
2 *She **spends** a lot of time working in the garden.*
pass, occupy, fill
To spend time doing something useless is to **waste** it.

spill verb
1 *Katie **spilled** her juice all over the table.*
overturn, upset, tip over
2 *Milk **spilled** on to the floor.*
overflow, pour, slop, slosh, splash
3 *The treasure chest fell open, **spilling** gold coins everywhere.*
shed, tip, scatter, drop

spin verb
*The rear wheels of the jeep **spun** round.*
turn, rotate, revolve, whirl, twirl

spine noun
1 *Your **spine** runs down the middle of your back.*
backbone, spinal column
*The bones in your spine are your **vertebrae**.*
2 *A porcupine has sharp **spines**.*
needle, quill, point, spike, bristle

spirit noun
1 *He carried a charm to keep evil **spirits** away.*
ghost, ghoul, phantom, spectre, demon
2 *The orchestra played the piece with great **spirit**.*
energy, liveliness, enthusiasm, vigour, zest, zeal, fire
3 *There is a real **spirit** of cooperation in the team.*
feeling, mood, atmosphere

spiteful adjective
*He made some really **spiteful** comments.*
malicious, malevolent, ill-natured, hostile, venomous, vicious, nasty, unkind
OPPOSITE kind

splash verb
1 *The bus **splashed** water over us.*
shower, spray, spatter, sprinkle, squirt, slop, slosh, spill, (informal) splosh
2 *The children **splashed** about in the playing pool.*
paddle, wade, dabble, bathe

splendid adjective
1 *There was a **splendid** banquet on the eve of the wedding.*
magnificent, lavish, luxurious, impressive, imposing, grand, great, dazzling, glorious, gorgeous, elegant, rich, stately, majestic
2 *That's a **splendid** idea!*
excellent, first-class, admirable, superb, wonderful, marvellous

splinter verb
*The glass **splintered** into pieces.*
shatter, smash, fracture, chip, crack, split

split verb
1 *He **split** the log in two.*
chop, cut up, crack open, splinter
2 *He **split** his trousers climbing over the fence.*
rip open, tear
3 *The pirates **split** the gold between them.*
distribute, share out
4 *The path **splits** here.*
branch, fork, separate
to split up
*The search party decided to **split up**.*
break up, part, separate, divide
*If a married couple splits up, they may **divorce**.*

split noun
*He had a **split** in the seat of his trousers.*
rip, tear, slash, slit

spell

spoil verb
1 *Bad weather* **spoiled** *the holiday.*
ruin, wreck, upset, mess up, mar, scupper
2 *The grafitti* **spoils** *the look of the new building.*
damage, harm, hurt, disfigure, deface
3 *His parents have* **spoiled** *him since he was a baby.*
indulge, pamper, make a fuss of

sport noun
see panel below

spot noun
1 *There were several* **spots** *of paint on the carpet.*
mark, stain, blot, blotch, smudge, dot, fleck, speck
Small brown spots on your skin are **freckles***.*
A small dark spot on your skin is a **mole***.*
A mark you have had on your skin since you were born is a **birthmark***.*
A small round swelling on your skin is a **pimple***.*
A lot of spots is a **rash***.*
2 *We felt a few* **spots** *of rain.*
drop, blob, bead
3 *Here's a nice* **spot** *for a picnic.*
place, position, location, site, situation, locality

spot verb
1 *Nina* **spotted** *her friend in the crowd.*
see, sight, spy, catch sight of, notice, observe, make out, recognise, detect
2 *The tyres were* **spotted** *with mud.*
mark, stain, blot, spatter, fleck, speckle, mottle

sprawl verb
1 *We* **sprawled** *on the lawn.*
flop, lean back, lie, loll, lounge, recline, relax, slouch, slump, spread out, stretch out
2 *New houses have started to* **sprawl** *across the countryside.*
spread, stretch

spray verb
A passing bus **sprayed** *mud over us.*
shower, spatter, splash, sprinkle, scatter

spread verb
1 *I* **spread** *the map on the table.*
lay out, open out, fan out, unfold, unfurl, unroll
2 *The milk spilled and* **spread** *all over the floor.*
expand, extend, stretch, broaden, enlarge, swell
3 *The school website is a good way of* **spreading** *news.*
communicate, circulate, distribute, transmit, make known, pass on, pass round
4 *She* **spread** *jam on a piece of toast.*
smear
5 *He* **spread** *the seeds evenly over the ground.*
scatter, strew

spring verb
Suddenly a rabbit **sprang** *over the fence.*
jump, leap, bound, hop, vault
When a cat springs at a mouse, it **pounces***.*
to spring up
Weeds **spring up** *quickly in damp weather.*
appear, develop, emerge, shoot up, sprout

sprinkle verb
She **sprinkled** *flakes of chocolate over the cake.*
scatter, shower, spray, dust, powder

spurt verb
Water **spurted** *from the hole in the pipe.*
gush, spout, shoot out, stream, squirt, jet

WORD WEB

sport noun
I enjoy playing **sport** *at the weekend.*
exercise, games

American football

TEAM SPORTS INCLUDE
American football, baseball, basketball, bowls, cricket, football or soccer, hockey, lacrosse, netball, polo, rounders, rugby, volleyball, water polo

INDIVIDUAL SPORTS INCLUDE
angling, archery, athletics, badminton, billiards, boxing, bowling, canoeing, climbing, croquet, cross-country running, cycling, darts, diving, fencing, golf, gymnastics, horse racing, jogging, judo, karate, motor racing, mountaineering, orienteering, pool, rowing, sailing, show jumping, snooker, squash, surfing, swimming, table tennis, tae kwon do, tennis, waterskiing, weightlifting, windsurfing, wrestling

WINTER SPORTS INCLUDE
bobsleigh, curling, ice hockey, ice skating, skiing, snowboarding, speed skating, tobogganing

PEOPLE WHO TAKE PART IN SPORT
athlete, coach, competitor, player, sportsman or sportswoman

PLACES WHERE SPORT TAKES PLACE
arena, field, ground, park, pitch, pool, ring, rink, run, slope, stadium, track

boxing

SOME ATHLETIC EVENTS
cross-country, decathlon, discus, heptathlon, high jump, hurdles, javelin, long jump, marathon, pentathlon, pole vault, relay race, running, shot, sprinting, steeplechase, triathlon, triple jump

snowboarding

baseball

tennis

basketball

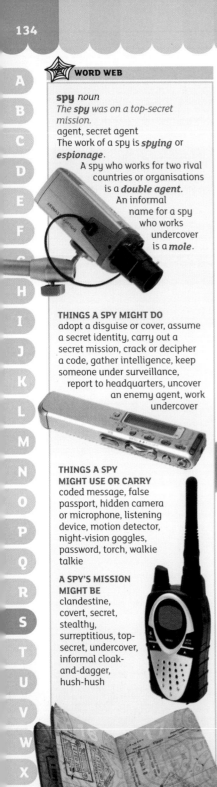

⭐ **WORD WEB**

spy noun
The **spy** was on a top-secret mission.
agent, secret agent
The work of a spy is **spying** or **espionage**.
A spy who works for two rival countries or organisations is a **double agent**.
An informal name for a spy who works undercover is a **mole**.

THINGS A SPY MIGHT DO
adopt a disguise or cover, assume a secret identity, carry out a secret mission, crack or decipher a code, gather intelligence, keep someone under surveillance, report to headquarters, uncover an enemy agent, work undercover

THINGS A SPY MIGHT USE OR CARRY
coded message, false passport, hidden camera or microphone, listening device, motion detector, night-vision goggles, password, torch, walkie talkie

A SPY'S MISSION MIGHT BE
clandestine, covert, secret, stealthy, surreptitious, top-secret, undercover, informal cloak-and-dagger, hush-hush

---

squabble verb
The twins are always **squabbling** in the car.
argue, fight, quarrel, bicker, wrangle

squash verb
1 My sandwich got **squashed** at the bottom of my schoolbag.
crush, flatten, press, compress, mangle
To squash food deliberately is to **mash** or **pulp** or **purée** it.
2 We **squashed** our sleeping bags into our rucksacks.
squeeze, stuff, force, cram, pack, ram

squat verb
We **squatted** on the ground to watch the puppet show.
crouch, sit

squat adjective
The alien had a **squat** little body on three short legs.
dumpy, stocky, plump, podgy, portly

squeeze verb
1 She **squeezed** the water out of the sponge.
press, wring, compress, crush
2 Five of us **squeezed** into the back of the car.
squash, cram, crowd, stuff, push, ram, shove, wedge
3 Holly **squeezed** her sister affectionately.
clasp, hug, embrace, cuddle
To squeeze something between your thumb and finger is to **pinch** it.

squeeze

squirt verb
My little brother made the tap water **squirt** all over me.
spurt, spray, gush, spout, shoot, jet

stab verb
1 He **stabbed** the sausage with his fork.
spear, jab, pierce, impale
2 She **stabbed** a finger at him.
stick, thrust, push, jab

stab noun
Jake felt a sudden **stab** of pain in his chest.
pang, prick, sting

stable adjective
1 The ladder doesn't look very **stable**.
steady, secure, firm, fixed, solid, balanced
OPPOSITE wobbly, shaky

---

2 He's been in a **stable** relationship for years.
steady, established, lasting, durable, strong
OPPOSITE temporary

stack noun
There were **stacks** of books all over the floor.
pile, heap, mound, tower
Another word for a stack of hay is a **rick** or **hayrick**.

stack verb
Stack the papers on the desk.
gather, assemble, collect, heap up, pile up

staff noun
There was a party at the hospital for all the **staff**.
workers, employees, personnel, workforce, team
The staff on a ship or aircraft are the **crew**.

stage noun
1 They went up on the **stage** to collect their prizes.
platform
2 The final **stage** of the journey was made by coach.
leg, step, phase, portion, stretch
3 At this **stage** in her life, she wants to try something new.
period, point, time, juncture

stagger verb
1 The wounded knight **staggered** and fell.
reel, stumble, lurch, totter, sway, falter, waver, wobble
2 We were **staggered** at the size of the pyramid.
amaze, astonish, astound, surprise, flabbergast, stupefy, startle, stun

stain noun
There were several coffee **stains** on the tablecloth.
mark, spot, blot, blotch, blemish, smear, smudge

stain verb
Her trainers were **stained** with mud.
discolour, mark, soil, dirty, blacken, tarnish

stale adjective
The bread had gone **stale**.
dry, hard, old, mouldy, musty
OPPOSITE fresh

stalk verb
1 The cheetah **stalked** its prey.
hunt, pursue, track, trail, follow, shadow, tail
2 Miss Foster turned and **stalked** out of the room.
stride, strut

stammer verb
Angela went red and started ***stammering***.
stutter, falter, stumble, splutter

stamp verb
1 *He* ***stamped*** *on the flower by mistake.*
step, tread, trample
2 *The librarian* ***stamped*** *my library book.*
mark, print
To stamp a postmark on a letter is to ***frank*** it.
To stamp a mark on cattle with a hot iron is to ***brand*** them.

stand verb
1 *The newborn pup was too weak to* ***stand***.
get to your feet, get up, rise
2 *They* ***stood*** *the ladder against the wall.*
put, place, set, position, station, erect
3 *The offer still* ***stands***.
remain valid, be unchanged, continue
4 *I can't* ***stand*** *the smell any longer.*
bear, abide, endure, put up with, tolerate, suffer
to stand for something
1 *She won't* ***stand for*** *any nonsense.*
put up with, tolerate, accept, allow, permit
2 *What do these initials* ***stand for***?
mean, indicate, signify, represent
to stand out
Among all the photographs, this one really ***stood out***.
catch your eye, stick out, be prominent
to stand up for someone
He always ***stands up for*** *his friends.*
support, defend, side with, speak up for
(informal) stick up for

standard noun
1 *Their writing is of a very high* ***standard***.
grade, level, quality
2 *He considered the book good by any* ***standard***.
guidelines, ideal, measurement, model
3 *The soldiers carried their* ***standard*** *proudly.*
colours, flag, banner

standard adjective
The teacher showed us the ***standard*** *way to write a letter.*
normal, usual, common, conventional, typical, customary, accepted, approved, established, orthodox, regular, traditional
OPPOSITE abnormal

star noun
1 *Astronomers study the* ***stars***.
A word meaning 'to do with stars' is ***stellar***.
A night sky in which you can see stars is ***starry*** or ***star-studded***.
A mark in the shape of a star in a piece of writing is an ***asterisk***.
2 *Several Hollywood* ***stars*** *attended the premiere of the film.*
celebrity, idol, superstar

stare verb
The guard ***stared*** *straight ahead, not blinking.*
gaze, gape, peer, look
to stare at someone
The wolf was ***staring*** *hungrily* ***at*** *us.*
gaze at, gawp at, goggle at, eye, ogle, scrutinise, watch
To stare angrily at someone is to ***glare*** at them.

start verb
1 *The new course will* ***start*** *in the autumn.*
begin, commence
(informal) get going, get cracking, kick off
OPPOSITE finish, end
2 *We are planning to* ***start*** *a book club.*
create, set up, establish, found, institute, originate, introduce, initiate, open, launch
OPPOSITE close
3 *The horses* ***started*** *when the gun went off.*
jump, flinch, jerk, twitch, recoil, wince

start noun
1 *Try not to miss the* ***start*** *of the film.*
beginning, opening, introduction, commencement
OPPOSITE end, close, finish
2 *She has been with the theatre company right from the* ***start***.
beginning, outset, creation, inception, birth, dawn, launch
3 *The explosion gave us all a nasty* ***start***.
jump, jolt, shock, surprise

startle verb
The sudden noise ***startled*** *the deer.*
alarm, panic, frighten, scare, make you start, make you jump, surprise, take you by surprise

starving adjective (informal)
What's for dinner? I'm ***starving***!
hungry, famished, ravenous
To be slightly hungry is to be ***peckish***.

state noun
1 *The roof of the cottage is in a bad* ***state***.
condition, shape
The state of a person or animal is their ***fitness*** or ***health***.

2 *He gets into a terrible* ***state*** *before an exam.*
panic, fluster
(informal) flap
3 *The queen is the head of* ***state***.
country, nation

state verb
Her passport ***states*** *that she is an Australian citizen.*
declare, announce, report, say, proclaim, pronounce, communicate

stay verb
1 *Can you* ***stay*** *there while I park the car?*
wait, hang about, remain
OPPOSITE leave, depart
2 *We tried to* ***stay*** *warm by stamping our feet.*
keep, carry on being, continue
3 *Do you plan to* ***stay*** *in America for long?*
live, reside, dwell, lodge, settle, stop

stay noun
Our friends came for a short ***stay***.
visit, stopover, holiday, break

steady adjective
1 *You need a* ***steady*** *hand to be a surgeon.*
stable, balanced, settled, secure, fixed, firm, fast, solid
A common simile is ***as steady as a rock***.
OPPOSITE unsteady, shaky
2 *The plants need a* ***steady*** *supply of water.*
continuous, uninterrupted, non-stop, consistent
OPPOSITE intermittent
3 *The runners kept up a* ***steady*** *pace.*
regular, constant, even, smooth, rhythmic, unvarying
OPPOSITE irregular

steal verb
1 *The thieves* ***stole*** *several valuable paintings.*
rob, thieve, take, lift, make off with
(informal) pinch, nick, swipe, snaffle
2 *The children* ***stole*** *quietly upstairs.*
creep, sneak, tiptoe, slip, slink

steep *adjective*
The bus inched its way slowly up the **steep** *slope.*
abrupt, sudden, sharp
A cliff or drop which is straight up and down is **sheer** or **vertical**.
OPPOSITE gradual, gentle

steer *verb*
She **steered** *the car into the parking space.*
direct, guide
To steer a vehicle is to **drive** it.
To steer a boat is to **navigate** or **pilot** it.

step *noun*
1 *The baby took her first* **steps** *yesterday.*
footstep, pace, stride
2 *Be careful not to trip on the* **step**.
doorstep, stair
A set of steps going from one floor of a building to another is a **staircase**.
A folding set of steps is a **stepladder**.
The steps of a ladder are the **rungs**.
3 *The first* **step** *in making a cake is to weigh the ingredients.*
stage, phase, action

step *verb*
Don't **step** *in the puddle!*
put your foot, tread, walk, stamp, trample
to step something up
They have **stepped up** *security at the airport.*
increase, intensify, strengthen, boost

stern *adjective*
The coach gave each of the players a **stern** *look.*
disapproving, unsmiling, severe, strict, hard, harsh, grim
OPPOSITE lenient

stick
noun
1 *They collected* **sticks** *to make a fire.*
twig, branch, stalk
2 *The elderly patient walked with a* **stick**.
cane, rod, staff, pole
A stick used by a conductor is a **baton**.

A stick carried by a police officer is a **truncheon**.
A magic stick used by a witch or fairy is a **wand**.

stick *verb*
1 *He* **stuck** *his fork into the potato.*
poke, prod, stab, thrust, dig, jab
2 *She tried to* **stick** *the broken pieces of china together.*
glue, paste, cement, bond, join, fasten
3 *The stamp wouldn't* **stick** *to the envelope.*
adhere, attach, cling
4 *The wheels of the caravan* **stuck** *fast in the mud.*
jam, wedge, become trapped
to stick out
The shelf **sticks out** *too far.*
jut out, poke out, project, protrude
to stick up for someone
(informal) She **stuck up for** *him when he was in trouble.*
support, defend, side with, stand up for, speak up for

sticky *adjective*
1 *Someone had left a blob of* **sticky** *toffee on the chair.*
tacky, gummy, gluey
(informal) gooey, icky
2 *I don't like hot* **sticky** *weather.*
humid, muggy, clammy, close, steamy, sultry
OPPOSITE dry

stiff *adjective*
1 *Stir the flour and water to a* **stiff** *paste.*
firm, hard, solid
A common simile is **as stiff as a poker**.
OPPOSITE soft
2 *He mounted the picture on* **stiff** *card.*
rigid, inflexible, thick
OPPOSITE pliable
3 *Her muscles were* **stiff** *after the long walk.*
aching, achy, painful, taut, tight
OPPOSITE supple
4 *The team will face* **stiff** *competition in the final.*
strong, powerful, tough, difficult
OPPOSITE easy

5 *His* **stiff** *manner made him hard to talk to.*
unfriendly, cold, formal, awkward, wooden
OPPOSITE relaxed
6 *The judge imposed a* **stiff** *penalty.*
harsh, severe, strict, hard
OPPOSITE lenient
7 *A* **stiff** *breeze was blowing.*
strong, brisk, fresh
OPPOSITE gentle

stifle *verb*
1 *We were almost* **stifled** *by the fumes from the exhaust pipe.*
choke, suffocate, smother
To kill someone by stopping their breathing is to **strangle** or **throttle** them.
2 *She tried to* **stifle** *a yawn.*
suppress, muffle, hold back, repress, restrain

still *adjective*
1 *The prisoner sat* **still** *and said nothing.*
motionless, unmoving, stationary, static, inert
2 *It was a beautiful* **still** *evening.*
calm, peaceful, quiet, tranquil, serene, hushed, silent, noiseless, windless

sting *verb*
The smoke made our eyes **sting**.
smart, hurt, prick, prickle, tingle

stingy *adjective(informal)*
He's too **stingy** *to give anyone a birthday card.*
mean, miserly, selfish, uncharitable
(informal) tight-fisted, penny-pinching
OPPOSITE generous

stink *verb*
The dungeon **stank** *of unwashed bodies.*
reek, smell

stink *noun*
The mouldy cheese gave off a dreadful **stink**.
odour, stench, reek, bad smell

stir *verb*
1 *Stir the mixture until it is smooth.*
mix, beat, blend, whisk
2 *The giant* **stirred** *in his sleep.*
move slightly, shift, toss, turn
to stir something up
The bandits were always **stirring up** *trouble.*
arouse, encourage, provoke, set off, trigger, whip up

stir *noun*
The news caused quite a **stir**.
fuss, commotion, excitement, hullabaloo

stomach *noun*
He rolled over and lay on his **stomach**.
belly, gut, paunch
(informal) tummy

steps

The part of the body that contains the stomach is the **abdomen**.

stone noun
The columns of the temple were carved from stone.
A large lump of stone is a **rock**.
A large rounded stone is a **boulder**.
Small rounded stones are **pebbles**.
A mixture of sand and small stones is **gravel**.
Pebbles on the beach are **shingle**.
Round stones used to pave a path are **cobbles**.

stoop verb
We had to stoop to go through the tunnel.
bend, duck, bow, crouch

stop verb
1 *I'll go into town when the rain stops.*
end, finish, cease, conclude, terminate
OPPOSITE start
2 *Can you stop talking for a minute?*
give up, cease, suspend, quit, leave off, break off
(*informal*) knock off, pack in
OPPOSITE continue, resume
3 *Guards, stop that man!*
hold, detain, seize, catch, capture, restrain
4 *You can't stop me from going.*
prevent, obstruct, bar, hinder
5 *How do you stop this machine?*
turn off, immobilise
6 *The bus will stop at the school gates.*
come to a stop, halt, pull up, draw up
7 *If you tighten the valve, it will stop the leak.*
close, plug, seal, block up, bung up

stop noun
1 *Everything suddenly came to a stop.*
end, finish, conclusion, halt, standstill
2 *They drove down through France, with a short stop in Paris.*
break, pause, stopover, rest

store verb
Squirrels need to store food for the winter.
save, set aside, stow away, hoard, reserve, stockpile
(*informal*) stash

store noun
1 *The building is now used as a grain store.*
storeroom, storehouse, repository, vault
A store for food is a **larder** or **pantry**.
A store for weapons is an **armoury** or **arsenal**.
2 *He kept a large store of wine in the cellar.*
hoard, supply, quantity, stock, stockpile, reserve
3 *He's the manager of the local grocery store.*

storm noun
1 *Crops were damaged in the heavy storms.*
squall, blizzard, gale, thunderstorm, hurricane, typhoon
An old word for storm is **tempest**.
When a storm begins to develop it is **brewing**.
2 *Plans to close the library caused a storm of protest.*
outburst, outcry, uproar, clamour

storm verb
The soldiers stormed the castle.
charge at, rush at

stormy adjective
1 *It was a dark, stormy night.*
blustery, squally, tempestuous, wild, windy, rough, choppy, gusty, raging
OPPOSITE calm
2 *Fighting broke out at the end of a stormy meeting.*
bad-tempered, quarrelsome, turbulent, violent

stout adjective
1 *The doctor was a stout man with grey hair.*
fat, plump, chubby, dumpy, tubby, portly, stocky, beefy, burly
OPPOSITE thin
2 *You will need a pair of stout walking boots.*
strong, sturdy, tough, robust, sound, substantial
OPPOSITE weak
3 *The enemy put up a stout resistance.*
brave, courageous, spirited, plucky, determined, staunch, resolute, firm
OPPOSITE cowardly

straight adjective
1 *They walked in a straight line.*
direct, unswerving
A common simile is **as straight as an arrow**.
OPPOSITE crooked
2 *It took a long time to get the room straight.*
neat, orderly, tidy
OPPOSITE untidy
3 *She found it difficult to get a straight answer from him.*
honest, plain, frank, straightforward
OPPOSITE indirect, evasive

strain verb
1 *The dog was straining at its lead.*
pull, tug, stretch, haul
2 *People were straining to see what was going on.*
struggle, strive, make an effort, try, attempt
3 *Take it easy and don't strain yourself.*
weaken, exhaust, wear out, tire out, tax

strain noun
The strain of her job was making her ill.
stress, tension, worry, anxiety, pressure

stranded adjective
1 *A whale lay stranded on the beach.*
run aground, beached, marooned
2 *He was stranded in London without any money.*
abandoned, deserted, helpless, lost, stuck
(*informal*) high and dry

strange adjective
1 *A strange thing happened this morning.*
funny, odd, peculiar, unusual, abnormal, curious, extraordinary, remarkable, singular, uncommon
OPPOSITE ordinary, everyday
2 *Did you hear strange noises in the night?*
mysterious, puzzling, baffling, mystifying, perplexing, bewildering, inexplicable
3 *The professor showed us his strange inventions.*
weird, eccentric, peculiar, bizarre
(*informal*) oddball, wacky
4 *I find it hard to get to sleep in a strange bed.*
unfamiliar, unknown, new, alien
OPPOSITE familiar

strangle verb
The victim had been strangled.
throttle

strap noun
The trunk was fastened with a leather strap.
belt, band

stray verb
Some sheep had strayed on to the road.
wander, drift, roam, rove, straggle, meander, ramble

a b c d e f g h i j k l m n o p q r s t u v w x y z

stretch

streak *noun*
1 *The horse had a white **streak** on his muzzle.*
band, line, stripe, strip, smear, stain
2 *There is a **streak** of meanness in his character.*
element, trace

streak *verb*
1 *Rain had begun to **streak** the window.*
smear, smudge, stain, line
2 *A group of motorbikes **streaked** past.*
rush, speed, dash, fly, hurtle, flash, tear, zoom

stream *noun*
1 *The climbers dipped their feet in a cool mountain **stream**.*
brook, rivulet
(*Scottish*) burn
2 *The raft was carried along with the **stream**.*
current, flow, tide
3 *A **stream** of water poured through the hole.*
cataract, flood, gush, jet, rush, torrent
4 *The museum had a steady **stream** of visitors.*
series, string, line, succession

stream *verb*
*Warm sunlight **streamed** through the window.*
pour, flow, flood, issue, gush, spill

strength *noun*
1 *Hercules was said to have enormous **strength**.*
power, might, muscle, brawn, toughness, force, vigour
2 *The main **strength** of the team is in scoring goals.*
strong point, asset, advantage
OPPOSITE weakness

strengthen *verb*
1 *Regular exercise **strengthens** your muscles.*
make stronger, build up, toughen, harden
2 *Concrete was used to **strengthen** the tunnel.*
fortify, reinforce, bolster, prop up

stress *noun*
1 *The hospital staff were working under a lot of **stress**.*
strain, pressure, tension, worry, anxiety
2 *My piano teacher puts great **stress** on the need to practise.*
emphasis, importance, weight

stress *verb*
*She **stressed** the need for absolute secrecy.*
emphasise, draw attention to, highlight, underline

stretch *verb*
1 *He **stretched** the rubber band until it snapped.*
expand, extend, draw out, pull out, elongate, lengthen
2 *She **stretched** her arms wide.*
extend, open out, spread out
3 *The road **stretched** into the distance.*
continue, extend

stretch *noun*
1 *He had a two-year **stretch** in the army.*
spell, period, time, stint
2 *There are often accidents on this **stretch** of road.*
section, length, piece
3 *It's a beautiful **stretch** of countryside.*
area, tract, expanse, sweep

strict *adjective*
1 *The club has **strict** rules about who can join.*
rigid, inflexible
(*informal*) hard and fast
OPPOSITE flexible
2 *The sergeant was known for being **strict** with his men.*
harsh, severe, stern, firm
OPPOSITE lenient
3 *He used the word in its **strict** scientific sense.*
exact, precise, correct
OPPOSITE loose

stride *noun*
*The robot took two **strides** forward.*
pace, step

strike *verb*
1 *Roy **struck** his head on the low ceiling.*
bang, bump, hit, knock, thump, collide with
(*informal*) wallop, whack
2 *The enemy could **strike** again at any time.*
attack

striking *adjective*
*The most **striking** feature of the mermaid was her iridescent tail.*
conspicuous, noticeable, prominent, remarkable, memorable, extraordinary, outstanding, impressive
OPPOSITE inconspicuous

string *noun*
1 *She tied some **string** round the parcel.*
rope, cord, twine
2 *They have received a **string** of complaints.*
series, succession, chain, sequence

string verb
We **strung** the fairy lights on the Christmas tree.
hang, arrange, thread

strong

strip verb
1 Lottie **stripped** the paper off her present.
peel, remove
OPPOSITE cover, wrap
2 He **stripped** and got into the bath.
get undressed, undress
OPPOSITE dress

strip noun
In front of the house was a narrow **strip** of grass.
band, length, ribbon, piece, bit

stripe noun
The tablecloth was white with blue **stripes**.
line, strip, band, bar

stroke noun
1 He split the log with a single **stroke**.
blow, hit, action, movement, effort
2 She added a few quick pencil **strokes** to her drawing.
line, mark

stroke verb
Jess was curled up on the sofa, **stroking** the cat.
pat, caress, rub, touch, fondle, pet

stroll verb
The children **strolled** quietly home.
walk slowly, amble, saunter

strong adjective
1 Crocodiles have **strong** jaws
powerful, muscular, mighty, well-built, beefy, brawny, burly, strapping
OPPOSITE weak, puny
2 The tent is made from **strong** material.
robust, sturdy, tough, hard-wearing, durable, stout, substantial
OPPOSITE thin, flimsy
3 The fugitive was caught in the **strong** beam of a searchlight.
bright, brilliant, dazzling, glaring
OPPOSITE weak, pale
4 I smelt the **strong** aroma of roasting coffee.
overpowering, pronounced, pungent, piquant
OPPOSITE faint, slight
5 The police have **strong** evidence of his guilt.
convincing, persuasive, effective, sound, solid, valid
OPPOSITE weak, feeble, flimsy
6 Zelda takes a **strong** interest in fashion.
enthusiastic, keen, passionate, fervent, avid, zealous
OPPOSITE slight

struggle verb
1 The captives **struggled** to get free.
strain, strive, wrestle, writhe about, tussle, fight, battle
2 The expedition had to **struggle** through a snowstorm.
stagger, stumble, flounder, labour

struggle noun
The rebels surrendered without a **struggle**.
fight, battle, combat, clash, contest

stubborn adjective
She's too **stubborn** to admit that she was wrong.
obstinate, pig-headed, strong-willed, uncooperative, inflexible, wilful
A common simile is **as stubborn as a mule**.
OPPOSITE compliant

stuck-up adjective (informal)
Nobody likes Ernest—he's so **stuck-up**.
arrogant, conceited, haughty, proud, snobbish, superior
(informal) snooty, toffee-nosed
OPPOSITE humble

study verb
1 He went to university to **study** medicine.
learn about, read, research into
2 The spy **studied** the document carefully.
examine, inspect, analyse, investigate, look closely at, scrutinise, survey
3 She has to **study** for her exams.
revise, cram
(informal) swot

stuff noun
1 What's that sticky **stuff** on the carpet?
matter, substance
2 You can put your **stuff** in one of the lockers.
belongings, possessions, things, gear

stuff verb
1 We managed to **stuff** everything into the boot of the car.
pack, push, shove, squeeze, ram, compress, force, cram, jam
2 The cushions are **stuffed** with foam rubber.
fill, pad

stuffy adjective
1 Open a window—it's **stuffy** in here.
airless, close, muggy, humid, stifling, musty, unventilated
OPPOSITE airy
2 I found the book a bit **stuffy**.
boring, dull, dreary, pompous, stodgy
OPPOSITE lively

stumble verb
1 He **stumbled** on a tree root and twisted his ankle.
trip, stagger, totter, flounder, lurch
2 The actress **stumbled** over her words.
stammer, stutter, falter, hesitate
to stumble across something
I **stumbled across** some old photos.
come across, encounter, find, unearth, discover

stun verb
1 The pilot was alive but **stunned**.
daze, knock out, knock senseless, make unconscious
2 The whole town was **stunned** by the news.
amaze, astonish, astound, shock, stagger, stupefy, bewilder, dumbfound

stupid adjective
1 Trolls are often very **stupid**.
foolish, unintelligent, dense, dim, dim-witted, brainless, dumb, slow, thick, feeble-minded, half-witted, simple, simple-minded, dopey, dull
2 It would be **stupid** to go snowboarding without a helmet.
senseless, mindless, idiotic, unwise, foolhardy, silly, daft, crazy, mad
OPPOSITE intelligent

sturdy adjective
1 Shetland ponies are short and **sturdy**.
stocky, strong, robust, athletic, brawny, burly, healthy, hefty, husky, muscular, powerful, vigorous, well-built
OPPOSITE weak
2 She bought some **sturdy** walking boots.
durable, solid, sound, substantial, tough, well made
OPPOSITE flimsy

stutter verb
He tends to **stutter** when he's nervous.
stammer, stumble, falter

style noun
1 I don't like that **style** of jeans.
design, pattern, fashion
2 The book is written in an informal **style**.
manner, tone, way, wording
3 The actress always dresses with great **style**.
elegance, stylishness, taste, sophistication

subject noun
1 Do you have any strong views on the **subject**?
matter, issue, question, point, theme, topic
2 Her passport shows that she is a British **subject**.
citizen, national

subtle adjective
1 There was a **subtle** smell of roses in the air.
faint, slight, mild, delicate

a
b
c
d
e
f
g
h
i
j
k
l
m
n
o
p
q
r
s
t
u
v
w
x
y
z

2 *His jokes are too **subtle** for most people.*
ingenious, sophisticated
3 *I tried to give her a **subtle** hint.*
gentle, tactful, indirect

subtract verb
*If you **subtract** 5 from 20, you will have 15 left.*
take away, deduct, remove
OPPOSITE add

succeed verb
1 *You have to work hard if you want to **succeed**.*
be successful, do well, prosper, flourish, thrive
(*informal*) make it
2 *Everyone hoped that the plan would **succeed**.*
be effective, produce results, work
(*informal*) catch on
OPPOSITE fail
3 *Edward VII **succeeded** Queen Victoria.*
come after, follow, take over from, replace

success noun
1 *She talked about her **success** as an actress.*
achievement, attainment, fame
2 *They congratulated the team on their **success**.*
victory, win, triumph
3 *The **success** of the mission depends on the astronauts.*
effectiveness, successful outcome, completion

successful adjective
1 *She owns a very **successful** chain of restaurants.*
thriving, flourishing, booming, prosperous, profitable, popular
2 *The supporters cheered the **successful** team.*
winning, victorious, triumphant
OPPOSITE unsuccessful

suck verb
to suck something up
*A sponge will **suck up** water.*
soak up, draw up, absorb

sudden adjective
1 *Maria felt a **sudden** urge to burst into song.*
unexpected, unforeseen, impulsive, rash, quick
OPPOSITE expected
2 *The bus came to a **sudden** halt.*
abrupt, sharp, swift
OPPOSITE gradual

suffer verb
1 *He **suffers** terribly with his back.*
feel pain, hurt
2 *He will **suffer** for his crime.*
be punished, pay

3 *The home team **suffered** a humiliating defeat.*
experience, undergo, go through, endure, stand, bear, tolerate

suffocate verb
*The firefighters were nearly **suffocated** by the fumes.*
choke, stifle
To stop someone's breathing by squeezing their throat is to **strangle** or **throttle** them.
To stop someone's breathing by covering their nose and mouth is to **smother** them.

suggest verb
1 *Mum **suggested** going to the zoo.*
propose, advise, advocate, recommend
2 *Her comments **suggest** that she's not happy.*
imply, hint, indicate, signal

suggestion noun
*They didn't like his **suggestion**.*
proposal, plan, idea, proposition, recommendation

suit verb
1 *Would it **suit** you to stay here overnight?*
be convenient for, be suitable for, please, satisfy
OPPOSITE displease
2 *His new haircut doesn't **suit** him.*
look good on, become, flatter

suitable adjective
1 *Please wear clothes **suitable** for wet weather.*
appropriate, apt, fitting, suited (to), proper, right
OPPOSITE unsuitable
2 *Is this a **suitable** time to have a chat?*
convenient, acceptable, satisfactory
OPPOSITE inconvenient

sulk verb
*I was **sulking** because I wasn't allowed to play outside.*
be sullen, mope, brood, pout

sulky adjective
*Ron had turned into a **sulky** teenager.*
moody, sullen, brooding, moping, mopey

summarise verb
*Can you **summarise** the main points of the story?*
sum up, outline, review
(*informal*) recap

summary noun
*We each wrote a **summary** of the poem.*
synopsis, précis, outline

summon verb
*The king **summoned** his knights from far and wide.*
call, send for, order to come, bid to come

To ask someone politely to come is to **invite** them.

sunny adjective
*It was a beautiful **sunny** day.*
fine, clear, cloudless
OPPOSITE cloudy

sunrise noun
*The magic spell wears off at **sunrise**.*
dawn, daybreak
OPPOSITE sunset

sunset noun
*They arranged to meet in the churchyard at **sunset**.*
sundown, dusk, twilight, evening, nightfall
OPPOSITE sunrise

superb adjective
*Brazil scored another **superb** goal.*
excellent, outstanding, exceptional, remarkable, impressive, magnificent, marvellous, splendid, tremendous, wonderful
(*informal*) brilliant, fantastic, terrific, fabulous, sensational, super

supervise verb
*Children must be **supervised** by an adult in the park.*
oversee, superintend, watch over, be in charge of, be responsible for, direct, manage
To supervise candidates in an exam is to **invigilate**.

supple adjective
*The moccasins are made of **supple** leather.*
flexible, pliable, soft
OPPOSITE stiff, rigid

supply verb
*The art shop can **supply** you with brushes and paints.*
provide, equip, furnish

supply noun
*They had a good **supply** of fuel for the winter.*
quantity, stock, store, reserve
supplies
*We bought **supplies** for the camping trip.*
provisions, stores, rations, food, necessities

support noun
1 *She thanked them for their **support**.*
assistance, backing, aid, cooperation, encouragement, help
A support for a shelf is a **bracket**.
A support built against a wall is a **buttress**.
A support for someone with an injured leg is a **crutch**.
A bar of wood or metal supporting a framework is a **strut**.
A support put under a board to make a table is a **trestle**.

2 *The cinema was reopened with **support** from local businesses.*
donations, contributions, sponsorship

support *verb*
1 *The rope couldn't **support** his weight.*
bear, carry, stand, hold up
2 *The beams **support** the roof.*
prop up, strengthen, reinforce
3 *His friends **supported** him when he was in trouble.*
aid, assist, help, back, encourage, stand by, stand up for, rally round
4 *She had to work to **support** her family.*
maintain, keep, provide for
5 *He **supports** several local charities.*
donate to, contribute to, give to
6 *Which team did you **support** in the World Cup?*
be a supporter of, follow

supporter *noun*
1 *The home **supporters** cheered their team.*
fan, follower
2 *She is a well-known **supporter** of animal rights.*
champion, advocate, backer, defender

suppose *verb*
1 *I **suppose** you want to borrow some money.*
expect, presume, assume, guess, believe, think
2 ***Suppose** a spaceship landed in your garden!*
imagine, pretend, fancy
to be supposed to do something
*The bus is **supposed to** leave at 9 o'clock.*
be meant to, be due to, be expected to, ought to

sure *adjective*
1 *I'm **sure** that I'm right.*
certain, convinced, confident, definite, positive
OPPOSITE unsure, uncertain
2 *He's **sure** to phone tonight.*
bound, certain
OPPOSITE unlikely

surface *noun*
1 *The **surface** of Mars is barren and rocky.*
exterior, outside
The surface of something may be covered with a ***crust*** or ***shell*** or ***skin***.
A thin surface of expensive wood on furniture is a ***veneer***.
OPPOSITE centre
2 *A dice has dots on each **surface**.*
face, side
OPPOSITE inside

3 *Oil floated on the **surface** of the water.*
top
OPPOSITE bottom

surface

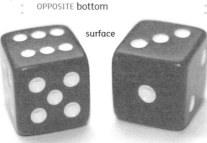

surge *verb*
1 *Massive waves **surged** around the tiny raft.*
rise, roll, swirl, heave, billow
2 *The crowd **surged** forward.*
rush, push, sweep

surprise *noun*
*The news that Sara was married came as a **surprise**.*
amazement, astonishment, revelation, shock, wonder
(*informal*) bombshell

surprise *verb*
1 *I was **surprised** by how well she could sing.*
amaze, astonish, astound, stagger, startle, stun, take aback, take by surprise, dumbfound
(*informal*) bowl over, flabbergast
2 *He **surprised** the burglars as they came through the window.*
discover, come upon, catch unawares, catch offguard, catch red-handed

surprised *adjective*

surprising *adjective*
*There are a **surprising** number of errors in the book.*
amazing, astonishing, astounding, extraordinary, remarkable, incredible, staggering, startling, stunning, unexpected
OPPOSITE predictable

surrender *verb*
1 *The band of outlaws refused to **surrender**.*
admit defeat, give in, yield, submit, capitulate
2 *Please **surrender** your ticket to the driver.*
give, hand over

surround *verb*
1 *The garden was **surrounded** by a stone wall.*
enclose, fence in, wall in
2 *The pack of wolves **surrounded** its prey.*
encircle, ring, hem in, besiege

surroundings *plural noun*
*The hotel is set in very pleasant **surroundings**.*
setting, location, environment

survey *noun*
*They did a **survey** of local leisure facilities.*
review, investigation, study
A survey to count the population of an area is a ***census***.

survey *verb*
1 *You can **survey** the whole valley from the top of the tower.*
view, look over, look at, observe
2 *They **surveyed** the damage done by the storm.*
inspect, examine, scrutinise, study

survive *verb*
1 *He managed to **survive** alone on the island for six months.*
stay alive, last, live, keep going, carry on, continue
OPPOSITE die
2 *Will the birds **survive** this cold weather?*
endure, withstand, live through, weather

suspect *verb*
1 *The police **suspected** his motives.*
doubt, mistrust, have suspicions about
2 *I **suspect** that the shop will be closed on Sundays.*
expect, imagine, presume, guess, sense, fancy

suspend *verb*
1 *The meeting was **suspended** until the next day.*
adjourn, break off, discontinue, interrupt
2 *For the party, we **suspended** balloons from the ceiling.*
hang, dangle, swing

suspense *noun*
*The film was a thriller, full of action and **suspense**.*
tension, uncertainty, anticipation, expectancy, drama, excitement

a
b
c
d
e
f
g
h
i
j
k
l
m
n
o
p
q
r
s
t
u
v
w
x
y
z

suspicion noun
I have a **suspicion** that he is lying.
feeling, hunch, inkling, intuition, impression

suspicious adjective
1 There is something about him which makes me **suspicious**.
doubtful, distrustful, mistrustful, unsure, uneasy, wary
OPPOSITE trusting
2 What do you make of his **suspicious** behaviour?
questionable, suspect, dubious, shady
(informal) fishy

swagger verb
The lead actor **swaggered** about on stage.
strut, parade

swallow verb
The bread was so dry that it was hard to **swallow**.
gulp down
to swallow something up
As it climbed higher, the rocket was **swallowed up** by the clouds.
envelop, engulf, cover over, absorb

swamp verb
A huge wave threatened to **swamp** the ship.
overwhelm, engulf, inundate, flood, submerge

swamp noun
Much of the land near the coast is **swamp**.
marsh, bog, mire, fen, quicksand, quagmire

swap or **swop** verb
We **swapped** seats so I could sit in the aisle.
change, exchange, switch, substitute

swarm verb
Hundreds of people **swarmed** around the film star.
crowd, flock
to swarm with
The garden is **swarming with** ants.
be overrun by, be crawling with, be infested with, teem with

sway verb
The tall grass **swayed** in the breeze.
wave, swing, rock, bend, lean

swear verb
1 The knight **swore** that he would protect the unicorn.
pledge, promise, vow, give your word, take an oath
2 The player **swore** when he bashed his knee.
curse

sweat verb
He **sweats** a lot in hot weather.
perspire

sweep verb
1 She **swept** the floor with an old broom.
brush, clean, dust
2 The bus **swept** past.
shoot, speed, zoom

sweet adjective
1 The pudding is too **sweet** for me.
sickly, sugary, sweetened, syrupy
OPPOSITE acid or bitter or savoury
2 The **sweet** smell of roses filled the room.
fragrant, pleasant
OPPOSITE foul
3 Fergus heard the **sweet** sound of a harp.
melodious, pleasant, soothing, tuneful
OPPOSITE ugly
4 What a **sweet** little cottage!
attractive, charming, dear, lovely, pretty, quaint
OPPOSITE unattractive

swerve verb
The car **swerved** to avoid a hedgehog.
turn aside, veer, dodge, swing

swift adjective
1 They set off at a **swift** pace.
fast, quick, rapid, speedy, brisk, lively
2 She received a **swift** reply to her email.
quick, fast, immediate, instant, prompt, speedy, snappy

swing verb
1 A glass chandelier **swung** from the ceiling.
hang, dangle, sway, flap, wave about
2 She **swung** round when I called her name.
turn, twist, veer, swerve

swirl verb
Clouds of dust **swirled** up in the desert wind.
spin, twirl, whirl, churn

switch verb
1 Please remember to **switch** off the light.
turn
2 The teams will **switch** ends at half-time.
change, swap, exchange, shift

swoop verb
The owl **swooped** and caught the mouse.
dive, drop, plunge, plummet, descend, pounce

symbol noun
The dove is a **symbol** of peace.
sign, emblem, image
The symbols we use in writing are **characters** or **letters**.
The symbols used in ancient Egyptian writing were **hieroglyphics**.
The symbol of a club or school is their **badge**.
The symbol of a firm or organisation is their **logo**.

symbol

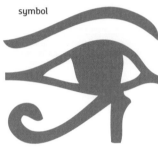

sympathetic adjective
They were **sympathetic** when my mother was ill.
understanding, compassionate, concerned, caring, comforting, kind, supportive
OPPOSITE unsympathetic

sympathise verb
to sympathise with
We **sympathised with** those who had lost their homes.
be sympathetic towards, be sorry for, feel for, commiserate with

sympathy noun
Did you feel any **sympathy** for the characters in the story?
understanding, compassion, pity, fellow-feeling, tenderness

system noun
1 The city has an archaic transport **system**.
organisation, structure, network, framework
(informal) set-up
2 Do you understand the new cataloguing **system**?
procedure, process, scheme, arrangement, method, routine

swarm

tactful *adjective*
*She gave him a **tactful** reminder about her birthday.*
subtle, discreet, diplomatic, sensitive, thoughtful
OPPOSITE tactless

take *verb*
1 *Naomi **took** her sister's hand.*
clutch, clasp, take hold of, grasp, grip, seize, snatch, grab
2 *The soldiers **took** many prisoners.*
catch, capture, seize, detain
3 *Someone has **taken** my pen.*
steal, remove, make off with
(*informal*) swipe, pinch
4 *The guide will **take** you to the edge of the forest.*
conduct, escort, lead, accompany
5 *The bus **took** us right to the station.*
bring, carry, convey, transport
6 *It'll **take** two people to lift that table.*
need, require
7 *The caravan can **take** six people.*
hold, contain, accommodate, have room for
8 *He couldn't **take** the heat of the midday sun.*
bear, put up with, stand, endure, tolerate, suffer, stomach
9 *He **took** their names and addresses.*
make a note of, record, write down
10 *The magician asked me to **take** a card.*
pick, choose, select

tame

11 *Take 2 from 8 and you get 6.*
subtract, take away, deduct

talent *noun*
*She has a great **talent** for music.*
gift, ability, aptitude, skill, flair, knack
Unusually great talent is **genius**.

talented *adjective*
*He's a very **talented** dancer.*
gifted, able, accomplished, capable, skilled, skilful, clever, brilliant
If you are talented in several ways, you are **versatile**.

talk *verb*
1 *Doug was trying to teach his parrot to **talk**.*
speak, say things, communicate, express yourself
2 *The two old friends had a lot to **talk** about.*
discuss, converse, chat, chatter, gossip
(*informal*) natter

talk *noun*
1 *I need to have a **talk** with you soon.*
conversation, discussion, chat
The talk between characters in a story is the **dialogue**.
2 *There is a **talk** about Egyptian art at lunchtime.*
lecture, presentation, speech, address
A talk in church is a **sermon**.

talkative *adjective*
*You're not very **talkative** this morning.*
chatty, communicative, vocal, forthcoming, articulate
An informal name for a talkative person is a **chatterbox**.

tall *adjective*
1 *Jasmine is **tall** for her age.*
big
OPPOSITE short
2 *Singapore has many **tall** buildings.*
high, lofty, towering, soaring, giant
Buildings with many floors are **high-rise** or **multi-storey** buildings.
OPPOSITE low

tame *adjective*
1 *The guinea pigs are **tame** and used to people.*
domesticated, broken in, docile, gentle, obedient, manageable
OPPOSITE wild
2 *The film seems very **tame** nowadays.*
dull, boring, tedious, bland, unexciting, uninteresting
OPPOSITE exciting

tamper *verb*
to tamper with something
*Someone has been **tampering with** the lock.*
meddle with, tinker with, fiddle about with, interfere with

tap *verb*
*Someone **tapped** three times on the door.*
knock, rap, strike

tape *noun*
*The stack of old letters was tied up with **tape**.*
ribbon, braid, binding

target *noun*
1 *Her **target** was to swim thirty lengths.*
goal, aim, objective, intention, purpose, hope, ambition
2 *She was the **target** of his jokes.*
object, victim, butt

task *noun*
1 *The robot was given a number of **tasks** to do.*
job, chore, exercise, errand
2 *The soldiers' **task** was to capture the hill.*
assignment, mission, duty, undertaking

taste *verb*
1 ***Taste** the soup to see if it needs salt.*
sample, try, test, sip
2 *The curry **tastes** quite mild.*

taste *noun*
1 *I love the **taste** of ginger.*
flavour
2 *May I have a **taste** of the cheese?*
mouthful, bite, morsel, nibble, bit, piece, sample
3 *Her **taste** in clothes is a bit odd.*
choice, preference, discrimination, judgement

tasteless *adjective*
1 *He apologised for making a **tasteless** remark.*
crude, tactless, indelicate, inappropriate
OPPOSITE tasteful
2 *The sprouts were overcooked and **tasteless**.*
flavourless, bland, insipid
OPPOSITE flavourful

tasty *adjective*
*That pie was very **tasty**.*
delicious, appetising
OPPOSITE unappetising

taunt *verb*
*The gladiator **taunted** his opponent.*
barrack, insult, jeer at, laugh at, make fun of, mock, ridicule, sneer at

taut *adjective*
*Make sure the rope is **taut**.*
tight, tense, stretched
OPPOSITE slack

taut

a
b
c
d
e
f
g
h
i
j
k
l
m
n
o
p
q
r
s
t
u
v
y
z

teach *verb*
*My dad is **teaching** me to play the guitar.*
educate, inform, instruct
To teach people to play a sport is to **coach** or **train** them.
To teach one person at a time or a small group is to **tutor** them.

teacher *noun*
*We have a new ballet **teacher**.*
tutor, instructor, trainer
Someone who teaches you to play a sport is a **coach**.
In the past, a woman who taught children in a private household was a **governess**.

team *noun*
*She's been picked for the junior hockey **team**.*
side

tear *verb*
1 *The tree branch **tore** a hole in our kite.*
rip, snag, gash, shred, split, slit
2 *He **tore** home to watch his favourite TV programme.*
run, rush, dash, hurry, race, sprint, speed

tear *noun*
*There was a **tear** in one of the sails.*
cut, rip, rent, split, gash, hole, opening, slit, gap

tease *verb*
*They **teased** him about his new haircut.*
taunt, make fun of, poke fun at, mock, ridicule, laugh at

tell *verb*
1 ***Tell** us what you can see.*
describe, explain, reveal, report, say, state
2 ***Tell** me when you are ready.*
let you know, inform, notify, announce, communicate
3 *He **told** them to stop making so much noise.*
order, command, direct, instruct
4 *We **told** each other scary ghost stories.*
narrate, relate
5 *He **told** me he would buy the tickets.*
assure, promise
6 *She couldn't **tell** where she was in the dark.*
make out, recognise, identify, perceive

tear

7 *Can you **tell** one twin from the other?*
distinguish, separate
to tell someone off
*She **told them off** for being late.*
scold, reprimand, reproach
(*informal*) tick off

temper *noun*
1 *Mr Black had been in a bad **temper** all morning.*
mood, humour, state of mind
2 *The chef is always flying into a **temper**.*
rage, fury, fit of anger, tantrum
to lose your temper
*When she **loses her temper**, her cheeks go red.*
get angry, get annoyed, fly into a rage

temporary *adjective*
*They made a **temporary** shelter for the night.*
makeshift, provisional
OPPOSITE permanent

tempt *verb*
*Can I **tempt** you to have more pudding?*
coax, entice, persuade, attract
To tempt someone by offering them money is to **bribe** them.
To tempt an animal into a trap is to **lure** it.

tender *adjective*
1 *Frost may damage **tender** plants.*
delicate, fragile
OPPOSITE hardy, strong
2 *Cook the meat slowly until it is **tender**.*
soft, succulent, juicy
OPPOSITE tough
3 *The bruise is still **tender**.*
painful, sensitive, sore
4 *She gave him a **tender** smile.*
affectionate, kind, loving, caring, warm-hearted, compassionate, sympathetic, fond
OPPOSITE uncaring

tense *adjective*
1 *The muscles in her shoulders were **tense**.*
taut, tight, strained, stretched
2 *The crowd were **tense** as they waited to hear the results.*
anxious, nervous, apprehensive, edgy, on edge, fidgety, jumpy, jittery
(*informal*) uptight
3 *It was an extremely **tense** moment for all of us.*

nerve-racking, stressful, worrying
OPPOSITE relaxed

tension *noun*
*The **tension** of waiting was almost unbearable.*
stress, strain, anxiety, nervousness, suspense, worry

terrible *adjective*
*We heard there had been a **terrible** accident.*
awful, dreadful, horrible, appalling, shocking, ghastly, horrific, frightful

terrific *adjective* (*informal*)
1 *The footprint of the yeti was a **terrific** size.*
big, huge, immense, enormous, giant, gigantic, colossal, massive
2 *She's a **terrific** tennis player.*
excellent, first-class, first-rate, superb, marvellous, wonderful
(*informal*) brilliant, fantastic, fabulous

terrify *verb*
*The dogs were **terrified** by the thunder.*
frighten, scare, startle, alarm, panic, horrify, petrify

terror *noun*
*Her eyes filled with **terror** as she described the ghost.*
fear, fright, horror, panic, alarm, dread

test *noun*
*How did you do in the maths **test**?*
exam, examination, assessment, appraisal, evaluation
A set of questions you answer for fun is a **quiz**.
A test for a job as an actor or singer is an **audition**.
A test to find the truth about something is an **experiment** or **trial**.

test *verb*
1 *I made an appointment to have my eyes **tested**.*
examine, check, evaluate, assess, screen
2 *He is **testing** a new formula for invisible ink.*
experiment with, try out, trial

thankful *adjective*
to be thankful for something
*We were **thankful for** her help.*
grateful for, appreciative of, pleased about, relieved about
OPPOSITE ungrateful

thanks plural noun
*She sent them a card to show her **thanks**.*
gratitude, appreciation

theme noun
*What is the **theme** of the poem?*
subject, topic, idea, gist, argument

theory noun
1 *The detective has a **theory** about the case.*
explanation, hypothesis, view, belief, idea, notion, suggestion
2 *She bought a book about musical **theory**.*
laws, principles, rules

thick adjective
1 *The Roman wall was about 2 metres **thick**.*
wide, broad
OPPOSITE thin
2 *The cabin was made from **thick** logs of wood.*
stout, chunky, heavy, solid, substantial
OPPOSITE thin, slender
3 *The explorers hacked their way through the **thick** jungle.*
dense, close, compact
4 *His boots got stuck in a **thick** layer of mud.*
deep, heavy
OPPOSITE thin, shallow
5 *The guide spoke with a **thick** Polish accent.*
heavy, noticeable
OPPOSITE slight
6 *(informal) Fortunately, the giant was rather **thick**.*
stupid, brainless, foolish
OPPOSITE intelligent

thief noun
*The police managed to catch the **thief**.*
robber
Someone who steals from people's homes is a **burglar** or **housebreaker**.
Someone who steals from people in the street is a **pickpocket**.
Someone who steals from shops is a **shoplifter**.
Someone who used to steal from travellers was a **highwayman**.

thin adjective
1 *The prisoners were dreadfully **thin**.*
lean, skinny, bony, gaunt, spare, slight, underweight
Someone who is thin and tall is **lanky**.
Someone who is thin but strong is **wiry**.
Someone who is thin but attractive is **slim** or **slender**.

thin

Thin arms or legs are **spindly**.
A common simile is *as thin as a rake*.
OPPOSITE fat
2 *The fairy wore a **thin** cloak of spider's silk.*
fine, light, delicate, flimsy, sheer, wispy
A thin line is a **fine** or **narrow** line.
A thin book is a **slim** book.
OPPOSITE thick
3 *The icing should be **thin** enough to spread.*
runny, watery
OPPOSITE thick

thick

thing noun
1 *What's that green **thing** on the floor?*
item, object, article
2 *We had a lot of **things** to talk about.*
matter, affair, detail, point, factor
3 *A lot of **things** had happened since we spoke.*
event, happening, occurrence, incident
4 *I have only one **thing** left to do.*
job, task, act, action
things
*Put your **things** in one of the lockers.*
belongings, possessions, stuff, equipment, gear

think verb
1 ***Think** before you do anything rash.*
consider, contemplate, reflect, deliberate, reason
To think hard about something is to **concentrate** on it.
To think quietly and deeply about something is to **meditate**.
To keep thinking anxiously about something is to **brood** on it.
2 *Do you **think** this is a good idea?*
believe, feel, consider, judge, conclude
3 *What do you **think** this ring is worth?*
reckon, suppose, imagine, estimate, guess, expect
to think about something
*I need some more time to **think** about it.*
consider, reflect on, ponder, muse on, mull over
to think something up
*They **thought up** a good plan.*
invent, make up, conceive, concoct, devise

thirsty adjective
*They were **thirsty** after their long walk.*
dry, parched
If someone is ill through lack of fluids, they are **dehydrated**.

thorough adjective
1 *The doctor gave him a **thorough** examination.*
comprehensive, full, rigorous, careful, methodical, systematic, meticulous, painstaking, conscientious
OPPOSITE superficial
2 *He's made a **thorough** mess of things!*
complete, total, utter, absolute, downright

thought noun
1 *She gave a lot of **thought** to the problem.*
consideration, deliberation, study
2 *The detective spent some time in **thought**.*
thinking, contemplation, reflection, meditation
3 *What are your **thoughts** on modern art?*
opinion, belief, idea, notion, conclusion

thoughtful adjective
1 *Mr Levi had a **thoughtful** expression on his face.*
pensive, reflective, absorbed, preoccupied
OPPOSITE blank, vacant
2 *She added some **thoughtful** comments in the margin.*
well-thought-out, careful, conscientious, thorough
OPPOSITE careless
3 *It was very **thoughtful** of you to visit me in hospital.*
caring, considerate, kind, friendly, good-natured, unselfish
OPPOSITE thoughtless

thoughtless adjective
*It was **thoughtless** of him to mention her dead husband.*
inconsiderate, insensitive, uncaring, unthinking, negligent, ill-considered, rash
OPPOSITE thoughtful

thrash verb
1 *The rider **thrashed** and spurred his horse to go faster.*
hit, beat, whip, flog
(informal) whack, wallop
2 *The crocodile **thrashed** its tail in the mud.*
swish, flail, jerk, toss
3 *(informal) The visitors **thrashed** the home side 6–0.*
beat, defeat, trounce

threat noun
1 *She made a **threat** about phoning the police.*
warning
2 *Earthquakes are a constant **threat** in California.*
danger, menace, hazard, risk

a b c d e f g h i j k l m n o p q r s t u v w x y z

threaten *verb*
1 *The bandits* **threatened** *him when he tried to escape.*
make threats against, menace, intimidate, terrorise, bully, browbeat
2 *The forecast* **threatened** *rain.*
warn of
3 *Wild tigers are* **threatened** *with extinction.*
endanger, put at risk

thrill *noun*
Kim loves the **thrill** *of rock climbing.*
adventure, excitement, sensation, tingle
(*slang*) buzz, kick

thrill *verb*
The thought of seeing a real shark **thrilled** *him no end.*
excite, exhilerate, electrify, rouse, stir, stimulate
OPPOSITE bore

thrilled *adjective*
I was **thrilled** *to be invited to the wedding.*
delighted, pleased, excited, overjoyed, ecstatic

throb *verb*
She could feel the blood **throbbing** *through her veins.*
beat, pound, pulse, pulsate

throw *verb*
1 *I* **threw** *some bread into the pond for the ducks.*
fling, cast, pitch, sling, toss
(*slang*) bung, chuck
To deliver the ball in cricket or rounders is to **bowl**.
To throw the shot in athletics is to **put** the shot.
To throw something high in the air is to **lob** it.
To throw something heavy is to **heave** it.
To throw something with great force is to **hurl** it.
If someone throws a lot of things at you, they **pelt** you.
2 *The horse* **threw** *its rider.*
throw off, shake off, dislodge

thrill

to throw away
We **threw away** *a pile of old junk.*
get rid of, dispose of, discard, scrap
(*informal*) dump, ditch

thrust *verb*
1 *Drew* **thrust** *his hands into his pockets.*
push, force, shove
2 *The bandit* **thrust** *at him with a dagger.*
lunge, jab, prod, stab, poke

thump *verb*
'Silence!' he rasped, **thumping** *his fist on the table.*
bang, bash, pound, hit, strike, knock, rap
(*informal*) whack, wham

tidy *adjective*
I like to keep my office **tidy**.
neat, orderly, uncluttered, trim, smart, spruce, straight
OPPOSITE untidy

tie *verb*
1 *Zoe* **tied** *a pink ribbon round the parcel.*
bind, fasten, hitch, knot, loop, secure
To tie up a boat is to **moor** it.
To tie up an animal is to **tether** it.
OPPOSITE untie
2 *The two teams are still* **tied**.
be equal, be level, draw

tight *adjective*
1 *The lid was too* **tight** *for him to unscrew.*
firm, fast, secure
If it is so tight that air cannot get through, it is **airtight**.
If it is so tight that water cannot get through, it is **watertight**.
OPPOSITE loose
2 *They squeezed into the* **tight** *space.*
cramped, compact, small, narrow, poky, snug
OPPOSITE spacious
3 *Make sure that the ropes are* **tight**.
taut, tense, stretched, rigid
A common simile is **as tight as a drum**.
OPPOSITE slack

tighten *verb*
1 *She* **tightened** *her grip on his hand.*
increase, strengthen, tense, stiffen
2 *You need to* **tighten** *the guy ropes.*
make taut, pull tighter, stretch
3 *He tried to* **tighten** *the screw.*
make tighter, screw up
OPPOSITE loosen

tilt *verb*
The caravan **tilted** *to one side.*
lean, incline, tip, slant, slope, angle
When a ship tilts to one side, it **lists**.

time *noun*
1 *Is this a convenient* **time** *to talk?*
moment, occasion, opportunity
2 *Autumn is my favourite* **time** *of the year.*
phase, season
3 *He spent a short* **time** *living in China.*
period, while, term, spell, stretch
4 *Shakespeare lived in the* **time** *of Elizabeth I.*
era, age, days, epoch, period
5 *Please try to keep* **time** *with the music.*
tempo, beat, rhythm
on time
Please try to be **on time**.
punctual, prompt

time

timid *adjective*
At first, the mermaid was too **timid** *to say anything.*
shy, bashful, modest, nervous, fearful, shrinking, retiring, sheepish
A common simile is **as timid as a mouse**.
OPPOSITE brave, confident

tiny *adjective*
The ladybird was so **tiny** *that you could hardly see it.*
little, minute, miniature, microscopic, minuscule
(*informal*) teeny, titchy
OPPOSITE big, large

tip *noun*
1 *The* **tip** *of his nose felt cold.*
end, point
The tip of an ink pen is the **nib**.
2 *The* **tip** *of the mountain was covered in snow.*
cap, peak, top, summit, pinnacle, crown
3 *He gave them some useful* **tips** *on first aid.*
hint, piece of advice, suggestion, clue, pointer
4 *They took a load of rubbish to the* **tip**.
dump, rubbish heap

tip *verb*
1 *The caravan **tipped** to one side.*
lean, tilt, incline, slope, slant
When a ship tips slightly to one side, it **lists**.
When a ship tips right over, it **capsizes**.
2 *Sophie **tipped** the box of crayons on to the table.*
empty, turn out, dump, unload
to tip over
*He **tipped** the milk jug **over** by accident.*
knock over, overturn, topple, upset

tired *adjective*
*Have a lie down if you're **tired**.*
exhausted, fatigued, weary, worn out, listless, sleepy, drowsy
(*informal*) all in
to be tired of something
*I'm **tired of** watching TV.*
bored with, fed up with, sick of
If you are not interested in anything, you are **apathetic**.

title *noun*
1 *She couldn't think of a **title** for the story.*
name, heading
The title above a newspaper story is a **headline**.
A title or brief description next to a picture is a **caption**.
2 *The form asks you to fill in your name and **title**.*
form of address, designation, rank
The ordinary title used before a man's name is **Mr**.
The ordinary title used before a woman's name is **Miss** or **Mrs** or **Ms**.
A polite way to address someone whose name you don't know is **sir** or **madam**.

tolerant *adjective*
*Molly was very **tolerant** towards other people.*
understanding, easygoing, open-minded, sympathetic, charitable, forgiving, lenient, indulgent, long-suffering
OPPOSITE intolerant

tolerate *verb*
1 *He won't **tolerate** sloppy writing.*
accept, permit, put up with
2 *Cactus plants can **tolerate** extreme heat.*
bear, endure, stand, abide, suffer, stomach
(*informal*) stick

tomb *noun*
*Inside the **tomb** were several ancient skeletons.*
burial chamber, crypt, grave, mausoleum, sepulchre, vault

An underground passage containing several tombs is a **catacomb**.
A tomb is often marked by a **tombstone**, **gravestone** or **headstone**.

tone *noun*
1 *There was an angry **tone** to her voice.*
note, sound, quality, intonation, manner
2 *The room is painted in subtle **tones**.*
colour, hue, shade, tint
3 *Eerie music created the right **tone** for the film.*
feeling, mood, atmosphere, spirit, effect

✏️ **WRITING TIPS**

tooth *noun*
You can use these words to describe **teeth** or **jaws**
jagged, serrated, razor-sharp, needle-sharp, pincer-like
TEETH MAY
bite, chew, grind, munch, chomp, gnash, snap, tear, rip, puncture

---

top *noun*
1 *They climbed to the **top** of the hill.*
peak, summit, tip, crown, crest, head
OPPOSITE bottom, base
2 *The desk **top** was covered with newspapers.*
surface
3 *The **top** of the jar was screwed on tightly.*
lid, cap, cover, covering

top *adjective*
1 *Their office is on the **top** floor.*
highest, topmost, uppermost, upper
OPPOSITE bottom, lowest
2 *She got **top** marks in her exam.*
most, best, highest
3 *The skiers set off at **top** speed.*
greatest, maximum
4 *He is one of Europe's **top** chefs.*
best, leading, finest, foremost, principal, superior
OPPOSITE junior

top *verb*
1 *Mum **topped** the cake with fudge icing.*
cover, decorate, garnish, crown
2 *The athlete is hoping to **top** her personal best.*
beat, better, exceed, outdo, surpass

topic *noun*
*What was the **topic** of the conversation?*
subject, talking-point, issue, matter, question

topical *adjective*
*The website often discusses **topical** issues.*
current, recent, up-to-date

toss *verb*
1 *He **tossed** a coin into the wishing-well.*
throw, cast, hurl, fling, pitch, sling
(*informal*) chuck
2 *Let's **toss** a coin to see who'll go first.*
flip, spin
3 *The little boat **tossed** about in the storm.*
lurch, pitch, roll, heave, rock, bob
4 *She **tossed** and turned, unable to get to sleep.*
thrash about, flail, writhe, wriggle

total *noun*
*A **total** of 15 million people live in Tokyo.*
sum, whole, entirety, amount

total *adjective*
1 *The bill shows the **total** amount due.*
full, complete, whole, entire
2 *The party was a **total** disaster.*
complete, utter, absolute, thorough, downright, sheer

total *verb*
*The donations **total** almost 300 euros.*
add up to, amount to, come to, make

touch *verb*
1 *Some animals don't like to be **touched**.*
feel, handle, stroke, fondle, caress, pat, pet
2 *The car just **touched** the gatepost.*
brush, graze, contact
3 *The speed of the racing car **touched** 200 miles per hour.*
reach, rise to
4 *I was **touched** by the poem that she wrote.*
move, affect, stir

touch *noun*
1 *I felt a light **touch** on my arm.*
pat, stroke, tap, caress, contact
2 *There's a **touch** of frost in the air.*
hint, trace, suggestion

a b c d e f g h i j k l m n o p q r s t u v w x y z

touchy adjective
Be careful what you say—he's very **touchy**.
easily offended, sensitive, irritable, quick-tempered

tough adjective
1 *You'll need* **tough** *shoes for hiking.*
strong, sturdy, robust, durable, stout, hard-wearing, substantial
Common similes are *as tough as nails* and *as tough as old boots*.
OPPOSITE flimsy
2 *The meat was very* **tough**.
chewy, leathery, rubbery
OPPOSITE tender
3 *They played against* **tough** *opposition.*
strong, stiff, powerful, resistant, determined, stubborn
OPPOSITE weak, feeble
4 *The police deal with some* **tough** *criminals.*
rough, violent, vicious, hardened
5 *It was a* **tough** *job to clean the oven.*
demanding, laborious, strenuous, gruelling, tiring, exhausting
OPPOSITE easy
6 *The crossword puzzle was too* **tough** *for him.*
difficult, hard, puzzling, baffling, knotty, thorny
OPPOSITE easy

tower noun
A small tower on a castle or other building is a **turret**.
A church tower is a **steeple**.
The pointed structure on a steeple is a **spire**.
The top part of a steeple with a bell is a **belfry**.
The tall tower of a mosque is a **minaret**.

tower verb
to tower above something
The castle **towers above** *the village.*
rise above, stand above, dominate, loom over

Eiffel Tower

trace noun
1 *The burglar left no* **trace** *of his presence.*
evidence, sign, mark, indication, hint, clue, track, trail
A trace left by an animal might be its **footprint** or **scent** or **spoor**.
2 *They found* **traces** *of blood on the carpet.*
tiny amount, drop, spot

trace verb
She is trying to **trace** *her distant ancestors.*
track down, discover, find, uncover, unearth

track noun
1 *A rough* **track** *leads past the farm.*
path, pathway, footpath, trail
2 *They followed the deer's* **tracks** *for miles.*
footprint, footmark, trail, scent
3 *They are laying the* **track** *for a new railway.*
line, rails
4 *The athletes are warming up on the* **track**.
racetrack, circuit, course

track verb
Astronomers are **tracking** *the path of the comet.*
follow, trace, pursue, chase, tail, trail, hunt, stalk
to track someone or something down
They **tracked down** *the owner of the car.*
find, discover, trace, hunt down, sniff out, run to ground

tradition noun
It's a **tradition** *to sing 'Auld Lang Syne' on New Year's Eve.*
custom, convention, habit, routine, fashion

traditional adjective
1 *The African drummers wore* **traditional** *costumes.*
national, regional, historical

2 *They chose to have a* **traditional** *wedding.*
conventional, customary, established, time-honoured, habitual, typical, usual

tragedy noun
The accident at sea was a terrible **tragedy**.
disaster, catastrophe, calamity, misfortune

tragic adjective
He died in a **tragic** *accident.*
catastrophic, disastrous, calamitous, terrible, appalling, dreadful, unfortunate, unlucky

trail noun
1 *We walked along a* **trail** *through the woods.*
path, pathway, track, route
2 *The police were on the* **trail** *of the bank robbers.*
track, chase, hunt, pursuit
The trail left in the water by a ship is its **wake**.

trail verb
1 *The detective* **trailed** *the suspect all day.*
follow, chase, tail, track, pursue, shadow, stalk, hunt
2 *She* **trailed** *her suitcase behind her.*
pull, tow, drag, draw, haul
3 *He is already* **trailing** *behind the front runners.*
fall behind, lag, straggle, dawdle

train verb
1 *He* **trains** *the football team every Saturday.*
coach, instruct, teach, tutor
2 *They are* **training** *hard for the Commonwealth Games.*
practise, exercise, prepare yourself, (*informal*) work out

tramp verb
They **tramped** *across the muddy fields.*
march, hike, trek, trudge, plod, stride

trample verb
Don't **trample** *the flowers!*
crush, flatten, squash, tread on, walk over, stamp on

transfer verb
Some paintings have been **transferred** *to the new gallery.*
move, remove, shift, relocate, convey, hand over

transform verb
They **transformed** *the attic into an office.*
change, alter, turn, convert, adapt, modify

transmit verb
1 *The spy* **transmitted** *her messages in code.*
send, communicate, relay, emit, broadcast

WORD WEB

transport noun
TRANSPORT BY AIR
aeroplane, airship, helicopter, hot-air balloon

TRANSPORT BY ROAD
bicycle, bus, car, coach, horse, jeep, lorry, minibus, taxi, van

TRANSPORT BY RAIL
monorail, train, tram, underground

TRANSPORT BY WATER
barge, boat, canoe, ferry, punt, raft, ship, yacht

bicycle

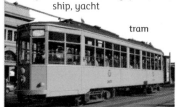
hot-air balloon

tram

VEHICLES WHICH CARRY PEOPLE
bus, cab, camper, car or motorcar, caravan, coach, jeep, minibus, minicab, people carrier, rickshaw, taxi, train, tram, trolleybus

VEHICLES USED FOR WORK
ambulance, bulldozer, dustcart, fire-engine, hearse, HGV or heavy goods vehicle, horsebox, lorry, milkfloat, removal van, pick-up truck, police car, steamroller, tank, tanker, tractor, truck, van

VEHICLES WHICH TRAVEL ON SNOW OR ICE
sled or sledge, sleigh, skidoo, snowplough, toboggan

coach

OLD HORSE-DRAWN VEHICLES
carriage, cart, chariot, coach, gig, stagecoach, trap, wagon

boat

To transmit a programme on radio or TV is to **broadcast** it.
OPPOSITE receive
2 *Can the disease be **transmitted** to humans?*
pass on, spread, carry

transparent adjective
*The box had a **transparent** lid.*
clear
(*informal*) see-through
Something which is not fully transparent, but allows light to shine through, is **translucent**.

trap noun
1 *The animal was caught in a **trap**.*
snare, net, noose, booby trap
2 *The police set up a **trap** to catch the robbers.*
ambush

trap verb
*They tried to **trap** the mouse.*
capture, catch, snare, corner

tread verb
*Please **tread** carefully.*
step, walk, proceed
to tread on
*Don't **tread on** the wet cement!*
walk on, step on, stamp on, trample, crush, squash

treasure noun
*The **treasure** was buried somewhere on the island.*
hoard, riches, wealth, fortune
A hidden store of treasure is a **cache**.

treasure verb
*She **treasures** the photograph of her grandmother.*
cherish, prize, value

treat verb
1 *The old woman had always **treated** him kindly.*
behave towards, deal with
2 *She is being **treated** for minor injuries.*
give treatment to

To treat a wound is to **dress** it.
To treat an illness or wound successfully is to **cure** or **heal** it.

treatment noun **1** *The hospital is for the **treatment** of sick animals.*
care, nursing, healing
2 *He is trying a new **treatment** for back pain.*
remedy, therapy, medication
Emergency treatment at the scene of an accident is **first aid**.
3 *The sculpture has been damaged by careless **treatment**.*
handling, use, care, management

tremble verb
*The little fairy was **trembling** with cold.*
shake, shiver, quake, quiver, shudder

tremendous adjective
1 *They heard a **tremendous** roar issue from the cave.*
big, enormous, great, huge, immense, massive, mighty, fearful
2 *Winning the cup was a **tremendous** achievement.*
marvellous, magnificent, wonderful, superb, terrific, sensational, spectacular, stupendous, extraordinary, outstanding

trend noun
1 *There is a general **trend** towards healthier eating.*
tendency, movement, shift, leaning
2 *This type of computer game is the latest **trend**.*
fashion, style, craze, fad, vogue

trial noun
1 *Scientists are conducting **trials** on a new space probe.*
test, experiment

WORD WEB

travel verb
*She prefers to **travel** to work by bus.*
go, journey, move along, proceed, progress

VARIOUS WAYS TO TRAVEL
cruise, cycle, drive, fly, go by rail, hike, hitch-hike, motor, pedal, ramble, ride, roam, row, sail, tour, trek, voyage, walk, wander

When birds travel from one country to another they **migrate**.
When people travel to another country to live there they **emigrate**.

PEOPLE WHO TRAVEL AS A WAY OF LIFE
itinerant, nomad, traveller

OTHER PEOPLE WHO TRAVEL
astronaut, commuter, cyclist, driver or motorist, explorer, hitch-hiker, holidaymaker, motorcyclist, passenger, pedestrian, pilot or aviator, rambler or walker, sailor, tourist

A person who travels to a religious place is a **pilgrim**.
A person who travels illegally on a ship or plane is a **stowaway**.
A person who likes travelling round the world is a **globetrotter**.

a b c d e f g h i j k l m n o p q r s t u v w x y z

2 *The **trial** will be heard in a crown court.*
case, hearing
*A military trial is a **court martial**.*

trick noun
1 *Stephie played a **trick** on her brother.*
joke, practical joke, prank
*Tricks which a magician performs are **conjuring tricks**.*
2 *The Trojans never guessed that the wooden horse was a **trick**.*
deception, pretence, fraud, cheat, hoax
(*informal*) con

trick verb
*He **tricked** them into believing he was a police officer.*
deceive, dupe, fool, hoodwink, cheat, swindle
(*informal*) con

trickle verb
*Water **trickled** from the tap.*
dribble, drip, leak, seep, ooze
OPPOSITE gush

tricky adjective
*There were a couple of **tricky** questions in the exam.*
difficult, complicated, awkward, intricate, involved, ticklish
OPPOSITE straightforward, easy

trip noun
*They went on a **trip** to the seaside.*
journey, visit, outing, excursion, jaunt, expedition

trip verb
*He **tripped** on the loose carpet.*
catch your foot, stumble, fall, slip, stagger

trivial adjective
*Don't bother me with **trivial** details.*
unimportant, minor, insignificant, trifling, negligible, petty, silly, slight, frivolous
OPPOSITE important

trouble noun
1 *The family has had a lot of **trouble** recently.*
difficulty, hardship, suffering, unhappiness, distress, misfortune, pain, sadness, sorrow, worry
2 *The police dealt with **trouble** in the crowd.*
disorder, unrest, disturbance, commotion, fighting, violence
3 *The **trouble** with this computer is that it's very slow.*
problem, difficulty, disadvantage, drawback
to take trouble
*He **took trouble** to remember all our names.*
bother, make an effort, take pains

trouble verb
1 *What's **troubling** you?*
distress, upset, bother, worry, concern, pain, torment, vex
2 *I don't want to **trouble** her if she's busy.*
disturb, interrupt, bother, pester
3 *Nobody **troubled** to tidy up the room.*
bother, make an effort, take trouble

true adjective
1 *Do you think the newspaper report is **true**?*
accurate, correct, right, factual, authentic, undeniable
OPPOSITE untrue, false
2 *This is a **true** copy of my birth certificate.*
genuine, real, actual, faithful, exact
OPPOSITE false
3 *Esther has always been a **true** friend.*
faithful, loyal, constant, devoted, sincere, steady, trustworthy, dependable, reliable
OPPOSITE unreliable

trust verb
*I **trusted** her to keep my identity a secret.*
rely on, depend on, count on, bank on, believe in, be sure of, have confidence in, have faith in

trust noun
1 *The director has **trust** in her acting ability.*
belief, confidence, faith
2 *They put their lives in the **trust** of the pilot.*
responsibility, safe-keeping, hands

truth noun
1 *The detective doubted the **truth** of her story.*
accuracy, authenticity, correctness, genuineness, reliability, truthfulness, validity
OPPOSITE inaccuracy or falseness
2 *Are you sure you're telling the **truth**?*
facts
OPPOSITE lies

truthful adjective
1 *She is normally a **truthful** person.*
honest, frank, sincere, straight, straightforward, reliable, trustworthy
2 *He gave a **truthful** answer.*
accurate, correct, proper, right, true, valid
OPPOSITE dishonest

try verb
1 *I'm going to **try** to beat my dad at chess.*
aim, attempt, endeavour, make an effort, strive, struggle
2 *Would you like to **try** a larger size?*
test, try out, evaluate, experiment with

try noun
1 *We may not succeed, but it's worth a **try**!*
attempt, effort, go, shot
2 *Would you like a **try** of my mango smoothie?*
trial, test, taste

trying adjective
*The way he keeps asking questions is very **trying**.*
tiresome, irritating, annoying, wearing, wearisome

tuck verb
*He **tucked** his t-shirt into his jeans.*
push, insert, stuff

tug verb
1 *It annoys me when my brother **tugs** my hair.*
pull, yank, jerk, pluck, wrench
2 *We **tugged** the sledge up the hill.*
drag, pull, tow, haul, lug, draw, heave

tune noun
*Can you play the **tune** to 'Happy Birthday'?*
melody, song, air, theme

turn verb
1 *A wheel **turns** on its axle.*
go round, revolve, rotate, roll, spin, swivel, pivot, twirl, whirl
2 *The van **turned** into a side street.*
change direction, corner
To turn unexpectedly is to **swerve** or **veer** off course.
If you turn to go back in the direction you came from, you **do a U-turn**.
If marching soldiers change direction, they **wheel**.
3 *He **turned** a curious shade of green.*
become, go, grow
4 *They **turned** the attic into a spare bedroom.*
convert, adapt, change, alter, modify, transform, develop
to turn something down
*She **turned down** the offer of a part in the play.*
decline, refuse, reject
to turn something on or **off**
*He **turned on** the radio.*
switch on or off
to turn out
*Everything **turned out** well in the end.*
end up, come out, happen, result
to turn over
*The boat **turned over**.*
capsize, overturn, turn upside down, flip over, keel over
to turn up
*A friend **turned up** unexpectedly.*
arrive, appear, drop in

turn *noun*

1 *She gave the handle a **turn**.*
twist, spin, whirl, twirl
A single turn of wheel is a
revolution.
The process of turning is **rotation**.
2 *The house is just past the next
turn in the road.*
bend, corner, curve, angle, junction
A sharp turn in a country road
is a **hairpin bend**.
3 *It's your **turn** to do the washing
up.*
chance, opportunity, occasion, time,
slot, go
4 (*informal*) *Seeing the skeleton
gave her quite a **turn**.*
fright, scare, shock, start, surprise

twinkle *verb*

*The stars **twinkled** in the sky.*
sparkle, shine, glitter, glisten,
glimmer, glint

twist *verb*

1 *She **twisted** a bandage round her
wrist.*
wind, loop, coil, curl, entwine
2 ***Twist** the handle to open the door.*
turn, rotate, revolve, swivel
3 *The road **twists** through the hills.*
wind, weave, curve, zigzag
4 *He **twisted** and turned in his
sleep.*
toss, writhe, wriggle
5 *I tried to **twist** the cap off the
bottle.*
unscrew
6 *Heat can **twist** metal out of shape.*
bend, buckle, warp, crumple, distort

twisted *adjective*

*The trunk of the olive tree was
twisted with age.*
knarled, warped, buckled, misshapen,
deformed

twitch *verb*

*The dog **twitched** in his sleep.*
jerk, jump, start, tremble

type *noun*

1 *What **type** of films do you like to
watch?*
kind, sort, variety, category, class,
genre
2 *The book was printed in large
type.*
print, lettering, letters, characters

typical *adjective*

1 *The weather is **typical** for this
time of year.*
normal, usual, standard, ordinary,
average, predictable, unsurprising
OPPOSITE unusual
2 *The pointed arch is **typical** of
Gothic architecture.*
characteristic, representative
OPPOSITE uncharacteristic

ugly *adjective*

1 *The princess had to kiss a fat,
ugly toad.*
grotesque, hideous,
unattractive, repulsive,
revolting, monstrous
OPPOSITE beautiful
2 *The room was
filled with
ugly furniture.*
unattractive, unsightly,
displeasing, tasteless,
horrid, nasty
OPPOSITE beautiful
3 *The crowd was in an **ugly** mood.*
unfriendly, hostile, menacing,
threatening, angry, dangerous
OPPOSITE friendly

ugly

unavoidable *adjective*

*The accident was **unavoidable**.*
inevitable, bound to happen, certain,
destined

unaware *adjective*

unaware of
*They were **unware of** the dangers
that lay ahead.*
ignorant of, oblivious to,
unconscious of

unbearable *adjective*

*The stench in the cave was
unbearable.*
unendurable, intolerable,
impossible to bear

unbelievable *adjective*

1 *The account of the UFO sighting
was **unbelievable**.*
unconvincing, unlikely, far-fetched,
improbable, incredible
2 *She scored an **unbelievable** goal.*
amazing, astonishing, extraordinary,
remarkable, sensational,
phenomenal

uncertain *adjective*

1 *I was **uncertain** what to do next.*
unsure, doubtful, in two minds,
unclear
2 *They are facing an **uncertain**
future.*
indefinite, unknown, undecided,
unpredictable

uncomfortable *adjective*

1 *She complained that her shoes
were **uncomfortable**.*
restrictive, cramped, hard, stiff, tight,
tight-fitting
2 *He spent an **uncomfortable** night
sleeping on the floor.*
restless, troubled, disagreeable,
uneasy

unconscious *adjective*

1 *The patient had been
unconscious for two days.*
If you are unconscious because of a
hit on the head, you are **knocked out**.
If you are unconscious for an
operation, you are **anaesthetised**.
If you are unconscious because of
an accident or illness, you are **in a
coma**.
2 *She's **unconscious** of the effect
she has on other people.*
ignorant, unaware
3 *They laughed at her **unconscious**
slip of the tongue.*
accidental, unintended, unintentional
OPPOSITE conscious
unconscious of
*He's **unconscious** of all the trouble
he's caused.*
unaware of, ignorant of, oblivious to

uncover *verb*

1 *Archaeologists have **uncovered**
two more skeletons.*
dig up, unearth, expose, reveal, show,
disclose

a b c d e f g h i j k l m n o p q r s t **u** v w x y z

To uncover your body is to **strip** or **undress**.

2 He **uncovered** the truth about his family's past.

detect, discover, come across

OPPOSITE cover up, hide

understand verb

1 I don't **understand** what you mean.

comprehend, grasp, follow, see, take in, realise, appreciate, recognise, work out, fathom

2 Can you **understand** this writing?

read, interpret, make out, make sense of

To understand something in code is to **decode** or **decipher** it.

3 I **understand** they're moving to Sydney.

believe, hear

understanding noun

1 The robot has limited powers of **understanding**.

intelligence, intellect, sense, judgement

2 The course will increase your **understanding** of science.

appreciation, awareness, knowledge, comprehension, grasp

3 The two sides reached an **understanding**.

agreement, deal, settlement, arrangement, accord

4 She treats her patients with **understanding**.

sympathy, compasssion, consideration

undo verb

1 I'll have to **undo** this row of knitting.

unfasten, untie, unravel, loosen, release

To undo stitching is to **unpick** it.

2 Sue **undid** the wrapping on the parcel.

open, unwrap, unfold, unwind, unroll, unfurl

3 The good witch tried to **undo** the spell.

reverse, cancel out, wipe out

unemployed adjective

Since the factory closed, he has been **unemployed**.

out of work, jobless

(informal) on the dole

To be unemployed because there is not enough work to do is to be **redundant**.

OPPOSITE employed, working

uneven adjective

1 The ground was very **uneven** in places.

rough, bumpy, rutted

OPPOSITE smooth

uncover

2 Their performance has been **uneven** this season.

erratic, inconsistent, irregular, variable, unpredictable

OPPOSITE consistent

3 It was a very **uneven** contest.

one-sided, unbalanced, unequal, unfair

OPPOSITE balanced

unexpected adjective

Her reaction was totally **unexpected**.

surprising, unforeseen, unpredictable, unplanned

OPPOSITE expected

unfair adjective

1 Do you think that the umpire's decision was **unfair**?

unjust, unreasonable, wrong, one-sided, imbalanced, impartial, biased

OPPOSITE fair, just

2 I felt that her criticism of my work was **unfair**.

undeserved, unmerited, uncalled-for, unjustified

OPPOSITE fair, deserved

unfamiliar adjective

The astronauts looked on an **unfamiliar** landscape.

stange, unusual, curious, novel, alien

unfamiliar with

They were **unfamiliar with** the local customs.

unaccustomed to, unused to, unaware of

unfortunate adjective

1 The **unfortunate** couple had lost all their possessions.

unlucky, poor, unhappy, hapless, wretched, ill-fated

2 The goalkeeper made one **unfortunate** error.

disastrous, calamitous, unwelcome

OPPOSITE fortunate, lucky

3 He made an **unfortunate** remark about her cooking.

regrettable, inappropriate, tactless, unsuitable, untimely

unfriendly adjective

The housekeeper greeted us with an **unfriendly** glare.

unwelcoming, inhospitable, unsympathetic, unkind, impolite, uncivil, unhelpful, hostile, cold, cool, distant, standoffish, aloof, unsociable, unneighbourly

OPPOSITE friendly, amiable

unhappy adjective

You look **unhappy**—what's the matter?

brokenhearted, dejected, depressed, desolate, despairing, dismal, distressed

(informal) down, downcast, downhearted, forlorn, gloomy, glum, grave, heartbroken, in low spirits, miserable, regretful, sad, sorrowful, sorry, tearful, troubled, upset, wistful, woeful, wretched

OPPOSITE happy

unhealthy adjective

1 One of the calves has been **unhealthy** since birth.

unwell, ill, sick, diseased, infirm, sickly, poorly, weak, delicate, feeble, frail

OPPOSITE healthy, strong

2 He eats an **unhealthy** diet of junk food.

unwholesome, unnatural, harmful, unhygienic

OPPOSITE healthy, wholesome

unhelpful adjective

The shop assistant was most **unhelpful**.

uncooperative, unfriendly, inconsiderate, reluctant to help

OPPOSITE helpful

unimportant adjective
*Don't worry about **unimportant** details.*
insignificant, minor, trivial, trifling, irrelevant, secondary, slight, small, negligible, worthless, petty
OPPOSITE important

unique adjective
*Each person's fingerprints are **unique**.*
distinctive, different, individual, special, peculiar
(*informal*) one-off

unite verb
1 *King Bluetooth **united** the kingdoms of Denmark and Norway.*
combine, join, merge, link, integrate, unify, amalgamate, bring together
OPPOSITE separate
2 *People of all ages **united** to celebrate Chinese New Year.*
collaborate, cooperate, join forces
To unite to do something bad is to *conspire*.
OPPOSITE compete

unkind adjective
*It was a thoughtless and **unkind** remark.*
callous, hard-hearted, cruel, thoughtless, heartless, uncaring, unfeeling, inconsiderate, unsympathetic, unfriendly, uncharitable, harsh, mean, nasty, selfish, spiteful, vicious, malicious
OPPOSITE kind

unknown adjective
1 *The letter was in an **unknown** hand.*
unidentified, unrecognised
OPPOSITE known
2 *The author of the story is **unknown**.*
anonymous, nameless, unnamed, unspecified
OPPOSITE named
3 *The explorers entered **unknown** territory.*
unfamiliar, alien, foreign, undiscovered, unexplored, uncharted
OPPOSITE familiar
4 *The part was played by an **unknown** actor.*
little known, unheard of, obscure
OPPOSITE famous

unlikely adjective
*No one believed her **unlikely** excuse.*
unbelievable, unconvincing, improbable, implausible, incredible, far-fetched
OPPOSITE likely

unlucky adjective
1 *Some people think that 13 is an **unlucky** number.*
unfavourable, ill-omened, ill-starred, jinxed

2 *By an **unlucky** chance, their plan was discovered.*
unfortunate, unwelcome, untimely

unnecessary adjective
*I'm deleting any **unnecessary** files from my computer.*
inessential, non-essential, uncalled for, unwanted, excessive, superfluous, surplus, extra, redundant
OPPOSITE necessary

unpleasant adjective
1 *Mr Smallweed was a thoroughly **unpleasant** man.*
disagreeable, unfriendly, unkind, bad-tempered, nasty, malicious, spiteful, hateful
2 *Being lost in the jungle had been an **unpleasant** experience.*
uncomfortable, disagreeable, awful
3 *The smell from the drain was very **unpleasant**.*
disgusting, foul, repulsive, revolting, horrible, horrid, repellent, offensive, objectionable

unpopular adjective
*The new manager was **unpopular** at first.*
disliked, hated, despised, unloved
OPPOSITE popular

untidy adjective
1 *Our house is the one with the **untidy** garden.*
messy, disorderly, cluttered, jumbled, tangled, littered, chaotic
(*informal*) higgledy-piggledy, topsy-turvy
2 *His work was **untidy** and full of mistakes.*
careless, disorganised, slapdash
(*informal*) sloppy
3 *She arrived looking **untidy** and flustered.*
dishevelled, bedraggled, rumpled, unkempt, scruffy, slovenly

unusual adjective
1 *The weather was **unusual** for the time of year.*
abnormal, out of the ordinary, exceptional, remarkable, extraordinary, odd, peculiar, singular, strange, unexpected, irregular, unconventional, unheard-of
OPPOSITE ordinary
2 *Ebenezer is an **unusual** name.*
uncommon, rare, unfamiliar
OPPOSITE common

upset verb
1 *Something in the letter had **upset** her.*
distress, trouble, disturb, displease, unsettle, offend, dismay, grieve, fluster, perturb
2 *Bad weather **upset** the train timetable.*
disrupt, interfere with, interrupt, affect, throw out

3 *The baby **upset** a whole bowl of cereal.*
knock over, spill, tip over, topple
4 *A fallen tree branch **upset** the canoe.*
overturn, capsize

urge verb
*He **urged** her to reconsider her decision.*
advise, counsel, appeal to, beg, implore, plead with, press
To urge someone to do something is also to *advocate* or *recommend* it.
OPPOSITE discourage

urge noun
*I had a sudden **urge** to burst into song.*
impulse, compulsion, longing, wish, yearning, desire, itch
(*informal*) yen

urgent adjective
1 *She had **urgent** business in New York.*
pressing, immediate, essential, important, top-priority
OPPOSITE unimportant
2 *He spoke in an **urgent** whisper.*
anxious, insistent, earnest

use verb
1 *She **used** a calculator to add up the figures.*
make use of, employ, utilise
To use your knowledge is to *apply* it.
To use your muscles is to *exercise* them.
To use a musical instrument is to *play* it.
To use an axe or sword is to *wield* it.
To use people or things selfishly is to *exploit* them.
2 *Can you show me how to **use** the photocopier?*
operate, work, handle, manage
3 *You've **used** all the hot water.*
use up, go through, consume, exhaust, spend

use noun
1 *Would these books be any **use** to you?*
help, benefit, advantage, profit, value
2 *A sonic screwdriver has many **uses**.*
function, purpose, point

useful adjective
1 *A flask is **useful** for keeping food warm.*
convenient, handy, effective, efficient, practical
2 *The website offers some **useful** advice.*
good, helpful, valuable, worthwhile, constructive, invaluable
OPPOSITE useless

a b c d e f g h i j k l m n o p q r s t u v w x y z

useless *adjective*
1 *This old vacuum cleaner is **useless**.*
ineffective, inefficient, impractical, unusable
OPPOSITE useful, effective
2 *Her advice was completely **useless**.*
worthless, unhelpful, pointless, futile, unprofitable, fruitless
OPPOSITE useful
3 (*informal*) *I'm **useless** at drawing.*
bad, poor, incompetent
(*informal*) rubbish, hopeless
OPPOSITE good

usual *adjective*
1 *I'll meet you at the **usual** time.*
normal, customary, familiar, habitual, regular, standard
2 *It's **usual** to knock before entering.*
common, accepted, conventional, traditional

vacant *adjective*
1 *The house over the road is still **vacant**.*
unoccupied, uninhabited, deserted
OPPOSITE occupied
2 *The receptionist gave me a **vacant** stare.*
blank, expressionless, mindless, absent-minded, deadpan
OPPOSITE alert

vague *adjective*
1 *The directions she gave me were rather **vague**.*
indefinite, imprecise, broad, general, ill-defined, unclear, woolly
OPPOSITE exact, detailed

2 *A **vague** shape could be seen through the mist.*
blurred, indistinct, obscure, dim, hazy, shadowy
OPPOSITE definite

vain *adjective*
1 *The duchess was **vain** about her appearance.*
arrogant, proud, conceited, haughty, self-satisfied
OPPOSITE modest
2 *He made a **vain** attempt to tidy the room.*
unsuccessful, ineffective, useless, worthless, fruitless, futile, pointless
OPPOSITE successful

valuable *adjective*
1 *Apparently the painting is very **valuable**.*
expensive, costly, dear, precious, priceless
2 *He gave her some **valuable** advice.*
useful, helpful, constructive, good, worthwhile, invaluable
OPPOSITE worthlessNotice that invaluable is not the opposite of **valuable**.

value *noun*
1 *The house has recently increased in **value**.*
price, cost, worth
2 *He stressed the **value** of taking regular exercise.*
advantage, benefit, merit, use, usefulness, importance

value *verb*
1 *He had always **valued** her advice.*
appreciate, respect, esteem, have a high opinion of, set great store by
To value something highly is to **prize** or **treasure** it.

2 *A surveyor was sent to **value** the house.*
price, cost, rate, evaluate, assess

vanish *verb*
*With a flick of his wand, the wizard **vanished** into thin air.*
disappear, go away, fade, dissolve, disperse
OPPOSITE appear

vanity *noun*
*His **vanity** is such that he never admits he's wrong.*
arrogance, pride, conceit, self-esteem, self-importance

variety *noun*
1 *The centre offers a **variety** of leisure activities.*
assortment, mixture, array
2 *The supermarket has over thirty **varieties** of pasta.*
kind, sort, type, make, brand
A variety of animal is a **breed** or **species**.
3 *There is not much **variety** in her choice of words.*
variation, change, difference, diversity

vast *adjective*
1 *The miser accumulated a **vast** fortune.*
large, huge, enormous, great, immense, massive
2 *A **vast** stretch of water lay between them and dry land.*
broad, wide, extensive, sweeping

version *noun*
1 *The two newspapers gave different **versions** of the accident.*
account, description, story, report

view

2 *It's an English **version** of a French play.*
adaptation, interpretation
A version of something which was originally in another language is a **translation**.
3 *A new **version** of the computer game will be released in May.*
design, model, form, variation

very *adverb*
*Carl is a **very** talented juggler.*
extremely, highly, enormously, exceedingly, truly, intensely, especially, particularly, remarkably, unusually, uncommonly, outstandingly, really
(*informal*) terribly
OPPOSITE slightly

vibrate *verb*
*I pulled a lever and the whole engine began to **vibrate**.*
shake, shudder, tremble, throb, judder, quake, quiver, rattle

vicious *adjective*
1 *This was once the scene of a **vicious** murder.*
brutal, barbaric, violent, bloodthirsty, cruel, merciless, pitiless, ruthless, callous, inhuman, malicious, sadistic, atrocious, barbarous, murderous, villainous, wicked
2 *Male baboons can be **vicious** if provoked.*
fierce, ferocious, violent, savage, wild

victory *noun*
*Hannibal won several **victories** over the Romans.*
win, success, triumph
OPPOSITE defeat

view *noun*
1 *There's a good **view** from the top of the hill.*
outlook, prospect, scene, panorama, scenery
2 *What are your **views** on animal testing?*
opinion, thought, attitude, belief, conviction, idea, notion

view *verb*
1 *Thousand of tourists come to **view** Niagara Falls each year.*
look at, see, watch, observe, regard, contemplate, gaze at, inspect, survey, examine, eye
2 *Wanda **viewed** her cousin with extreme dislike.*
think of, consider, regard

vile *adjective*
1 *The professor gave us a **vile** concoction to drink.*
disgusting, repulsive, revolting, foul, horrible, loathsome, offensive, repellent, sickening, nauseating
OPPOSITE pleasant

2 *Murder is a **vile** crime.*
dreadful, despicable, appalling, contemptible, wicked, evil

villain *noun*
*Detectives are on the trail of an infamous **villain**.*
criminal, offender, rogue, wrongdoer
An informal word for the villain in a story is **baddy**.
OPPOSITE hero

violence *noun*
1 *The marchers protested against the use of **violence**.*
fighting, might, war, brute force, barbarity, brutality, cruelty, savagery
OPPOSITE non-violence, pacifism
2 *The **violence** of the storm uprooted trees.*
force, power, strength, severity, intensity, ferocity, fierceness, fury, rage
OPPOSITE gentleness, mildness

violent *adjective*
1 *There were **violent** clashes in the streets.*
aggressive, forceful, rough, fierce, frenzied, vicious, brutal
OPPOSITE gentle, mild
2 *The bridge was washed away in a **violent** storm.*
severe, strong, powerful, forceful, raging, tempestuous, turbulent, wild
OPPOSITE weak, feeble

visible *adjective*
*There were no **visible** signs that the door had been forced.*
noticeable, obvious, conspicuous, clear, distinct, evident, apparent, perceptible, recognisable, detectable
OPPOSITE invisible

visit *verb*
*They're **visiting** friends in Toronto for a few days.*
call on, come to see, drop in on, go to see, pay a call on, stay with

visit *noun*
1 *My grandmother is coming for a **visit**.*
call, stay
2 *We are planning a short **visit** to Paris.*
trip, excursion, outing

visitor *noun*
1 *They've got some Polish **visitors** staying with them.*
guest, caller
2 *Rome welcomes millions of **visitors** every year.*
tourist, holidaymaker, sightseer, traveller

vivid *adjective*
1 *Gaugin often painted in **vivid** colours.*
bright, colourful, strong, intense, vibrant, dazzling, brilliant, glowing, striking, showy

2 *He gave a **vivid** description of his travels in Mexico.*
lively, clear, powerful, evocative, imaginative, dramatic, lifelike, realistic, graphic
OPPOSITE dull

voice *noun*
*The robot spoke with a slow, metallic **voice**.*
speech, tone, way of speaking

> ✎ **WRITING TIPS**
>
> You can use these words to describe a **voice**:
> croaky, droning, gruff, high-pitched, husky, low, shrill, soft-spoken, squeaky, throaty *A **gruff** voice cried, 'Who dares to enter my cave?'*

voluntary *adjective*
*She does **voluntary** work for a charity.*
optional, unpaid
OPPOSITE compulsory

vomit *verb*
*The smell made him want to **vomit**.*
be sick, heave, retch
(*informal*) throw up

vote *verb*
*Everyone has a right to **vote** in the election.*
cast your vote
to vote for someone or **something**
*I haven't decided who to **vote for**.*
choose, opt for, nominate, elect

vote

vote *noun*
*The results of the **vote** will be known tomorrow.*
ballot, election, poll, referendum

vulgar *adjective*
1 *The new colour scheme just looks **vulgar** to me.*
tasteless, unsophisticated, cheap, tawdry
(*informal*) tacky
OPPOSITE tasteful
2 *The book sometimes uses **vulgar** language.*
indecent, offensive, rude, coarse
OPPOSITE decent

a b c d e f g h i j k l m n o p q r s t u v w x y z

wail *verb*
Upstairs, the baby began to wail.
cry, howl, bawl, cry, moan, shriek

wait *verb*
Please wait here until I get back.
remain where you are, stay, stop, rest, pause, linger
(*informal*) hang about or around, hold on

wait *noun*
There was a long wait before the show began.
interval, pause, delay, hold-up

wake, **waken** *verbs*
1 *Hagor the giant woke from a deep sleep.*
awake, awaken, become conscious, come round, rise, arise, stir, wake up
2 *The alarm clock woke me at 6 a.m.*
rouse, arouse, awaken, disturb

walk *verb*
1 *I walked down the lane, humming a tune.*
amble, crawl, creep, dodder, pace, plod, saunter, step, stroll, wander
2 *A squat little troll walked towards the forest.*
hobble, limp, lope, lurch, shamble, shuffle, stagger, stumble, toddle, totter, waddle
3 *The robot walked its way up the stairs.*
clump, pound, stamp, traipse, tramp, trudge, wade
4 *The burglar walked away into the shadows.*
mince, pad, patter, prowl, slink, stalk, steal, tiptoe
5 *Captain Flint walked on board the ship.*
march, parade, stride, strut, swagger, trot
6 *They are planning to walk across the Himalayas.*
hike, trek, ramble
7 *The children walked into the classroom.*
file, troop

walk *noun*
1 *We went for a walk in the country.*
stroll, saunter, ramble, hike, trek, tramp, trudge
2 *There are some lovely walks through the forest.*
path, route

wander *verb*
1 *Sheep wandered about the hills.*
stray, roam, rove, range, ramble, meander, travel, walk

2 *We must have wandered off the path.*
stray, turn, veer, swerve

want *verb*
1 *He desperately wants to win a medal.*
wish, desire, long, hope
2 *Gayle had always wanted a pony of her own.*
wish for, desire, fancy, crave, long for, yearn for, hanker after, pine for, set your heart on, hunger for, thirst for
3 *That floor wants a good scrub.*
need, require

war *noun*
The war between the two countries lasted many years.
fighting, warfare, conflict, strife, hostilities

warm *adjective*
1 *It was a warm September evening.*
Weather which is unpleasantly warm is *close* or *sultry*.
Water or food which is only just warm is *lukewarm* or *tepid*.
A common simile is *as warm as toast*.
OPPOSITE cold
2 *Sandy put on a warm jumper.*
cosy, thick, woolly
OPPOSITE thin
3 *The fans gave the singer a warm welcome.*
friendly, warm-hearted, welcoming, kind, affectionate, genial, amiable, loving, sympathetic
OPPOSITE unfriendly

warm *verb*
She sat by the fire, warming her hands and feet.
heat, make warmer, thaw out
OPPOSITE chill

warn *verb*
The guide warned us to keep to the path.
advise, caution, alert, remind
To warn people of danger is to *raise the alarm*.

warning *noun*
1 *There was no warning of the danger ahead.*
sign, signal, indication, advance notice
2 *The traffic warden let him off with a warning.*
caution, reprimand

wash *verb*
1 *It took Rapunzel a long time to wash her hair.*
clean
To wash something with a cloth is to *mop*, *sponge* or *wipe* it.
To wash something with a brush is to *scrub* it.
To wash something in clean water is to *rinse*, *sluice*, or *swill* it.

To wash yourself all over is to **bath** or **shower**.
2 *Waves washed over the beach.*
flow, splash

waste *verb*
Let's not waste any more time.
squander, misuse, throw away, fritter away
OPPOSITE save

waste *noun*
A lot of household waste can be recycled.
rubbish, refuse, trash, garbage, junk, litter
Waste food is **leftovers**.
Waste metal is **scrap**.

wasteful *adjective*
It's wasteful to cook more food than you need.
extravagant, uneconomical, prodigal, lavish, spendthrift
OPPOSITE economical, thrifty

watch *verb*
1 *I could sit and watch the sea for hours.*
gaze at, look at, stare at, view, contemplate
2 *Watch how the batsman holds the bat.*
observe, take notice of, keep your eyes on, pay attention to, attend to, heed, note
3 *Could you watch my bag for a few minutes?*
keep an eye on, keep watch over, guard, mind, look after, safeguard, supervise, tend

---

✏️ **WRITING TIPS**

water *noun*
You can use these words to describe **how water moves**:
bubble, cascade, dribble, drip, flood, flow, froth, gurgle, gush, jet, ooze, overflow, ripple, roll, run, seep, shower, spill, spatter, splash, spout, spray, sprinkle, spurt, squirt, stream, surge, sweep, swirl, swish, trickle, well up

---

wave *verb*
1 *The tall grass waved in the breeze.*
move to and fro, sway, swing, flap, flutter
2 *I tried to get their attention by waving a newspaper.*
shake, brandish, flourish, twirl, wag, waggle, wiggle

wave *noun*
1 *We watched the waves break on the shore.*
breaker, roller, billow
A very small wave is a *ripple*.
A huge wave caused by an earthquake is a *tidal wave* or *tsunami*.

A number of white waves following each other is **surf**.
The top of a wave is the **crest** or **ridge**.
2 *A* **wave** *of anger spread through the crowd.*
surge, outbreak

wavy adjective
The mermaid combed her long **wavy** *hair.*
curly, curling, rippling, winding, zigzag
OPPOSITE straight

way noun
1 *Can you show me the* **way** *to the bus station?*
direction, route, road, path
2 *Is your house a long* **way** *from here?*
distance, journey
3 *This is the best* **way** *to make porridge.*
method, procedure, process, system, technique
4 *What a childish* **way** *to behave!*
manner, fashion, style
5 *In some* **ways**, *the brothers are very alike.*
respect, particular, feature, detail, aspect
6 *Things are in a bad* **way**.
state, condition

weak adjective
1 *The footbridge was old and* **weak** *in places.*
fragile, flimsy, rickety, shaky, unsound, unsteady, unsafe, decrepit
2 *The patient was too* **weak** *to walk very far.*
feeble, frail, ill, sickly, infirm, delicate, puny
3 *The nobles plotted against the* **weak** *king.*
timid, spineless, ineffective, powerless, useless
4 *The film was fun, but the plot was a bit* **weak**.
feeble, lame, unsatisfactory, unconvincing
5 *He asked for a mug of* **weak** *tea.*
watery, diluted, tasteless, thin
(*informal*) wishy-washy
OPPOSITE strong

weakness noun
1 *He pointed out the* **weakness** *in their plan.*
fault, flaw, defect, imperfection, weak point
2 *Eve has a* **weakness** *for toffee apples.*
liking, fondness (*informal*) soft spot

wealthy adjective
They say that he comes from a very **wealthy** *family.*
rich, well-off, affluent, prosperous, moneyed, well-to-do
(*informal*) flush, loaded
OPPOSITE poor

wear verb
1 *Can I* **wear** *my new dress to the party?*
dress in, be dressed in, have on
2 *The rug in the hallway is starting to* **wear**.
fray, wear away, wear out
3 *Those tyres have* **worn** *well.*
last, endure, survive

weather noun see panel opposite

weird adjective
1 **Weird** *noises have been heard in the tower at midnight.*
eerie, ghostly, unearthly, mysterious, uncanny, unnatural
(*informal*) spooky, creepy
OPPOSITE ordinary, natural
2 *My big sister has a* **weird** *taste in music.*
strange, odd, peculiar, bizarre, curious, quirky, eccentric, outlandish, unconventional, unusual
(*informal*) wacky, way-out
OPPOSITE conventional

welcome noun
The landlady gave us a friendly **welcome**.
greeting, reception
welcome adjective
1 *A cup of tea would be very* **welcome**.
pleasant, pleasing, agreeable, appreciated, desirable, acceptable
OPPOSITE unacceptable
2 *You're* **welcome** *to use my bike.*
allowed, permitted, free
OPPOSITE forbidden
welcome verb
An elderly butler **welcomed** *us at the door.*
greet, receive, meet, hail

well adverb
1 *The whole team played* **well** *on Saturday.*
ably, skilfully, expertly, effectively, efficiently, admirably, marvellously, wonderfully
OPPOSITE badly
2 *It's cold outside, so you'd better wrap up* **well**.
properly, suitably, correctly, thoroughly, carefully
3 *I know her brother* **well**.
closely, intimately, personally
well adjective
Mrs Orr looks surprisingly **well** *for her age.*
healthy, fit, strong, sound, robust, vigorous, lively, hearty
OPPOSITE ill

well-known adjective
A **well-known** *athlete will open the new sports shop.*
famous, celebrated, prominent, notable, renowned, distinguished, eminent
OPPOSITE unknown, obscure

WORD WEB

weather noun
The typical weather in a particular area is the **climate**.
A person who studies and forecasts the weather is a **meteorologist**.

SOME TYPES OF WEATHER
fog: mist, (Scottish) haar, haze, smog; ice and snow: blizzard, frost, hail, ice, sleet, snowstorm light rain: drizzle, shower heavy rain: cloudburst, deluge, downpour, monsoon, torrent sun: drought, heatwave, sunshine storm: squall, tempest light wind: breeze, gust strong wind: cyclone, gale, hurricane, tornado, typhoon, whirlwind

WRITING TIPS

You can use these words to describe **weather**.

TO DESCRIBE *CLOUDY WEATHER*
dull, grey, overcast, sunless

TO DESCRIBE *COLD WEATHER*
arctic, bitter, chilly, frosty, icy, nippy, perishing, raw, snowy, wintry

TO DESCRIBE *SNOW*
crisp, powdery, slushy
TO DESCRIBE *HOT WEATHER*:
baking, humid, melting, roasting, sizzling, sticky, sultry, sweltering

TO DESCRIBE *STORMY WEATHER*
rough, squally, tempestuous, turbulent, violent, wild
***THUNDER* MAY:**
boom, crash, resound, roar, rumble

TO DESCRIBE *SUNNY WEATHER*
bright, cloudless, fair, fine, springlike, summery, sunny, sunshiny

TO DESCRIBE *WET WEATHER*
damp, drizzly, raining cats and dogs, showery, spitting, torrential
***RAIN* MAY:**
lash or pelt down, pour, teem
(*informal*) bucket, tip down

TO DESCRIBE *WINDY WEATHER*
biting, blowy, blustery, breezy, gusty
***WIND* MAY:**
batter, blast, buffet, howl, moan, wail

wet *adjective*
1 *Archie took off his **wet** clothes and had a hot bath.*
damp, soaked, soaking, drenched, dripping, sopping, wringing wet
2 *The pitch was too **wet** to play on.*
waterlogged, saturated, sodden, soggy, dewy, muddy, boggy
3 *Take care—the paint is still **wet**.*
runny, sticky, tacky
4 *It was cold and **wet** all afternoon.*
rainy, showery, pouring, drizzly, misty

whip *verb*
1 *The jockey **whipped** his horse to make it go faster.*
beat, hit, lash, flog, thrash
2 ***Whip** the cream until it is thick.*
beat, whisk

whirl *verb*
*The snowflakes **whirled** in the icy wind.*
turn, twirl, spin, twist, circle, spiral, reel, pirouette, revolve, rotate

whisper *verb*
*What are you two **whispering** about?*
murmur, mutter, mumble
OPPOSITE shout

whole *adjective*
1 *I haven't read the **whole** book yet.*
complete, entire, full, total, unabbreviated
OPPOSITE incomplete
2 *The dinosaur skeleton appears to be **whole**.*
in one piece, intact, unbroken, undamaged, perfect
OPPOSITE broken, in pieces

wicked *adjective*
1 *Cinderella had a **wicked** stepmother.*
evil, cruel, vicious, villainous, detestable, mean, corrupt, immoral, sinful, foul, vile
OPPOSITE good, virtuous
2 *They hatched a **wicked** scheme to take over the world.*
evil, fiendish, malicious, malevolent, diabolical, monstrous, deplorable, dreadful, shameful
3 *The goblin had a **wicked** grin on his face.*
mischievous, playful, impish, naughty

wide *adjective*
1 *The hotel is close to a **wide** sandy beach.*
broad, expansive, extensive, large, spacious
OPPOSITE narrow
2 *She has a **wide** knowledge of classical music.*
comprehensive, vast, wide-ranging, encyclopedic
OPPOSITE limited

wield *verb*
*The lumberjack was **wielding** his axe.*
brandish, flourish, hold, use

wild *adjective*
1 *I don't like seeing **wild** animals in captivity.*
undomesticated, untamed
OPPOSITE tame
2 *The hedgerow was full of **wild** flowers.*
natural, uncultivated
OPPOSITE cultivated
3 *To the west is a **wild** and mountainous region.*
rough, rugged, uncultivated, uninhabited, desolate
OPPOSITE cultivated
4 *The crowd were **wild** with excitement.*
riotous, rowdy, disorderly, unruly, boisterous, excited, noisy, uncontrollable, hysterical
OPPOSITE calm, restrained
5 *The weather looked **wild** outside.*
blustery, windy, gusty, stormy, turbulent, tempestuous
OPPOSITE calm

willing *adjective*
1 *She is always **willing** to help.*
eager, happy, pleased, ready, prepared
2 *I need a couple of **willing** volunteers.*
enthusiastic, helpful, cooperative, obliging
OPPOSITE unwilling

wilt *verb*
*The flowers **wilted** in the heat.*
become limp, droop, flop, sag, fade, shrivel, wither
OPPOSITE flourish

win *verb*
1 *Who do you think will **win**?*
come first, be victorious, succeed, triumph, prevail
To win against someone is also to **beat**, **conquer**, **defeat** or **overcome** them.
OPPOSITE lose
2 *She **won** first prize in the poetry competition.*
get, receive, gain, obtain, secure
(*informal*) pick up, walk away with

wind *verb*
1 *She **wound** the wool into a ball.*
coil, loop, roll, turn, curl
2 *The road **winds** up the hill.*
bend, curve, twist and turn, zigzag, meander

wilt

windy *adjective*
*It was a cold, **windy** day.*
breezy, blustery, gusty, squally, stormy
OPPOSITE calm

wink *verb*
*The lights **winked** on and off.*
flash, flicker, sparkle, twinkle

winner *noun*
*The **winner** was presented with a silver cup.*
victor, prizewinner, champion, conqueror
OPPOSITE loser

wipe *verb*
*I **wiped** the table with a cloth.*
rub, clean, polish, mop, swab, sponge
to wipe something out
*Pompeii was **wiped out** by the eruption of Mount Vesuvius.*
destroy, annihilate, exterminate, get rid of

wink

wire *noun*
*Several **wires** protruded from the robot's head.*
cable, lead, flex
A system of wires is **wiring**.

wise *adjective*
1 *The soothsayer was very old and **wise**.*
sensible, reasonable, intelligent, perceptive, knowledgeable, rational, thoughtful
2 *I think you made a **wise** decision.*
good, right, proper, sound, fair, just, appropriate
OPPOSITE foolish

wish *noun*
*Her dearest **wish** was to travel to the Amazon.*
desire, want, longing, yearning, hankering, craving, urge, fancy, hope, ambition
(*informal*) yen

wish *verb*
*I **wish** that everyone would sit still for a minute!*
If you wish something would happen, you can say that you **want** or **would like** it to happen.

wither *verb*
*The flowers had **withered** and died.*
shrivel, dry up, shrink, wilt, droop, sag, flop
OPPOSITE flourish

witness *noun*
*A **witness** said that the car was going too fast.*
bystander, observer, onlooker, eyewitness, spectator

A B C D E F G H I J K L M N O P Q R S T U V **W** X Y Z

witty *adjective*
He gave a **witty** account of his schooldays.
humorous, amusing, comic, funny
OPPOSITE dull

wizard *noun*
1 The **wizard** cast a spell over the whole palace.
magician, sorcerer, enchanter
2 My sister is a **wizard** with computers.
expert, specialist, genius
(*informal*) whizz

wobble *verb*
1 The cyclist **wobbled** all over the road.
sway, totter, tetter, waver, rock
2 The jelly **wobbled** as I carried the plate.
shake, tremble, quake, quiver, vibrate

wobbly *adjective*
1 The baby giraffe was a bit **wobbly** on its legs.
shaky, tottering, unsteady
2 This chair is a bit **wobbly**.
loose, rickety, rocky, unstable, unsafe

woman *noun*
A polite word for a woman is **lady**.
A married woman is a **wife**.
A woman who has children is a **mother**.
An unmarried woman is a **spinster**.
A woman whose husband has died is a **widow**.
A woman on her wedding day is a **bride**.
A woman who is engaged to be married is a **fiancée**.
Words for a young woman are **girl** and **lass**.
Old words for a young woman are **maid** and **maiden**.

wonder *noun*
The sight of the Taj Mahal filled them with **wonder**.
admiration, awe, reverence, amazement, astonishment

wonder *verb*
I **wonder** why she left in such a hurry.
be curious about, ask yourself, ponder, think about

wonderful *adjective*
1 It's **wonderful** what computers can do these days.
amazing, astonishing, astounding, incredible, remarkable, extraordinary, marvellous, miraculous, phenomenal
2 We had a **wonderful** time at the party.
excellent, splendid, great, superb, delightful
(*informal*) brilliant, fantastic, terrific, fabulous, super
OPPOSITE ordinary

wood *noun*
1 All the furniture in the room was made of **wood**.
timber, lumber, planks, logs
2 We followed a nature trail through the **wood**.
woodland, woods, forest, trees

word *noun*
1 What's the French **word** for 'birthday'?
expression, term
All the words you know are your **vocabulary**.
2 You gave me your **word**.
promise, assurance, guarantee, pledge, vow
3 There has been no **word** from him for several weeks.
news, message, information

work *noun*
1 Digging the garden involves a lot of hard **work**.
effort, labour, toil, exertion
2 Do you have any **work** to do this weekend?
task, assignment, chore, job, homework, housework
3 What kind of **work** does she do?
occupation, employment, job, profession, business, trade, vocation

work *verb*
1 She's been **working** in the garden all day.
be busy, exert yourself, labour, toil, slave
2 He **works** in the bookshop on Saturdays.
be employed, have a job, go to work
3 My watch isn't **working**.
function, go, operate
4 Is the TV easy to **work**?
operate, run, use, control, handle

world *noun*
1 Antarctica is a remote part of the **world**.
earth, globe
2 Scientists are searching for life on other **worlds**.
planet

worried *adjective*
You look **worried**. Is something the matter?
anxious, troubled, uneasy, distressed, disturbed, upset, apprehensive, concerned, bothered, tense, strained, nervous
OPPOSITE relaxed

worry *verb*
1 There's no need to **worry**.
be anxious, be troubled, be disturbed, brood, fret

world

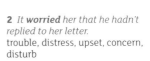

2 It **worried** her that he hadn't replied to her letter.
trouble, distress, upset, concern, disturb

worry *noun*
1 He's been a constant source of **worry** to her.
anxiety, distress, uneasiness, vexation
2 I don't want to add to your **worries**.
trouble, concern, burden, care, problem

worthwhile *adjective*
It may be **worthwhile** to get a second opinion.
helpful, useful, valuable, beneficial, profitable
OPPOSITE useless

wound *noun*
He is being treated in hospital for a head **wound**.
injury, cut, gash, graze, scratch, sore

wound *verb*
The fox was **wounded** in the leg and bleeding.
injure, hurt, harm

wrap *verb*
1 She **wrapped** the presents in shiny gold paper.
cover, pack, enclose, enfold, swathe
To wrap water pipes is to **insulate** or **lag** them.
2 The mountain was **wrapped** in mist.
cloak, envelop, shroud, surround, hide, conceal

a
b
c
d
e
f
g
h
i
j
k
l
m
n
o
p
q
r
s
t
u
v
w
x
y
z

wreck verb

1 *His bicycle was **wrecked** in the accident.*
demolish, destroy, crush, smash, shatter, crumple
2 *The injury **wrecked** her chances of becoming a dancer.*
ruin, spoil

wreckage noun

*Divers have discovered the **wreckage** of an old ship.*
debris, fragments, pieces, remains
The wreckage of a building is **rubble** or **ruins**.

wriggle verb

*The prisoner managed to **wriggle** out of his bonds.*
twist, writhe, squirm, worm your way

wrinkle noun

*The old hag's face was covered in **wrinkles**.*
crease, fold, furrow, line, ridge, crinkle, pucker, pleat
A small hollow on someone's skin is a **dimple**.

wrinkle verb

*The creature **wrinkled** its nose and sniffed.*
pucker up, crease, crinkle, crumple, fold
OPPOSITE smooth

write verb

1 *My granny **wrote** a diary when she was a girl.*
compile, compose, draw up, set down, pen
To write letters or emails to people is to **correspond** with them.
To write a rough version of a story is to **draft** it.
2 *He **wrote** his address on the back of an envelope.*
jot down, note, print, scrawl, scribble

To write on a document or surface is to **inscribe** it.
To write your signature on something is to **autograph** it.

writer noun

A person who writes books is an **author**.
A person who writes novels is a **novelist**.
A person who writes plays is a **dramatist** or **playwright**.
A person who writes scripts for films or television is a **scriptwriter** or **screenwriter**.
A person who writes poetry is a **poet**.
A person who writes about someone else's life is a **biographer**.
A person who writes for newspapers is a **correspondent**, **journalist**, or **reporter**.
A person who writes music is a **composer**.

writing noun

1 *Can you read the **writing** on the envelope?*
handwriting
Untidy writing is a **scrawl** or **scribble**.
The art of beautiful handwriting is **calligraphy**.
2 *The **writing** on the stone was very faint.*
inscription
3 (*often plural*) *She introduced me to the **writings** of Roald Dahl.*
literature, works

 WORD WEB

writing noun
VARIOUS FORMS OF WRITING AND LITERATURE
autobiography, biography, children's literature, comedy, crime or detective story, diary, drama or play, essay, fable, fairy story or fairy tale, fantasy, fiction, film or TV script, folk tale, ghost story, historical fiction, history, journalism, legend, letters or correspondence, lyrics, myth, newspaper article, non-fiction, novel, parody, philosophy, poetry or verse, prose, romance, satire, science fiction or sci-fi, spy story, thriller, tragedy, travel writing, western

wrong adjective

1 *It was **wrong** to take the book without asking.*
bad, dishonest, irresponsible, immoral, sinful, wicked, criminal, unfair, unjust

2 *His calculations were all **wrong**.*
incorrect, mistaken, inaccurate
3 *Did I say the **wrong** thing?*
inappropriate, unsuitable, improper
4 *There's something **wrong** with the TV.*
faulty, defective, not working, out of order
OPPOSITE right
to go wrong
*The professor's plan began to **go wrong**.*
fail, backfire
(*informal*) flop, go pear-shaped
OPPOSITE succeed

yell verb

*I **yelled** to attract their attention.*
call out, cry out, shout, bawl, bellow

young adjective

1 *A lot of **young** people went to the concert.*
youthful, juvenile
OPPOSITE older, mature
2 *I think this book is a bit **young** for you.*
childish, babyish, immature, infantile
OPPOSITE adult, grown-up
A young person is a **child** or **youngster**.
A young adult is an **adolescent** or **youth**.
A very young child is a **baby** or **infant**.
A young bird is a **chick**, **fledgling**, or **nestling**.
Young fish are **fry**.
A young plant is a **cutting** or **seedling**.
A young tree is a **sapling**.

young plural noun

*The mother bird returned to feed her **young**.*
offspring, children, young ones, family
A family of young birds is a **brood**.
A family of young cats or dogs is a **litter**.

zero noun

*Four minus four makes **zero**.*
nothing, nought
A score of zero in football is **nil**; in cricket it is a **duck**, and in tennis it is **love**.